BUDDHISM IN THE HISTORY OF INDIAN IDEAS

Buddhism in the History of Indian Ideas

N.N. BHATTACHARYYA

MANOHAR
2026

First published 1993
Reprinted 2026

ISBN 978-81-7304-017-7

Published by
Ajay Kumar Jain *for*
Manohar Publishers & Distributors
4753/23 Ansari Road, Daryaganj
New Delhi 110 002

Printed at
Replika Press Pvt. Ltd.

CONTENTS

ABBREVIATIONS

ABORI	*Annals of the Bhandarkar Oriental Research Institute*, Poona.
ADV	*Advayavajrasaṃgraha*, ed. by MM. H.P. Sastri, GOS, No. XL Baroda 1929.
Ait. Ar.	*Aitareya Āraṇyaka*, ed. with Eng. trans. by A.B. Keith, Oxford 1909.
Ait. Br.	*Aitareya Brāhmaṇa*, ed. with com. of Sāyana by S. Samasrami, Calcutta 1894-1906; Eng. trans. by A.B. Keith, HOS, Cambridge Mass, XXV, 1920.
Ait. Up.	*Aitareya Upaniṣad*, ed. Nirnaya Sagar Press, Bombay 1948; S. Radhakrishnan *Principal Upaniṣads*, London 1953.
Aṅguttara	*Aṅguttara Nikāya*, ed. R. Morris and E. Hardy, 6 Vols. with Index by M. Hunt, London 1885-1900; Eng. trans. by F.L. Woodward and E.M. Hare, *The Book of Gradual Sayings*, PTS, London 1935-36.
Āpas. SS.	*Āpastamba Śrautasūtra*, ed. with Rudradatta's com. by R. Garbe, Calcutta 1881-1903.
ASB	Asiatic Society of Bengal.
ASI	Archaeological Survey of India.
ASIAR	*Archaeological Survey of India: Annual Report*
AV	*Atharvaveda*, Eng. trans. by W.D. Whitney, Cambridge Mass, 1905.
BEFEO	*Bulletin de l'École Française d'Extreme Orient.*
Bib. Ind.	Bibliotheca Indica.
BIPM	*Bronze Images of the Patna Museum*, Patna 1961.
BM	*Buddhist Monuments*, by Debala Mitra, Calcutta 1971.
BMGM	*Bulletin of the Madras Government Museum.*
Br.	Brāhmaṇa.
BSOAS	*Bulletin of the School of Oriental and African Studies.*

BST	Buddhist Sanskrit Texts, Mithila Institute, Darbhanga.
Chāndogya	*Chāndogya Upaniṣad*, ed. NSP. R.A. Hume, *Thirteen Principal Upanisads*, Oxford 1921.
CII	*Corpus Inscriptionum Indicarum.*
Com.	Commentary.
CSS	Calcutta Sanskrit Series.
DHB	*History of Bengal*, Vol. I. Dacca University, ed. R.C. Majumdar, Calcutta 1943.
Dīgha	*Dīgha Nikāya*, ed. T.W. Rhys Davids, 3 Vols. 1880, 1903, 1911; Eng. trans. *Dialogues of the Buddhaa*, by T.W. Rhys Davids, London 1899, 1910, 1921.
DS	Dharmasūtra.
edn.	edition.
EIB	*East Indian Bronzes*, Calcutta University 1979.
Ep. Ind.	*Epigraphia Indica.*
ERE	*Encyclopaedia of Religion and Ethics*, ed. J. Hastings, Edinburgh 1902 ff.
GNB	*Gods of Northern Buddhism*, by Alice Getty, Oxford 1914.
Gobhila G.S.	*Gobhila Gṛhyasūtra*, Eng. trans. by H. Oldenberg in *SBE* XXX.
GOS	Gaekwads Oriental Series.
HIIA	*History of Indian and Indonesian Art*, by A.K. Coomaraswamy, London 1927.
Hir GS	*Hiraṇyakeśi Gṛhyasūtra*, Eng. trans. by Ḥ. Oldenberg in *SBE* XXXI.
IBI	*Indian Buddhist Iconography*, by B.T. Bhattacharyya, Calcutta 1968.
IBBSDM	*Iconography of the Buddhist and Brahmanical Sculptures in the Dacca Museum*, by N.K. Bhattasali, Dacca 1929.
IHQ	*Indian Historical Quarterly.*
IMG	*Indian Mother Goddess*, by N.N. Bhattacharyya, New Delhi 1977.
Ind. Ant.	*Indian Antiquary.*
ITL	*The Iconography of Tibetan Lamaism*, by A.K. Gordon, New York 1939.
JAOS	*Journal of the American Oriental Society.*
JASB	*Journal of the Asiatic Society of Bengal.*
JBORS	*Journal of Bihar and Orissa Research Society.*

JBTS	*Journal of the Buddhist Text Society.*
JDL	*Journal of the Department of Letters*, Calcutta University.
JISOA	*Journal of the Indian Society of Oriental Arts.*
JPTS	*Journal of the Pali Text Society.*
JRASB	*Journal of the Royal Asiatic Society of Bengal.*
JUPHS	*Journal of the U.P. Historical Society.*
Kārikā	*Sāṅkhyakārikā* of Īśvarakṛṣṇa.
Kat SS	*Kātyāyana Śrautasūtra*, ed. V.D. Sharma, Benaras 1933-37.
Kośa	*Abhidharmakośa*, ed. by La Vallee Poussin, London 1918.
Lāt SS.	*Lātyāyana Śrautasūtra*, ed. by A.C. Vedantavagisa, Calcutta 1872.
Lalita	*Lalitavistara*, ed. and Eng. trans. by R.L. Mitra, Calcutta 1877, 1886.
Laṅkā	*Laṅkāvatārasūtra*, Sans. ed. by B. Nanjio, Kyoto 1923; Eng. trans. by D.T. Suzuki, London, 1932.
List	Lüders' "List of Brahmi Inscriptions" in *Ep. Ind.* Vol. X.
MASI	*Memoirs of the Archaeological Survey of India.*
MMK	*Āryamañjuśrīmūlakalpa*, ex. by Ganapati Sastri, 3 Vols. Trivandrum 1920-25.
Majjhima	*Majjhima Nikāya*, ed. by V. Trenckner and R. Chalmers, 3 Vols. PTS, London 1888-89; Eng. trans. by I.B. Horner, *Middle Length Savings*, PTS, 1954-59.
NSP	*Niṣpannayogāvalī* of Abhayākaragupta, ed. by B.T. Bhattacharyya, GOS, No. 109, Baroda 1949.
NS	*Nyāya Sūtra*, ed. with Eng. trans. by S.C. Vidyabhusana, Allahabad 1911.
ORC	*Obscure Religious Cults*, by S.B. Dasgupta, Calcutta 1969.
PMC	*Patna Museum Catalogue of Antiquities*, Patna 1965.
PTS	Pali Text Society.
RAS	Royal Asiatic Society.
Rockhill	*The Life of Buddha*, by W.W. Rockhill, 2nd edn. London 1884.
RV	*Ṛgveda*, ed. by Vaidika Samsodhana Mandala, 4 Vols. Poona 1933 ff; Eng. tans. by R.T.H. Griffith, Benares 1915.

SBE	*Sacred Books of the East.*
SDM	*Sādhanamālā*, ed. B.T. Bhattacharyya, 2 Vols. GOS, Baroda 1925-28.
Śāṅ. GS	*Śāṅkhyāyana Gṛhyasūtra*, Eng. trans. by H. Oldenberg in SBE XXIX.
SS	Srautasutra.
Saṃyutta	*Saṃyutta Nikāya*, ed. by L. Feer, 5 Vols. PTS, London 1884-91, Eng. trans. ***Book of Kindred Sayings***, by C.A.F. Rhys Davids and F.L. Woodward, London 1917-30.
Śat. Br.	*Śatapatha Brāhmaṇa*, Eng. trans. by J. Eggelling, *SBE*, XII, XXVI, XLI, XLIII, XLIV, Oxford 1882-1900.
Sum Vil.	*Sumaṅgalavilāsinī*, ed. by T.W. Rhys Davids et al., PTS, London 1931.
Saddharma	*Saddharmapuṇḍarīka*, Eng. trans. by H. Kirn in *SBE*, 1909.
Taitt. Ār.	*Taittirīya Āraṇyaka*, ed. by R.L. Mitra, Calcutta, 1872.
TSS	Trivandrum Sanskrit Series.
TAA	*Tantrayāna Art: An Album*, by S.K. Saraswati, Calcutta 1977.
Up.	Upaniṣad.
Uttara	*Uttarādhyayana Sūtra*, Eng. trans. by H. Jacobi in *SBE*. XLV.
ZDMG	*Zeitschrift der Deutschen Morgenlandischen Geschen Gesselschaft.*

I

INTRODUCTION: A SURVEY OF BUDDHIST RESEARCHES

Since their very inception modern researches on Buddhism have rested upon studies of corresponding manuscripts in at least four languages—Pali, Sanskrit, Tibetan and Chinese. The earliest known European to come to the East to study Pali was the Danish scholar R.K. Rask who reached Ceylon in 1821 where he studied not only Pali but also Sinhalese and acquired a rich collection of palm-leaf manuscripts. In 1824, Benjamin Clough made a study of Pali grammar and vocabulary; following this, in 1826, was the publication of *Essai sur le Pali* in French by Eugene Burnouf and Christian Lassen.[1] The edition in Roman characters with an English translation of the first thirty-eight chapters of the *Mahāvaṃsa* in 1837 by George Turner marked the first important attempt to introduce the treasures of Pali literature to the scholars of the West. Subsequently the subject was taken up with much interest by N.L. Westergaard and F. Spiegel. In 1855 Vincent Fausböll of Copenhagen prepared an edition and a Latin translation of *Dhammapada* which was subsequently rendered into German in 1860. Between 1869 and 1880, a good number of texts belonging to the Sutta and Vinaya category were edited and translated by R.C. Childers, V. Fausböll, I.P. Minayeff, J.D. Alwis, T.W. Rhys Davids, Th. Steele, J.F. Dickson, Sir Coomaraswamy, P. Grimbolt, R. Pischel, H. Oldenberg and others.[2] An important advance was marked by the publication of the well-known *Pali Dictionary* in 1875 by R.C. Childers. The Danish scholar V. Trenckner published his edition of the *Milindapañho* in 1880. In 1881, T.W. Rhys Davids founded the Pali Text Society (PTS). In his own words: 'The sacred books of the early Buddhists have preserved to us the sole record of the only religious movement in the world's history which bears any close resemblance to

Christianity, and it is not too much to say that the publication of this unique literature will be no less important for the study of history and especially of religious history than the publication of the Vedas has always been.' The PTS brought about a qualitative change in the study of Pali and Buddhism by publishing critical editions of the texts and their commentaries as well as their dependable English translations and a good number of journals containing scholarly articles on Buddhism and on Pali language and literature.[3]

Interestingly, in the eighteenth century and in the first quarter of the nineteenth century when Buddhism was practically unknown in Europe, a modern critical study of it was introduced in Asia by the Japanese scholars Tominage Chuki (1715-45) and Jiun Sonja (d. 1803). The latter studied Sanskrit by himself in the pre-Meiji period, and having examined the fragmentary Sanskrit MSS of the Horiyuji and other monasteries and having compared them with their Chinese versions, published the Sanskrit editions of a number of Sūtras. B.H. Hodgson who stayed in Nepal between 1821 and 1843 made a collection of manuscripts which he presented to the libraries of London, Paris and Calcutta. The manuscripts sent by him to Paris offered Burnouf a great scope for studying Sanskrit materials directly. In 1839 he translated into French the *Saddharmapuṇḍarika*, which was printed in 1841. Subsequently, other works in Sanskrit pertaining to the pro-Mahayanic, Mahayanic and Tantric systems were collected, edited and translated.[4] Since no complete canon of Sanskrit Buddhist works was found in India, scholars had to depend on Tibetan and Chinese sources. At the dawn of Buddhalogical studies, there ensued a controversy between the French scholar E. Burnouf and the Russian scholar V. Vasilev on the question whether Buddhism could be better understood from the Indian or also from the Chinese and Tibetan sources. According to the former, only Indian sources provided evidence on genuine Buddhism while the latter held that Buddhism in the totality of its development could be understood only from Tibetan and Chinese sources. Fragments of manuscripts discovered in Central Asia provided a fresh fillip to the study of the lost Sanskrit Buddhist canon.[5]

Francesco Orazio della Penna, a Capuchin missionary who lived in Lhasa from 1716 to 1732, compiled a Tibetan dictionary and translated Tson-kha-pa's *Lam-rim-chen-mo* and the *Prātimokṣa*. Another Jesuit missionary, Ippolito Desideri, who stayed in Lhasa from 1717 to 1721, wrote a book in 1729 on Tibetan custom and religion. As early as in 1827, E. Burnouf had referred to the Tanjur and Kanjur in a note on Tibetan literature. In the third decade of the nineteenth century

Alexander Csoma de Koros gave an introduction to these collections in his writings on Tibetology. In 1845 J.J. Schmidt brought out an index of the Kanjur collection. Studies on the Tibetan sources were subsequently taken up by Anton Schiefner, V.P. Vasilev, Ph. E. Foucaux, C.F. Köppen, Sarat Chandra Das, A.I. Vostrikov and others. After Sarat Chandra Das, Rahul Sankrityayana and Giuseppe Tucci undertook several expeditions to Tibet and brought many valuable materials on Tibetan Buddhist literature and art. The Peking edition of the Tanjur was catalogued by P. Cordier (1909-15), and after his death his unfulfilled project of preparing an index to the *Catalogue* was completed by M. Lalou (1933).[6] As early as in 1804-05 Benjamin Bergaman translated several Kalmyk texts and published a volume which became an important source for the study of religion and rituals as practised by the Kalmyks living between the Volga and the Don, and of Lamaism in general.[7] J.J. Schmidt made a thorough study of the Mongolian sources on which he published several articles between 1832 and 1837. Such studies provided the basis of the emergence and development of the Russian School of Buddhalogy. Studies in the Sinhalese, Burmese and Siamese sources were initiated respectively by R. Spence Hardy, P. Bigandet and H. Alabaster.

In the modern sense, study of the Chinese sources was inaugurated with the publication of C.J. Neumann's work (1833) on the Buddhist pilgrims who came to India, which was followed by A. Remusat's translation of Fa-hien's account (1836). Gabet and Huc's French translation of the Mongol version of Kaśyapa Mataṅga's *Sūtra* came out in 1848 and St. Julien's translation of Hiuen Tsang's works and that of the Chinese version of the Avadānas came out between 1853 and 1859. Texts from the Chinese Buddhist canon were translated by S. Beal in a series of works done during the period between 1871 and 1878.[8] Studies in Chinese sources received a fresh momentum in 1883 after the publication of Bunyiu Nanjio's *Catalogue of the Chinese Tripiṭaka*. Japanese scholars contributed immensely to the study of Indian Buddhism and they worked especially on the Chinese sources.[9] In the field of Chinese sources the researches of Paul Pelliot and Paul Demieville deserve special mention.[10] In 1926, S. Levi came to Japan and laid the foundation of a centre of Buddhist research which came to be known as Maison Franco Japanaise. Here he sponsored a project of compiling an encyclopaedic dictionary, the *Hobogirin*. His collaborators were Takakusu, Anesaki, Inoue, Suziyama and others. Demieville acted as its chief editor.

Besides the well known bibliographical works such as the *Deutsche Bibliographie des Buddhismus* (1916), the *Bibliographie Bouddhique* (which began to be published from 1928) and others, attempts were made to present the results of studies in different fields of Buddhism from time to time.[11] Apart from the textual studies which formed the substratum of all subsequent researches, the main emphasis of the earlier writers of Buddhism was on clarifying various traditions, so different from one another, in connection with the sources; on examining with the purpose of making a distinction between the mythical and historical elements contained in the legendary data in regard to the life and achievements of the Buddha; and on distinguishing a primitive Buddhism from the doctrines supposed to have been grossly altered at a later period. The growth of different Buddhist sects and their doctrines, the rise of Mahāyāna with its increasing emphasis on the extreme form of philosophical idealism, and a corresponding mythological development to this speculative approach were also brought to light. Attempts were also made to prove that early Buddhism was by its very nature opposed to Brahmanism and that its followers formed a congregation, the object of which was to realise a perfect life into which members were admitted only after the performance of certain vows and rites and from which they could not return without becoming renegades. The historical process through which the geographical expansion of Buddhism in and outside India was possible was also understood to a considerable extent.

In 1834 James Prinsep deciphered the Aśokan inscriptions which had marked the beginnings of the studies in Indian palaeography and epigraphy. The Aśokan inscriptions which are of great importance to the study of Buddhism were dealt with by Burnouf, Kern, Cunningham, Senart, Bühler and Hultzsch.[12] The Annual Reports of the Archaeological Survey of India which began to be published by Cunningham since 1871 and the *Epigraphia Indica* which was started by James Burgess in 1892 contained materials for Buddhist archaeology. In 1833 Burgess himself published a book under the title *The Buddhist Caves and Inscriptions*. In 1910 H. Lüders published a *List of Brahmi Inscriptions*[13] which documented the geographical distribution of the Mahāsaṅghikas, Caityakas or Śailas, Haimavatas, Sarvāstivādins, Kāśyapiyas, Vātsiputriyas, Sautrāntikas, Dharmottarīyas, Bhadrayānīyas and Sāmmitiyas. Likewise from Sten Konow's *Kharoṣṭhi Inscriptions* (1929) geographical distribution of the Mahāsaṅghikas, Sarvāstivadins, Kāśyapiyas and Bahuśrutiyas is clearly understood[14] while J. Ph. Vogel's study of the Nagarjunikonda inscriptions[15] provides information on the Tāmraparṇakas, Mahīśāsakas, Bahuśrutiyas, Aparaśailas and Mahāsaṅghikas. Such works contributed a great deal to the understanding of the sectarian history of Buddhism as we come across in the later works of N. Dutt, M. Walleser, A. Bareau, E. Lamotte and others. Studies in Buddhist archaeology were initiated by Sir Alexander Cunningham and his colleagues of the Archaeological Survey of India[16] and in Buddhist art and iconography by Ritter, Cunningham, Grünwedel, Fergusson, Burgess, Foucher and others.

E. Conze has divided the course of Buddhist researches into three distinct schools: the older Anglo-German school of Rhys Davids and Hermann Oldenberg which based itself solely on the Pali canon and which is believed to have presented the Buddha's doctrines more faithfully than any other; the Russian school headed by Minayeff, Rosenberg, Stcherbatsky and others which depended on the scholastic literature on Buddhism and interpreted its different aspects in close dependence not only on the Indian commentaries but also on the continuous living tradition of Tibet, Mongolia, China and Japan; and the Franco-Belgian school headed by Levi, Vallee Poussin, Przyluski and others which continued on the Russian line but used other sources also supplementing their philosophical and philological analysis with the data of ethnology, sociology, etc. This division was based upon the preference and insistence of each school of scholars in relation to the typical nature of the source materials they were in the habit of using. In the earlier stages of Buddhist researches, the comparative study of the Sanskrit and Pali redactions was made for settling the question of their relative age and authority, and accordingly Sanskrit came to be regarded as the sacred language of the Northern Buddhists (i.e. those of Nepal, Tibet, China, Japan, Vietnam, Cambodia and Indonesia) and Pali as that of the Southern (i.e. of Ceylon, Burma and Siam). It should be pointed out in this connection that although the existence of Pali started being recognised by European scholars from 1826, in the earlier phases of Buddhist research Sanskritic sources (i.e. those translated into Chinese, Tibetan and Mongolian) played a more prominent role.

The changes that have taken place in the study of Buddhism are largely due to the piecemeal way in which the original documents have been brought to light. Remusat and Schmidt, the predecessors of Burnouf, drew all their inspiration respectively from Chinese and Tibeto-Mongolian sources. Burnouf himself depended more on Sanskritic sources of the later period. The situation, however, changed after the discovery of a complete canon in Pali. This new development contributed to a number of theoretical formulations among the Buddhist researchers which eventually led to a kind of grouping, one claiming for the absolute authority of the Pali canon in determining the original character of Buddhism, and the other depending mainly on the Sanskritic sources. Because it had a complete canon, Pali came to enjoy a special position, and despite the recognition on the basis of Tibetan and Chinese translations of the existence of a complete Sanskrit canon of the Sarvāstivāda, fragments of which have come to light, the claim of the Sanskritists remained rather feeble until Vallee Poussin and Stcherbatsky pointed out that mere existence of the complete Theravāda canon does not prove its relative antiquity and primitivity.[17] Subsequent researches prove that although some Pali works were translated into Sanskrit, a good number of other works may be cited which bear neither the stamp of Sanskrit Mahāyāna, nor that of Pali Theravāda. These belong to the canon of the Sarvāstivāda and other kindred schools. These schools might have translated their scriptures not from the Pali of the Theravādins but from the Prakrit dialects in which they were originally composed. Even the Pali canon might have been the development of a still earlier canon composed in some form of Prakrit.[18]

The fact that there was a long time gap between the days of the Buddha and the formation of canonical literature, that the present three-fold division was artificial made only after the actual production of the majority of the texts concerned, and that something must have existed as the original canon before the days of Aśoka—all these had been taken seriously into account by all critical scholars of Buddhism, and all of them unanimously held that a comparative study of the texts belonging to different Buddhist sects was necessary to settle the points of resemblance and divergence in their contents by which a chronological stratification for the reconstruction of the history of the earliest phase of Buddhism could be possible and that some idea of the original Buddhist canon, supposed to have existed before the days of Aśoka, could be obtained. Previously the task of comparison between the Pali and Sanskrit texts for the sake of establishing the older and common elements was undertaken by Burnouf, Senart, Oldenberg and Windisch. The discovery of the Sanskrit fragments in Central Asia and their comparison with parallel texts in Pali, Chinese and Tibetan has in some cases yielded tangible results.

E. Frauwallner[19] sought to prove that before the time of Aśoka was produced a great work, the *Skandhaka*, which divided and arranged the enormous materials concerning monastic rules according to a well-conceived plan and also regulated and formulated institutions of

Buddhist monastic life, the admission to the order, the confession ceremonies, the retirement during the rainy season and at the same time discussed clothing, food and drugs for the sick as well as the rules to be observed in the punishment of the offenders. This formulation was rejected by Lamotte[20] on certain technical grounds though the hypothesis in itself cannot be ruled out. The main problem is whether within the accepted Tripiṭaka things which are earlier and which are later can be distinguished. So far as the Pali texts are concerned, this is possible to a certain extent. The study in Vinaya in itself has some initial advantages. Since there is in the Chinese the Mahāsaṅghika recension of the *Vinaya Piṭaka* the position is more favourable for it than for the Sūtras. The Mahāsaṅghika Vinaya compared with that of the Sthaviras shows that both the versions are in close agreement regarding the major disciplinary rules. Other fragmentary Vinayas of different schools also point in the same direction. The present forms of the texts and, where texts are not available, or available only in fragments, those of the translations, bear testimony of additions, interpolations and accretions, and since there was no centralised control to prevent this they came to disagree on numerous points. There cannot, however, be any categorical answer to the question whether their disagreement affected the fundamental doctrines.

The researches of Franklin Edgarton on Buddhist Hybrid Sanskrit have also thrown significant light on the process of the formation of Buddhist canon[21] and evoked much interest among the scholars.[22] Edgarton divided the Buddhist Hybrid Sanskrit into three classes: the first containing texts entirely in Hybrid Sanskrit; the second containing verses in Hybrid Sanskrit but the prose portion showing a few signs of middle Indic phonology and morphology with vocabulary basically of the Hybrid Sanskrit; and the third containing text Sanskritised, the vocabulary only showing relics of Hybrid Sanskrit tradition. From this Edgarton concluded that the Buddhist Hybrid Sanskrit tradition went back to an early Buddhist canon which was originally composed in a middle Indic language containing a dialect mixture. This mixture of dialects was subjected to a process of Sanskritisation when the Buddhist Hybrid texts were written. Some of his critics agreed with him on this point, but they were not willing to accept that the prose of the works of the third class belong to the Buddhist Hybrid Sanskrit tradition. According to them these texts were written in a class of Sanskrit which contains some elements of Hybrid forms.[23] Another objection raised against Edgarton relates to his use of Nepalese manuscripts, scribal errors of which are likely to be confused with Hybrid Sanskrit.

Earlier attempts to reconstruct the historical biography of the Buddha, to separate facts from legends, were not crowned with success.[24] As early as in 1856, H.H. Wilson held it "not impossible after all, that Śākya Muni was an unreal being, and that all that is related of him is as much a fiction as his preceding migration."[25] The difficulties relating to the historical biography of the Buddha, confronted by the earlier writers and also by the subsequent researchers, were due to the fact that the available documents did not in themselves form a basis for an historical account. Senart in his *Essai sur la legende du Buddha* (1875) held that the Buddha was an allegorical figure who was originally a sun-god. Like the sun issuing from the clouds of night, the Buddha was produced from the dark womb of Māyā. The death of Māyā, immediately after the birth of the Buddha, resembled the vanishing of the morning cloud before the sun's rays. Like the sun-hero conquering the thunder-demon the Buddha vanquished Māra and after his victory he set in motion the 'Wheel of Law' that marched triumphantly across the firmament, until at last the day declined and the sun-god succumbed to darkness. The destruction of the Śākyas was the dying away of the power of sun in the blood-red tints of the evening clouds. J.H.C. Kern[26] had also followed a line similar to that of Senart and reduced the whole to an astronomical account. According to him the twelve *nidānas* symbolised the twelve months, the six heretical teachers the planets, rebellion of Devadatta, the struggle between the sun and the moon, and so on. The view of Kern was to a great extent supported by Barth who did not even hesitate to consider courtesans as the mother goddesses.

On the other hand C.F. Köppen (1857-59) who happened to be a close friend of Marx and Engels went many steps forward, even far beyond the range of speculation that might be provided through the then available materials, and declared that the Buddha was not only an historical person but also the greatest emancipator of the oppressed, the greatest revolutionary and the greatest political innovator of his time. H. Oldenberg (1881)[27] and E.W. Hopkins (1895)[28] ridiculed the view of Senart that even the career of Napoleon or Max Müller could be explained in terms of a sun myth. Rhys Davids and Oldenberg tried to separate the legendary elements of the Buddhist tradition on the basis of Pali sources and corresponding historical evidence and tried to present a reliable account of facts concerning the Buddha's life. But the situation changed very little. In 1915, R.O. Franke said:

> I should wish to make it appear as if I believed that we know even the very least about the founder of this doctrine. Naturally

> somebody (or somebodies) has (or have) created it, otherwise it would not be there. But who this somebody was, and whether there were not rather several somebodies, we have no knowledge.[29]

E.J. Thomas in his *Life of Buddha as Legend and History* (1927) says:

> The matter stands just as in the case of any historical person, say Socrates, Muhammad or Bonaparte. We have many records, many related facts, dates and archaeological remains, as well as the actually existing Buddhist peoples with their systems. Do these data point to an origin in the growth and spread of a myth, in which the religious belief in a god has been gradually converted into an apparently historical event, or is the basis of a historical person who lived in the sixth century B.C.?

Thomas himself was inclined to insist on the second proposition that the events related to an historical person were converted into mythological narratives and not the reverse. In 1947, E. Lamotte in his *Legende du Bouddha*[30] raised the old question once again and held that since the Buddha legends had no tinge of reality what the historians should do in this field was not to extract history from these legends, but to stratify the legends and remain content by studying their successive stages.[31]

As regards the so-called 'original' doctrine of the Buddha, there has been no dearth of variety in scholarly speculations. Oldenberg who thought it unnecessary to look for any other thing as original Buddhism beyond the normal suggestivity of the Pali sources held that Buddhism was evolved out of the necessity to define the relation between the all-perfect, all-pervading and all-beautiful *ātman* (the individual Self equated with the universal Self) and a painful world, full of hunger and thirst, sorrow and confusion, old age and death.[32] According to Mrs. C.A.F. Rhys Davids, who was also a great exponent of the Pali school, the period of the genesis of Buddhism was absolutely different from the picture as provided in the earliest records. The name of Buddhism had become connotative of the later monkish accretions on a primitive, tribal and unsophisticated kernel which should better be called Sākya.[33] Unfortunately her works have exhausted themselves in the most masterly criticism of the sources and in brilliant outlining of methodology, but she gives very little about the reconstructed form of the primitive Śākya religion on which she laid so much emphasis (see ch. II). Stcherbatsky on the other hand insisted on the exact meaning of the technical terms found in the scholastic literature of Buddhism which he believed to be nearer to the original doctrine. According to him the *dharma* theory was the basis of all forms of Buddhism which meant an interplay of plurality of elements without a real entity—a conception which must have been in existence in pre-Buddhist traditions.[34] Maryla Falk, St. Schayer and C. Regamey tried to penetrate what they called pre-canonical Buddhism by taking into account those ideas which despite their conflict and clash with the orthodox theories of the Theravādins and Sarvāstivādins were taken up and developed by the Mahāyāna. E. Conze tried to show that Buddhism from its very beginning upheld a doctrine of mystic experience to be attained by its followers through the symbolism of rituals, and this approach became popular among some later writers in this field.

Minayeff's *Recherches* (1884) contained detailed but controversial accounts of the Buddhist councils and the growth of the sects with the conclusion that the councils had an historical value from a double point of view. They contained an ancient nucleus of an authentic tradition, i.e. discussions on the point of discipline which were not necessarily anterior to all canonical codification and resumed under the symbolical aspect of a regular council the work of compilation and arrangement of scriptures.[35] In 1908, Louis de la Vallee Poussin having critically examined all hitherto published materials and arguments put forward by previous scholars admitted the validity of Minayeff's conclusions about the functional reality of the earlier councils as the source of the diversification of Buddhist thoughts and practices ultimately culminating in the formation of different schools and sects.[36] Jean Przyluski in his *Le Legende de l'Empereur Aśoka* (Paris, 1923)[37] adduced convincing grounds for believing that the traditions found in the *Aśokāvadāna* were older than those of the Vinaya of the Mūlasarvāstivādins and distinguished three phases in the history of the progress of Buddhism and the Buddhist church from the lower valley of the Ganges to the tableland of Upper Asia, each of which corresponded to a distinctive period in the history of Buddhist literature. In his *Le Concile de Rājagṛha* (Paris, 1926) he had given French translations of the accounts of the First Council as found in the *Kia-Yeh-Kie-King* and the *Ta-Che-Tu-Luen* and dealt with the geographical distribution and doctrinal intricacies of various Buddhist sects. Przyluski identified the Kāśyapīyas with the Haimavatas and held that the Kāśyapīyas had a canon similar to that of the Dharmaguptakas.[38]

In 1925, J. Masuda published the translation of the Chinese version of Vasumitra's treatise on eighteen sects of Buddhism in India, which was supplemented by the Tibetan texts on the eighteen schools by Bhavya and Vinītadeva.[39] Texts of various traditions were comparatively studied also in M. Walleser's *Sekten des Alten Buddhismus* (1927). In his introduction to the French translation of the *Abhidharmakośa* (1923-31) Vallee Poussin dealt with the basic theoretical aspects of the Sautrāntika school.[40] Information on the Dārṣṭāntikas was supplied by K'ouci-ki, one of the disciples of Hieun Tsang. That Kumāralāta was the founder of this school was stressed by Sylvain Levi in 1929 who tried to prove that the *Dṛṣṭāntamālya* or *Dṛṣṭāntapaṅkti* of the Tanjur collection was a fragment of the *Kalpanāmaṇḍitikā*.[41] Among the three Chinese versions of Vasumitra's treatise, the one translated and interpreted by Paramārtha was reproduced by Paul Demieville in his *L'Origine des sectes bouddhiques d'apares Paramārtha* (1931-32).[42] Paramārtha's account of the Second Buddhist Council refers to the controversy provoked by the five points of Mahādeva leading to the division of the Saṅgha into Sthavira and Mahāsaṅghika groups. Following Paramārtha, Demieville has shown that among the offshoots of the Mahāsaṅghikas, the Ekavyavahārikas held that all composite objects were unreal and fictitious, the Lokottaravādins held that all mundane *dharmas* were unreal and the supramundane *dharmas* were real, and the Kaurukullukas held the view that only the Abhidharma contained the real teachings of the Buddha.

In 1946, M. Höfinger[43] said that the Council of Vaiśāli was not a fiction. The account of the conflict about the disciplinary rules between the monks of Vaiśāli, the Vajjiputtakas, and the rest of the community was almost identical in all the Vinaya texts and it assumed the existence of a protocanonical account very close to the time of its occurrence. Other traditions, claiming various causes of dissension, were superimposed later. The growth of such traditions might well be divided into two categories, the first representing the account of the Mahāsaṅghika Vinaya and the second by the accounts in other Vinaya texts. In 1955, A. Bareau[44] suggested that Aśoka was associated with Sthaviravāda school which was threatened during his reign with a schism of the Sarvāstivādins, the main points of difference centering round the understanding and interpretation of the Abhidharma. He dealt with the different traditions about the origin of the sects and divided them chronologically in three epochs, the first consisting of the sects mentioned in the Ceylonese *Dīpavaṃsa*, the second of those mentioned in the Sāmmitiya tradition of Bhavya and the third of those mentioned in the Kashmirian sources like the Chinese translation of *Sāriputraparipṛcchā* of the Mahāsaṅghikas, the *Samaya-*

bhedaparacanacakra of Vasumitra and *Mañjuśripariprcchā* available only in the Chinese translation. Lamotte (1958) suggested that the Vātsiputrīyas made extensive studies on the Abhidharma and the difference of interpretations gave rise at least to four new schools, each of which appended its own interpretation to sections of the Abhidharma. These four new schools were known as Dharmottarīya, Bhadrayānīya, Sāmmitīya and Sannagārika. Lamotte also furnished us with a tabular statement of the geographical distribution of several schools on the basis of the inscriptions discovered so far.[45]

A.K. Warder in the second part of his *Indian Buddhism* (1970) tried to show that all the eighteen schools of early Buddhism elaborated their doctrines out of a common kernel. His treatment of the individual sects was mainly historical in nature, which also insisted on the socio-political conditions and art activities of different ages. He also dealt with the sectarian migrations or expansions in South East Asia. N. Dutt in his *Buddhist Sects* (1970) made an analytical study of the treatises of Vasumitra, Bhavya and Vinītadeva, the *Kathāvatthu* and its commentary, the *Abhidharma-Kośavyākhyā*, the Sāmmitīya *Nikāya Śāstra*[46] and the Gilgit manuscripts containing the original Mūlasarvāstivādin Vinaya. The *Kathāvatthu* which actually deals with the points of controversies on doctrinal and other issues which existed among different Buddhist sects, was handled with critical details by S.N. Dube (1980)[47] who gave a vivid and faithful elucidation of its diverse contents. He also tried to refute on the basis of the points of controversies, as recorded in the *Kathāvatthu*, the view of certain earlier scholars that the so-called Buddhist sects were not sects in the proper sense of the term, being no more than branches of the universal Saṅgha without distinctive organisations and doctrinal divergences.

Earlier works on Buddhism were based mainly upon the Mahayanic sources because the Tibetan and the Chinese texts were the first to reach the European scholars. The long series of important texts in the *Bibliotheca Buddhica* of Leningrad, edited and translated by the colleagues of Minayeff, led a host of scholars to devote themselves to the study of Mahāyāna Buddhist texts. The Franco-Belgian school headed by Levi, Poussin and others contributed in no small measure to the study of Mahayanism. The works of Kuroda, Suzuki, McGovern, Kimura, Dutt and others,[48] published between the last decade of the nineteenth century and the first quarter of the twentieth, no doubt purport to present in an historical outline the origin and development of Mahayanic ideas and practices, but the vast and varied theoretical formulations, as found in the scholastic literature of Mahāyāna, the immense mythological and cultic speculations, the ritualistic intricacies deriving their ingredients from the varied levels of culture and other components involved therein, made the penetration into it a matter of proverbial difficulty. Conze seems to be right when he says in regard to Mahāyāna: "Our picture of it is still that of the old nineteenth century map of Africa, with some patches here and there at the edges, but with the vast interior left empty and white, filled only with conjecture and surmise."

We have already referred to the edition and translation of a good number of Mahayanic texts while dealing with the Sanskrit, Tibetan and Chinese sources. The philosophical treatises of various schools of Mahāyāna were edited, translated and interpreted by Max Müller, Kasawara, Wenzel, Beal, Vallee Poussin, Yamaguchi, Schaffer, Johnston, Kunst, Kajiyama, Bendal, Rouse, H.P. Sastri, V. Bhattacharyya, Stcherbatsky and others. The publication of the Mahāyāna Sūtras and the works of different philosophical schools opened a new horizon in the field of study of Buddhist philosophy from different points of view, despite Conze's criticism that only five per cent of the Mahayanic Sūtras had so far been rightly edited and two per cent intelligibly translated. Studies in this field got a new start with the publication of Max Walleser's *Die buddhistische philosophie* (1904-14) and Y. Sogen's *Systems of Buddhist Thought* (1912). Aspects of different schools of Mahayanic thought, especially the doctrine of the void as developed by Nāgārjuna and his commentators, were treated in St. Schayer's *Vorarbiten zur Geschichte der Mahāyānistischen* (1921). O. Rosenberg's *Die Probleme der buddhistische philosophie* (1924) formulated a special *dharma* theory, doctrine of elements, as the basic ingredient of all forms of Buddhist systems, and the views expressed in this work subsequently became the guideline of the Russian school.[49]

Stcherbatsky's *Theory of Knowledge and Logic according to the Later Buddhist Texts* was published in two volumes between 1903 and 1909. During these years apart from Dharmakīrti's *Nyāyavindhu* and Dharmottara's commentary on it, very few original works on Buddhist logic were known to the academic world. Tuccis's *Pre-Dignāga Buddhist Texts on Logic from Chinese Sources* (1929) included two logical treatises of the early schools retranslated from Chinese into Sanskrit known as *Fang-pien-sin-louen* (*Upāyahṛdaya*) and *Jou-che-louen* (*Tarkaśāstra*). Some Sanskrit fragments of Dignāga's *Pramāṇasamuccaya* were collected and published by Randle in 1926. The original Sanskrit text of Dharmakīrti's *Pramāṇavārtika* was discovered by Rahula Sankrityayana during his expeditions to Tibet (1934-36). Stcherbatsky had to depend mainly on the Tibetan sources for the reconstruction of the Sanskrit originals, and in this way on the basis of the writings of Dignāga, Dharmakīrti and a host of their commentators, the reconstruction finally culminated in his two volumes of *Buddhist Logic* (1931-32). What is most remarkable about Stcherbatsky was that long before Rahula's discovery of the *Pramāṇavārtika* practically the entire tradition of Buddhist logic was reconstructed by him.[50]

The concept of Nirvāṇa which was previously dealt with by Childers, D'Alwais, Rhys Davids, Frankfurter et al., was subsequently interpreted by Dhalman, Eklund, Vallee Poussin and Stcherbatsky. Mrs. Rhys Davids brought to light much of the Theravāda Abhidharmic conceptions. Stcherbatsky expounded the logical and epistemological theories while Vallee Poussin did invaluable work in making accessible the Abhidharma of the Indian schools and the intricacies of Vijñānavada. Studies in the so-called Tantric elements in Mahāyāna Buddhism began with Köppen's *Die lamaische Hierarchie und Kirche* (1859) and Schlagintwait's *Buddhism in Tibet* (1863). The works of Rockhill, Waddell and others contributed to a great extent to the study of Tantric Buddhism which was also facilitated by the efforts of the great Indian explorer Sarat Chandra Das who returned from his travels into the interior of Tibet in 1882, where he had collected a great deal of material from the ancient libraries of the Sakya and Sam-ye monasteries of Lhasa.

The *Pañcakrama* which is an extract of the *Guhyasamāja* was edited by Vallee Poussin in 1896 who also edited the *Ādikarmapradīpa* in 1898 with an introduction and analysis of its contents. According to B.T. Bhattacharyya there seems to be a historical connection between the Yogācāra school and the rise of the Vajrayāna form of Mahāyāna Buddhism. S. Levi thought he could detect allusions to Tantric rites in the *Mahāyānasutrālaṅkāra*. Studies in the *Abhisamayālaṅkāra* contributed a great deal to the understanding of Tantric Buddhism.[51] In 1916 H.P. Sastri published a Bengali work under the title *Bauddha Gān O Dohā* which was a collection of the mystic ritual songs, known as the *caryā* songs written in a language which may be regarded as the oldest form of Bengali and other Eastern languages. These songs were collected by Sastri from Nepal. Subsequently P.C. Bagchi discovered from the Tanjur collection the Tibetan translation of all these songs (1938) and published more Dohās composed by Sarahapāda, Kānhapāda and Tillopāda.[52] As early as in 1903 F.W. Thomas had brought to light a good number of Sanskrit and Tibetan Sādhanas,[53] a few of which were utilised by A. Foucher in 1905 in his *Etude sur l'iconographie*

Bouddhique. The Tibetan version of the *Cakrasaṃvara*, sometimes also known as *Ḍākinijāla*, was partially edited and translated by Kazi Dawa Samdup under the title *Śrīcakrasambhāra-tantra* (1919).[54] The *Mañjuśrīmūlakalpa* was edited by T. Ganapati Sastri (1920-22).[55] H.P. Sastri's *Advayavajrasaṃgraha*, a collection of works supposed to be written by the celebrated Tantric teacher Advayavajra, was published in 1927. Indrabhūti's *Jñānasiddhi* and Anaṅgavajra's *Prajñopāyaviniścaya-siddhi* was edited by B.T. Bhattacharyya in 1929. The oldest extant Buddhist Tantra, the *Tathāgataguhyaka* or *Guhyasamāja* was also edited by him (1931). The *Ḍākarṇava* was edited by N.N. Chaudhuri (1935) while the *Mahāvairocana* was translated in parts in French by Tajima (1936). The volumes of the *Gilgit Manuscripts* which began to be published from 1939 contained edited versions of a good number of Buddhist Tantric texts. There is a Sanskrit manuscript of the *Kālacakra* in Cambridge (Add. no. 1346). Its Tibetan version was worked out by A.I. Vostrikov who made a Russian rendering of the text in the thirties. Its commentary made by Nāḍapāda was known as *Sekoddeśaṭīkā* which was edited by M.E. Carelli (1941). There was another commentary on the *Kālacakra* (Asiatic. Soc. Ms. no. 4727) known as *Vimalaprabhā* which was edited by B. Banerjee. Abhayākaragupta's *Niṣpannayogāvali* was edited by B.T. Bhattacharyya in 1949, while Snellgrove's edition and translation of the *Hevajratantra* came out in 1959.

L.A. Waddell's *The Buddhism of Tibet or Lamaism* (1895) sought to establish that a cult of demoniacal Buddhas was incorporated into the Mahāyāna practices. These demoniacal Buddhas under the names of Kālacakra, Heruka, Acala, Vajrabhairava etc. were to be conciliated by constant worship of themselves and their female energies, the dreadful Ḍākini fiendesses, with offerings and sacrifices, magic circles, special *mantra*-charms, etc. H. Zimmer in his *Kunstform und Yoga in indischen Kultbild* (1926) dealt with the questions relating to meditation and to the male and female principles which found expression in Tantric Buddhist art forms.[56] B.T. Bhattacharyya's *Buddhist Esoterism* (1924, 1932) found little similarity between the Hindu and the Buddhist Tantras, either in subject-matter or in philosophical doctrines inculcated in them or in religious principles. W.V. Evans-Wentz in his *Tibetan Yoga and Secret Doctrines* (1935) held that the Buddhist Tantras represented "a philosophy comprehensive enough to embrace the whole of knowledge, a system of meditation which will produce the power of concentrating the mind upon anything whatsoever, and an art of living which will enable one to utilize each activity (of body, speech and mind) as an aid to the path of liberation." Historical studies of Vajrayāna and kindred doctrines, their origins, development and metamorphosis were made by H.V. Glasenapp (1936), S.B. Dasgupta (1946,1950) and N.N. Dasgupta (1947).[57]

Three of the more important strands of the Tibetan tradition have become better known: the Gelugpa by the information which Alex Wayman provided on Tsongkhapa's *Stages on the Path of Enlightenment* (1952); the Nyingmapa through Evans-Wentz's *The Tibetan Book of Great Liberation* (1954); and the *Kahgyupta* by H.V. Guenther's translation of Sgam-po-pa's *The Jewel Ornament of Liberation* (1959). In his *Yuganaddha : The Tantric View of Life* (1952) Guenther had endeavoured to prove that the followers of Tantric Buddhism tried to view life neither as an indulgence in passion nor as an escape from it. Bisexuality is inherent in all beings and hence sexual partnership is the best expression for the most intimate relation between the two opposites.[58] Of other works dealing with the Tantric tradition in relation to Tibetan and Indian Buddhism mention may be made of D.N. Snellgrove's *Buddhist Himalayas* (1957), Lāma Anagarika Govinda's *Foundation of Tibetan Mysticism* (1959), G. Tucci's *The Theory and Practice of the Maṇḍalas* (1961) and Ariane Macdonald's *Le Maṇḍala du Mañjuśrīmūlakalpa* (1962).[59] In his subsequent work *Yoga of the Guhyasamāja Tantra* (1977) Wayman had used published Sanskrit texts, the *Pradīpoddyotana* Ms., relevant texts translated into Tibetan and thirteen Tibetan works on Tantra by Tsongkhapa, the founder of the Gelugpa sect. Eva Dargyay's *The Rise of Esoteric Buddhism in Tibet* (1978) analysed the tradition of the old school of Tibetan Buddhism. More than twenty biographies were dealt with in this volume.[60] Recently there has been an overflow of works on Tibetan Buddhism dealing mostly with the life and teachings of the celebrated saints.

Besides the works of the well-known scholars on the history of Buddhism in India,[61] the volumes on Indian history and civilization sponsored by various academic organisations contained chapters on historical development of Buddhism in India in a chronological sequence.[62] These works mostly contain the life and activities of the Buddha; the principal doctrines, the monastic rules; the councils; the development of the sects; the advent of Mahāyāna, its ethics, monasticism and doctrines; the concept of Bodhisattva; the geographical distribution of Hīnayāna and Mahāyāna; the four philosophical schools; doctrinal changes; emergence of Tantric Buddhism; Vajrayāna, Kālacakrayāna and Sahajayāna; and art and iconography; etc. Studies in the field of the regional histories of Buddhism in India were inspired by the archaeological discoveries connected with the sites of Buddhism in different parts of India.[63] Apart from such historical works, there was another class of studies in which Buddhism was treated from a comparative point of view. Thus Stcherbatsky tried to understand some philosophical concepts of Buddhism in the light of Kantian terminologies like 'thing-in-itself', 'the schematism of categories', 'the synthesis of apperception' and so on. In the writings of the medieval Buddhist philosophers he had discovered Bergson's 'duration', Russell's 'sense data' and a host of ideas of European philosophy.[64] A good number of comparative works on Buddhism and Christianity were published in which greater emphasis was laid on the similarity of moral precepts, monasticism and Christianization of certain Buddhist legends. Likewise Marxism offered a two-fold approach to the Buddhist studies: a comparative analysis of the philosophical contents of Marxism and Buddhism, and the materialistic interpretation of the genesis and expansion of Buddhism in India and abroad.[65]

Studies in Buddhist iconography, initiated by Grünwedel, Foucher, B.T. Bhattacharyya, N.K. Bhattasali and others received a new dimension in the hand of A.K. Coomaraswamy[66] who challenged the theory of the non-Indian origin of the Buddha image and held that the standing Buddha was derived from the standing Yakṣa primitives of the type of Parkham, Patna and Deoria whereas the seated Buddha had its prototype in the Yogī-like figures of the Bharut reliefs as well as in the similar effigies found on earlier coins. He analysed the well-known symbols of Buddhist art and observed that all of them represented a universal religious symbolism and a set of theological concepts which could be traced back even to the Vedas. Subsequent works on Buddhist iconography were mostly descriptive in character in which the identification of the deities on the authority of the iconological texts formed the sole basis of study. Since in Tantric Buddhism there was a variety of forms and conceptions of deities, a good number of works on Buddhist iconography banked on this phase of Buddhism. Among important specialised works in this field, mention should be made of Marie T. Mallmann's study of Avalokitesvara (1948) and Manjusri (1964), Conze's study of the iconography of Prajñāpāramitā (1949, 1951), B.N. Misra's study of the Bodhisattvas from Nalanda (1953), Lohuizen de Leeuw's study of the Paṭṭikera Cundā (1966), etc.[67]

Köppen, Oldenberg and the Rhys Davids couple believed that the study of Buddhism should be correlated with that of the Indian social history and that the social contents of the Buddha's teachings and those of the Buddhist tradition should be brought to light. Richard Fick's socio-economic study of the Jātakas (1897)[68] may especially be referred to in this connection. That the Buddhist Saṅghas were modelled on the patterns of tribal democracies and meant to be the ideal substitutes for a vanished way of life was demonstrated by a number of scholars.[69] Narendra Wagle followed a new methodology to analyse the social structure of the Buddha's time from the works of a relatively late period. He analysed the terms of address used by different members of the society and thus outlined social groupings and rankings. On the basis of certain terms of habitation he tried to explain the patterns of settlement and economic life of the period.[70] Uma Chakravarti (1987) dealt with the social dimensions of early Buddhism examining the principles on which the Buddhist system of social stratification was based and the changing position of the *gahapatis* who appear prominently in early Buddhist literature and analysed the role of power and the conceptualization of the ideal socio-political system as envisaged in Buddhism. Despite such works, there has been no serious attempt to deal with what Buddhism actually did in Indian social history. To what extent could Buddhism transform the existing pattern of society? What was its impact upon Indian society and life? How far could Buddhism change the caste-based society, the patriarchal values, the political and economic set-up? What were the relations between Buddhist doctrines and political theories and also between Buddhism and the state from the viewpoint of practical politics? Many such questions may be raised and we must get answers to them. From the surviving Buddhist states such relations have to a certain extent been traced and identified,[71] but how all these relations functioned in ancient India under the Buddhist and non-Buddhist kings is a subject of vast enquiry.

Notwithstanding numerous works on different aspects of Buddhism, there are some basic questions to which we have no satisfactory answer yet. The first and foremost of all such questions is: what is Buddhism? Is it possible to supply a definition of it? The answer is bound to be in the negative, since what is presented to us as Buddhism is no more than a variable thought-complex, always in a state of flux. Can Buddhism be called a religion? Of course not in the sense of Judaism, Christianity and Islam. How can a floating mass of ideas be described as a religious system? A world view in which the world has no real existence, things are neither transient nor eternal, cannot be the basis of a religion. Mādhavācārya was perfectly right when he described Buddhism as one of the sixteen Indian philosophical systems in his *Sarvadarśanasaṃgraha*. When he dealt with Buddhism and Jainism he considered them merely as different schools of thought belonging to the same category as the Mīmāṃsā or the Sāṅkhya or the Vedānta. He never thought that these were different religious systems. Oldenberg and Kern, and subsequently Coomaraswamy, pointed out that the Buddhist ideas were not stranger to those of pre-Buddhist Hinduism, rather they were logical consequences of it. Pre-Buddhist Hinduism, as it was revealed in the Vedic texts, anticipated Buddhism in diction as well as in thought. The conception of metempsychosis, the endless cycles of births and deaths, and the doctrine of *karman* as the power of predetermining the course of the migration of becoming from one state of being to another—the ideas by which the main tenets of Buddhism are characterised—belong to the pre-Buddhist thought-complex and are shared alike by all the religio-philosophical systems of India. Even the reward of good action is impermanence which arises out of some kind of desire, and hence the doctrine of deliverance gradually came to be based upon the conquest of all desire through the knowledge of impermanence of everything. The Buddha was not the only person to teach all these.

The close proximity of Buddhism to other system of Indian thought is more convincingly revealed in the later logical, epistemological and metaphysical literature of the Buddhists. So, the question with which one is naturally confronted is: Why, despite the admittance of the basic concordance of Buddhism with other streams of what is known as Hinduism, was the former treated as an essentially different type of religion and why was an anti-Hindu flavour added to it? This question has been dealt with in detail in the seventh chapter of this volume in which an attempt is made to explain the 'identity-in-difference' approach of the Western scholars and many of their Indian counterparts in dealing with the relation between Buddhism and (the religious phenomena which came to be known as) Hinduism. This was primarily due to the fact that Buddhism was initially known to the Western world through non-Indian sources as well as through the contact of the European nations with the Buddhist countries of Asia. A cult of the Buddha observed in Mongolia and China by the European travellers and Christian missionaries was designated as Buddhism at a period when the Europeans had no idea about the Indian sources of Buddhism. It was not known to them that what they knew as Buddhism went to different Asian countries from India. Secondly in most Asian countries outside India Buddhism had acquired a quasi-religious character under diverse historical and cultural conditions, though in India it remained in the form of a thought-complex in conformity with other systems. Its universality and wide acceptance in most Asian countries brought it at par with other universal religions, such as Islam or Christianity, in the eyes of the

Western scholars. The new dimension it achieved in the course of its historical development outside India blurred to a considerable extent its basic affiliations with Hinduism, and there were also political considerations behind treating it as a separate religious system.

Buddhism was mentioned for the first time in Clement of Alexandria's *Stromaties* which was composed about AD 200. About two centuries after Clement, the Buddha was mentioned by Hieronyus (AD 347-419) who said that the Buddha was born from the side of a virgin's body. In medieval Europe the legend of Barlaam and Josaphat was very popular. The legend had a direct bearing on the legend of the Buddha's *mahāniṣkramaṇa* or great renunciation. The first contacts of the Western world with Buddhism in Asia took place in the thirteenth century when Pope Innocent IV sent the Franciscan and Dominican friars as envoys to the Mongol Khan. Informations on Buddhism were given by the Franciscan friar Willem van Ruyksbroeck who spent six months in 1254 in Karakorum. In his *Itinerarium* he had geven description of Lamaism and Lamaistic formulas. Marco Polo's account, composed about the end of the thirteenth century, contained more details of Buddhism. In the fourteenth century a number of Papal envoys came to China, and the accounts they wrote contained information on Buddhism. In the fifteenth and sixteenth centuries missionaries went to China, Japan, Ceylon and South East Asia. In 1548 the Spanish Jesuit Franciscus Xaverius met a Japanese merchant named Yagiro who explained to him and other missionaries the doctrines of Buddhism. Information thus obtained from him was sent to Europe in letters written by Xaverius himself and also by Csome de Torres, the Father of Goa, and Father Nicolas Lancilotto between 1548 and 1549.

Hinduism, the term by which all the varied forms of Indian religious ideas, beliefs, customs, cults and rituals are denoted, may be compared to a strange river, constituted by numerous tributaries coming from different sources, which in course of its flow has created many affluents branching out in different directions towards different goals. Jainism and Buddhism were the first to branch out from the main stream as very forceful affluents, but while the former was able to maintain mostly a unilinear course with not more than two or three breaks, the latter had a multi-channelled progress in various directions through the ages until each of its courses rejoined the main stream at different periods of history. Therefore the question of the decline and extinction of Buddhism in India cannot rise at all. Various causes have been attributed by the scholars to its so-called decline such as the infection of Tantrism, exhaustion, internal corruption, sectarianism, social failure, withdrawal of royal patronage, Muslim invasion and so forth.[72] But the point which has been overlooked in this connection is that, like its own basic doctrine, the history of Buddhism in India was also in a perpetual flux, nothing but metamorphoses of ideas, each stage of its transformation being marked by a qualitative change. Here we come across the working of a process, the principle of negation, somewhat similar to the Hegelian dialectics which expresses continuity of development, the connection of the new and the old in the process of the replacement of some qualitative changes by others. The role of Buddhism as a thought-complex was similar, if not the same, to that of the Vedānta in generating the growth of multifarious spiritual systems, and as such its decline and extinction become meaningless since there is a difference between generated objects and the generating principle.

We have presented a brief survey of the nature of works on Buddhism. In fact all the major aspects of Buddhism have been studied by competent scholars. But this does not mean that there should not be any further work on Buddhism. In fact the scope of new interpretation, new findings and reassessment of the earlier formulations always remains. In the present work Buddhism has been viewed as a thought-complex. To stigmatise it as a single religious system is bound to be unhistorical and fallacious. An integrated study of the Indian religio-philosophical ideas and practices would clearly reveal that some key-concepts in this field were formulated in space and time under diverse historical circumstances, and these key-concepts were adopted by all the spiritual disciplines of India including Buddhism. The differences were in the area of interpretation and emphasis. And in this crisscross process of the multi-angled interpretations, every spiritual discipline was in a state of flux. This happened not only to Buddhism but to other systems as well, which has been demonstrated in the present volume. While in this introductory chapter a general survey of the history of researches on Buddhism has been made, in the second chapter we have tried to make a reassessment of the views on the origins of Buddhism forwarded by such eminent scholars on Buddhism as Jacobi, Oldenberg, T.W. and C.A.F. Rhys-Davids, Vallee Poussin, Stcherbatsky, Rosenberg, St. Schayer, B.M. Barua, Coomaraswamy, N. Dutt, Radhakrishnan, S.N. Dasgupta, G.C. Pande, D.D. Kosambi, Debi Prasad Chattopadhyaya, R.S. Sharma, V.P. Varma and others. Apart from their views, special emphasis has been laid on the evidences they cited in favour of their views and the mode of their arguments in the cross-current of which some positive conclusions appear to have emerged.

The third chapter which deals with the ideological background of Buddhism is basically a textual study in which the key concepts of Buddhism as found in the earlier Vedic texts have been traced, identified and documented. While dealing with the concepts which served as the ingredients of Buddhism, various scholarly views on these have also been taken into account and it has been established that the doctrines of the Buddha and his contemporaries were aspects of a single body of teaching. Specifically their views may be different but generically they belong to the same category. This was due to the fact that the Buddha, Mahāvīra and their contemporaries belonged to the same age and to the same region and they inherited the same spiritual, mythical, ritualistic and intellectual tradition of the past. They responded and reacted, in their own ways, which were more or less similar, to the same stimuli arising out of the stupendous intellectual, moral and sociopolitical transformation which were taking place in their time.

The fourth chapter deals with the Hindu substrata of Buddhist mythology. Here the term Hindu has been used in the sense of traditional Indian which includes pre-Vedic, Vedic, Puranic, regional, tribal and allied elements. It has been shown that just as the Vedic gods were subordinated to Yajña in the Brāhmaṇa literature and to the *brahman* in the Upaniṣads, so also they were subordinated to the Buddha in the Buddhist mythology. The earlier Buddhist attempt to create a mythology projecting the Buddha on top of the traditional and innovatory gods, however, failed to make any impact on popular imagination. An artificial Śakra endowed with endless noble qualities could hardly be a proper match for his vigorous and lively Puranic counterpart. The roots of the deified abstractions of the Mahayanists and their further Tantric ramifications have also been traced and it has been shown how the gods belonging to the Vedic and Puranic tradition and how the inducted powerful local and folk deities eventually survived owing to their agelong association with the masses while the earlier Buddhist fanciful innovations or the abstract meditative figurations belonging to the clan of the new-fangled Dhyānī Buddhas and their emanations gradually shrank into non-entities.

The fifth chapter which is the longest deals with the most important question of how Buddhism was viewed by the non-Buddhist philosophers and logicians. It has been demonstrated that there was a structural unity in all forms of Indian thought and that the non-Buddhist thinkers of all ages had a thorough acquaintance with the doctrines and philosophical intricacies of Buddhism. There were convergences as well as divergences. The Jains, for example, differed from the Buddhists in regard to the doctrines of momentariness, causal efficiency, atomism and the problems of knowledge. But their knowledge of Buddhism was not superficial. Some Jain authors even wrote commentaries on Buddhist works. The Vedantists were critical of Buddhism, but they were also influenced by Buddhist ideas. The philosophical views of Gauḍapāda were openly based on Buddhism and the term 'crypto-Buddhist' attributed to Śaṅkara was not without any base. Kumārila of the Mimāṃsā school was a severe critic of the Buddhist epistemological and ontological theories, but Prabhākara, another exponent of the Mimāṃsā school, was really a 'bastard son of Buddhism' in the language of Stcherbatsky. The closest relation of the Buddhists was, however, with the Nyāya-Vaiśeṣikas. Vātsyāyana's critique of Buddhism marked the beginning of an ideological combat between the Buddhists and the Nyāya-Vaiśeṣikas which lasted for a period of more than six hundred years, and in course of this combat both sides enriched themselves very much. On the Buddhist side there were such intellectual luminaries as Dignāga, Dharmakīrti, Dharmottara, Vinītadeva, Śāntarakṣita, Kamalaśīla and others while the Nyāya-Vaiśeṣika was represented by Uddyotakara, Vācaspati Miśra, Jayanta and Śrīdhara. The doctrinal, epistemological and ontological critique of Buddhism vis-a-vis the standpoints maintained by the Jains, Vedāntists, Mīmāṃsakas and Nyāya-Vaiśeṣikas clearly suggest that Buddhism was viewed by its opponents as a thought-complex comprising four philosophical schools and not a distinct religious system. The Buddhist teachers and their views were held in high esteem by their opponents and they never concealed what they borrowed from Buddhism in order to enrich or sharpen their viewpoints.

The sixth chapter is an historical study of the Buddhist sects, their geographical distribution and doctrinal peculiarities. It has been pointed out how factionalism, arising out of personality clashes eventually led to doctrinal centrifugality. The rise of Mahāyāna has specially been treated with insistence on its extra-Buddhist sources.

The seventh chapter deals with the final transformation of Buddhism with reference to its basic character as the crucible for generating various ideas and practices on the one hand and as an instrument of bringing uniformity and integrity of various spiritual disciplines on the other. It has been stressed that the period which has been stigmatised by most historians as that of the decline and disappearance of Buddhism was in reality the only period in its long history in India in which it was able to come out of its dry academic shell and renovate all the existing traditional and popular spiritual disciplines by its own spirit. Apart from these seven chapters, there is a big appendix on iconography which deals with the origin and development of the Buddhist iconology in an historical outline.

NOTES

1. According to Burnouf the first to mention Pali was Simon de la Loubere who visited Siam in 1687-88 as envoy of king Louis XIV. In the last quarter of the eighteenth century William Chambers and J.Ph. Wesdin published a few notices on Pali. The latter in his *Systema brahmanicum* (1791) quoted an Italian translation of the *Kammavācā* made from original Pali in 1776.
2. For the contribution of these scholars in the promotion of Pali see N.N. Bhattacharyya, *History of Researches on Indian Buddhism*, (New Delhi, 1981), 110 ff.
3. Besides the *PTS*, other organisations came forward to publish Pali texts and their translations. A good number of them were published in the Harvard Oriental Series. German translations were done by K.N. Neumann, P. Dhalke, K. Seidenstucker *et al.* In Sri Lanka the Mahābodhi Society, in Burma the Buddha Sāsana Council, and in Cambodia the Buddhist Institute of Pnom-Penh undertook the task of publishing Pali texts with translations in local languages. A complete edition of the Tripiṭaka in 39 volumes and in Siamese character was printed by the order of king Culālaṅkaraṇa in 1894. In 1925 an edition of the Jātakas in 10 volumes and in subsequent years as many as 45 volumes of the Tripiṭaka, 30 volumes of the Aṭṭhakathās and 10 volumes of the Prakaraṇas were published in the Siamese script. Pali texts were translated in Japan in 65 volumes under the supervision of J. Takakusu and M. Nagai. In India, Pali texts were studied, edited and translated by individual scholars mostly without any organisational support. Subsequently the University of Bombay, the Buddhist Centre of Nalanda, the Mahābodhi Sabhā at Sarnath, the Mahābodhi Society at Calcutta and other organisations took active interest in publishing the Pali texts and their translations.
4. Mention may be made in this connection to Senart's edition of the *Mahāvastu* (1882-97); R.L. Mitra (1877), S. Levi (1892) and E.B. Cowell's (1893) edn. and trans. of the *Lalitavistara*; Cowell and Neil's edn. of the *Divyāvadāna* (1891); Kern's edn. of the *Jātakamālā* (1891); S.C. Das's edn. of the *Suvarṇaprabhāsa* (1898); S.B. Samasrami (1873) and S.C. Sastri's edn. of the *Kāraṇḍavyūha* (1898); Max Müller's edn. of the *Sukhāvativyūha* (1881); Nanjio's edn. (1923) and Suzuki's trans. (1932) of the *Laṅkāvatārasūtra*; Rahder's

edn. of the *Daśabhūmika* (1926); Works on the Prajñāpāramitā literature including edns. and trs. by Max Müller (1881), R.L. Mitra (1888), R. Ghosh (1902-14), Leumann (1912), Max Walleser (1914). Tucci (1923), Stcherbatsky and Obermiller (1929), S. Konow (1941), Lamottee (1944-49), Hikata 1958), Conze (1954-68); etc. also B.T. Bhattacharyya's edn. of the *Sādhanamālā* (1925, 1928), the *Jñānasiddhi* and *Prajñopāya* (1929), the *Guhyasamāja* (1931) and the *Nispannayogāvali* (1949); Ganapati Sastri's edn. of the *Mañjuśrīmūlakalpa* (1920-22); H.P. Sastri's edn. of the *Advayavajrasaṃgraha* (1927); Carelli's edn. of the *Sekoddeśa* commentary on the *Kālacakra* (1941); Snellgrove's edn. and tr. of the *Hevajra*, etc. should be mentioned. For details see N.N. Bhattacharyya, *op.cit.*, 51 ff.

5. See A.F.R. Hoernle, *Manuscript Remains of Buddhist Literature in Eastern Turkestan* (London, 1916). The earlier discoveries of manuscripts in Central Asia led to the organisation of several expeditions—three expeditions between 1900 and 1916— conducted by Sir Aurel Stein, four German expeditions led by Albert Grünwedel and Georg Huth (1902-03), Von Le Cog (1904-05), Le Cog and Grünwedel (1905-07), and Von Le Cog (1913-14), one French expedition led by Paul Pelliot (!906-08), three Japanese expeditions (1902-04, 1908-09, 1910-13), and three Russian expeditions, the first by D. Klementz (1898), the second and third led by Serge Oldenburg (1909-10, 1914-15). Other expeditions are mentioned by Jack A. Dabbs, *History of the Discovery and Explorations of Chinese Turkestan* (The Hague, 1963). A bibliography of the earlier Central Asiatic studies was published in *Monumenta Serindica* (Kyoto, 1958), I, 53-87. All Sanskrit fragments published by the German scholars from 1904 to 1964 are listed in Waldschmidt's *Sanskritbandschriften aus des Turfanfunden* (Wiesbaden, 1965). (For the year from 1964 to 1970 see Ibid, III, 1971, 275-76). Sanskrit fragments from the Pelliot collection in Paris were edited by Bernard Pauly in *Journal Asiatique*, 1965, 83-121, 183-87; 1966, 245-304; 1967, 231-41. Yamada's *Bongo butten no shobunken* (Kyoto, 1959), contains list of Sanskrit fragments belonging to the London, Leningrad and Japan collections. After the death of Petroffsky and Oldenburg, work on Leningrad collection was neglected until the early 1950s, when V.S. Vorolyov-Desyatovsky revived the studies. For details see N.N. Bhattacharyya, *op.cit.*, 100 ff.

6. In 1972 Alaka Chattopadhyaya in her *Catalogue of Indian Texts in Tibetan Translation* rearranged the essential information contained in Cordier's *Catalogue* and made an improvement of Lalou's *Index*. Over 4,500 works of Indian Buddhists, the Indian originals of which are largely lost, survive in meticulous Tibetan translation. These are contained in the great Tibetan collections called the Kanjur and the Tanjur. Apart from these, the so-called 'histories of religion' (*Chos-*

'byun) are very important Tibetan sources for the study of Buddhism. Among works of this category Buston's *History*—passages form which were translated by Th. Stcherbatsky, Sarat Chandra Das, L.A. Waddel, Charles Bell et al.—was rendered into English by E. Obermiller. *Tāranātha's History of Buddhism in India* was translated into Russian by V.P. Vasilev (1866-69), into German by Anton Schiefner (1869), into Japanese by Enga Teramoto (1928) and into English by Harinath De (1911 in parts), N. Dutt and U.N. Ghoshal (from Schiefner's German in *IHQ*) and Lama Chimpa and Alaka Chattopadhyaya (1970). Sarat Chandra Das (1908) published the first and second part of the Tibetan text of Sumpa's *Pag-Sam-Jon-Zang* with translation of selected passages. The *Blue Annals* was translated by G. Roerich (1949-53) and portions of the *Red Annals* by G. Tucci (1969). For details see S.C. Chaudhuri's *Bibliography of Tibetan Studies* (Calcutta, 1971).

7. *Nomadische Streiferein unter den Kalmüken* (reprint), Oosterhout, 1969); cf. *Indo-Iranian Journal*, XIV, 1972, pp. 265-67.
8. He published the accounts of Fa-hien and Sung Yun (1869) and translated the *Si-yu-ki* (1885) and Hiuen Tsang's *Life* by Shaman Hwui Li from Chinese (1888). Works of I-tsing were rendered into French and English respectively by E. Chavannes (1894) and J. Takakusu (1896). J.H. Legge's account of Fa-hien's travels came out in 1896 while that of H.A. Giles in 1923. T. Watters' translation of Hiuen Tsang's account was published in 1904-05. Mention should also be made here of T.M. Chau's *Hiuen Tsang: Pilgrim and Scholar* (Nhatrang, 1963).
9. Cf. Kasahara's *Dharmasaṃgraha* (1885), Takakusu's *Pali Chrestompathy with Chinese Equivalents* (1906), Anesaki's *Concordance of Pali Texts with their Chinese Version* (1908), Kimura's *Studies in Abhidharma* (1926), Anakuma's *The Comparative Catalogue of the Chinese Āgamas and Pali Nikāyas* (1920) and *A Dictionary of Proper Names in Indian Buddhism* (1930), texts edited by Wogihara, Yamaguchi and Kondo (1932- 36), Ono's *Dictionary of Buddhist Bibliography* (in Japanese, 12 Vols., 1933-35), etc. Among works of Indian scholars P.C. Bagchi's *Deux Lexiques Sanskrit-Chinois* (1929, 1937) and *Canon Bonddhique in Chine* (1937-38) deserve special mention.
10. Pelliot's contribution to Buddhist studies has been recorded in the *Bibliographie Bouddhique*, IV-V, (Paris, 1934), 3-19 and also in Demieville's *Paul Pelliot* (Paris, 1946) 29-54. For the researches of Paul Demieville, see *Choix d'etudes bouddhiques* (Leiden, 1973).
11. Ernst Windisch's work (*Geschichte der Sanskrit-Philologie* in Grundriss Series) on Indian philology and literature (1917-21) contained informations on Buddhist studies in the nineteenth century Europe. Among subsequent works mention may be made of the

following: Henri de Lubac, *La rencontre du bouddhisme et de l'Occident* (Paris, 1952); L.H. Hammerich, 'Studies of Buddhism in Denmark' in *Mahābodhi*, LXX, 1962, 227-32; I.B. Horner, 'PTS's Contribution to the spread of Buddhism' in *Ibid.*, LXXIV, 1966, 101-11; N. Dutt, 'Introduction to Pali Studies in India' in *Ibid.*, LXXV, 1967, 138 ff; E. Conze, *Thirty Years of Buddhist Research* (London, 1967); A. Pyatgorsky, 'Buddhalogy in the USSR' in *Mahābodhi*, LXXVI, 1968, 82 ff; A. Haldar, 'Buddhist Studies: A Brief Survey' in *Buddhist Yearly*, 1968-69, 21 ff; G.M. Bongard Levin, 'On Buddhist Studies in USSR' in *Journal of the Asiatic Society*, IX, 1969, 6 ff.; W. Schumann, 'Buddhism and Buddhist Studies in Germany' in *Mahābodhi*, LXXIX, 1971, 54-64; W. Peiris, *The Western Contribution to Buddhism* (Delhi, 1973); J. Kolmas, 'Buddhist Studies in Czechoslovakia' in *Bulletin of Tibetology*, IX, 1974, 5-10; J.W. de Jong, *A Brief History of Buddhist Studies in Europe and America* (Varanasi, 1976) and N.N. Bhattacharyya, *History of Reseaches on Indian Buddhism* (New Delhi, 1981).

12. Burnouf, *Le Lotus de la Bonne Loi* (Paris, 1852), App. X, 652 ff.; Kern, *Chronology of the Southern Buddhists and the Monuments of Aśoka*, in Dutch (Amsterdam, 1873); Cunningham, *Corpus of Aśokan Inscriptions* (Calcutta, 1877); Senart, *Les inscriptions de Piyadasi*, (Paris, 1881-86) also in *Revue in Deux Mondes*, XCII, 1889, 67-108; Bühler in *Ind. And.*, 1890 ff., *ZDMG*, 1883, 1887, *Ep. Ind.* II, 87., 366 ff.; Hultzsch, *Corpus Inscriptionum Indicarum*, I, (Calcutta, 1925). Cf. R.V. Sharma, *Piyadasi Inscriptions* (Muradpur, 1915); D.R. Bhandarkar and S.N. Majumdar, *Inscriptions of Aśoka* (Calcutta, 1920), etc. For a list of such works see M.A. Mehendale, *Aśokan Inscriptions in India* (Bombay, 1948). Subsequent works of B.M. Barua, D.C. Sircar and others also deserve mention.
13. The list appeared as an Appendix to the tenth volume of *Ep. Ind.* B.M. Barua and G. Sinha published *Bharhut Inscriptions* in 1928. The Kharosthi inscriptions discovered by Sir Aurel Stein in Chinese Turkestan in 1901, 1906-07 and 1913-16 were edited and published by E.M. Boyer and E.J. Rapson under the general editorship of E. Senart (Oxford, 1920-29).
14. N.G. Majumdar also published a list of Kharosthi inscriptions in *JRASB*, XX, 1-39.
15. *Ep. Ind.*, XX, 1-37.
16. Apart from his earlier works like *The Bhilsa Topes* (1854), Cunningham published 24 volumes as *Reports of the Archaeological Survey of India* (1861-85). Thirteen volumes were written by Cunningham himself and the rest by his assistants, J.D. Beglar and A.C.L. Carlleyle. Cunningham's *Ancient Geography of India* (1871) was mostly based on the travel reports of the Chinese pilgrims. His *Stūpa of Bharhut* (1879) and *Mahābodhi* (1892) were important

contributions to the study of Buddhist archaeology. James Burgess, who succeeded Cunningham as Director General of the ASI in 1886, made Western and Southern India the area of his special study. Reports on the former were published in 12 volumes (1874-91) and on the latter in 10 volumes (1884-1903). The *Annual Reports* of the ASI which began to be published shortly afterwards contained results of the explorations and excavations of Buddhist sites, monuments inscriptions and images and these provided source-materials for subsequent studies in different branches of Buddhalogy, including Buddhist art and architecture.

17. The following had expressed great doubt about the authenticity of the Pali canon. Minayeff, *Recherches sur le Bouddhisme*, (Paris, 1894); A. Barth in *Revue de l'histoire des Religious* (Paris, 1882-1900), Tomes 5, 28, 42; V.A. Smith in *Ind. Ant.*, XXXII, 1903, 364 ff.; Vallee Poussin in *Le Museon*, 1905, 213 ff., *Ind. Ant.* XXXVII, 1908, 1 ff., 81 ff., *ERE*, IV, 179 ff., *Bouddhisme* (Paris 1909), 29 ff., 155, 166 ff., 248; R.O. Franke in *JPTS*, 1908, 1-80; A.B. Keith, *Buddhist Philosophy in India and Ceylon* (Oxford, 1923), 3, 16 ff.
18. This view was previously put forward by M. Winternitz in his *History of Indian Literature*, II, 12 ff., and subsequently stressed by H. Lueders in his *Beobachtungen Uber die Sprache des buddhistischen kanons* (Berlin, 1954), who defended the view that the Pali and Sanskrit Buddhist texts show traces of the existence of a primitive canon written in an eastern dialect which may be called Ardhamagadhi.
19. *Earliest Vinaya and the Beginnings of Buddhist Literature* (Rome, 1956).
20. *Histoire du Bouddhisme Indien* (Louvain, 1958), I, 194-97.
21. *Buddhist Hybrid Sanskrit Grammar and Dictionary* (New Haven, 1953). For Edgarton's articles on Buddhist Hybrid Sanskrit see *Harvard Journal of Asiatic Studies*, I, 1936, 65-83; *BSOAS*, VIII, 1936, 501-16; *Kuppuswami Sastri Commemoration Volume*. (Madras, 1936); *Language*, XIII, 1937, 107-22, XXII, 1946, 94-102; *JAOS*, LVII, 1937, 16-34, 185-88; LXVI, 1946, 197-206; LXXII, 1952, 114-17; LXXVII, 1957, 227-32 etc. For a complete bibliography of his publications see *Language*, XI, 1964, 116-23.
22. Akira Yuyama in his bibliography of the *Sanskrit Texts of the Saddharmapuṇḍarīka* (Canberra, 1970), 80-81 records 19 reviews of Edgarton's *Grammar and Dictionary* and several articles written in its reaction. His views have been seriously discussed and analysed, often with criticisms, by Helmer Smith (1953-55), E. Waldschmidt (1960), H. Bechert (1961), F. Bernhard (1965), etc.
23. Cf. J. Brough in *BSOAS*, XVI, 1954, 351-75; L. Renou, *Histoire de la langue sanskrite* (Paris, 1956), 209; C. Regamey in *Asiatica: Festschrift Friedrich Weller* (Leipzig, 1954), 514-27.

24. Hodgson in *Trans. of the RAS*, II, 1830, 222 ff.; Csoma de Koros, *Notices on the Life of Sakya* (Calcutta, 1836); Burnouf, *Introduction a l' Histoire du Bouddhisme Indien* (Paris, 1844); Schiefner, *Eine Tibetische Lebensbeschreibung Cakyamuni's* (St. Petersburg, 1845), Foucaux, *Rgya-Tcher-Rol-pa* (Fr. tr. of *Lalita- vistara* from Tib.), (Paris, 1847); Hardy, *Eastern Monachism* (London, 1850); Schoebel, *Le Buddha et la Bouddhisme* (Paris, 1857); C.F. Köppen, *Religion des Buddha*, 2 Vols. (1857-59); Bigandet, *Life or Legend of Gaudama, the Buddha of the Burmese* (London, 1858); V.P. Vasilev, *Buddhizm: ego dogmati, istoria i literatura* (St. Petersburg, 1859) (German version 1860, French by La Comme 1865); Saint Hilaire, *Le Buddha et sa Religion* (Paris, 1860); T.D. Alwis, *Buddhism: Its Origin, History and Doctrine* (London, 1862); Alabaster, *Wheel of Law* (London, 1872); S. Beal, *Romantic Legends of Śākya Buddha* (London, 1875); T.W. Rhys Davids, *Buddhist Birth Stories* (London, 1878); W. Rockhill, *Life of Buddha* (London, 1884); etc.
25. *JRAS*, 1856, 229.
26. *Geschiedents van hat Buddhisme in Inde*, 1882-84; German trans. 1884; French trans. 1901-03.
27. *Buddha, sein Leben, seine Lehre, seine Gemeinde* (1881); Eng. trans. by W. Hoey, London, 1882.
28. *Religions of India*, Boston, 1895, 299.
29. *ZDMG*, 1915, 455, quoted from E.J. Thomas, *Life of Buddha as Legend and History*, London, 1927, 233-34.
30. *Revue de l'histoire des Religions*, CXXIV, 31-71.
31. See Andre Bareau, *Recherches sur la biographie de Buddha* (Paris, 1963, 1970-71); D. Snellgrove, 'In Search of the Historical Sākyamuni' in *South East Asian Review*, VII, 1975, 151-58; N.N. Bhattacharyya, 'A Note on the Historical Biography of the Buddha' in *Journal of Indian History*, LIII, 1975, 1-12.
32. *Buddha* (London 1882), 16-59; Cf. H. Kern, *Manual of Indian Buddhism* (Strassburg 1896), 11-12.
33. *Śākya or Buddhist Origins* (London, 1931).
34. *The Central Conception of Buddhism* (Leningrad, 1927).
35. This view was contested by Oldenberg in *ZDMG*, LII, 1898, 613-94 and R.O. Franke in *JPTS*, 1908, 59ff.
36. *Ind. Ant.*, XXXVII, 1908, 1-18, 91-106.
37. Eng. trans. by D.K. Biswas (Calcutta, 1967); Cf. E. Huber in *BEFEO*, VI, Nos 1-2; S. Levi in *Journal Asiatique*, II, 1914, 494 ff.
38. As early as in 1881, S. Beal published *The Vinaya of the Dharmaguptas according to the Chinese Version*. De Groot in his *Code du Mahāyāna* remarked that the Prātimokṣa of the Dharmaguptakas was actually in use in all the centres of China. Pa-Chow's *Comparative Study of the Prātimokṣa* (1955) uncovered much of the disciplinary rules of the Dharmaguptakas.

39. See *Asia Major*, II, 1-78.
40. The *Kramasiddhiprakaraṇa* of Vasubandhu, also a Sautrāntika treatise, was translated from its Tibetan version by E. Lamotte in 1936.
41. *Journal Asiatique*, 1929, 270 ff.
42. *Melanges Chinois et Bouddhiques*, I, 1931-32.
43. *Le Museon*, XX, 1946.
44. *Les premiers conciles bouddhiques* (Paris, 1955); *Les Sectes Bouddhiques du petit Vehicule* (Saigon, 1955).
45. *Histoire du Bouddhisme Indien* (Louvain, 1958).
46. The text was retranslated from the Chinese translation into Sanskrit by K. Venkataramanan in *Viśvabhārati Quarterly*, V, 1953.
47. *Cross Currents in Early Buddhism* (New Delhi, 1980). See its review by the present author in *Indian Historical Review*, VIII, 1981-82, 135-39.
48. S. Kuroda, *Outlines of Mahāyāna* (London, 1893); D.T. Suzuki, *Outlines of Mahāyāna Buddhism* (London, 1907); W.M. McGovern, *Introduction to Mahāyāna Buddhism* (London, 1922); R. Kimura, *Historical Studies of the Terms Hīnayāna and Mahāyāna and Outline of Mahāyāna Buddhism* (Calcutta, 1927); N. Dutt, *Aspects of Mahāyāna Buddhism and Its Relation to Hīnāyāna* (London, 1930); B.L. Suzuki, *Mahāyāna Buddhism* (London, 1938).
49. The following works on Buddhist philosophy deserve special mention. B.M. Barua, *Prolegomena to the History of Buddhist Philosophy* (1918); McGovern, *Manual of Buddhist Philosophy* (1923); Keith, *Buddhist Philosophy of India and Ceylon* (1923); Oltramare, *La theosophie bouddhique* (1923); Masuda, *Der individualistiche Idealismus der Yogācara-Schule* (1926); Wolff, *Zur Lehre vom Bewnsstsein den spatuen Buddhisten* (1930); Tucci, *On Some Aspects of the Doctrine of Maitreya and Asaṅga* (1930); Ñāṇatiloka, *Guide through the Abhidhamma Piṭaka* (1938); Takakusu, *Essentials of Buddhist Philosophy* (1947); Conze, *Buddhism: Its Essence and Development* (1951); Murti, *Central Philosophy of Buddhism* (1955), A.K. Chatterjee, *Yogācāra Idealism* (1962); A.K. Sarkar, *Changing Phases of Buddhist Thought* (1968), etc.
50. While Stcherbatsky was working on *Buddhist logic*, Satis Chandra Vidyabhusana worked on the same subject as another pioneer. His first monograph on this subject, *History of the Medieval School of Indian Logic* appeared in 1909 and this was followed by his bigger work, *A History of Indian Logic* (1921). No wonder, Stcherbatsky freely used Vidyabhusana's work, but while the latter's approach was that of a confirmed historian, the former wanted to rationalise Buddhist logic in modern terminology and to offer a vigorous philosophical defence of it. Among subsequent works H.K. Ganguli's *Philosophy of Logical Construction* (1963) was a critical examination of logical atomism and logical positivism in the light

of philosophies of Bhartṛhari, Dharmakīrti and Prajñākaragupta. Mention may also be made in this connection of K.N. Jayatilaka's *Early Buddhist Theory of Knowledge* (1963); J.N. Shah's *Akalaṅka's Criticism of Dharmakīrti's Philosophy* (1966); D.N. Shastri's *The Philosophy of Nyāya-Vaiśeṣika and its Conflict with the Buddhist Dignāga School* (1964); R.S.Y. Chi's *Buddhist Formal Logic: A Study of Dignāga's Hetucakra* and K'uai-Chi's *Great Commentary on the Nyāyapraveśa* (1969).

51. The Tibetan and Sanskrit versions of this text were edited by Stcherbatsky and Obermiller in 1929; the English translation was done by E. Conze 1954. The most helpful for the understanding of this text are Obermiller's *Doctrine of Prajñāpāramitā as Exposed in the Abhisamayālaṅkāra* (1932-33) and his incomplete *Analysis of the Abhisamayālaṅkāra* (1933-43). The Sanskrit edition of Haribhadra's commentary known as *Abhisamayālaṅkāraloka* was published by Tucci (1932) and Wogihara (1932-35).

52. *Dohākoṣa*, Calcutta 1938; *JDL*, XXVIII, 1-180, XXX, 1-156. The songs of Kānha and Saraha were translated with interpretations by M. Shahidullah in his *Les Chants Mystiques de Kanha et Saraha*, Paris, 1928. Rahul Sankrityayana had discovered and published many more Dohās of Sarahapāda (1957). See also Bagchi and S.B. Sastri, *Caryāgitīkoṣa*, with the commentary of Munidatta (1956).

53. *Le Museon*, IV(1). The complete text was edited by B.T. Bhattacharyya (1925, 1928), GOS, XXVI, XLI; cf. V. Bhattacharyya and K.S. Ramaswami Sastri in *IHQ*, II, 1926, 626 ff.; III, 1927, 161 ff.

54. Published in *Tantric Texts*, VII (intro. and Eng. trans.) and XI (Tibetan text).

55. TSS, LXX, LXXVI; cf. J. Przyluski in *BEFEO*, XXIII, 1923, 301 ff. A Tibetan text known as *Mañjuśrīnāmasaṅgīti* was edited by Minayeff (1887).

56. In fact Tantric Buddhist art and iconography had always evoked the interest of the scholars, pioneers in which field were Grünwedel (*Buddhistische Kunst in Indien*, 1893) and Foucher (*L'Iconographie Bouddhique* 1900-1906). Among subsequent important works mention may be made of A. Getty's *Gods of Northern Buddhism* (1914), B.T. Bhattacharyya's *Indian Buddhist Iconography* (1924, rev. ed. 1958), N.K. Bhattasali's *Iconography of the Buddhist Sculptures of the Dacca Museum* (1929), A.K. Coomaraswamy's *Elements of Buddhist Iconography* (1935), E. Clark's *Two Lamaistic Pantheons* (1934), A.K. Gordon's *Iconography of Tibetan Lamaism* (1939), etc.

57. Glasenapp, *Die Entestehung des Vajrayāna* (1936); *Buddhistische Mysterien* (1940); S.B. Dasgupta, *Obscure Religious Cults* (Calcutta,

1946); *Introduction to Tantric Buddhism* (Calcutta, 1950); N.N. Dasgupta, *Bāṅgalāy Bauddhadharma* (in Bengali), 1947.

58. Guenther's other works are *Philosophy and Psychology of Abhidharma* (1957); *The Life and Teaching of Naropa* (Oxford, 1963); *Treasures of the Tibetan Middle Way* (Leiden, 1966); *Buddhist Philosophy in Theory and Practice* (London, 1972).

59. Cf. Erik Haarh, 'Contributions to the Study of Maṇḍala and Mudrā in *Acta Orientalia*, 1958, XXIII, 57-91. A complete bibliography of Tucci's writings from 1911 to 1970 is to be found in the *Opera Minora* I (Rome, 1971). Tsongkhapa's *Tantra in Tibet* was edited and translated by J. Hopkins (London, 1977). Lessing and Wayman published translation of Mkhan-grub-rje's *Fundamentals of the Buddhist Tantras* (The Hague, 1968).

60. Among earlier biographical works G. Roerich's *Biography of Dharmasvāmin* (1950), Guenther's *Life and Teaching of Naropa* (1963) and Alaka Chattopadhyaya's *Atīśa and Tibet* (1967) deserve special mention.

61. For the recent works on the history of Buddhism in India see S. Dutt's *The Buddha and Five After Centuries* (1957); E. Lamotte's *Histoire du bouddhisme Indien* (1958); A. Mitra-Sastri's *Outline of Early Buddhism* (1963); rev. ed. of N. Macnicol's *The Living Religions of the Indian People* (1964); A Bareau in *Die Religionen Indiens*, III (1964); L.M. Joshi's *Buddhistic Culture of India during the Seventh and Eighth Centuries* A.D. (1967); B.N. Chaudhuri's *Buddhist Centres in Ancient India* (1969); A.K. Warder's *Indian Buddhism* (1970); V.P. Varma's *Early Buddhism and its Origins* (1973); etc.

62. Cf. *The History and Culture of the Indian People* Series, *The Comprehensive History of India* Series; *The Cultural Heritage of India* Series, etc. In 1956 on the occasion of the Buddha Jayanti a few useful collections on Buddhism were published such as the *Buddha Jayanti Souvenir* (ed. S.L. Sharma), *2500 years of Buddhism* (ed. P.V. Bapat). *The Path of Buddha* (ed. K.W. Morgan), etc. On the same occasion the Lanka Buddha Mandalaya with the cooperation of the Government of Srilanka planned the publication of an *Encyclopaedia of Buddhism* in 15000 pages under the general editorship of G.P. Malalasekera, a few volumes of which have hitherto been published.

63. Among the regional histories mention should be made of N.N. Dasgupta's *Bāṅglāy Bauddhadharma*, in Bengali (1947); S. Chaudhuri's *Bāṅgalādeśe Bauddhadharma*, in Bengali (1974); N.N. Vasu's *Modern Buddhism and its Followers in Orissa* (1911); N.K. Sahu's *Buddhism in Orissa* (1958); P. Mukherjee's *The Buddhist Remains in Orissa* (1961); P.C. Chaudhuri's *History of the Civilization of the People of Assam* (1966); S. Saśananda's *Buddhism in Assam* (1985); P.C. Alexander's *Buddhism in Kerala* (1949); A. Aiyappan and P.R. Srinivasan's *The Story of Buddhism*

with Special Reference to South India (1966); G.N. and P.N. Ganhar's *Buddhism in Kashmir and Ladakh* (1956); J. Nandon's *Les Bouddhistes Kashmiriens* (1961); S. Khosla's *History of Buddhism in Kashmir* (1972); F.M. Hassnain's *Buddhist Kashmir* (1973); D.L. Snellgrove and T. Skorupski's *The Cultural Heritage of Ladakh* (1977); N. Dutt and K.D. Bajpai's *Buddhism in Uttar Pradesh* (1956); U. Thakur's *Buddhism in Mithila* (1964); D.C. Ahir's *Buddhism in Northern India* (1972); S.M. Pahadia's *Buddhism in Malwa* (1976); B.G. Gokhale's *Buddhism in Maharashtra* (1976); etc.

64. Among works of this category mention should be made of P. Dahlke's *Buddhist Essays* (1908); *Buddhism and Science* (1927); *Buddhism and its Place in the Mental Life of Mankind* (1927); E. Holmes's *The Creed of Buddha* (1908); G. Grimm's *Die Wissenschaft des Buddhismus* (1923); etc.

65. Cf. R. Sankrityayana, *Buddhism: The Marxist Approach* (New Delhi, 1970). The interpretations of Kosambi, Debiprasad and other Marxist writers will be discussed later.

66. *History of Indian and Indonesian Art* (1927); *Yaksas* (1928, 1931); *Elements of Buddhist Iconography* (1935).

67. For recent iconographical studies see Mallmann's *Introduction a l'Etude d'Avalokiteśvara* (1948), *Etude Iconographique sur Mañjuśrī* (1964); D. Barrett's, *Sculptures from Amravati in the British Museum* (1954); P.R. Ramachandra Rao's *Art of Nagarjunikonda* (1956); W. Kirfel's *Symbolik des Buddhismus* (1969); D.A. Saunders' *Mudrā: A Study of Symbolic Gestures* (1960); D. Seckel's *Art of Buddhism* (1964, Eng. tr. Ann E. Keep); R.S. Gupte's *Iconography of the Buddhist Sculptures of Ellora* (1964); Debala Mitra's *Buddhist Monuments* (1971); D.C. Bhattacharyya's, *Tantric Buddhist Iconographic Sources* (1974), *Studies in Buddhist Iconography* (1978); S.K. Sarasvati's *Tantrayāna Art Album* (1978); D.L. Snellgrove's *The Image of Buddha* (1978); N.N. Bhattacharyya, 'Buddhist Iconography' in *East Indian Bronzes* (Calcutta University, 1979); Debala Mitra's *Bronzes from Achutarajapur* (1978), *Bronzes from Bangladesh* (1980), Mallar Ghosh's *Development of Buddhist Iconography in Eastern India* (1980); Ratan Parimoo's *Life of Buddha in Indian Sculpture* (1982); Lokesh Chandra's *Buddhist Iconography* (1987), etc.

68. *Die sociale Gliederung im nordöstlichen Indien zu Buddha's Zeit*, Eng. tr. by S.K. Mitra (Calcutta, 1920).

69. R.C. Majumdar, *Corporate Life in Ancient India* (1922); K.P. Jayaswal, *Hindu Polity* (1924); N.C. Bandyopadhyaya, *Development of Hindu Polity and Political Theories* (1927, 1938); G.D. De, *Democracy in Early Buddhist Sangha* (1955); Debiprasad Chattopadhyaya, *Lokāyata* (1959), etc.

70. *Society at the Time of the Buddha* (1968). Among other works bearing on socioeconomic aspects mention should be made of U. Dharmaratna's *Buddha and the Caste System* (1955); S. Dutt's *Buddhist Monks and Monasteries* (1963); Angnelal's *Indian Life in Sanskrit Buddhist Literature* (1968); D.K. Barua's *Vihāras in Ancient India* (1969) and *Analytical Study of the Nikāyas* (1972); G.S.P. Misra's *The Age of Vinaya* (1972), Uma Chakravarti's *Social Dimensions of Early Buddhism* (1987) etc.

71. Cf. H. Bechart, *Buddhismus, Staat und Gesellschaft in dem Ländem des Theravāda Buddhismus* (1966); W.H. Wrigging, *Ceylon: Dilemmas of a New Nation* (1960); J. Gernet, *Les economiques du Bouddhism dans la societe Chinoise* (1956); R.J. Miller, *Monasteries and Cultural Change in Inner Mongolia* (1959); E. Sarkisyanz, *Buddhist Backgrounds of the Burmese Revolution* (1965); D.E. Smith, *Religion and Politics in Burma* (1965); M.E. Spiro, *Buddhism and Society: A Great Tradition and Its Burmese Vicissitudes* (1970); E. Benz, *Buddhism or Communism : Which holds the Future of Asia?* (Eng. trans. 1965), etc.

72. R.C. Mitra, *The Decline of Buddhism in India* (Visvabharati, 1954); P.N. Bose, *Indian Teachers of Buddhist Universities* (Madras, 1923), 144 ff.; V.A. Smith, *Early History of India*, third ed., 363 ff.; S. Radhakrishnan, *Indian Philosophy* (London, 1923), 609 ff.; B.M. Barua, *Prolegomena to the History of Buddhist Philosophy* (Calcutta, 1918), 19 ff; P.C. Bagchi in *Asutosh Mukherjee Volume*, III, 412 ff.; U. Mishra in *Journal of the G.N. Jha Research Institute* IX(1) 111 ff.; S. Levi, *Le Nepal,* II, 317 ff; G.C. Pande, *Bauddha Dharma*, 491 ff.; C. Eliot, *Hinduism and Buddhism*, II, 120; R.C. Majumdar (ed), *History of Bengal* (Calcutta, 1948), I, 422 ff.; in *Cultural Heritage of India*, IV, 47-48; *B.C. Law Volume* pt. I, 75 ff., 669 ff.; N.N. Dasgupta, *Bāṅglāy Bauddhadharma* (Calcutta, 1947); L.A. Govinda in P.V. Bapat (ed), *2500 Years of Buddhism* (Delhi, 1956), 313-14; L.M. Joshi, *Studies in the Buddhisic Cultures of India* (New Delhi, 1957), 379-418; P.V. Kane, *History of Dharmasāstra*, V (2), (Poona, 1962), 1003-30; E. Conze, *A Short History of Buddhism* (London, 1960), 86; K.W. Morgan, *Path of the Buddha* (New York, 1956), 48; Edkins, *Chinese Buddhism*, 99; A.K. Warder, *Indian Buddhism*, Delhi 1970, 514 ff.; S.R. Goyal, *A History of Indian Buddhism* (Meerut, 1987), 383-404, etc.

II

ON THE ORIGINS: AN ASSESSMENT

In the case of Indological researches certain ideas have always predominated over others not because their historical validity is conclusively established but because they are popular and acceptable to the modern mind. One such idea is that the malignant growth of the Brahmanical ritualism and the corrupt practices of the priestly class of the later Vedic age created a social reaction out of which evolved a new intellectual movement led by the sophists of that age known as the Śramaṇas who rejected the Vedas and the authority of the Brāhmaṇas, ridiculed the complicated rituals and upheld the ideals of personal purity, renunciation, asceticism and intuitional knowledge. The Buddha belonged to this new movement of philosophy, and though apparently not the first, by far the most important and successful of the Śramaṇa schools was that founded by him.[1]

This understanding of the rise of Buddhism, if we judge from the viewpoint of formal logic, does not appear to be unlikely or inconsistent, and herein probably lies the reason of its wide acceptance. To substantiate this view, its supporters depended on the Upaniṣads in which they found sparks of a new intellectual revolution sponsored by the Kṣatriya kings and nobles who were supposed to have been disgusted with Brahmanical ritualism and sacrificial cults, and also on the post-Aśokan Buddhist and Jain texts which refer to the wandering ascetics, the teachers and sophists engaged in conversational discussions on matters of ethics and philosophy, and different schools of thought.[2] But when the growth of this Śramaṇism in general and Buddhism in particular is viewed in terms of a rationalistic philosophical movement arising out of the so-called irrationalism and commercialism of the existing Brahmanical tradition, the hypothesis cannot at once be regarded as valid, so long as we do not make a thorough check-up of the real contents of the two traditions.

It should be pointed out that in most cases the vision of the historian is circumscribed by the dominant outlook of his own age. The Western scholars with their Christian preoccupations wanted to see in the Vedic literature a transition from naturalistic polytheism to a kind of distinctive monotheism. So did their Indian counterparts who under the influence of Brahmoism and various forms of neo-Hinduism wanted to prove that Hinduism at all periods of its long history was basically monotheistic, devotional and ethical. The vast ritualistic literature was considered to be a tumorous overgrowth created by the Brāhmaṇa priestly class solely for the purpose of exploiting people in the name of religion, and it was against this priestly exploitation of the masses in the name of Yajña that the Upaniṣadic thinkers raised their voice, that Kṛṣṇa in the *Bhagavadgītā* formulated his devotional religion and that the Buddha and Mahāvīra introduced new systems based on humanism and rationalistic morality. All this sounds very well, but till today nobody has been able to say what Yajña was and what it did really mean to its performers. Scholars have made a thorough study of the Yajñas and their intricacies as found in the Vedic literature by applying the principles of anthropology, sociology, psychology, mythology, physical science and other disciplines, have written volumes after volumes, but have failed to provide even a bare definition of it.[3]

While dealing with the origins of Buddhism one point is generally ignored. The Hīnayānists, even in their earlier stages, recognised twenty-four bygone Buddhas. In the Mahāyāna tradition names of thirty-two earlier Buddhas have been recorded. The last seven Buddhas are more frequently known. They are Vipaśyin, Śikhi, Viśvabhū, Krākucchanda, Kaṇakamuni, Kaśyapa and Śākyasiṃha or Gautama. This reminds us of the corresponding Jain concept of twenty-four Tīrthaṃkaras. To stigmatize the earlier Buddhas or the earlier Tīrthaṃkaras simply as mythical persons involves the risk of an oversimplified approach towards the problem. There is no reason to disbelieve in the historical probability of the existence of a succession of teachers. Just as Lord Mahāvīra was not the first to proclaim Jainism, so also Gautama might have adopted and spread a doctrine which he found in the religio-philosophical tradition of India. He, indeed, is reported to have emphatically disowned the authorship of new teaching, but claimed to be the follower of a doctrine established long ago by the former Buddhas. It should be noted in this connection that Buddhism, as is known to us, appeared as a conglomerate of a number of religio-philosophical complexes, and it may not be unreasonable to suppose that some of these were introduced by the earlier Buddhas.

There is no genuine evidence to show that when Gautama Buddha formulated his philosophy of suffering, the four noble truths, he had any thought in his mind about the reactionary role of Brahmanism. Rather, the earlier concepts of metempsychosis, the endless cycles of births and deaths, the doctrine of *karma* and other kindred ideas found in the Brahmanical texts helped him to formulate his views on suffering and cessation of suffering, the problems with which he seemed to have been directly concerned. An extensive influence of the Sāṅkhya, which also insists on three categories of suffering (*ādhibhautika*, *ādhidaivika* and *ādhyātmika*), was suggested by Jacobi who had derived the chain of causation (*paṭiccasamuppāda*) from the series found in the Sāṅkhya system in its original form. In the *Buddhacarita* (xii, 17 ff) we find that, according to Āḷāra Kālāma, one of the teachers of the Buddha, the primal cause is *prakṛti* and there is also a soul (*ātman*) which is conscious of the body. A being (*sattva*) is constituted by the evolutes (*vikāra*) of *prakṛti* which manifests itself in five great elements (*pañcabhūta*) in their subtle states (*tanmātra*), egoism (*ahaṃkāra*) and intellect (*mahān* or *buddhi*). The first evolute of *Prakṛti* is *buddhi* or intellect which becomes individualised as *ahaṃkāra* or egoity. It is parallel to the Buddhist *vijñāna* (consciousness) which is the cause of *nāmarūpa* (name and form, individuality). Again, according to the Sāṅkhya, from egoity proceed the organs (*indriyas*) with the mind (*manas*) and the five subtle elements from which proceed five gross elements (*mahābhūtas*). These correspond to the *dharmas* of the Buddhists which are actually existing things. According to Jacobi the derivative character of Buddhism is clearly shown because for *avidyā* and *saṃskāra* "an intellect must be assumed which Buddhism admits after the *saṃskāra*, in the form of *vijnāna*" and the Buddhist *dharmas* correspond practically to the outer world, which is contained in the *mahābhūtas*, the gross elements of the Sāṅkhya-Yoga.[4]

Jacobi also held that the Brahmanic ascetic was the model of the monastic orders of the Jains and the Buddhists and this view was shared alike by Max Müller, Kern and Bühler. T.W. Rhys Davids said that "Gautama was born and brought up, lived and died a Hindu".

> There is not much in the metaphysics and principles of Gautama that cannot be found in one or other of the orthodox systems, and a great deal of his morality could be matched from the earlier and later Hindu books. Such originality as Gautama possessed lay in

> the way in which he adopted, enlarged, ennobled and systematised that which had already been well said by others : in the way in which he carried out to their logical conclusion principles of equity and justice already acknowledged by some of the most prominent Hindu thinkers. The difference between him and other teachers lay chiefly in his deep earnestness and in his broad public spirit of philanthropy.[5]

Oldenberg, too, thought that "it is certain that Buddhism has acquired as an inheritance from Brahmanism not merely a series of its most important dogmas, but what is not less significant to the historian, the bent of its religious thought and feelings, which is more easily comprehended than expressed in words".[6]

Oldenberg held that the gospel of the Buddha was deeply influenced by the teachings of the Upaniṣads. According to him the problem of early Brahmanical speculations was to define the relation between *ātman* and the external world. A world which is finite, imperfect and painful in all respects when equated with the infinite, perfect and ever-blissful *ātman* would naturally give birth to absolute pessimism.[7] This pessimism resulted in making Buddhism almost comatose. According to Oldenberg, the so-called Aryan migration took place in two waves,[8] the first settlers being driven by a more vigorous second wave dispersed to the forbidden eastern region beyond the river Sadānīrā where they finally settled. In these sultry moist tropical lands, the people who were in the prime of youthful vigour when they penetrated hither from the north (where they took flesh and milk and stayed in a nicer climate) ceased to be stout and strong and became victim of numerous tropical diseases. The rate of their mortality increased to such a fantastic level that they became disinterested in life. The reality of disease, infirmity and death made them unworldly and they resorted to the illusion of the other world, to the ideas of rebirth, transmigration and metempsychosis, which were all supplied by the Buddha as the way out of the miseries of human existence.[9]

Mrs. C.A.F. Rhys Davids[10] held that the original teaching of the Buddha were somewhat different from what they are traditionally reported to have been and even admitted the possibility of the existence of some 'unknown co-founders' of Buddhism. She expressed herself as being quite convinced that the Pali scriptures as they now stand represent the monkish thoughts of times much later than the Buddha's, and if we are to discover his original teachings we must extract it from the scriptures by a process of criticism and discrimination. She believed that the fragments of these teachings could be discovered here and there in the Pali canon and be differentiated from the surrounding material which must lead to the earliest period which was so different from the picture ordinarily found that she preferred to call it Śākya and not Buddhism. She held that in all great religions man is considered imperfect and immature, but he also has the potentiality of overcoming these shortcomings and as such the starting point of the Buddha's teachings could not have been merely the negative one of avoiding the evil propensities. Such a negativist version owed its origin to monkish accretions. For example, the concept of *dukkha* or suffering pertains to the ills of mind and body (mentally to be confronted with the unpleasant and separated from the pleasant; and physically old age, disease and death). It may be a good gospel for the work of a psychologist or a doctor, but not of any religion. She pointed out some fundamental differences between the earliest form of Buddhism and its monkish development. While the Dharma meant to the monks external doctrines, in the earlier doctrine it meant 'inner guide' which was not only immanent, but served as an 'ideal', 'conscience', 'duty', 'the ought and ought not'. She regarded the title Paṭiccasamuppāda as "almost certainly a name given by the compilers of the Sutta Piṭaka at a later date" to what Gotama called 'the doctrine of the middle'. Likewise Mārga which ordinarily meant the eightfold path was considered by Mrs. Rhys Davids to be the working of later systematizing tendency. She advocated the view that the Buddha did not preach the 'no-soul' theory at all, but that it was a later monkish innovation under the impact of the Sāṅkhya, the growth of a narrow world-view and hostility towards the Brāhmaṇas. In the monkish tradition Nirvāṇa was misinterpreted as the extinction of a man's self, but to the Buddha it meant the extinction of passion. The Buddha taught neither the Four Noble Truths, nor *nirvāṇa*, nor *anātman*. These were later developments.

Louis de la Vallee Poussin held that "Buddhism has been, from the beginning, a religion, properly so called, that is, there have been, from the beginning, Buddhists for whom Buddha was a god and who did not hope for a better state, a rebirth in Buddha's heaven, but this Buddhist religion has nothing or little to do with the most authentic teaching of Śākyamuni. Old Buddhism is essentially a discpline of salvation."[11] Poussin held that faith in the Buddha was essential to early Buddhist belief. Together with Keith he viewed the Buddha's silence on metaphysical questions as the result of his agnostic approach to all such problems. He regarded the doctrines of *nairātmya* and *karmaphalasam-*

bandha as the two most important thesis of primitive Buddhism. He said that the concept of *nirvāṇa* as the way of attainment of immortality was absurd. Logically viewed in terms of *anattā* it could denote annihilation. "The doctrine of annihilation was not an original purpose, it was a result." But in the original Buddhism it meant cessation of suffering. According to him Mahayanism was not a later development. It was the logical culmination of primitive Buddhism, and from the very beginning it had a tendency to place the lay supporters on the side of, if not above, the monks.

While Mrs. Rhys Davids held that the *pudgalanairātmya*, *śūnyavāda* and *vijñānavāda* are three consecutive stages of Buddhist thought, Schayer who insisted on precanonical Buddhism considered these to be three distinctive developments of ideas current in unsystematic form in early Buddhist circles. According to him the doctrine of *anityatā* is not the whole doctrine of early Buddhism. The fact is that the Pali Abhidhamma differs from the classification of Vasubandhu in the *Abhidharmakośa* in that it treats as *rūpadharmas* the four *saṃskṛta-lakṣaṇas*, which the Sarvāstivadins assign to the group of *rūpacit-taviprayukta-saṃskāras* and thus confines to *rūpa* the characteristics of origination, of maintenance, of growing old and impermanence. According to Schayer in precanonical Buddhism the elements of *rūpa* alone were considered impermanent. This view, according to Keith, is confirmed by the fact that the Mahāsaṅghika, Ekavyavahārika, Lokottaravādin and Kaukkuṭika schools place in the category of eternal non-contingent elements the four realms belonging to the *ārūpyadhātu* together with the two forms of extinction recognised by them. As opposed to *rūpadhātu*, therefore, we have the *dharmadhātu* as the eternal supersensual reality which can be discerned by mind alone. The distinction between *rūpa* and *dharma* has not been clearly recorded in the scholastic literature of Buddhism in which *dharma* is the generic term for elements, while *rūpa* is a category among *dharmas*. According to Schayer, there is a trace of the old antithesis in the fact that in the enumeration of the twelve *āyatanas* and the eighteen *dhātus* the *dharmāyatana* and the *dharmadhātu* contain only non-rūpa elements. Therefore it is certainly legitimate to suppose that the distinction of *dharma* and *rūpa* was originally clearly drawn.[12]

Keith's study of precanonical Buddhism[13] should be treated in more details. According to him, it is impossible to accept as coming from the Buddha himself any special set of the remarkably varying doctrines which we find current later. The systems which we have are relatively late in date, and they show very different appreciation of ideas which were no doubt strongly held in early Buddhism. For example, the *anātmavāda* is interpreted in very different ways, and is treated as perfectly consistent with the holding of opinions which might well be deemed as *ātmavāda*. There are various canonical passages where we have explanations of *nirvāṇa* which echo the ideas of the Upaniṣads regarding the ultimate reality. In the early Buddhist circles the idea of the ultimate reality, as something akin to the Brahmanical conception of the absolute, was in circulation. From these early speculations in Buddhist schools we may see a natural development direct to the absolute which is developed in the Mahāyāna, and to the consciousness theory of the Vijñānavāda. Agreeing with Schayer, Keith holds that the doctrine of impermanence need not be traced to the Buddha himself on the score of its universal acceptance and that the theory of four general functions (*sāmānyalaksaṇa*) which are manifestations of elements always present every moment in the stream of life process (*jāti*, *sthiti*, *jarā* and *anityatā*) held by the Sarvāstivādins, is manifestly inconsistent with true momentary existence. It was left to the Sautrāntikas who tried to evolve the doctrine of momentariness in a somewhat intelligible from. Here we have clear example of the manner in which a simple fact— the impermanence of physical things originally insisted upon as a means of inviting the attention of the hearers to the importance of that which is permanent—was developed by scholasticism into a metaphysical theory of pronounced difficulty. Likewise, according to Keith, the *dharmas* of Buddhist speculation arose from some much less elaborate idea. Various efforts of the schools to present list of *dharmas* afford little satisfaction. We have various *asaṃskṛta* and *saṃskṛta dharmas*, and the gulf between them is impossible logically to cross. The superimposition of the doctrine of atoms on the *dharmas* at a later date created a more confusing position. The theory that the *dharmas* were borrowed from the *guṇas* does not appear to rest on anything more solid than this general comparison, which seems sadly lacking in cogency. The concept of *dharma* bears obvious traces of reduction from something more concrete. It is not without anthropomorphic traits such as those which affect the structure of the picture of the *ātman* itself. It is impossible to form any intelligible conception of the *dharmas*, as Vasubandhu admitted in his own way. There is also no reason to hold that the Buddhist doctrine of causality was adopted from the Sāṅkhya, because the development of the *satkāryavāda* theory lay not in the Sāṅkhya school itself but in a philosophical debate which has its roots in the *Ṛgveda* itself. The chain aimed at explaining the origin of evil and the interest in causation was only a subordinate phenomenon. The early Buddhist doctrine of the chain of causality need not be ascribed to the Buddha, but it certainly was current early, and it has no relation whatsoever to the philosophical doctrine suggested as his. It may be difficult to understand the Buddhist doctrine of the world, but it is not fair to ascribe to the Buddha the concept of evanescent entities in beginningless commotion, steering to quiescence and annihilation, because that may be a modern interpretation of the universe. Nothing is more unhistorical than to read the minds of early Indian thinkers as if they were products of the twentieth century. According to Keith, we should give up the unscientific attempt to ascribe any definite doctrine to the Buddha and confine ourselves to the perfectly legitimate question of the development of the doctrines, without concerning ourselves with the insoluble question how far they can be carried back to their supposed founder.

Rosenberg[14] had claimed to have established the exact meaning of the basic technical terms of Buddhism, e.g., the term *dharma* meaning elements of existence, the term *saṃskāra* meaning co-operating elements of existence and the term *pratītyasamutpāda* meaning cooperation of the elements of existence. The three terms referred to one and the same system of pluralistic empiricism, which was the core of early Buddhism. Rosenberg had given to Buddhism the name of Dharma theory and declared that Buddhism in the three main forms of its development was nothing but a theory of *dharmas*, i.e., a system of a plurality of ultimate elements of reality to which a monistic foundation had been added in the Mahāyāna. It should be mentioned in this connection that Geiger considered that the concept of *dharma* had originally a supra-mundane and divine implication in the sense of the Upaniṣadic *brahman*. There are certain passages in the Nikāyas in which *dharma* is conceived of as the 'highest impersonal being' and as such the concept of *dharma* may conveniently be associated with that of *brahman*. Mrs. Rhys Davids also advocated a similar opinion. Keith found in the concept of *dharmas* anomalies and contradictions caused by scholastic interpretations. "The *dharmas* may in their ultimate origin have traits of souls, deprived of all concrete character; any real assurance as to their character seems impossible, and their philosophical importance is historical only."[15]

Stcherbatsky[16] who interprets the central conception of Buddhism as a radical pluralism traces the concept of *dharma*, meaning vital essential, super-subtle elements. He claimed that the *dharmas* were infra-atomic dynamic unities of forces or elements whose interdependence according to causal laws constituted the illusive objects of our phenomenal life. He insisted on the exact meaning of the Buddhist technical terms which, according to him, were translated just anyhow, either on the basis of etymology or of common sense. Stcherbatsky's methodology was to depend on what the Buddhist materials themselves had to say on the terms and concepts. His chief source was not the Pali canon, but a later work, the *Abhidharmakośa* of Vasubandhu. According to him, although late, the *Abhidharmakośa* was a systematic exposition of such earlier work which must have preserved the original doctrine very faithfully. Stcherbatsky held that the *dharma* theory was the basis of all forms of Buddhism and the starting point of all later developments. By *dharma* is meant a fundamental principle, viz. the idea that existence is an interplay of a plurality of subtle, ultimate, and not further analysable elements of matter, mind and forces. We do not know of any form of Buddhism without this doctrine and its corollary classification of elements into *skandha*, *āyatana* and *dhātu*, and the law of their interconnection (*pratītysamutpāda*). This doctrine of elements was current in pre-Buddhistic systems and in Buddhism they received a changed significance. According to Stcherbatsky, the idea of self or soul as a psychophysical entity, arising out of the rudimentary doctrine of elements, was not unknown in the earlier traditions. But the idea of an immortal soul, called *ātmavāda* by the Buddhists, was accepted by the subsequent philosophical systems except the materialists and the Buddhists whose sole emphasis was on the older tradition with considerable amendment. By the *anātmavāda* of the Buddhists we understand a plurality of separate elements without real entity, a conception which must have been in existence in pre-Buddhist traditions. According to Stcherbatsky, the basis of the Hīnayāna and Mahāyāna ideas was the same, which drew its main impulses from the earlier traditions. To him, the origin of Buddhism, therefore, was a matter of philosophy, to be traced to the history of ideas, and the Buddha was a representative of a spiritual succession established long ago by the former Buddhas.

B.M. Barua[17] had identified six distinct stages in the development of early Buddhism as a religion, each of which was related to the different phases in the evolution of the Saṅgha. He did not deny the possibility that there was a *lokottara* or supramundane conception of the Buddha from the earliest period which was meant for the laymen. He traced the Upaniṣadic sources of the Buddha's ideas at great length and held that Bhāradvāja, the propounder of the *Muṇḍakopaniṣad*, paved the way for the rational teachings of the Buddha. He called Bhāradvāja a transcendentalist who was the first to lead an anti-Brahmanic crusade. A.K. Coomaraswamy[18] found that the characteristics of the Buddha were similar to those of the Vedic god Agni, both of whom were omniscient and precocious. The abstract concept of causality as the fundamental principle of the phenomenal world was more clearly understood by the Buddha. The roots of the theory of *karman* were already found in the Vedic concept of *ṛta*, and the theory had its further development in later Vedic literature, but it was the Buddha who imparted a very wide and comprehensive significance to *karman*. According to Coomaraswamy the concept of 'becoming' was common to both the Upaniṣads and Buddhism in the sense of organic existence. The so-called pessimism of the Vedānta and Buddhism was not owing to a decline of material civilization, but to the accumulation of experience. Coomaraswamy sought the roots of Buddhism in the entirety of preBuddhist Indian thought, Vedic and non-Vedic. "Just as with the history of the various Brahmanical *darśanas*, so with Buddhism as a sect there remains much to be accomplished in historical elucidation and in exegesis and interpretation. But a more important task has hardly been envisaged: the connected historical study of Indian thought as an organic entirety" (*Gospel*, 219). His valuable work on the Yakṣas clearly demonstrated the popular substratum of the Buddha cult. N. Dutt insisted that the law of causation was the original theoretical basis of Buddhism, since all the schools of Buddhism were agreed on the central importance of *paticcasamuppāda* which had been identified with Dharma and the Buddha in ancient as well as later texts of Buddhism.[19]

Radhakrishnan's approach was categorical. He found no difference between the Upaniṣadic concept of *brahman* and the Buddhist concept of *dharma* which he considered to be essentially an ethical value on the empiric plane. According to him, "Buddhism helped to democratise the philosophy of the Upaniṣads, which was till then confined to select few.... It was Buddha's mission to accept the idealism of the Upaniṣads at its best and make it available for the daily needs of mankind. Historical Buddhism means the spread of the Upaniṣadic doctrine among the people ... such democratic upheavals are common features of Hindu history." He held that the Buddha belonged to the group of Upaniṣadic teachers and said : "The Upanisads arrive at the ground of all things by stripping the self of veil after veil of contingency. At the end of this process they find the universal self, which is none of these finite entities, though the ground of them all. Buddha holds the same view, though he does not state it definitely." Regarding the *anātmavāda* Radhakrishnan said : "Buddha clearly tells us what the self is not, though he does not give any clear account of what it is. It is however wrong to think that there is no self at all according to Buddha....

Buddha is silent about the *ātman* enunciated in the Upaniṣads. He neither affirms nor denies its existence."[20] It should be mentioned in this connection that Mrs. C.A.F. Rhys Davids also thought that the Buddha accepted a soul of the Upaniṣadic type.

S.N. Dasgupta,[21] on the other hand, though he admitted in a general way the influence of the Upaniṣads on Buddhism, had subscribed to the average view of the historians that it was in opposition to the Brahmanical sacrificial cults. He referred to the magical elements in the sacrifice and held that in the time of the Buddha freedom of thought, especially relating to the problems of life and the universe, was absolutely regimented owing to the mechanical sacerdotalism of the priestly class. According to him, the Upaniṣads prepared the ground of intellectual freedom which was cultivated with profit by the Buddha. He modernised the earlier concepts like *karman* which was "rooted in the Indian mind from the earliest days in the tribal belief in the efficacy of magical operations, incantations and the like, and it was only extended at a large stage into the ethical field." He held that early Buddhism as interpreted in the Theravāda school did not show any positive conception of Nirvāṇa. According to him the original Buddhism was based on 'sturdy universal rationalism' and simple morality and it was only in the subsequent stages that the mystic beliefs in the essenceless state of Nirvāṇa as the ultimate and highest state to be attained by the extinction of cravings and by the knowledge gained through Yoga came to be established.

Vidhusekhar Bhattacharya[22] tried to make an historical analysis of the earlier streams which influenced the teachings of the Buddha. He did not subscribe to the view that the Upaniṣadic *brahmavidyā* was developed in the hands of the Kṣatriya princes who were opposed to the Brahmanical rituals. Nor he was ready to accept the view that the original purpose of Buddhism was to raise emphatic protest against the contemporary bloody sacrifices. He held that the Buddhist polemics against the sacrificial cult and priesthood were only of secondary importance. He pointed out that the Vedic Yajñas had their own logic and their special mechanism was meant for achieving definite external purposes, the social importance of which could hardly be minimised. He was probably the first to point out that the Vedic Yajñas had an altogether different implication, as was evident from the tradition of the Mīmāṃsakas. The concept that God has no mastery of worldly objects and is utterly incapable of bestowing them to the worshippers was probably borrowed by the Buddha from the earlier ritualistic traditions. Vidhusekhar insisted on the role of the ascetics and free thinkers who flourished before and during the age of the Buddha and also on the influence of the Upaniṣads and the Sāṅkhya on the ideological formulations of the Buddha. The Buddhist concept of *avidyā* as the basic cause of suffering had its origin in the Upaniṣads in which it was defined as the knowledge for material enjoyments as opposed to *parā-vidyā* which was the science of spiritual happiness.

One of the most remarkable studies on the origins of Buddhism was made by G.C. Pande.[23] His approach needs to be discussed at a greater length. According to him, at the very outset we have to realize that even the earliest available collections within the Buddhist canon are of uncertain date and heterogeneous contents. They contain within themselves seeds of multiform growth. From what we know about the Chinese Āgamas it appears safe to draw a similar general conclusion about them. An historical approach to ancient Buddhism, therefore, most certainly entails the stratifaction of the Nikāyas and the Āgamas. An examination of the Bharhut and Sanchi inscriptions shows that some time before the second century B.C. there was already a collection of Buddhist texts, which was called 'Piṭakas' and was divided into five Nikāyas, that there were 'Suttas' in which the 'Dhamma' was preached, that some of these agreed with those contained in our Tripiṭaka, and that Jātakas of exactly the same kind as those contained in the Tripiṭaka, already belonged to the stock of Buddhist literature. It may therefore be asserted that the growth of the Nikāyas falls between the fifth and the third centuries B.C. The silence of the Vinaya over the third Council suggests that it had reached completion in the first two centuries after the Buddha. The silence of the canon over Aśoka which contrasts so strongly with later tradition is also significant in this respect and suggests its antiquity.[24]

Pande made a stratification of the Nikāyas and to a certain extent he was able to detect their earlier and later contents. According to him the stratification of the Sūtras should appear as a *sine qua non* of future progress in the direction of discovering ancient Buddhism. Previously Oldenberg[25] had held that the *Pātimokkha* and part at least of the liturgical formulae embedded in the *Khandakas* framed the earliest stratum. As regards the Sutta Piṭaka, he supposed, on the analogy of liturgical formulae, that the earliest expression of the Dhamma must have been in dogmatic paragraphs consisting of such formulae as the Four Noble Truths, the Twelve Nidānas, etc., and devoid of all narrative details. But Pande says that the analogy does not hold and that formulae, technicalities and systems etc., must be of secondary consequence. The original concepts mostly at first express themselves quite nebulously, taking frequently the aid of myth. According to T.W. Rhys Davids the four

Nikāyas "had been put together out of older material at a period halfway between the death of the Buddha and the accession of Aśoka".[26] The course of evolution he had outlined in ten stages. He also insisted on the importance of the test from vocabulary, of "words used in one sense in the older strata of the literature and in another sense in the later strata".[27]

Pande says :

> The evolution of the Nikāyas falls between the age of the Upaniṣads and that of the Abhidharma and other Buddhist sectarian literature. This provides us with a general sense of direction in trying to discover what is early and what is late in the Nikāyas. The growth of monastic learning and of philosophical analysis and controversy led to increased complexity, subtlety and system in the realm of ideas till the message of Buddha was converted into a stupendous scholastic philosophy. At the same time the spread of Buddhism among the people led it to imbibe many elements of popular religion and helped the apotheosis of Buddha. *Pari Passu* with this orientation in doctrinal change there was a corresponding change in the style of expression which tended to lose simplicity and spontaneity and poetic vigour in favour of dry-as-dust abstract scholarly formulae. Linguistically, too, the change may be seen in the use of the new technical terms and in the development of new technical senses for old words.[28]

Quoting Carpenter he says like the Gospel the Nikāyas "grew up in the dark, and their history can only be recovered in the form of a series of conjectures to account for the facts which they exhibit".[29]

Having made a distinction between the earlier and later portions of Vinaya and the Nikāyas in his own way on the basis of internal textual analysis, the general ideological trends, interpolations, vocabulary and linguistic features, historical background and geographical considerations, Pande holds in opposition of Stcherbatsky and Mrs. Rhys Davids, that the concept of the Four Truths was an integral part of the original doctrine. Regarding the theory of Mrs. Rhys Davids that the monkish accretions inverted the original teachings of the Buddha, he says that although the fact of negativist monkish 'more wording' seems undeniable, it is perhaps not unreasonable to suggest that this process had its distant roots in the character of the original mandate itself. The development appears to have been more of a one-sided accentuation than a radical inversion. He holds that the understanding of the concept of *dukkha* or suffering in terms of birth, disease, old age and death should be understood symbolically not literally. He holds that Stcherbatsky's view of *dukkha* is bounded up with his view of Nirvāṇa "If *dukkha* is the 'commotion' of 'elements', it is something 'objective', a real pervasive feature of the Universe, and escape from it can come, consistently with the denial of *uccheda*, only through non-experience. Nirvāṇa becomes akin to endless sleep"![30] According to Pande, *dukkha* in the Nikāyas seems to mean primarily pain or disagreeable feeling, actual or potential, and secondarily, through extension of meaning, what may proximately or remotely cause such a feeling.

The law of dependent origination (*paṭiccasamuppāda*) has been regarded by Pande as one of the fundamental doctrines of early Buddhism, but he does not agree with the widely accepted view of T.W. Rhys Davids[31] that it was the first clear enunciation in history of the principle of natural causality in all phenomena on the ground that such formulations would make the Buddha a forerunner of Comte or of modern psychology. He also rejects the view of Mrs. Rhys Davids[32] that the Buddha utilised the causal idea in favour of his Gospel of the way as a becoming better through the exercise of will, since perception of causal uniformities could become an aid in realising the ideals. According to Pande, it is curious, indeed, that the Buddha should need the cosmic consciousness of the Enlightment in order ot discover a principle which naturalist philosophers have speculatively discovered in all ages. He also dismisses Coomaraswamy's[33] interpretation of the origin of suffering in terms of the involvement of the spirit in the contingent life of Nature. According to Pande, these views are valuable but cannot be equated with the Buddha's own idea which was so comprehensive and so non-technically phrased that it became the source of diverse interpretations.[34] Paṭiccasamuppāda has a double aspect—a primary and general aspect including the fundamental ground of *dukkha* and an applied and secondary aspect which indicates the proximate cause of *dukkha* in psychological terms. The Buddha universalised and impersonalised causality, omitting a personal creator as the First Cause, and treated it not as a relation between substances based on the expression of personal or material energy but as an invariance of order between events and their conditions. Pande's final conclusion is that the treatment of Paṭiccasamuppāda repudiates the assumption that it was the result of deliberate thought on the part of any one individual. Apart from the central idea, the formula has grown through accretions, fusions and analysis.[35]

Regarding the question of the historical origins of Buddhism Pande holds that in the sixth century B.C. the age of 'migrations and settlements' was over, and that the territorial element had attained preponderance over the tribal in the organisation of the state. A trial of strength was taking place between the monarchies and also between the monarchical and non-monarchical forms of government. The contest plainly showed the decline of republics, the rise of absolutism and the growing success of Magadhan imperialism. The growth of towns and commerce and the organisation of trade and craft into guilds made the social landscape of the age quite distinct from that of the preceding period. The origins of Buddhism and Jainism must have been linked with these changes. In the atmosphere of the town life much of the symbolism of the older Vedic religion, derived from natural phenomena and pastoral and agricultural functions, would become dim, the gods less convincing, and the ritual obscure and even pointless. A sharp contrast had developed between its prevailing tendency, which was formalistic, ritualistic, and at heart quite worldly, and the new departure of the Upaniṣads, which tended increasingly in an esoteric and ascetic direction. Ritualism was worsted in its struggle with ascetic renunciation and creed of a life of virtue and devotion.[36] Both Buddhism and Jainism derived their main impulses from this new trend. Pande, however, holds that Buddhism and Jainism can hardly be looked upon as reforming movements. Undoubtedly these systems were to a certain extent influenced by their contemporary social changes, but the latter could not have been the cause of their origins.[37]

As regards the question of the social origins of Buddhism the views of the scholars differ from one another. Certain passages found in the Buddhist texts pertaining to social equality and social justice led some historians, social and religious reformers and even political activists to view the Buddha as a social revolutionary, a crusader against the Brahmanical ritualism and an emancipator of the oppressed. Such an approach is found in the writings of the nineteenth-century Indian intelligentsia. The theory that Buddhism as a religion heralded a Kṣatriya revolt against the Brahmanical theology, metaphysics and ritualism was zealously supported by modern religious reformers like Svāmī Vivekananda[38] and political thinkers like M.N. Roy[39] and Jawaharlal Nehru.[40] Among Buddhalogists, C.A.F. Rhys Davids[41] holds that "the frequency with which we find the Buddha consulted on the growing social claims were a burning question of the day. His own positions tracing the origin of social divisions or 'classes' to some primitive norm or standard (*dhamma*) arising through division of labour, and recognising only an aristocracy of intellect and virtue, must have appealed strongly to those who were dissatisfied with the Brahmin's assumptions." Monier-Williams[42] held that the Buddha "was a Hindu of the Hindus and he remained a Hindu to the end". He was the first to establish some kind of a "universal monastic communism", but he had very little to do with the social issues. Although Oldenberg[43] quoted certain sayings of Buddha pertaining to social justice, of which we have already had the occasion to refer, he denied the Buddha the role of a social reformer.

The origin of Buddhism has also been linked with the emergence of the trading communities and the consequent rise of urbanism in the time of the Buddha. Among the followers of the Buddha there were many business magnates, besides the royal converts, who liberally financed the monastic organisation. P.L. Narsu[44] holds that "the time of the full sway of the guilds coincides with the period of the greatest Buddhist influence and it was in the provinces where Buddhism was strongest that the merchant guilds were most firmly established." N. Dutt[45] demonstrates that the Vaiśya community of Rajgir furnished the largest number of converts. According to Max Weber[46] "Like Jainism, but even more clearly, Buddhism presents itself as a product of the time of urban development, of urban kingship and city nobles.... Oldenberg drew attention to the fact that rural surroundings, cattle and pasture were characteristic of the ancient Brahmanical teachers and schools, at least in the early times of Upaniṣads, whereas the city and the urban palace with its elephant riding kings were characteristic of Buddha's time." Elsewhere he says that Buddhism began as a salvation doctrine of a privileged intellectual class and in its initial stages it had very little to do with the non-privileged.[47] Among the Marxist scholars, D.D. Kosambi[48] held that the Vaiśyas and the Śūdras had the task of producing the surplus which the priests and the warriors took away by natural right, originally for the good of tribes, but soon for the good of the upper castes. The Vedic ritual was formulated in pastoral age where large herds collectively owned were the main form of property. The new society had gone over to agriculture, so that the slaughter of more and more animals at a growing number of sacrifices meant a much heavier drain upon producer and production, telling upon trading class and the new economic set-up. Herein lies the economic reason of the Buddhist and Jain emphasis on *ahiṃsā* or non-killing. Truth, justice, not encroaching upon the possession of others, and similar values show that a totally new concept of private individual property had arisen. The *ahiṃsā* doctrine first expressed the basic fact that agriculture can support at least ten times the number of people per square mile than a pastoral economy in the same territory. The doctrine of *karman* was a religious extension of the elementary concept of agricultural economy. It could grow and ripen like a seed planted in a previous season, or mature like a debt, while it never failed to pay in exact proportion. Buddhism did not fight to abolish all castes from society even though the Śramana himself renounced caste. Though the Buddhist monastic order functioned along the lines of a tribal *sabhā* council, the Buddhist precepts were meant for a class society far beyond the tribe, caste or cult.

The views of Kosambi were basically accepted and modified to a considerable extent by two Marxist scholars, Debiprasad Chattopadhyaya and R.S. Sharma. Debiprasad[49] sought to explain the origin of Buddhism in the light of the great social transformation, the rise of class society and state power, that took place during the lifetime of the Buddha. According to him, the Buddha was overwhelmed by the stupendous social transformation and wholesale bloodshed of his time; and so also were his contemporaries who, however, thought that there was nothing to be done at all about these. The Buddha on the other hand asked the people to join the Saṅghas, which were modelled on the patterns of tribal democracies and meant to be the ideal substitutes for a vanished way of life. It should be mentioned in this connection that many of the earlier scholars such as Rhys Davids, Oldenberg, Monier-Williams, K.P. Jayaswal, R.C. Majumdar and others thought it necessary to use the term 'communistic' to describe the functioning of the early Buddhist Saṅghas. The Saṅghas were run strictly on the basis of democratic rules. All decisions were to be unanimous, and if that was not possible the verdict of the majority was to be respected. There was no such thing as private property within the Saṅghas. The monks could only use three garments, stitched from rags, an almsbowl, needle and thread, and a razor, but these were not his private possessions. The monks were forbidden ownership of houses, fields, cattle, the touch of gold and silver and trade. They lived on alms which amounted to a single meal a day. Wherefrom did the Buddha imitate such a model? According to Debiprasad this model was basically tribal. How thoroughly did the Buddha imitate the tribal model had been shown by Debiprasad who, having dealt elaborately with the facts relating to (i) the procedure of entry into Saṅgha, (ii) the internal administration of the Saṅgha and (iii) the personal or private property within the Saṅgha, came to the conclusion that at a critical stage of Indian history, while the free tribes of the times were being ruthlessly exterminated and, within the orbits of the expanding state powers people were experiencing the rise of new values on the ruins of tribal equality, the Buddha was modelling his Saṅgha on the basic principles of tribal society and was advising the brethren of his order to mould their lives according to these principles. This point is crucial. In building up his own Saṅgha, the Buddha could provide the people of his times with the illusion of a lost reality of the dying tribal collective. And it was only the great genius of the Buddha which could have built this coherent and complete illusion. Not only did he successfully build up his Saṅgha on the model of the preclass society, but he took great care to see that the members therein—the *bhikṣus* within the Saṅgha—lived a perfectly detached life, i.e. detached from the great historical transformation going on in the society at large, whose course was obviously beyond his power to change. And at the same time the Buddha had to face the dual requirement of his age, and this alone explains why a considerable number of contemporary aristocrats and business magnates formed his front-rank associates. This explains why Buddhism had given moral support to the interest of the trading class. In fact, the Buddha had to act as an unconscious tool of history and it was not possible for him to change the course of historical transformation and what he could do under such a condition was to boost up some of its progressive features in public life and to revive some of the beneficial aspects of tribal life in a class society.

Another Marxist scholar R.S. Sharma[50] held that the primary factor that revolutionised the material life of the people around 700 B.C. in Eastern U.P. and Bihar, the birth place of Buddhism, was the use of iron which initiated plough agriculture with iron ploughshare, and consequently created a new social set-up, a class society marked by the rise of state power, in which cattle in the form of private wealth, to be increased by commercial activities, gained much importance, and its senseless destruction for the purpose of non-vegetarian food and also for the purpose of Brahmanical sacrificial cults came to be discouraged. The voice of protest was raised by the trading class and was given theoretical and moral support by the Buddha and his contemporaries. The most emphatic protest against animal sacrifice is registered in the early Pali texts. The Brahmanical attitude towards trade was not helpful. The traders were not encouraged and they were assigned a lower place in society. The Buddha took up the cause of this emergent class, having something new to contribute during its rise to power, and that is why traders of the first rank became his associates, and Buddhism lent all moral support to the financial and other interest of the trading class.[51]

A comprehensive work on the origins of Buddhism was subsequently made by V.P. Varma[52] who held that inspite of having social, economic and political consequences, the Buddha's movement was primarily ethical and religious. According to him, it is true that the Buddha obtained some deep and profound illumination (*bodhi*) in state of mystic absorption. But the philosophical formulation of the pratītyasamutpāda and the four Aryan truths can only be studied with reference to the various currents and crosscurrents of India's religious history from about the tenth century B.C. onwards. The picture of early Buddhist teachings that we get in the Vinaya and Sutta Piṭaka can, in several aspects, be shown to be influenced by the process of the decline of the Vedic religion also. A great religious movement is not ushered in all at once. Sometimes it may be that for centuries dominant ideas incubate and thus the background is prepared for a very long time. The general currents and crosscurrents in the social and religious history of India from a very early period were working in a direction which, by the inevitable law of historical causation, culminated in the Buddhist movement.

At the same time Varma holds that the stress on the situational background of a big religious movement does not imply that we should neglect the determining influence of the world-moving personality of the Buddha on the genesis of early Buddhism. But the study of the situational background helps us to appreciate the forces amidst which a great religious personality flourishes and with reference to which his teachings are oriented. Hence along with the study of the philosophy and ethics of early Buddhism, the historical evolution of ancient Indian religion should also be shown. According to Varma, it is essential to apply the historical method to the study of the growth of moral, philosophical and religious concepts and propositions from the Vedic days onwards; second, textual study of the early Buddhist scriptures for the determination of the successive layers of the contents of the books; and third, application of the historical method to early Buddhism for analysing the entire social, political and economic background of the movement and for discovering the forces which helped to determine the crystallisation and growth of Buddhism as a religious association and movement.

While Max Müller, Deussen, Oldenberg, Schayer, Keith and Barua undertook the study of the influence of the Upaniṣads on Buddhism, Varma has tried to trace the roots of Buddhism in the Vedic Saṃhitās themselves. This he claims to be one of the main contributions which his work may make to knowledge. The Vedas contain several types of thought and different layers of poetic collections. According to him, there is no dearth of sceptical and critical elements in the Saṃhitās. Even during the days of the Upaniṣads there are references to the doctrines of *asadvāda*. The Buddha seems to continue the critical, rational and protestant elements in ancient Indian thought. There must have been a continuity from the later Vedic days, in the succession of teachers who sponsored a critical and sceptical attitude against ritualism, and the Buddha belonged to this tradition. It is a mistake, in the opinion of the author, to represent early Buddhism as a philosophical carrying forward of the streams of Upaniṣadic thought. The Buddha was an ethical teacher who stressed *dhyāna*, *samādhi* and *nirvāṇa*, but he also challenged some of the essential propositions of Brahmanism. But although early Buddhism was critical in its attitude to contemporary Brahmanism, and although it used some negative phraseology as *anātman*, *nairātmya* and *nirvāṇa*, possibly to differentiate and to keep its system apart from the Brahmanism of those days, it had solid positive teachings of its own.

The psychological factors in the origin of religions have also been considered by Varma with special reference to Buddhism. According to him, if the Indian national mind did accept the teachings of the Vedānta and Buddhism, it does indicate that some important individuals and groups must have had the deep desire to make a search after immortality and must have believed that through the acquisition of supernormal Yogic powers immortality could be obtained. Varma's second proposition is that it is an important problem of psychology of religion to study the motivations that led people like Bimbisāra and Prasenajit to become so deeply attached to the new gospel of Buddhism. What were the motivational compulsives that led rich traders accept Gautama's teachings? Were they thus seeking 'compensations' for guilty conscience at their being rich while the masses suffered or were they anxious to unravel the mysteries of the beyond because the present was seized with the prospect of death? Psychological factors are present not only in the acceptance of moral and metaphysical truths but also in the interpretations that are put on religious and metaphysical notions in successive ages. One of the fundamentals of early Buddhism was the stress on the 'anxiety' element as the impelling basis of man's existence. Although the problem of the Buddha started at a psychological level, it is eternal in the sense that death, disease, dismay and final disaster are the permanent destiny of all human beings. The Buddha wanted an escape and he found the way in the theory and practice of the negation and neutralisation of the human ego.

The present author considers Buddhism as one of the numerous offshoots of the Vedic religious tradition. It wanted to project the 'enlightened one' (*buddha*) far above the natural gods of the Vedas. In Jainism too we find that the known Vedic and non-Vedic gods have been superseded by the 'enlightened ones', the Tīrthaṃkaras or Jinas. The process of such supersession began in the post-Ṛgvedic age when the early Vedic nature-gods were first subordinated to Yajña, elevated to the position of the world principle in the Brāhmaṇa literature, and then to *brahman*, the all-pervading cosmic self of the Upaniṣads. Two common features are conspicuous in the whole process. The first is the marked decline in the position of the Vedic nature-gods which was probably caused by man's increasing mastery over nature. The second is the introduction of a personal or human element in the cosmic scheme. In the case of the undefined Yajña, gods are subordinated to human efforts. They can be coerced through appropriate rituals to obey the command of the performers. Although in a religious sense the concept of *brahman* later culminated in the growth of monotheism based on the equation of the sectarian Supreme Beings with the Upaniṣadic Absolute, the basic concept was based on the equation of the cosmic self with the human individual self. In Buddhism the concept of the 'enlightened one' was superimposed on the traditional deities either in the form of a supramundane Buddha humanly incarnated by the historical Buddha or in the form of the historical Buddha apotheosised to the status of the Supreme Being in course of time. Buddhism from its very beginning was basically and functionally a cult of the Buddha and of the pantheon of gods of which he was the patriarch. Both the Hīnayāna and the Mahāyāna texts attribute the characteristics of the Supreme Being to the Buddha. His worldly existence and even his 'great demise' did not disqualify him from becoming the Supreme Being. This is not an unusual feature in the history of religion. Kṛṣṇa was man and God in the same form; so were Christ and Virgin Mary.[53] During his lifetime Śrī Caitanya was regarded as the Rādhā-Kṛṣṇa combine. The same happened in the case of the Buddha who had combined in himself the elements of divinity and omniscience.[54]

NOTES

1. T.W. Rhys Davids, *Buddhism* (London,1877), 85-86; *Buddhism : Its History and Culture* (London, 1896); *Dialogues of the Buddha*, I, (London, 1899), 96 ff.; A. Barth, *Religions of India*, Eng. tr.

(London, 1882; rep. Delhi, 1969), 101-39; H. Oldenberg, *Buddha*, Eng. tr. (London, 1882; rep. Delhi, 1971), 1 ff.; M. Monier Williams, *Buddhism* (London, 1889); E.W. Hopkins, *Religions of India* (Boston, 1895) rep. New Delhi, 1970), 298-347; J.H.C. Kern, *A Manual of Indian Buddhism*, (Strassburg, 1896; rep. Delhi, 1968), 11 ff.; C. Eliot, *Hinduism and Buddhism*, I (London, 1921); N. Dutt, *Early Monastic Buddhism*, I (Calcutta, 1941); G.C. Pande, *Studies in the Origins of Buddhism* (Allahabad, 1957; see rev. ed. Delhi, 1974), 251-368; A.K. Warder, *Indian Buddhism* (New Delhi, 1970), 33-37; etc.

2. P. Deussen, *System Des Vedānta* (Leipzig, 1883), 18ff.; R. Garbe, *Beiträge zur indischen Kulturgeschichte* (Berlin, 1903), 1ff; R. Fick, *Social Organisation in NE India in Buddha's Time* (Eng. tr. S. Mitra), (Calcutta, 1920), 90 ff.; S.N. Dasgupta, *A History of Indian Philosophy* (Cambridge, 1922), I, 31; S.K. Belvalkar and R.D. Ranade, *History of Indian Philosophy* (Poona, 1927), II, 44 ff.; N. Dutt, *Early Monastic Buddhism* (1960 ed). 27-61; A.L. Basham, *History and Doctrine of the Ājīvikas* (London, 1951), 18 ff.; D.P. Chattopadhyaya, *Lokāyata* (Delhi, 1959), 504-24; G.C. Pande, op.cit., see rev. ed., 313-14, N.N. Bhattacharya, *Jain Philosophy : Historical Outline* (New Delhi, 1975) 51-80. The view that the Kṣatriyas had an essential share in the development of Upaniṣadic ideas was contested by H. Oldenberg, *Die Lehre der Upanishaden* (Gottingen, 1915), 166ff.; A.B. Keith, *Aitareya Āraṇyaka* (Oxford, 1919), 50; *JRAS*, 1915, 550; etc. According to G.C. Pande "the hypothesis of a conflict between the two has been sometimes put forward and the Kṣatriyas have been credited with the leadership of a revolt against Brahmanical religion and social supremacy. It is, however, difficult to see any real class basis of this conflict. Nor there is any definite evidence for the suggestion."

3. The term Yajña has always been vaguely translated as 'sacrifice' meaning 'the slaughter of animals or the surrender of a possession to a god for the purpose of pleasing him.' Behind such a rendering must have worked the impact of the Biblical legend of Abraham's sacrifice of his son to appease God—a legend to which the Western scholars were traditionally accustomed. Although this interpretation is fallacious, the same was also held by a good number of early Indian authorities. Śabara had to make enormous intellectual exercise to convince his contemporaries that Yajña had nothing to do with the propitiation of gods, since they had no ownership of worldly objects and were utterly incapable of bestowing them upon the performer. This shows that the significance of Yajña was misunderstood even in remote antiquity. It is also to be noted that a very sophisticated philosophical system like the Pūrva Mīmāṃsā which rejects the concept of God downright firmly believes in the efficacy of the Vedic

Yajñas. This proves that in the olden days the Yajñas were understood in quite a different sense.

4. Jacobi's conclusions were extended by Schayer who held that the chain was a *kosmische emanationsformel*. Deussen holds that *vijñāna* is cosmic and produces all reality. Keith (*IHQ*, XII, 1-20) tried to trace a parallel between the Buddhist concept of *nirvāṇa* and the Sāṅkhya concept of liberation while Radhakrishnan (*Indian Philosophy*, I, 472n) held that there was a close resemblance between the Buddhist *pratītyasamutpāda* and the Sāṅkhya *pratyasarga*. R Pischel, *Leben und Lehre des Buddha* (Leipzig, 1905; Eng. tr. B.H. Kapadia, 1965), held that theoretical Buddhism rested on Sāṅkhya-yoga and had borrowed from the latter everything. Garbe (*Die Sāṃkhya Philosophie*) held that the Buddha knew the Sāṅkhya in its complete form. Schrader (*Indian Culture*, I, 1934-35, 543 ff) held that the influence of Vedānta on Buddhism was peripheral while that of the Sāṅkhya total. S.N. Dasgupta (*HIP*, I, 78) also held that there was truth in the view that Buddhism drew much of its inspiration from the Sāṅkhya and the Yoga.
5. *Buddhism* (London, 1877), 83-84 (1925 ed.).
6. *Buddha* (London, 1882), 52.
7. A similar view was also expressed by Kern in his *Manual of Indian Buddhism* (Strassburg, 1896).
8. Cf. Hoernle-Grierson-Chanda theory of the Inner and Outer Bands of the Aryans.
9. *Buddha*, 16-59. Oldenberg tried, of course on the basis of un-founded assumptions, to view the teachings of the Buddha in the light of contemporary social life. But he did not subscribe to Köppen's evaluation of the Buddha as a social revolutionary, although he quoted a few says of the Buddha dealing with social inequalities. *Ibid.*, 64. His statement that Buddhism was the earliest beginning of the monastic movement in India does not seem to be valid from an historical point of view. His view that "the Brāhmaṇas, standing without the pale of the state, find themselves together in a great confederacy" is also not supported by evidence.
10. *Buddhism : A Study of the Buddhist Norm* (New York, 1912) rev. *Buddhism : Its Birth and Dispersal* (London, 1934); *Buddhist Psychology* (London, 1914, 1924; rev. *Birth of Indian Philosophy and Its Development*, London 1936); *Gotama the Man* (London, 1928; *Śākya Or Buddhist Origins* (London, 1931); 'Soul-Theory in Buddhism' in *JRAS*, 1903, 587-91; 'Dhyāna in Early Buddhism' in *IHQ*, III, 1927, 689-715; 'Man as Willer' in *Buddhistic Studies* (ed. B.C. Law), (Calcutta, 1931) 587-611; 'The Unknown Co-Founders of Buddhism' in *JRAS*, 1927, 193- 208. In her 'Relations between Early Buddhism and Brahmanism', *IHQ*, X, 1934, 276, Mrs. Rhys Davids said that "there was nothing in Brahmanism resembling the

ecclesiastical autocracy of the Holy Roman Church of the Middle Ages."

11. *The Way of Nirvāṇa* (Cambridge, 1917), 30; *Le Dogme et sa philosophie du Bouddhisme* (Paris, 1930).
12. *Archiv Orientalni*, VII, 120 ff.; *Ausgewählte Kapitel aus der Prasannapadā*, 83 ff.
13. *IHQ*, XII, 1936, 1-20; *Buddhist Philosophy* (Oxford, 1923), 27 ff.
14. *Die Probleme der buddhistischen Philosophie* (Berlin, 1924).
15. *IHQ*, XII,; Cf. Schayer in *Archiv Orientalni*, VII, 129-30.
16. "The Dharmas of the Buddhists and the Guṇas of the Sāṅkhya" in *IHQ*, X, 1934, 737-60; *The Central Conception of Buddhism* (Leningrad, 1927; rep. New Delhi, 1970), 65 ff.
17. *Prolegomena to the History of Buddhist Philosophy* (Calcutta, 1918); *A History of Pre-Buddhistic Indian Philosophy* (Calcutta, 1925); 'Early Buddhism' in the *Cultural Heritage of India*, I, 237 ff.
18. 'Rebirth and Omniscience in Pali Buddhism' in *Indian Culture*, III, 1936-37; *Buddha and the Gospel of Buddhism* (London, 1916).
19. *Early History of the Spread of Buddhism and the Buddhist Schools* (Calcutta, 1925); *Aspects of Mahāyāna and its Relation to Hinayāna* (Calcutta, 1930); *Early Monastic Buddhism* (Calcutta, 1941, 1945).
20. *Indian Philosophy* (Cambridge, 1922), 1, 340-476, 581-669. The quotations from *ibid.*, 386-89, 471.
21. *History of Indian Philosophy*, I, 78-168; *Hindu Mysticism* (London, 1927), 85-109; *Indian Idealism* (Cambridge, 1932), 76-108; *Philosophical Essays* (Calcutta, Univ., 1941), 117-50.
22. *The Basic Conception of Buddhism* (Calcutta, 1934).
23. *Studies in the Origins of Buddhism* (Allahabad, 1957).
24. *Ibid.*, 1-16. Rhys Davids concluded that the Nikāyas were put together out of older material at a period about half way between the death of the Buddha and the accession of Aśoka.
25. Intro. to the PTS ed. of the *Vinaya Piṭaka* and also Intro. to *SBE*, XIII (in collaboration with T.W. Rhys Davids).
26. *Cambridge History of India*, I, 95; Cf. B.C. Law, *History of Pali Literature*, I, 42.
27. *Dialogues of the Buddha*, III (IX).
28. *Op.cit.*, 27.
29. *Ibid.*, 28.
30. *Ibid.*, 404-05.
31. *Dialogues of the Buddha*, II. 42 ff.
32. *Śākya*, 148-62.
33. *Hinduism and Buddhism*, 80.
34. Pande, *op. cit.* 411-12.
35. *Ibid.*, 413 ff.
36. Cf. R.G. Bhandarkar, *Collected Works*, IV, 3ff.; Belvalkar and Ranade, *History of Indian Philosophy*, 443 ff.

37. Pande, *op. cit.*, 310 ff.
38. *Complete Works*, IV, 378.
39. *From Savagery to Civilization*, 9.
40. *The Discovery of India*, 95.
41. *Buddhism*, 115.
42. *Buddhism : Its Connection with Brahmanism and Hinduism* (London, 1890), 71 ff.
43. *Buddha*, 64 ff., 152 ff.
44. *The Essence of Buddhism* (Madras, 1912), 140.
45. *Early History of the Spread of Buddhism* (Calcutta, 1925).
46. *The Religion of India*, Eng. tr. by Gerth and Martindale (Illinois, 1958), 204-05.
47. *Sociology of Religion* (London, 1965), 116-17.
48. *Introduction to the Study of Indian History* (Bombay, 1956); *Culture and Civilization of Ancient India* (Bombay, 1965).
49. *Lokayata* (Delhi, 1959), 459ff.
50. *Das Kapital Centenary Volume*, ed. M. Sen (Delhi, 1970), 66ff. 'Material Milieu of the Birth of Buddhism', in 29th *International Congress of Orientalists* (Paris, 1973).
51. It may, however, be said that the earlier Chalcolithic elements continue to occur in a significant quantity at all the sites even after the beginning of the use of iron. But iron was the basic technological element from the sixth century B.C. onwards. In this connection I like to point out that in the Vedic texts there is practically no reference to iron and that iron is mentioned in the earlier Upaniṣads only twice. In the Upaniṣads we also come across clear evidence of an enormous amount of social surplus accumulated in the hands of the kings and aristocrats. Kings like Janaka could bestow as gifts thousands of cattle to those preaching the doctrine of *brahman*. The source of this surplus could only be two—either by a revolutionary change in the mode of production or by heavily exploiting the toiling masses. In any case, the sixth century B.C. was the greatest turning point of ancient Indian history. See N.N. Bhattacharyya, *Jain Philosophy: Historical Outline* (New Delhi, 1976), 54ff.
52. *Early Buddhism and Its Origins* (New Delhi, 1973).
53. From the spiritual and orthodox position it was held (i) that Jesus being the eternal son of God, became man, being conceived by the Holy Ghost and born of the Virgin Mary and (ii) that inasmuch as he is thus God and man in two distinct natures and one person for ever, so is *she*, his Mother, truly and properly described Theotokos and Virgo Deipara—the Mother of Our Lord and God, who was God when *he* issued from virgin womb, wearing the *manhood* which of her substance has been prepared for *him*, which *he* had taken to himself, which *he* carried with *him* to the cross. This argument is the part and

parcel of the faith of the whole Catholic Church. For details see my *India Mother Goddess* (New Delhi, 1977), 195-201.

54. Thus the Buddha may also be regarded as one the precursors of the *guruvāda* of later times according to which the *guru* or the preceptor or the founder of a sectarian system should be equated with the Supreme Being and worshipped by the devotees.

III

THE IDEOLOGICAL BACKGROUND: AN ENQUIRY

The proposition that the Buddha was averse to what is known as Brahmanical ritualism or Vedic sacrifices has been taken for granted, notwithstanding the abundance of ritualistic ingredients in Buddhism itself. We have already said that the term 'sacrifice' should not be regarded as the synonym of Yajña and that it is impossible to know at the present state of our knowledge what the Vedic Yajña really meant to the early Indians. Yajña has been considered by most scholars as a form of mechanical sacerdotalism invented by the Brāhmaṇas for the material gain of their own class. It is generally held that in the age of the *Ṛgveda* the main object of the Yajña was to draw the attention of the gods by offering them food and drink and that in the subsequent age of Brāhmaṇa literature this simple method of attracting the gods was so transformed by wily Brāhmaṇas that it became a show of meaningless extravagance and corrupt practices of the privileged class.[1]

But one should not fail to recall in this connection that the Mīmāṃsa school of Indian philosophy which completely rejects the concept of a creator god as logically irrelevant and ontologically repulsive categorically holds that the Veda in its entirety is meant for being used in Yajña which is the *summum bonum* of human existence. Now if the Yajñas meant nothing more than useless rituals invented by the Brāhmaṇas for the sake of their own mateial gain, a most intellectual and highly sophisticated system like the Pūrva Mīmāṃsā could not have been their staunch supporters. As we have already noted, the general belief is that the rituals are prescribed for pleasing the gods or for invoking their favour by offering something to them. But it is precisely such an idea that the Mīmāṃsakas want vigorously to reject. Śabara's arguments in this connection may be summarised as follows : From the performance of ritual acts originates that which was not before (*apūrva*). According to the Vedas, Yajña is the cause of yielding result and not the gods, because the result is the *puruṣārtha* which is obtained by human efforts and not by the grace of the gods. If it be said that Yajña is offering to any god, in that case the god concerned should possess a body and consume the food offered to him. It is not possible for the gods to assume human shape; the question of partaking of food does not even rise. If it be said that the gods being pleased with the performance of Yajña bestow the desired objects, this argument cannot also stand, because the gods have no mastery over the desired objects. The Yajñas are therefore efficacious by themselves.[2]

To stigmatise the Vedic rituals as the cunning devices of the priestly class and the Buddha's disapproval of these[3] as a mark of protest against the degradation of the Vedic religion in the age of the later Saṃhitās and Brāhmaṇas thus suffers from the logical fallacy of oversimplification. The Buddha could not have been unaware of the Brahmanical formulations and their interpretations regarding the efficacy of the Yajña rituals. Rather, he did not fail to observe how Yajña was elevated into a world principle, why the whole world was conceived of in terms of Yajña, why the gods were said to perform their functions through Yajña, why Prajāpati typified Yajña in his cosmogonic activities and why even the parts of the Yajña rituals were invested with cosmic significance. He even used the term Yajña to denote the principles he stood for. A careful scrutiny of the passages relating to the Brahmanical Yajñas in the Buddhist texts shows that the Buddha's objection was concerned mainly with the question of animal slaughter involved in certain forms of the ritual. The contents of the *Kuṭadanta Sutta* clearly indicate that the Buddha tried to give a new interpretation to the concept of Yajña, eliminating on the one hand the aspect of animal slaughter and adding on the other some ethical principles. The contents of the Sutta are as follows : A Brāhmaṇa named Kuṭadanta came to the Buddha and asked him about the procedure of performing a great Yajña which he wanted to do. The Buddha referred to the Yajña performed in olden times by king Mahāvijita in which, as per the advice of his Brāhmaṇa priest (who was no other than the Buddha himself in one of his previous existences), no animal was slaughtered and the king had obtained the desired results by performing some pious deeds beneficial to his subjects. The Buddha added that there were even better forms of Yajña which could be performed by making regular gifts to the meritorious persons, by constructing *vihāras*, by taking refuge in *triśaraṇa*, by adopting the *śikṣāpadas*, by absorbing into four forms of meditation, by acquiring knowledge and by abstaining from worldly desires.

This new interpretation of Yajña by the Buddha in terms of the spiritual and ethical doctrines preached by him was also foreshadowed in the Brahmanical texts. The concepts of the Yajñakratus came into existence which was outside the purview of the normal ritual and consisted of recitation in forest of specific *mantras* required for the Yajñas without corresponding oblations or offerings but with elaborate symbolic identifications of the various elements in the Yajña with the phenomena of the physical and intellectual worlds. Renewed emphasis was laid upon what the *Bhagavadgītā*[4] aptly calls Svādhyāya, Jñāna and Dhyāna Yajñas (pertaining to scripture, knowledge and meditation) in the place of Dravyamaya Yajña (pertaining to material desire). Thus while the earlier Yajñas seem to have been related somehow with the working of the secret causes underneath the surface of things and of the subtle correspondences that knit together the multiform personal and impersonal, animate and inanimate, small and great potencies of nature, the new-fangled interpretations of them were conducive to the concepts of penance and asceticism, transmigration, metempsychosis and search for liberation. The Buddhist concepts of *nāma* and *rūpa* might also have been adopted from the same concepts found in the later Saṃhitās and Brāhmaṇas meant for qualifying the earlier Vedic gods relegated to the position of associate deities in connection with the Yajña.[5]

It is apparent from the evidence of the Vedic sources that the principles and even the contents of the rituals of the later Tantric texts which made their way into Buddhism were not basically different from the Vedic ritualism and that they were already foreshadowed in the Vedas. In the Brāhmaṇa literature sexual union is not only regarded as the means of achieving spiritual happiness, but it is identified with the Yajña itself. The tasks of maintaining Agnihotra, performing consecration, constructing altars and even composing verses are conceived in terms of sexual symbolism.[6] In the Upaniṣads and the Sūtras, and also in the commentarial works, observance and performance of sexual union as a religious rite, are prescribed.[7] The Vedic texts prescribe Somayajñas and Haviryajñas which included the Srautāmaṇi using libation of drinks of intoxicating liquor. According to the *Śatapatha Brāhmaṇa* wine is always pure and hence purifies the performer of the Yajñas. It is *paramāhūti*, the nectar of immortality. The same work prescribes the measure and number of drinks to be offered or taken at a Yajña.[8] The *cakra* sitting of the Tantras has unmistakable similarity with the Vājapeya and Sautrāmaṇi. Even the Tantric transgression of caste bondage is foreshadowed in a passage of the *Aitareya Brāhmaṇa*[9] which states that while performing Yajña in company, the members of the company become Brāhmaṇas and there is no caste. The Tantric practice of *ācamana*, which is a form of ablution, in which certain parts of the body are touched with water, are found in the Vedic texts.[10] The ritual of purifying the body by uttering some *mantras* as *bijas* while contemplating the deities on certain parts of the body and touching such parts as found in the Vedic texts,[11] corresponds to Tantric *nyāsa*. The use of mystic sounds like *khaṭ*, *phaṭ*, *huṃ*, etc., are also found in the Vedic texts.[12]

All these have incipient appearnce in early Buddhism and are amply pronounced in later Buddhism. The *Guhyasamāja*,[13] one of the earliest extant Buddhist Tantras, puts forward a quick and short method for realising Buddhahood and for the attainment of miraculous powers such as killing of enemy with magical rites, causing rainfall in a drought, etc. and the methods for the attainment of *siddhi*. It knows of six black arts and allows the killing of animals, sex rites, etc. The *Sādhānamālā*[14] asserts that everything, even Buddhahood, can be accomplished by *mantras*. It mentions eight *siddhis* and states that by means of certain *mantras* the wealth of Kubera can be appropriated and that gods like Hari, Indra, Brahmā and others and also the heavenly damsels can be utilised as servants. These rites continue the primitive magical tradition, and a direct link can be established between the *Atharvaveda* and the Buddhist Tantras so far as the rituals are concerned. Belief in the efficacy of *mantra, maṇḍala, mudrā* etc., which is more pronounced in later Buddhism must have been a heritage of remote antiquity which found its way in all forms of Indian systems. The Buddhist texts record that the Buddha himself performed many miracles. Despite his personal aversion to magical practices he could not avoid them. These practices exerted a great influence even on his contemporaries. In the *Dīgha Nikāya*,[15] the Buddha mentions *pañca-kāma-guṇadittha-dhamma-nibbāna-vāda*—a philosophical view according to which the soul attains *nirvāṇa* through the full indulgence of the pleasures of the five senses. Likewise, the *Majjhima Nikāya*[16] mentions the view of a class of Śramaṇas and Brāhmaṇas according to whom sexual intercourse with youthful female ascetics was a way to achieve salvation. A passage of the *Kathāvatthu*[17] refers to the belief current among certain sects that *maithuna* or sexual union could have been a means of salvation. We learn from the *Tevijja Sutta* that there were some Śramaṇas and Brāhmaṇas who lived by teaching spells for preserving the body, procuring prosperity, causing adversity, removing sterility, and so on.

B.T. Bhattacharya[18] has observed that the Tantric rituals were able to make their way in Buddhism because some converts who previously accustomed to such practices could not give up their traditonal habits despite their conversion. It was among these people that Tantric rites were secretly maintained. Subsequently they made secret conclaves (*guhyasamājas*) within the Saṅgha, composed their own scriptures and got these sanctioned by the words of the Buddha. But there were other factors also. There are many passages in the Buddhist texts which associate the Buddha directly with the Tantric practices. The *Mahāpadāna Sutta*[19] which contains legends of the Buddha are full of miracles. The *Pāṭika Sutta*[20] describes the Buddha not only as taking part in the competition of making miracles but also as boasting of his miraculous powers. The stories of his transforming a dragon into an insect, of sending fire to the cold-stricken mendicants, of his walking on rivers, of his miracles at Sāṅkāsya and Śrāvastī, of his conversion of Nanda by showing him heavenly nymphs, etc., may be recalled in this connection. His celebrated disciple Moggalāna was also reputed to be famous for magical powers. In the *Lalitavistara*[21] it is stated that the Buddha himself practised *āsphānaka yoga*. In the *Majjhima Nikāya*[22] it is stated that the Buddha himself in his early days had stayed in a cemetery with bones as his pillow. The use of skulls as almsbowls by the Buddhist monks, referred to in the *Cullavagga*,[23] was evidently due to Tantric influence. In the same text[24] a *mantra* or charm is mentioned as being prescribed by the Buddha to be used as a means of warding off the fear of snakebite.

It appears that the stories of the miracles said to have been performed by the Buddha were invented in later times to glorify the Master, although it is possible that he did something which appeared to the ordinary person as miraculous. Belief in the wonder-working power of *mantras*, charms, etc., was a legacy of the past, the influx of which in Buddhism could not be stopped by the Buddha who was, however, personally opposed to all these. In the *Brahmajāla Sutta* we come across an interesting list of arts which the Buddha condemned as *teracchānavijjā*, *micchā* and *ajiva* and he asked not only his disciples but all good men not to encourage such things. The aspirant for *arhat*-hood attains some supernatural power called *ṛddhi* (*iddhi* in Pali), and the Buddha is said to have repeatedly warned his disciples not to utilise this power. In the *Vinaya Piṭaka*[25] it is stated that a monk doing this is guilty of a *dukkhaṭa* offence. While some of the metaphysical principles of the earlier Tantric tradition, especially the relation between the human body and the cosmos, the practical methods of disciplining the body, mind and intellect by various practices, the role of the preceptor as the spritual guide of the aspirant, the importance of initiation, etc., were taken into account and accepted with some modifications by the Buddha, he was probably against certain kinds of magical acts which he did not find as consistent with the doctrines which he himself propounded. It appears that one of the main sources of the Buddhist concept of *anātman* lay in the primitive Tantric tradition. The doctrine of *dehātmavāda* in which the existence of soul apart from the body is not recognised was a continuation of this tradition. Although in later Tantric texts the doctrine of soul independent of the body found a place owing to the influence of other systems, it is basically inconsistent with the main spirit of the Tantra which only recognises the human body as the source of all spiritual experience, the revitalisation of which, through certain physical processes, has been regarded as conducive to salvation.

The concept of *ātman* had much to do with the doctrinal development of Buddhism. What the Buddha really meant by the term *anātman* (commonly viewed as 'absence of soul') is difficult to say at the present state of our knowledge, though there is no dearth of its modern interpretations. It is not impossible that originally *ātman* was a relative and negative conception denoting the man's own body in contrast with the world outside, and later the term came to signify one's proper self or essence. The origin and development of the concept of *ātman* should be viewed in terms of various cosmogonical speculations of the Vedic age which had sought to know things as they were and to find out common origin of the diverse pohenomena of nature, in nature itself. The starting point was a unique First Principle, originally physical in character like earth, water, etc. In the famous creation hymn of the *Ṛgveda*[26] the question is raised whether the fathomless waters existed before the formation of the world and the answer is given in the affirmative. The mythological metamorphosis of this primitive empiricism is found in the Ṛgvedic conception of Hiraṇyagarbha or Golden Germ emanating from the primeval waters which is described as the lord of all things upholding heaven and earth.[27] Into this incipient source of existence, floating in the form of World Egg on the primordial waters were infused the personalities of two divinities, Prajāpati and Viśvakarmaṇ, and later the abstract principle *ātman*, when the earlier anthropomorphised forms of divinities were found inadequate to explain creation as an actual physical process. The space requires to get dissipated into the wind and other elements, the water to get hardened itself into the earth and so on. This could only be possible if the elements in question had the inner potentiality of such transformation and if that potentiality could be viewed in terms of their own self or *ātman*.[28]

Even in the Puruṣa-sukta of the *Ṛgveda* is found the idea of equation of one faculty of nature with another and their eventual identification with a macrocosmic principle, conceived of in the form of a Yajña. This has contributed a great deal to the subsequent notion that the human body is the microcosm of the universe. With the elaboration of this idea the physical conception of Puruṣa underwent significant changes, and it was identified with *ātman*, the inner self of all beings.[29] The earlier passages of the Upaniṣads equate the cosmic elements like fire, sun, etc., with the hand, eye and other limbs of the Puruṣa while the later passages turn each of the elements into a Puruṣa controlled by the *ātman* residing in all of them. The transition from the category of Puruṣa to that of *ātman* is clearly shown in many passages of the Upaniṣads.[30] Thus the conception of *ātman*, as the highest cosmogonical principle, had to pass through many stages of thought. In the *Chāndogya*[31] the sky, the sun, the wind, the space and the waters are equated respectively with the head, the eye, the breath, the body, and the bladder of *ātman*. In the next stage *ātman* is conceived as the unitary world-soul, the immanent reality of all things.[32]

In the *Bṛhadāraṇyaka*[33] longer descriptions of *ātman* as the basis of the unity implied in the usual correlations of the non-self and the self are met with as the precondition of the final identification of *ātman* with *brahman*. It is clear from the Upaniṣadic evidence that before their final identification these two concepts hovered near each other as designations of the ultimate world-ground. The Upaniṣads give a hierarchy of different grades of reality down from the all-embracing absolute.[34] The *Taittiriya Upaniṣad*[35] asks: "From whence verily all these beings spring forth? Through whom, having sprung forth, they continue alive? Unto whom they repair? And into whom are they absorbed?" The answer is given in terms of a First Principle, subject to restless shift, but capable of producing the effect, like water hardening itself into the earth. This restless shift is indicated variously in the Upaniṣads in terms of a steady but multifarious advance from a concrete physical First Principle like earth or water to non-material principle like *ākāśa*, to a ritualistic principle like Puruṣa, to a theistic principle like Prajāpati or Viśvakarman, to a physiological principle like *prāṇa*, but ultimately to the all-embracing psychophysical principle like *ātman*, revealing the macrocosm in the microcosm, the individual self equated with *brahman* or universal self, the last being the culminating point of the process.

All the concepts relevant for the development of the doctrine of *ātman* found necessary expression in Buddhism as well. The Buddha also held that the elements of the cosmos were found in the nature of the individual, the breath of the body corresponding to the wind of the world, the mind to the space of the universe, the gross body to the physical elements and so forth. But while formulating his own doctrine of *anātman* (which literally means absence of soul or self) he insisted not on the cosmic or metaphysical aspects of the concept of *ātman*, but simply on some of its ethical implications. He held that the equation of the individual self with Absolute was bound to create the notion of I-ness in an individual. And this I-ness is the root cause of human suffering. He was not also ready to subscribe to the view that every living being had a permanent soul, which remained unaffected by the actions of an individual and which was regarded as the carrier of the effects of *karma* and as the link between one life and another. He questioned: How can an eternal substance which is pure by nature and fully liberated be linked with another object which is evanescent, impure and unliberated?

In the *Brahmajāla-sutta* of the *Dīgha Nikāya* the refutation of the notion of *ātman* as a permanent and immaculate entity, existing within the human body unaffected by human deeds, has been attempted with reference to a number of philosophical schools said to have been in vogue during the time of the Buddha. Among these schools, the Śāśvatavāda held that the soul and the world existed eternally while according to the Aśāśvatavāda the body or the organs of sense were impermanent while the mind or consciousness was permanent. The Śāśvatavādins, according to the Nikāyas, are described as those who take *attā* (*ātman*) or the self as one of the five *khandas* or something apart from them and hold that it continues for ever without any change. The self, according to these schools, is the speaker, feeler and enjoyer of the fruits of good or bad actions and is permanent, fixed, eternal, unchangeable and steadfast.[36] Likewise various schools of the Uddhamāghatānikās hold, each following its own logic, that the soul was material (*rūpī*), non-material (*arūpī*), both material and non-material and neither material nor non-material. The Saññivādins, an offshoot of this school, believed in the existence of a conscious soul after death which might be limited or unlimited, both limited and unlimited, neither limited nor unlimited, which might be conscious of only one object (*ekatta*), many objects (*nānātta*), limited space or object (*paritta)* and unlimited space or object (*appamāna*) and might result in unmixed happiness (*ekānta-sukhī*), unmixed misery (*ekānta-dukkhī*), mixture of happiness and misery, and neither happiness nor misery. The Asaññivādins upheld the existence of unconscious but healthy soul after death, while according to the Nevasaññināsaññivādins the soul after death remained neither conscious nor unconscious.[37]

Among other philosophical schools mentioned in the *Brahmajāla-sutta* which exerted greater influence on the Buddhist ideas pertaining to the concept of the soul mention should be made of the seven classes of Ucchedavādins or Annihilationists. They had seven features of the soul: It has form (*rūpavā*), is made of the four elements, and in composition is similar to the human being; is heavenly remaining in the Kāmāvacara sphere; is of the same substance as mind (*manomaya*) possessing all parts of the physical body and organs of senses (*indriyas*); is of the same substance as beings of the Ākāśānañcāyatana, having neither perception of material objects (*rūpasaññā*) nor that of obstructing objects (*paṭighasaññā*); is of the same nature as beings of the Viññānanañcāyatana and identifies itself with infinite consciousness (*anantam viññānam*); is like the beings of the Akiñcaññāyatana; and is similar to the beings of the Nevasaññānāsaññāyatana in which state it is considered to be the best (*paṇita*) and the most tranquil (*śānta*). These seven features of the soul remind us of the sevenfold Buddhist classification of beings (*viññānaṭṭhitis*); two classes of Kāmāvacaras, one class of Rūpāvacaras and four classes of Arūpāvacaras. These conceptions of the Ucchedavādins amount to the identification of the soul with the body. The soul is made of elements that constitute one or the other of the above-mentioned category of beings. As the body of beings may be of seven different varieties, so also is the soul. Apart from the Ucchedavādins, the views of the Diṭṭhadhammanibbānavādins also had something to do with the Buddhist conceptions. They hold that the soul passes through four states (*jhānas*) in its way to the attainment of Nirvāṇa. In the first *jhāna* the soul becomes free from desires (*kāma*) and evil thoughts and actions (*akusaladhamma*); in the second, it becomes from reflection (*vitakka*) and judgement (*vicāra*); in the third it becomes indifferent to happiness and sorrow; and in the fourth, it attains a pure state having only equanimity (*upekkhā*) and memory (*sati*). In Buddhism, these four *jhānas* are regarded as the first four steps in the path of spiritual advancement.

That the Buddhists were greatly concerned with the doctrine of soul is attested by numerous passages of the Buddhist literature on it. They could not accept it owing to their insistence on the doctrine of momentariness and disbelief in the existence of a permanent entity. If they did so, as the *Nidāna-Saṃyutta* frankly asserted, it would push them to the position of the Śāśvatavādins.[38] But at the same time they could not deny or ignore it absolutely. According to the Buddhists, *attā* (*ātman*) is only a word of common usage and does not correspond to any real entity.[39] In the Pali texts it is said that the belief in the existence of a soul is due to misinterpretation or misapprehension of one of the five constituents (*khandas: rūpa, vedanā, saññā, saṅkhārā* and *viññāna*). There are four types of such misapprehensions, namely, *attā* is the same as *rūpa*, etc; it is possessed of *rūpa*, etc.; in it there is *rūpa*, etc. and, it is in *rūpa*, etc.[40] In many ways such misapprehensions take place. A person while meditating sometimes conceives of the object of meditation as identical with himself. It is like equating the flame of a burning lamp with its colour. A person may also think that the *khandas* belong to the self or soul, just as shadow belongs to a tree, or they exist in the self just as smell exists in a flower or they are the container of the self just as a casket is of the jewel.[41]

Thus, although they were repeatedly taught that the concept of self or soul is basically inconsistent with the principles of Buddhism, the concept was so popular with the Buddhists that the texts had to contain copious illustrations of the nature of the misconceptions relating to the existence of soul current among the followers. As a consequence to the mistaken identification of *attā* with one of the components of a being, the soul has been classified into three types, namely, *attā* of beings of Kāmadhātu; *attā* of beings of Rūpadhātu; and *attā* of beings of Arūpadhātu.[42] Though in the *Milindapañho*[43] *vijñāna* is often identified with *attā* or *jīva*, it is suggested that when the organs of senses cease to work, the function of the *attā* also ceases, so it cannot be said that it has a separate and independent existence of its own. Again, in the *Mahāvagga*[44] such expression as *attānaṃ gavesayyātha*, *attadipā viharatha*, *brahmabhūtena attanā*, etc. seem to suggest that here the concept of *attā* has been used in a more than merely reflexive sense. In the *Dhammapada*, *ātman* is described as a very near and dear entity, essentially independent, having potentialities for causing good or evil.[45]

Though Nāgārjuna tried from a logical point of view to demonstrate that if *ātman* be the same as the *skandhas*, it would be subject to origin and destruction and that if it be different from the *skandhas* it would be without the characteristics appertaining to the *skandhas*,[46] the Buddhists were always interested in the concept of the soul. This is attested by the fact that of all the issues of debate, the one on the existence of the soul seems to have occasioned probably the biggest controversy among the early Buddhists. The issue forms the subject-matter of the first controversy in the *Kathāvatthu*.[47] The Buddhists who advocated a soul theory were known as Pudgalavādins.[48] There were one or two

Buddhist schools of thought like the Vātsiputriyas who held that apart from the five *khandas*, there was a sixth ingredient, *pudgala* or *attā* (soul), the seat of I-ness. Otherwise, how could the Buddha say that in a previous existence he was such and such a being? According to the Pudgalavādins the relation between the *pudgalas* and the *khandas* was that of ineffability just as the relation between the flower and its scent. They interpreted such utterances as *sarve dharmā anātmānaḥ* as suggesting that one should not seek the self in what the self was not, and not that there was no self whatever.

Mrs. Rhys Davids,[49] as we have pointed out above earlier, held that the Buddha did not preach *anātman* theory. It was subsequently ascribed to him through monastic innovation which sought to challenge the Brahmanical worldview. Coomaraswamy[50] and Radhakrishnan[51] also thought on the same lines while Sogen[52] and Suzuki[53] held that Buddism had denied the *ātman* in the sense of a finite substantial individual but not in the sense of the absolute unity of the universe. According to Schrader[54] the Buddha appeared as a soul-denier to his contemporaries only because they conceived of the soul in an extremely anthropomorphic fashion. We have already had the occasion to refer to the view of Stcherbatsky[55] which holds that the idea of an immortal soul was unknown to the Vedas and earlier Upaniṣads. According to him, the concept of an immortal soul was a new fangled idea which was accepted by most Indian schools of thought. The Buddhist and the materialists rejected this doctrine as *ātmavāda* and resorted to the older tradition. They employed the term *anātmavāda* to denote the plurality of separate elements without real entity, a conception which must have been in existence in pre-Buddhist traditions. G.C. Pande[56] thinks that although some Nikāya texts can be found which appear to assume an *ātman* theory, and others which preach a theory of *anātman*, the Buddha's own standpoint seems to have been that ultimate reality belongs neither to the one nor to the other conception.

A.L. Basham[57] while dealing with the history of the Ājīvikas suggested that the doctrines of Gośāla, Puraṇa and Pakudha were aspects of a single body of teachings. This holds good also in the case of all their contemporaries, including the Buddha and Mahāvīra. On specific issues their views may be different, but generally they belong to the same category. In the Jain *Sūyagaḍa*[58] Purana Kassapa is mentioned as an Akriyāvādin, and Śīlāṅka, the commentator on the *Sūyagaḍa*, finds in his doctrine some ingredients of the Sāṅkhya. According to the Buddhist sources like the *Samaññaphala-sutta* his doctrine is that the soul remains inactive as in the Sāṅkhya and it is the body which acts or causes others to act. The soul is nothing but a passive spectator. It remains unaffected by the result of good and bad deeds of the body. B.M. Barua[59] on the basis of his supposed identification of Pakudha Kaccāyana with Kakudha or Kabandhī of the *Praśna Upaniṣad* says that according to Pakudha the roots of all things were matter and soul. In the *Sāmaññaphala-sutta*, Pakudha's philosophy is described as the doctrine of seven categories (*satta-kāyavāda*) while in the Jain *Sūyagaḍa*[60] as the doctine of soul as a sixth (*ātma-ṣaṣṭha-vāda*) which Śīlāṅka identified with the doctrine of *Bhagavadgītā* as well as with that of the Sāṅkhya. The materialist Ajita Keśakambalī on the other hand believed in *dehātmavāda* according to which there is no soul apart from the body.

It appears that Lord Mahāvīra also approached the question of the soul from a viewpoint similar to that of the early Buddhists. Śīlāṅka in his *Ācārāṅgaṭīkā*[61] has categorically stated that Jainism does not believe in the doctrine of *ātman* as the First Principle. Although there is a tendency among the scholars to explain *jīva* in terms of *ātman* or *puruṣa* of the other schools of Indian thought, etymologically it stands for 'what lives or is animate'. The concept bears a clear mark of formulation from observing the characteristics of life and not through the search after a metaphysical principle underlying individual existence.[62] Thus the word in the original sense stood for the vital principle rather than for the soul. Later on, however, the question of consciousness was emphasised[63] and the Jīvas were theoretically arranged in a continuous series according to the degrees of consciousness. On the top of this series were placed the perfect souls that had overcome all *karmas* and attained omniscience and at the bottom were placed imperfect souls inhabiting the bodies of earth, water, fire, air or vegetables.[64] It was conceived as existing permanently, acting and being acted upon as an experient (*bhoktā*) and agent (*kartā*).[65] Attempts were also made to solve the problem of its relation with the body and by postulating that during the period of its union with matter, its features are obscured, though not destroyed. Thus the soul is capable of expansion and contraction according to the dimensions of the physical body with which it is associated for the time being, just as a lamp which remaining the same illumines the whole of the space enclosed in a small or big room in which it happens to be placed.[66] Owing to the inclination generated by its past actions a soul comes to inhabit different bodies successively. Whilst the knowledge possessed by the soul may be boundless, that which it actually possesses is fragmentary due to the obscuration caused by *karma*. That is why it suffers and enjoys the fruits of its deeds.

The Buddha did not seem to posit the agency of the soul in the process of transmigration and rebirth. In pre-Buddhist thought also, prior to the maturity of the doctrine of *karma* the conceptual situation of eschatology was somewhat hazy. The celebrated funeral hymn of the *Ṛgveda*[67] conceives of the human body as the conglomeration of various material elements and there is a hint that after death each of these returns to the corresponding mass of great elements while the sense organs pass into space. Although the hymn has something more to suggest, the idea that after death the bodily elements are dissolved in the natural elements was accepted and logically asserted by the materialists. Ajita Keśakambalin, a senior contemporary of the Buddha, said: "There are in the world no recluses or Brāhmaṇas who have reached the highest point, who walk perfectly and who having understood and realised by themselves alone, both this world and the next, make their wisdom known to others. A human being is made of four elements. When he dies, the earthly in him returns and relapses into the earth, the fluid to the water, the heat to the fire, the wind to the air, and his faculties pass into the space."[68] According to Pakudha Kaccāyana, a being is composed of seven elements and its destruction means the transformation of one element into another. According to the materialists, especially the Brāhaspatyas or Lokāyatas or Cārvākas there is no heaven, no final liberation, nor any soul in another world; there are four elements—earth, water, fire and air; and from these elements alone is intelligence produced, just like the intoxicating power of *kinva*, etc. mixed together.[69] Some schools of thought like a few groups of the Diṭṭhadhammanibbānavādins of the Buddhist texts or the Samucchedavādins, Sāyavādins and Na-santi-paralokavādins of the Jain texts held that there is no separate existence of the soul which is the same as the body itself and it becomes extinct after the extinction of the body.

The conception of a life-principle, apparently distinct from the body, finds rudimentary expression in some passages of the *Ṛgveda*.[70] It is said that after death a man goes to the realm of the blessed where Yama or Varuṇa rules,[71] in the realm of Viṣṇu,[72] in 'the midst of heaven by the side of the ruddy morn',[73] in the company of gods drinking with them Soma or honey[74] and so forth. Companionship with the Sun and the gods, and immortality are the prized goals.[75] Two separate pathways along which all the moving creatures travel, namely the path of the Fathers and that of gods and mortals are spoken of.[76] But the concept of a soul or the idea of reward and punishment, after death, in exact correspondence to the good or bad deeds of a person in this life (which is the basis of the doctrine of *karma*) is absent in the *Ṛgveda*. In the eschatological speculations of the later Saṃhitās and Brāhmaṇas the doctrine of transmigration of soul and rebirth is not clear, though there are passages faintly foreshadowing such ideas.[77] Future existence, at least of a blessed character, is assured to a man only through the correct performance of Yajña. It is only through the correct knowledge of Yajña that one is born 'with eyes' in the other world. The Yajamāna is reborn from fire among the gods and enjoys immortal existence. The fire of Yajña burns away all one's sins and hence bestows prosperity and renown in the present world and a meritorious world hereafter.

All that the Brāhmaṇa literature wants to assure is a future existence only as a glorified continuation of present existence after death.[78] A probability of transmigration from one state to another is indicated but the linked agencies have not been specified. There are, however, references to the gradations of *karmas* and *yāgas* performed in this life with the hint that there is a corresponding gradation in the fruits of them enjoyable in the next world, and also allusions to a soul in man and similar spirits in trees, plants, birds, animals etc. The floating and disorganised elements of the incipient doctrine of *karma* which found sporadic expressions in the Brāhmaṇa literature were systematised and perfected by the thinkers of subsequent generations including the Buddha who insisted on the karmaic effects as the means of communication from one life to another. The Buddha was, however, unwilling to accept the intermediacy of soul in the process of rebirth. The idea of the soul as something distinct from the body, immortal and pure by nature was not fully developed in the age of the later Saṃhitās and Brāhmaṇas. It was still incapable of remaining dissociated from its outward trapping. In other words, the difference between *dehātmavāda* and *ātmavada* was not clearly recognised in the Brāhmaṇa literature.

In the *Bṛhadāraṇyaka Upaniṣad*[79] Jāratkārava asks Yājñavalkya about the condition of the self or soul when it leaves the human body, whether it thereafter leads an embodied or disembodied existence:

> When after the death of a man, the eye is dissolved into the sun, the mind into the moon, the ear into the space, the body into the earth, the speech into the fire, the hair into the plants and the blood into the waters what happens to the person that inhabits the mortal vesture which we call human body?

No clear answer to this question has been given by Yājñavalkya because the concept of soul from an absolutistic point of view was then yet to be formed. The same Upaniṣad[80] speaks of the formless creator as having entered the body right up to the tips of the nails and assumed therein the name and function of *prāṇa*, the life principle which is assigned a province and duration longer than that of one life, inasmuch as the transmigrating *ātman* or soul is laid to go from one to another.[81] In the Upaniṣads are laid down several stages leading to the development of the concept of the soul on the one hand to its becoming the ultimate world ground, the highest cosmic principle manifest in every individual as pure consciousness, and on the other to its intermediary role in the process of rebirth. Introspective knowledge of the soul in the first stage of its development was concerned with the essence of man conceived of in terms of the organic functions of the body such as the vital breath, consciousness or intellection, but in the next stage when the self or soul within was believed to transcend the normal organic functions and was in itself beyond the comprehension of any of these organs, the question as to the real nature of the self and the possibility or otherwise of its knowledge began to tax the thinkers of the day, such as the Buddha and his contemporaries, seriously.

The conception of an innately immaculate and immortal conscious principle subject to transmigration from one state of bodily existence to another was not fully crystallized even in the *Bṛhadāraṇyaka Upaniṣad*. Divergent eschatological doctrines in connection with a soul element have been furnished here. In one place[82] it is stated that Indra, assuming the form of an eagle, carries the souls of the pious performers of the Aśvamedha over a dangerous pathway not broader than the edge of a razor and hands them over to Vāyu who takes them to the abode of the blessed. Elsewhere in the same Upaniṣad[83] it is stated that when the individual soul leaves this body it goes to the wind. The latter makes room for it like the hole of a carriage-wheel and through it the soul soars higher up to the sun whence it reaches higher up to the moon which in turn sends it up to a still higher world where the soul dwells in eternal peace. A third theory[84] distinguishes between the two pathways: the one upwards to the realm of the gods from whence there is no return, and the other belonging to the Manes which involves a continual round of births and deaths. According to the doctrine of Five Fires,[85] when a man is cremated, from out of the cremation-fire which serves as altar, a lustrous person (soul) arises, who goes either to the world of the gods or to the world of the fathers. A clear-cut concept of rebirth in the human world in better or worse position quite in accordance with the merits or demerits accrued through the *karma* of the previous life is quite indistinct in the earlier Upaniṣads.

This explains why the Buddha did not resort to the soul concept in order to explain the process of rebirth. The Buddhist concept is that a living being composed of five *skandhas* is without any beginning. It is in a continuous state of flux. Each preceding group of *skandhas* gives rise to the subsequent group, and this process goes on ceaselessly in the present existence as also in the future. Just as a corn falling on the ground sprouts again without the help of a cultivator, so also one group of *skandhas* gives rise to another group without the mediacy of any soul or agent. The process is dependent on the law of causal sequence. According to the Buddhist view[86] the impressions (*saṅkhārā, saṃskāra*) left on the mind by *avijjā* (*avidyā*) or ignorance lead one to perform deeds of various kinds which have the propensities of rebirth consciousness (*paṭisanidhi-viññāna*). These impressions are the conative factors making for rebirth and persisting into another life. The concept of *saṅkhāra* is practically equivalent to that of *kamma* (*karma*). The *jāti* or rebirth is controlled in *kammabhava*[87] (existence according to one's past deeds) and not in *uppattibhava* (three planes of existence of *Kāma*, *Rūpa* and *Arūpa*). It is related to *bhava* or desire for existence in two ways: *kamma* (previous actions) and *upanissaya* (immediately effective cause). The deeds of past life are effected in rebirth.[88]

The doctrine of *karma* or of postmortem reward and punishments for the good or bad actions of an individual was probably inspired from the simple agricultural maxim: as you sow, so shall you reap. Every event of the life of an individual is due to the *karma* of his or her previous life. Birth and death, pleasure and pain, disease and suffering, everything is dependent on this peculiar concept of *karma*. Because of good or evil *karma* a living creature would be reborn into any species, particularly suited to and measured by the action from the vilest insect to a god. This emphasis on the doctrine of *karma* was certainly due to the corresponding emphasis on the ethical values. For this it was universally acceptable to all forms of Indian thought.

> Karma therefore was a religious extension of an elementary concept of abstract value, independent of the individual, caste or tribe. It could grow and ripen like a seed planted in the previous season, or mature like a debt, while it never failed to pay in exact proportion. It can be seen how this would appeal to peasant and traders, even to the Śūdra who might thus aspire to be a reborn king.[89]

Karma and its fruits are meant in the Vedas to be the performance of the Yajñas—not so much for any moral elevation, as for the achievement of objects of practical welfare. Happiness or absolute extinction of sorrow was not the goal. Knowledge to these earlier authorities meant only the knowledge of the Yajña and of the dictates of the Vedas. It was not taken in its widest and most universeal sense. These were the points on which Jainism and Buddhism had a significant departure from the Vedic line. An advance in the new line had, however, begun in the Upaniṣads which had anticipated some of the characteristics upheld in Buddhism and Jainism. In the Upaniṣads, the doctrine of *karma* is presented in two forms—simple and sophisticated. The simple form of this doctrine is that just as the good seeds bring a good harvest and bad seeds bad, so also a man becomes good by good deeds and bad by bad deeds. Its ethics is that every deed must produce its natural effect in the world and as such also leaves an impression on the mind. In the sophisticated level, however, *karma* is regarded as blind unconscious principle, governing the whole universe. It is not subject to the control even of God.[90]

The doctrine of *karma* is inextricably blended in later Indian tradition with that of transmigration of the soul and rebirth. In the *Ṛgvedic* eschatology, as we have seen above, there is no direct reference to the soul's transmigration or to the doctrine of rebirth in any form. In the Brāhmaṇa literature, however, we come across the idea of repeated births and deaths, but this idea has not been established in a perfect theoretical set-up. It is only in the Upaniṣads that we come across a clear development of the theory of transmigration of the soul in three distinct stages. In the first stage the earlier Vedic idea of heaven or the abode of Yama has been replaced by the conception of *yāna* or way, of the fathers (*pitṛ*) or of the gods (*deva*). In the second stage the doctrine of transmigration is presented without any reference to the idea of *karma* or reaping the fruits of deeds. In the final stage, however, we have a complete presentation of the transmigration of the soul strictly in terms of the doctrine of *karma*. According to the merits or demerits that a man earns through his actions, he will have to take birth again in this world. Good deeds in one life secure a better future for the next life, and this process continues until one achieves the final salvation. The Buddhist law of *karma* is only a special form of the more general law of causation. Since life is thought of as an unbroken stream of successive states which are causally connected, the present existence of an individual is in accordance with that of *karma*, the effect of the past. Rebirth is, therefore, not transmigration but a continuity in life-series in which process *karma* serves as a causal connection.

The contemporaries of the Buddha had also something to do with the doctrine of *karma*. Like the Buddha and Lord Mahāvīra they also formed their views on *karma*, not on the basis of the Upaniṣads (which in themselves show various stages and patterns) but of that of the earlier traditions interpreted and amplified in their own ways. Apart from Lord Mahāvīra, most contemporaries of the Buddha were Akriyāvādins who did not believe in the efficacy of *karma*, both in theory and in practice.[91] This Akriyāvāda is described in the *Majjhima Nikāya*[92] as Ahetuka (denying cause) and Akiriya (denying the effects of action) while in the *Aṅguttara Nikāya*[93] it is said to be a doctrine which denies the effects of deeds (*kamma)*, activity (*kiriya*) and energy (*viriya*). Gośāla Maṅkhaliputta, for example, held that there was no question of bringing unripe *karma* to fruition, nor of exhausting *karma* already ripened by conduct, by vows, by penance, or by charity.[94] However, according to the followers of the Kriyāvāda school it is through the agency of *karma* that the soul acts or is acted upon. The term *kriyā* which characterised the doctrines of these schools might have originally denoted the Vedic rituals. Subsequently with the progress of time it came to denote acts leading to human welfare, disciplining the body and controlling the mind from a moral point of view. Very naturally the doctrine of *karma* came within the purview of the Kriyāvādins. According to the *Sūyagaḍa*[95] the followers of Kriyāvāda maintain that misery is caused by oneself and not by any external agent. Liberation may be attained by knowledge and good conduct (*vijjā-caraṇam pāmokkham*). Fools are unable to stop the influx of evil actions, but the wise can do so by abstaining from wrong-doing.[96]

The term *Kiriyam* or *Kriyāvāda*, with some reservations, also applies to the Jain doctrines. It is interesting to note that the Jains developed a unique *karma* doctrine, basically different from others. Ordinarily *karma* means human action and is usually conceived by the Indian philosophers as leading to the good or bad results in this life or in another, which the performer of the action is to enjoy or suffer. But in Jainism *karma* is conceived as something essentially material and external which gets attached to the soul just as dust gets attached to the cloth.

> The defilement of the soul takes place in the following way. Subtle matter ready to be transformed into *karma* pours into the soul (i.e. Jīva); this is called influx (*āsrava*). In the usual state of things a soul harbours passion (*kaṣāya*) which acts like a viscous substance and retains the subtle matter coming into contact with

> the soul; the subtle matter thus caught by the soul enters, as it were, into a chemical combination with it; this is called binding (*bandha*) of *karma* matter. The subtle matter 'bound' or amalgamated by the soul is transformed into eight kinds of *karma*, and forms a kind of subtle body (*kārmaṇa-śarīra*) which clings to the soul in all its migrations and future births and determines the individual state and lot of that particular soul. . . . Now, when a particular *karma* has produced its effect in the way described, it is discharged or purged from the soul. The process of 'purging off' is called *nirjarā*. When this process goes on without interruption, *karma* matter will, in the end, be discharged from the soul, and the latter now freed from the weight which had kept it down before the time of its liberation (for matter is heavy and *karma* is material), goes up in a straight line to the top of the universe where the liberated soul dwells.[97]

The Jain approach to *karma* as the atomic essence of external material stimuli soiling the soul thus resembles some modern psychological theories, and its emphasis on resisting the influx of *karma* and on the clearance of what has already been stored is somewhat novel and radical. It is difficult to say why and how the Jains interpreted the earlier and contemporary traditions relating to the doctrine of *karma* to arrive at such an unconventional formulation.

But the Buddhist standpoint is based on easier principles. Notwithstanding their insistence on the concept of *anātman* —a concept which admits of various interpretations—the Buddhists agreed with the Upaniṣadic thinkers about the transmission of the effects of *karma* from one life to another. In the *Aṅguttara Nikāya*[98] it is stated that acts produce their effects wherever the being comes into existence, and the effects may appear in this existence or in the next, or in a still later existence. All beings are born of, and subject to their past deeds.[99] According to the law of causal sequence, the *saṃskāras* or impressions are the results of the non-realisation of truth and these are the immediately preceding conditions of the present existence. The *saṃskāras* represent the accumulation of the effects of *karma* left in a being before its rebirth. According to the *Aṅguttara Nikāya*,[100] *karma* is like a field and *vijñāna* is like the seed sown in it. This *vijñāna* or consciousness contains the residues of the previous impressions (*saṃskāra*) which give rise to the four mental factors (*nāma*) which take as their support (*ālambana*) the material elements (*rūpa*). It is in this way that the effects of *karma*, stored in the *saṃskāras* of past life, are transmitted to the next life. In the *Aṅguttara* passage referred to above *tṛṣṇā* (*tanhā*) or thirst is equated with *sneha* or water that nourishes the seed (*vijñāna*) in the field (*karma*). The thirst which the seed feels and the water by which it is quenched are both regualted by *avidyā* or ignorance and thereby settles the higher or lower states of future existence.[101]

Without a discussion of the views and standpoints of other eminent contemporaries of the historical Buddha it is not possible to have a full understanding of the ideological background of Buddhism. The most illustrious contemporary of the Buddha was Lord Mahāvīra, the last of the greatest exponents of Jainism. In their incipient stages, though not in the sophisticated, Buddhism and Jainism stood for same or similar principles. Both these systems deny the existence of an intelligent first cause but adore a pantheon of deities and deified saints, insist upon moral values, right conduct and self-discipline, maintain an ambivalence on the question of the authority of the Vedas and the supremacy of the Brāhmaṇas, and think it sinful to take life of the animals. Both these systems use similar, if not the same, terminology to denote their doctrinal concepts. That is why there was once a tendency among some of the nineteenth century European scholars to treat Jainism as an offshoot of Buddhism or latter as that of the former.[102] In the Buddhist texts there are numerous references to the Jains and their doctrines, just as in the Jain texts we have references to Buddhism. In the *Aṅguttara Nikāya*[103] we come across a reference to Lord Mahāvīra as one who knows and sees all things and claims perfect knowledge and faith and also to Jainism which teaches the annihilation by austerities of old *karma* and the prevention by inactivity of new *karma*. It is further stated that according to Jainism, when *karma* ceases misery ceases when misery ceases perception ceases; when perception ceases all sufferings come to an end, and a man is saved by complete annihilation of sin. Buddhaghoṣa[104] mentions the differences between Jainism and Ājīvikism and also treats the famous *Sāmaññaphala-sutta* passage[105] of the *Dīgha Nikāya* which mistakenly ascribes the four vows of Pārśva to Mahāvīra. Likewise in the earlier Jain works like the *Sūyagaḍa*[106] the Buddhists are described as believing in the doctrine of five *skandhas* and in that of momentary existence. In the later philosophical literature of the Buddhists and of the Jains we come across real philosophical debates on special issues like the doctrine of momentariness, determinate and indeterminate stages of perception, causal efficiency, self-revelatory character of cognition, nature of reality, atomism, etc., which will be dealt with in a subsequent chapter.

Among other contemporaries of the historical Buddha, Pūraṇa Kassapa, Pakudha Kaccāyana and Gośāla Maṅkhaliputta were associated with the genesis and development of the Ājīvika school which had a long and eventful career in the religious history of India. The Buddhist records speak of Pūraṇa Kassapa as a contemporary of the Buddha, an old, experienced and venerable teacher, the head of an order, the founder of a school having a large following.[107] Fragments of the doctrines of Pūraṇa which may be gleaned from different sources point to the fact that he believed in the doctrine of non-causation, and that is why later authorities like Ārya Śūra wanted to characterise him as a Svabhāvavādin.[108] The *Sāmaññaphala-sutta* regards him as a follower of the doctrine of non-action which is supported by Buddhaghoṣa.[109] In the Jain *Sūyagaḍa*[110] Pūraṇa is mentioned as an Akriyāvādin, and Śīlāṅka, the commentator on the *Sūyagaḍa*, finds in his doctrines some ingredients of the Sāṅkhya. From the Buddhist texts we learn that according to Pūraṇa when one acts or causes other to act, it is not the soul which acts or causes other to act. The soul is nothing but a passive spectator. In a passage of the *Aṅguttara Nikāya*,[111] Ānanda ascribes part of Gośāla's doctrine to Pūraṇa. This has led Basham to establish a common origin of the doctrines of these two great teachers. In the *Saṃyutta Nikāya*[112] the names of Makkhali Gośāla and Puraṇa Kassapa are significantly combined. In the *Aṅguttara* passage mentioned above Pūraṇa is said to have maintained the doctrine of six classes of men which also belonged to Gośāla. Besides, Basham[113] has drawn our attention to two significant sources—the Jain Tamil poem *Nīlakeci* and Guṇaratna's *Tarkarahasyadīpikā*. In the former, Pūraṇa is clearly described as the leader of the Ājīvikas, who received *Nīlakeci* and expounded his doctrines to her stating that Markali (Makkhali Gośāla) was the lord of the Ājīvikas. This shows that the Tamil Ājīvikas looked upon Pūraṇa as a great leader and second only to Gośāla himself. Guṇaratna refers to Pūraṇa as the upholder of the doctrine of destiny which is characteristic of Ājīvika philosophy. Buddhaghoṣa insists on the nakedness of Pūraṇa which is also confirmed by the *Divyāvadāna* in which he is described as a Nirgrantha. The story of Pūraṇa's suicide occurs in the *Dhammapada* Commentary[114] and in the *Divyāvadāna*.[115] A Tibetan version of the story also exists.[116] According to these accounts, the death of Pūraṇa took place at Śrāvastī, after a great miracle contest in which he was worsted by the Buddha.

According to Pakudha Kaccāyana, another important contemporary of the Buddha, a being is composed of seven elements which are neither created, nor moulded, which are barren and fixed as a rock or a stone pillar, do not produce anything, do not interact with one another, neither move nor change nor hinder one another so as to cause pain or pleasure. Hence there can be no killer or instigator of killing because, if a sword passes through the body of a being, it does not destroy it but only transforms one element into another. The seven elements are earth, water, fire, air, pleasure, pain and Jīva (being, life-principle, soul).[117] B.M. Barua,[118] on the basis of his supposed identification with Kakudha or Kabandhī of the *Praśna Upaniṣad* says that according to Pakudha the roots of all things were matter and soul, that in his six or seven categories one may trace a background of the Vaiśeṣika categories and that, as regards the broad outlines of his philosophy, Pakudha may be described as the Empedocles of India. How he has arrived at such a conclusion is difficult to understand since the *Sāmaññaphala-sutta* categorically states that according to Pakudha the seven categories are eternal and immutable elements. The *Majjhima Nikāya*[119] incorporates with Pakudha's doctrine part of Gośāla's fatalist creed and one of the Chinese versions of the *Sāmaññaphala-sutta*[120] describes Pakudha as a determinist. The southern Ājīvikas held a theory of elements very similar to that of Pakudha. "The three chief Tamil sources—*Maṇimekalai, Nīlakeci* and *Civañāṇacittiyar*—all declare that, according to the Ājīvika doctrine, there are five immutable atomic elements (*anu* or *porul*), earth, air, water, fire and life (*uyir* or *cīvam*). *Maṇimekalai*, however, the oldest of these sources, adds 'but joy and sorrow, these two are atoms'. *Nīlakeci* leaves the total of the elements at five, but *Civañāṇacittiyar* states: 'our lord declared to us the seven which we must consider, including these two which are joined with them, namely good and evil'. This is surely the seven-element theory of Pakudha Kaccāyana, with more moral categories *punna* and *pāpa* substituted for hedonistic *sukha* and *dukkha*."[121]

From the combined testimony of the Buddhist and Jain sources we learn, that, according to Gośāla Maṅkhaliputta, the greatest exponent of Ājīvikism, all beings are subject to a fixed and unchangeable series of existence, each of which has its own unalterable characteristic. He denies the effects of action and energy, since he holds that every being is helpless, unable either to help himself or others. This doctrine is described in the *Majjhima Nikāya*[122] as *ahetuka* (denying cause) and *akiriya* (denying the effects of action), while in *Aṅguttara Nikāya*[123] it is said to be a doctrine which denies the effects of deeds (*kamma*), activity (*kriyā*) and energy (*viriya*). According to Gośāla a person cannot attain perfection (*vimutti*) by exertion. He must transmigrate from one existence to another, and it is only after repeated existence that he attains emancipation (*śuddhi*). The consecutive existences of a being including the periods and types of existences are unalterably fixed (*niyata*). A complete view of Ājīvikism cannot be obtained owing to the fragmentary nature of data found in the Buddhist and Jain texts. But some Ājīvika terms and concepts have significant suggestivity such as *yoni-pamukha*, womb or birth; *karmas*, their number and classification; *paṭipadā*, paths (cf. *majjihima-paṭipadā* of the Buddhists); *antara-kappa*, ages of the world; *abhijāti*, classes of men; *puriṣa-bhūmi*, stages of human existence (cf. *bodhisattva-bhūmi*-s of the Buddhists); *manda*, bad; *khiddā*, pleasure; *vimaṃsā*, investigation; *samana*, monkhood; *jina*, enlightenment; *pañña*, the stage of the highest cognition; *suha*, joy; *dukkha*, suffering, etc. According to Gośāla, there is no cause either ultimate or remote for the depravity or rectitude of beings. The attainment of any given condition, of any character, does not depend either on one's own acts, or on the acts of another, or on human effort. All beings are bent this way and that by their fate, by the necessary conditions of the class to which they belong, by their individual nature; and it is according to their position in the one or the other of the six classes that they experience ease or pain. The Ājīvikas believed in the existence of seven elemental categories and the southern Ājīvikas developed a theory of atomism according to which the atoms move and combine densely or loosely to form things of different kinds. The combination of atoms occurs in fixed ratios. The soul and also pleasure or pain are conceived in terms of atomic combinations. Gośāla's Terasiya or three-membered dialectics (it may be; it may not be, and it may both be and not be) paved the way for Mahāvīra's seven-membered Syādvāda. The Ājīvikas believed in doctrine of re-animation (*pravṛtta-patihāra*), of natural and inevitable perfection through continuous transmigrations (*saṃsāra-śuddhi*) and six main types (*abhijātis*) of mankind based upon different colours of their subtle body: black (*kaṇha*) as bird-catchers, hunters, fishermen, etc; blue (*nīla*) as ascetics observing rigorous practices, including the Buddhists (*Sakyaputtīya Samanas*); red (*lohita*) as monks of the Jain order; yellow (*halidda*) as lay-devotees of Acelakas and Ājīvikas; white (*sukka*) as Ājīvika monks belonging to the earlier order of Nanda Vacca and Kisa Sankicca; and very white (*paramasukka*) as Ājīvika saints. "The fundamental principle of the Ājīvika philosophy", writes A.L. Basham, "was fate, called *niyati*. Buddhist and Jain sources agree that Gośāla was a rigid determinist who exalted *niyati* to the status of motive factor of the universe and sole agent of all phenomenal change. For him belief in free will was a vulgar error. The strong, the forceful, and the courageous, like the weakling, the idle and the coward, were all completely subject to the one principle which determined all things."[124]

A similar feeling, though expressed in a different way, has characterised the philosophy of Sañjaya Belaṭṭhiputta. A somewhat dubious tradition speaks of Sañjaya as the former preceptor of Sāriputta and Moggolāna, the chief disciples of the Buddha. Sañjaya is generally described as an agnostic (Ajñānavādin), a sceptic unwilling to give any definite answer to the ultimate problems which were, according to him, indeterminable.[125] Sixty seven kinds of Ajñānavadins are mentioned in the Jain texts. According to Lord Mahāvīra, the Ajñānavādins pretend to be intelligent, but in reality they do not know the truth. As teachers they mislead their pupils, because they are unfamiliar with truth and have not got rid of perplexity and contradictions (*aṇṇāniyā te kusalāvi saṃtā*; *asaṃthānya no vitigicchatiṇṇā*; *akoviyā āhu akoviyahim*; *ananuvi-ittu musaṃ vayanti*).[126] This school corresponds to the Amarāvikkhepikas or evasive disputants of the Buddhist texts who did not want to draw a line of demarcation between good and bad actions or give a categorical answer to the questions put to them.[127] These disputants thus had their own good reasons for the line of action followed by them in view of the fact that good (*kusala*) and evil (*akusala*) are relative terms, and no hard and fast line can be drawn between them. Although in the Buddhist and Jain texts the views of the Amarāvikkhepikas and Ajñānavādins are severely criticised, it can be said with certainty that the method of Sañjaya's arguments was partly accepted by the Buddha and Lord Mahāvīra. Both of them were unanimous in declaring that there are some mooted questions on which no opinion should be given. The Buddha seems to have counted the school of Sañjaya amongst the Aviruddhakas or 'non-hostile' systems.

Jacobi remarked:

> The similarity between some of these 'heretical' doctrines on the one side, and Jain and Buddhistic ideas on the other, is very suggestive, and favours the assumption that the Buddha as well as Mahāvīra owed some of his conceptions to these very 'heretics' and formulated others under the influence of the controversies which were continually going on with them.[128]

The last illustrious contemporary of the Buddha was Ajita Keśakambalin who declared that nothing was real that was not corporeal. Ajita's views come nearest to the views of the materialists like Cārvākas or Lokāyatas. This doctrine is sometimes styled the Bhūtavāda and from the numerous references to it in numerous texts it appears that this doctrine was developed into an orderly system of thinking from a very early period. According to the *Sāmaññaphala-sutta* version of Ajita's doctrine,

> there are in the world no recluses or Brāhmaṇas who have reached the highest point, who walk perfectly, and who having understood and realised by themselves alone, both this world and the next, make their wisdom known to others. A human being is made of four elements. When he dies, the earthly in him returns and relapses to the earth, the fluid to the water, the heat to the fire, and his faculties pass into space.[129]

That the Buddha was deeply concerned with the views of his contemporaries and that the entire thought-complex of his time had both positive and negative impact on the formulation of his own views are amply attested through the evidence furnished by the Buddhist texts. It appears that the historical Buddha had a negative approach in the beginning. Like Socrates he raised questions regarding the problems of life and the mysteries of the universe. This is testified by his polemics directed against many of his contemporary philosophical schools. Instead of presenting a complete worldview at first he set up some trends of thought which were subsequently processed and worked out in the Saṅghas instituted by him. That is why it took a longer time for his doctrines to receive public acceptance on a wider scale. For example, in the *Śvetāśvatara Upaniṣad*,[130] composed about the fifth or fourth century B.C., we come across various worldviews with Īśvara, Kāla, Svabhāva, Niyati, Yadṛcchā, Bhūta, Yoni and Puruṣa as the first principle, but with no reference to the Buddha or Buddhism. Pāṇini refers to the wandering ascetics of the Śramaṇa category and various groups like Kaukkuṭikas, Daṇḍājinikas, Ayaḥśūlikas, etc.,[131] but he has made no specific reference to the Buddhists. This non-mention is helpful in framing the hypothesis that the doctrines of the Buddha were not sufficiently popular even a century after their formulation. But this hypothesis should certainly not be taken as granted. There is another possibility also. It is not impossible that texts like the *Śvetāśvatara* have merely recorded quite in a mechanical way only such worldviews with which their authors were traditionally acquainted and that they did not care to take into account the new trends. The second probability seems to be more reasonable. For example, in the *Suśrutasaṃhitā*[132] which was composed about the fourth century A.D., the *Śvetāśvatara* list is quoted though its authors were not at all unaware of the other existing world-views.

The *Śvetāśvatara* list is thus suggestive of another set of anterior established ideas which the historical Buddha had to take into account in the course of the formulation of his own doctrines. The list supplements the schools of the Purvānta and Aparānta Kalpika categories of the Buddhist texts and those of the Kriyāvāda, Akriyāvāda, Ajñānavāda and Vinayavāda categories of the Jain texts. The *Śvetāśvatara* list begins with Īśvaravāda or absolute theism which was not, however, able to have a solid basis in Buddhism. The Buddhist cosmogonical ideas[133] made no room for a creator god, but left no stone unturned in projecting the Buddha as 'the omniscient one' enjoying the subordination of the existing gods, but unattached to the process of the formation and re-formation of the universe. In regard to the Buddha's omniscience the Buddhists took the stand which in a later period was adopted by the Nyāya-Vaiṣeśikas differing only on the point that omniscience should not have been the absolute monopoly of a supposed creator god. Regarding the latter the Buddhists did not subscribe to the Nyāya-Vaiṣeśika position, but sided with the Sāṅkhyas, Mīmāṃsakas and Jains to suggest that if god be considered an agent under bondage it cannot have the capacity to create and if considered as a free agent it cannot have the desire to create.

The doctrine of time or Kāla is very ancient in Indian philosophy. In the *Atharvaveda*[134] Kāla has been described as the cosmogonic agent and lord of everything. The *Śvetāśvatara*[135] also reviews the concept of time as the cause of the universe. According to Nīlakaṇṭha,[136] Kāla is the conductor of the knowledge of things. Time forms a part of the nine Nyāya-Vaiśeṣika categories of substance. It is also one of the nine *tattvas* of Jain philosophy which has been viewed as *anastikāya*, i.e. without any form.[137] Time comes within the purview of the Buddhist doctrine of *kṣaṇikatva* or momentariness. The Buddhists hold that the phenomenal objects are subject to change every moment, and within one moment take place their origin, duration and decay. Time is not here the first principle but the agent of continuity, because momentariness cannot be established by direct perception; it is the characteristic nature of effectiveness. But while in early Buddhism time is the receptacle of the dynamism of worldly objects, or ceaseless change that takes place in nature and wordly objects, in some forms of later Buddhism like the Kālacakrayāna time is conceived of as the ultimate immutable unchaging reality remaining in all the elements in their three kinds of existence.

It was Gośāla Maṅkhaliputta who raised the doctrine of Niyati to a philosophical level and was able to found a religious sect which came to be known as the Ājīvika. The doctrine of Niyati or destiny has been described in detail in a Prakrit work called *Gommatasāra*. In the Śaiva Āgamas, Kāla and Niyati have been described as the evolutes of Aśuddha Māyā. Though Buddhism in no way subscribes to the doctrine of destiny, some Ājīvika terms and concepts came to its fold. According to the Svabhāvavāda, of which Ajita Keśakambalin might have been a champion, the universe is law-governed and guided by cause-effect relations, while the doctrine of Yadṛcchā holds that everything is accidental. According to Guṇaratna,[138] the followers of the doctrine of Svabhāva believe that the transformation of a thing takes place owing to its inherent nature. Cotton cannot produce an earthenware and clay cannot produce cloth. This natural law is not recognised in the doctrine of Yadṛcchā which maintains that the world is a chaos and ascribes whatever order is seen in it to mere chance. The followers of the Svabhāvavāda had an ethic of their own and they were basically materialistic so far as their worldview was concerned (*svabhāvam bhūtacintakāḥ*).[139] In Indian tradition Svabhāvavāda is often equated with the Bārhaspatya, Cārvāka and Lokāyata doctrines.

In the *Śvetāśvatara* list the doctrines of Bhūta, Yoni and Puruṣa are mentioned. In the Suśruta, it will be remembered, Puruṣa is omitted and the term Prakṛti is used as a substitute for Bhūta and Yoni. These four concepts denote the earlier stages of the evolution of the Sāṅkhya which has been characterised by Nīlakaṇṭha[140] as a variety of the doctrine of Svabhāva (*svabhāva iti pariṇāmavādināṃ sāṅkhyānām*). Gauḍapāda says *sāṅkhyānāṃ svabhāvo nāma kaścit kāraṇamasti*.[141] Śaṅkara also categorically states that the Sāṅkhya is the other name of Svabhāvavāda.[142] The doctrine of Bhūta was an extension of Svabhāvavāda. This doctrine suggests that everything in the world is created by the combination of four or five elements. These elements are earth, water, fire, air and space. These are called the five *mahābhūtas* in the Sāṅkhya and are described as the evolutes of Prakṛti. The doctrine of elements has a significant role in Buddhism and its contemporary systems and it is also acknowledged in the Nyāya-Vaiśeṣika and Mīmāṃsa traditions. The first four—earth, water, fire and air—have colour and touchability while the fifth, i.e., space, is the container of sound.

The doctrines of the Buddha had thus a close bearing on the traditional Indian religio-ethical concepts of rebirth, efficacy of all action, bondage and emancipation. These concepts were universally accepted by most schools, including Buddhism, which seek within the framework of their respective philosophical tenets to bring these concepts in line with the notion of a conscious element. According to Buddhism, there lie at the root of the gross physical world two types of subtle elements, one physical and the other conscious, the former called *rūpa* and the latter *nāma*. There exist in the subtle world the physical series of states that originate and perish. The latter series are as much devoid of permanent substrata as the former series. Notwithstanding the existence of any permanent substance in the form of a fixed resting medium, the outgoing modification-moment, by its very nature, produces the incoming one. Only on this point does Buddhism show its special distinctiveness. But this applies only to one of its various philosophical aspects which may be studied with reference to other systems. Buddhism, as we have stated earlier, has always been a composite system and, unlike Islam or Christianity, which evolved through a unilinear thought-process, it represented a conglomeration of various features of the earlier traditions which the historical Buddha wanted to streamline. Many of such features have no basic relation with what is known to us as the general principles of Buddhism, but somehow they have been able to incorporate themselves within the framework of the composite system, as we shall see in the subsequent chapters.

NOTES

1. And the way in which the Buddha has been represented as a fireband crusader against the Yajña rituals provokes us to believe that he must have read the following assessment of Max Müller of the Brāhmaṇa literature which upholds the doctrine of Yajña: "No one should have supposed that at so early a period and so primitive a state of society there could have risen up a literature which for pedantry and downright absurdity can hardly be matched anywhere....The general character of these works is marked by shallow and insipid grandiloquence, by priestly conceit and antiquarian pendantry. It is most important to the historian that he should know how soon the fresh and healthy spirit of a nation can be blighted by priestcraft and superstition. It is most important that we should know that nations are liable to these epidemics in their youth as well as in their dotage." *Ancient Sanskrit Literature* (London, 1869), 389.
2. Śabara on *Mīmāṃsāsūtra* II.1.5; VI.1.2; VII.1.34; IX.1.6-10; X. 4.23.

3. Cf. The *Kūṭadanta* and *Tevijja Suttas* of the *Dīgha Nikāya; Yajña Sutta* of the *Saṃyutta Nikāya*; *Aṅguttara* II, 205; *Majjhima* (51), I, 342 ff; *Bhuridatta Jātaka* (Cowell, VI, No. 54), etc.
4. IV, 28ff.; Cf. *Ait. Br.* V.25; *Śat.Br.* XI.3.1.1. ff.; *Chāndogya* III. 17.1ff.
5. Cf. *Kāṭhaka Saṃ.* VIII.9; *Mait. Saṃ.* I.6.7; *Taitt. Br.* III. 8.14; *Ait.Br.* V.23; *Śat. Br.* I.2.3.1-5; VI.2.1:1ff. *Jaiminīya Up. Br.* III.6.4;etc.
6. Cf. *Śat. Br.* III.2.1.2; IV.6..7.9-10; VI.5.3.5; XI.6.2.10; *Ait. Br.* II.5.3; III.5.4; V.3.1; VI.5.10.
7. *Lāt.S.S.* IV.3.17; *Kāt.S.S.* XXII.42; *Taitt. Ār.* IV.7.50; *Ait. Br.* I.2.4.10; *Gobhila G.S.* II.5.6, 9-10; *Sāṅ.G.S.*I.19.2-6; *Hir.G.S.* I.24.3; *Āpas. S.S.*V.25.11; etc.
8. V.1.2.9; V.5.4.27; VI.6.3.7; XII.8.1.16; Cf. *Ait.Br.* III.1.5; VI.3.1; VII.5.7.
9. VII.1.4.
10. *Taitt. Ār.* II.17; *Gobhila G.S.* I.2.5.
11. *Ait. Ār.* III.2; *Ṛgvidhāna* II.16.
12. Cf. *Taitt. Ār.* IV.27.
13. Ed. B.T. Bhattacharyya, GOS, LIII, (Baroda, 1931), 31 ff.
14. *Sādhanas* 151, 155, 172, 256, 260, 296.
15. I, 157 ff.
16. I,305; *Culladhammasamādāna Sutta.*
17. XXIII.1-2.
18. *Buddhist Esoterism* (London, 1932), 22ff.
19. *Dīgha,* XIV.
20. *Ibid.,* XXIV.
21. ed. R.L. Mitra, *Bid. Ind.* 315.
22. I, 79; Chalmers, *Further Dialogues*, PTS, I, 35.
23. V.10.2; *SBE*, XX, 89.
24. V.6.
25. *Cullavagga,* VIII.2.
26. X.129. Thus the waters are said to have given birth to Agni or fire (*RV.* III.1.3; III.9.4, X.2.7; X.91.6), to Savitṛ or sun who is sometimes called apāṃ-napāt (*RV*, X.149.2), to Aditi, the mother of the luminaries and also to the gods (*RV*,X.63.2) and to Dyāvyā-Pṛthivī, i.e., Heaven and Earth (*RV*, X.185.1).
27. *RV.* X.121.
28. This is indicated in *Śat. Br.* X.6. 255 which seeks to explain the identity of the essence of the self within and the self without. In the *Ait. Ār.* II.1-3 *ātman* is conceived of as the fivefold *uktha*, the outer portion of which is formed by the five elements and inner by the body, the breath, the apertures, the blood-mucus, seed and the warmth. In the *Kaṭha Up.* IV.6. *ātman* is spoken of as born of old from the waters, while in the *Ait.Up.* I.1.3 it is stated that the *ātman*

after creating the waters drew forth from them a person from whose limbs the different parts of the world came into being. This reminds us of the Puruṣa-sukta. *RV*.X.90.

29. In the *Muṇḍaka Up*. II.1-10 Puruṣa is conceived as a primal person who is heavenly (*divya*), formless (*amūrta*), breathless (*aprāṇa*), mindless (*amanas*) and pure (*śubhra*). In the *Śvetāśvatara* I.2, Puruṣa is mentioned as the First Principle, described as the macrocosmic person with superhuman powers (III.11-19), often endowed with an animistic subtle corporeal appanage of the size of the thumb (Cf. *Kaṭha* IV. 12-13) and as identical with the inner soul or *antarātman*.
30. In the *Bṛhadāraṇayaka* I.4. it is stated that in the beginning this world was *ātman* alone in the form of Puruṣa. Elsewhere in the same text (III.9.26), *ātman* is designated as the Upaniṣadic Puruṣa. The Puruṣa in the earth and that in the body are same, both are alike declared to be no other than the immortal ātman or *brahman* (II.5.1ff). In the *Chāndogya* III.12.7. the space within the Puruṣa is equated with that within the heart.
31. The *Bṛhadāraṇyaka* II.4.7 and the *Maitri* VI.7, identify *ātman* with all gods and powers. In the former V.2. all things, cosmic and personal, are mutually correlated and identified with the *ātman*.
32. *Chāndogya* VI.9.15; *Śvetāśvatara* I.15; *Praśna* IV.7-9.
33. II.5, III.9,10-17; Cf. *Chāndogya* III.14.4.
34. *Taittirīya* II.1: From the self sprang the space, from space air, from air fire, from fire water, from water earth, from earth herbs, from herbs food, from food seed and from seed man.
35. III.1.
36. Cf. *Majjhima* (PTS), I, 98, 182; *Saṃyutta* (PTS), II.20; *Papañcasūdanī* (PTS), I.71.
37. *Dīgha* (PTS), I,31; *Majjhima*, II, 229.
38. *Saṃyutta* II.20; Cf. *Mādhyamikavṛtti*, ed. Poussin, 344. In the last chapter of the *Madhyamakārikā* Nāgārjuna says that if a person of the past could be shown to be the same that of the present, then only Sāsvatavāda could stand, but this is not possible as it would give rise to the contingency of permanence of a being as also to the possibility of a being, having a particular form of existence to assume different bodies. According to him if *ātman* is viewed as inseparable from *upādāna*, it means that the *ātman* of the previous existence is the same as the one in the present; from this it would follow that the *upādāna* of the previous existence is the same as that of the present. It is absurd. Again if *ātman* and *upādāna* be viewed as separate, one being the agent and the other its object, then also it is not proper to say that the object has changed but not its agent. Cf. *Mādhyamikavṛtti*, XVIII. Buddhaghoṣa in his *Sumaṅgalavilāsinī* (PTS) 118ff., associates various soul-schools mentioned in the *Brahmajāla Sutta* with different sects of the Buddha's time.

According to him those Saññivādins who believe that soul is material (*rūpī*) and remains conscious after death pertain to Ājīvikism while those who believe that soul is non-material (*arūpī*) but remains conscious after death belong to the sect of Mahāvīra.

39. *Dīgha*, I.202. In the Kosala-Saṃyutta (*Saṃyutta*, I.75) when it is stated that *attā* is the dearest in the whole world, the term *attā* seems to have been used in a conventional sense.
40. There is a fifth misapprehension: *attā* is something different from *rūpa*, etc. Cf. *Mādhyamikavṛtti*, 432.
41. *Patisaṃbhidāmagga* (PTS), I, 146-50.
42. *Dīgha*, I, 195.
43. ed. V. Trenckner, 55, 86.
44. I, 23 etc.
45. *Dhammapada*, attavaggo, also vv. 103-104, 258, 282, 315, 332, 379- 80.
46. *Mādhyamikavṛtti*, 341 ff.
47. For the *Kathāvatthu* account of the controversy see S.N. Dube, *Cross Currents in Early Buddhism* (New Delhi, 1980), 229-60.
48. There are at least four specific terms in Buddhism which approximate the soul concept. These are *ātman, jīva, sattva* and *pudgala*.
49. *Śākya* (London, 1931), 189ff.
50. *Hinduism and Buddhism*, 57-69, 71-73.
51. *Indian Philosophy* (London, 1927, reprinted 1948 ed.), 581ff.
52. *System of Buddhist Thought* (Calcutta, 1912), 9ff.
53. *Outlines of Mahāyāna Buddhism* (London, 1927), 150ff.
54. *Uber den Stand der Indischen Philosophie zur zeit Mahāvīras und Buddhas* (Berlin, 1902), 4-6.
55. 'Soul Theory of the Buddhists', in *Bulletin of the Academy of Sciences*, 1919, 823ff.
56. *Origin of Buddhism*, 484.
57. *History and Doctrine of the Ājīvikas* (London, 1951), 18.
58. I. 1.1.13.
59. *A History of the Pre-Buddhistic Indian Philosophy* (Calcutta, 1921), 281ff.
60. I.1.1.15-16.
61. ed. Dhanapati, 14.
62. Jacobi in *SBE*, XXII, 3n.
63. *Tattvārthādhigama*, II.8; Guṇaratna on *Ṣaḍdarśanasamuccaya*, 47.
64. *Ibid.*, II, 22-23.
65. *Nyāyāvatāra*, 31; *Dravyasaṃgraha* 2.
66. *Syādvādamañjari* 8, *Tattvārthādhigama* II.16.
67. X.16.
68. T.W. Rhys Davids, *Dialogues of the Buddha* (London, 1899), I, 73-74.

69. E.B. Cowell and A.E. Gough, The *Sarvadarśanasaṃgraha* (rep. 1974), 5-10.
70. I.113.16; I,140.8; VIII.100.5; X. 15.1; etc.
71. IX.113.7ff.
72. I.154.
73. X.14.8; X.15.7; etc.
74. X.154.1.
75. I.125.5; X.107.2.
76. X.88.15.
77. Cf. *Śat.Br.* XII.9.1.1; etc.
78. *Śat.Br.* II.3.3.8; *Jaiminīya Up.Br.* III.28.4; etc.
79. Ch. III.
80. I.4.7.
81. Cf. *Chāndogya*, II.13; *Bṛhadāraṇyaka* I.5.3; *Kauṣītaki* III.6ff.; *Praśna*, III.3.ff; *Taittirīya* II.2; *Aitareya* III; *Kena* I.4-8.
82. III. 3.
83. V.10.
84. VI.2.
85. *loc.cit.* Cf. *Chāndogya* IV.15.5-6; V.3-10.
86. *Visuddhimagga* (PTS), 538ff.
87. Cf. Karmabhava in *Kośa*, V.1.
88. Cf. *Majjhima*, III, 203.
89. Kosambi, *An Introduction to the Study of Indian History* (Bombay, 1956), 159.
90. For Upaniṣadic references to Karma see *Īśā* II, *Chāndogya*, III. 1.10, III. 14.1.
91. *Natthi kammam, natthi kiriyam, natthi viriyam.*
92. I. 409; II, 121.
93. I, 287.
94. Basham, *op.cit.*, 13-14.
95. I.12.4.
96. *Na kammaṇā kamma khaveṃti bālā, akammaṇā kamma khaviṃti dhiro.*
97. Jacobi in *ERE*, VII.168-69; for details see my *Jain Philosophy*, 88-165.
98. I, 134.
99. *Suttanipāta*, 653-54.
100. I, 223.
101. Cf. *Mahāvastu*, III, 62.
102. Cf. Barth, *Religions of India*, 148-50; Colebrooke, *Miscellaneous Essays*, II.276.
103. III, 74.
104. *Sumaṅgalavilāsinī*, I, 119, 168.
105. *Ibid.*, 57.
106. I.1,17.

107. *Dīgha*, I, 47.
108. *Jātakamālā*, ed. E.B. Cowell, 148-49.
109. *Sumaṅgala*, I. 162.
110. I.1.1.13.
111. III, 383ff.
112. I,66.
113. *History and Doctrine of the Ājīvikas*, 80ff.
114. Ed. Norman, III, 199ff.
115. Ed. Cowell and Neil, 143ff.
116. W.W. Rockhill, *Life of Buddha* (London, 1884).
117. Cf. Rhys Davids, *Dialogues of the Buddha* (London, 1889), I,74.
118. *Pre Buddhist Indian Philosophy* (Calcutta, 1921), 281ff.
119. I.513ff.
120. Rockhill, *op.cit.*, 255ff.
121. Basham, *op.cit.* 91.
122. I, 409; II, 121.
123. I, 287.
124. Basham, *op.cit.*, 224-25. The main sources of information regarding Gośāla and Ājīvikism are: the Jain *Sūyagaḍa* I.1.2.1-14; I.1.4.7-9; II.1.29; II.6 with Śīlāṅka's commentary; *Bhagavaī Sūtra* XV.1. with Abhayadeva's com; *Aupapātika*, sec. 118,120; the Buddhist Sāmaññaphala, *Dīgha*, I. 53-54 with Buddhaghoṣa's com; *Saṃyutta*, III, 69; *Aṅguttara*, I.286; *Mahasaccaka-sutta, Majjhima*, I, 231: Cf. I. 36; Chinese and Tibetan versions of the *Sāmaññaphala* tr. in Rockhill's *LB*; *Milindapanho*, Trenckner's ed. 5; *Mahābodhi Jātaka*, No. 528; etc. The Tamil sources are *Maṇimekalai*, *Nīlakeci* and *Civañāṇacittiyar*. Also see A.F.R. Hoernle's art. in *ERE*, I and B.M. Barua's 'Ājīvikas' in *Journal of the Dept. of Letters*, Calcutta University II, 1920.
125. For the mode of his arguments see Rhys Davids, *Dialogues of Buddha*, I.75.
126. *Sūyagaḍa*, I.12.2-4; II.2.79; *Uttara*, XVIII.23.
127. *Dīgha*, I, 25; *Sum. Vil.* I.116; *Majjhima*, I, 521.
128. *SBE*, XLV (ii), intro. xxvii.
129. Rhys Davids, *Dialogues*, I, 73-74.
130. I.1-2.
131. For a complete list see V.S. Agrawala, *India in the Age of Pāṇini*, 380ff.
132. *Śārirasthāna*, I.11. In this list Puruṣa is omitted and Bhūta and Yoni have been combined into Prakṛti.
133. See my *History of Indian Cosmogonical Ideas*, New Delhi, 1971, 74ff.
134. XIX.44.
135. VI.6.
136. Com. on *Mbh.* XIII.232.21.

137. For details see my *Jain Philosophy: Historical Outline* (New Delhi, 1975), 120ff.
138. *Tarkarahasyadīpikā*, 13-15.
139. *Laṅkāvatāra Sūtra*, Kyoto ed., 1923, 184; *Buddhacarita*, IX.52; *Mbh.* XII.179.222ff.
140. Com. on *Mbh.* XII. 232.21.
141. Com. on *Sāṅkhyakārikā*, XXVII.
142. Com. on *Brahmasūtra*, II.2.3-5.

IV

THE HINDU SUBSTRATA OF BUDDHIST MYTHOLOGY

Buddhism has an elaborate mythology adapted from the Vedic and anterior sources. In this mythology the erstwhile conceptions of the cosmos, heavens and hells, gods and goddesses, spirits and semi-divine beings—all have been retained, though an omniscient and omnipotent Buddha is projected on its top. Inevitably the Vedic characters are conspicuously present in Buddhist mythology but the forms in which they appear are very much stereotyped. They cannot be regarded as spontaneous expressions of natural religion, or representatives of social facts and relationships, or projections of the vital experiences of people, or archetypes buried deep in the popular mind. In fact, from the post-Ṛgvedic period, the natural attributes of the divinities began to sink into oblivion, and their extremely anthropomorphised forms studded with various abstractions, were subordinated to the ritualistic concept of Yajña, and still later to the all-pervading cosmic principle, *brahman*. Despite their subordination the mythological characters and events meant something to the masses—as they mean even today—which could not be ignored by the Buddha or his followers.

Although Buddhism insists on the doctrines of *karma* and rebirth, Buddhist mythology stresses on the concepts of heaven and hell. Even the inscriptions of Aśoka assure an individual a joyful life in heaven which can be attained through meritorious deeds in worldly life. In Buddhist mythology there are two broad categories of heaven—the Devaloka or the heaven of the gods and the Brahmaloka or the heaven of the Brahmas. Those who are righteous in body, speech and thought, hold the right view and do the right work, are moral, grateful, ardent, energetic, wise and blameless and have insight, are entitled to attain a heavenly life. Those who abstain from destruction of life, theft, lust, falsehood and liquor, who do not transgress *dharma* being led by desire, ill-will, delusion and fear, and those women who are faithful, modest, scrupulous, ungrudging, not wrathful, not envious, not stingy, not adulteresses are also destined to attain heaven.[1]

The Devaloka or the heaven of gods, also known as Kāmaloka or the abode of desire, comprises six worlds which are known as Cātummahārājika, Tāvatiṃsa, Yāma, Tuṣita, Nimmānarati and Paranimmitavasavatti.[2] The Cātummahārājika has four guardians for its four quarters—Dhatarattha to the east, Viruḷhaka to the south, Virupākkha to the west and Vessavana or Kubera to the north. They are all found in the Brahmanical mythologies as well and their retinue are the Gandhabbas, Kumbhaṇḍas, Nāgas and Yakkhas respectively. They are all protectors of the followers of the Buddha. Those who are pious, faithful, learned, charitable and wise go to this heaven.[3] The Tāvatiṃsa is above the Cātummahārājika, described as the world of the thirty-three, probably borrowed from the Vedic conception of thirty-three gods. The early Iranian concepts of thirty-three gods, found in the *Avesta*, may also have something to do with the Tāvatiṃsa heaven because it is said that it was originally the abode of the Asuras. It was Sakka or Indra who drove the Asuras out of this heaven, who later built their city, Asurabhavana, on the foot of the mount Sineru. To defend this heaven from the attack of the Asuras, Sakka built walls around it. This heaven is guarded by the Nāgas, Supaṇṇas, Kumbhaṇḍas, Yakkhas and Cātummahārājikadevas. All the Buddhas spend the *vassās* or rainy seasons in this heaven. Among the gods of the Tāvatiṃsa heaven Sakka, Vissakammā and Mātali very often visit the earth.[4] There are four other worlds in the ascending order known as Yāma, Tuṣita, Nimmānarati and Paranimmitavasavatti. These are inhabited by better persons, higher gods, Bodhisattvas and beings of higher spiritual plane.

While the spheres of the Devaloka are thus ruled by Pre-Buddhist divines, semi-divines and sages, in which the Buddha and his qualified followers are distinguished guests, the Brahmaloka is regarded as a still higher plane meant for the most outstanding ones. The concept of Brahmaloka evidently derived its main impulses from the parallel Upaniṣadic concept of *brahman*, the ultimate reality, the cosmic self variously identified with the individual self. But a more personalised form of *brahman* as the creative principle, often equated with Prajāpati was already foreshadowed in the Brāhmaṇa literature. In Buddhist mythology the number of *brahman* has been multiplied. At least twenty such *brahmans* are conceived, each of them being invested with the rulership of a special celestial region. The twenty regions of the Brahmaloka, from the lowest to the highest, are known as

Brahmapārisajja, Brahmapurohita, Mahābrahma, Parittābha, Appamāṇābha, Ābhāssara, Parittasubha, Appamānasubha, Subhakiṇha, Vehapphala, Asaññasatta, Avihā, Atappā, Sudassī, Sudassā, Akaniṭṭha, Ākāsānañcāyatana, Viññāṇañcāyatana, Akiñcaññāyatana and Nevasaññanāsaññayatana. The names are chosen at random, and as we proceed from the lowest to the highest region we find that the authors of the Buddhist texts are hopelessly and increasingly unable to determine the credentials of their inhabitants as also to provide them the amenities they should deserve as reward for their outstanding merit. The first sixteen of the twenty regions pertain to *rūpa* or the material level and the last four to *arūpa* or non-material level.[5]

Compared to the Buddhist heavens, the Vedic heaven is a world of material joys where the deceased enter upon a delectable life in which all desires are fulfilled. At the same time the concept of hell is not very conspicuous in the *Ṛgveda*. The *Atharvaveda*,[6] however, speaks of an underground black or dark chamber, the abode of female goblins and sorceresses, which is described as hell in contrast with the heavenly region, the realm of Yama. The torments of hell are not also clearly described in the Saṃhitās, and it appears that it is not till the period of the Brāhmaṇas that the notion of future punishment was developed. For the attainment of the Vedic heaven a person is not required to do any special spiritual exercise or any special meritorious act. Numerous are the channels through which the individuals can reach heaven, whence they meet their parents and relations, unite with wives and children and receive a life free from imperfections and bodily frailties, sickness and old age. In fact, the thoughts of the Vedic poets were more concerned with the joys of heavenly life, and they did not bother much about the questions relating to spiritual backwardness, sinful acts, human lapses and their consequences, the problem of evil, the cause of human misery, decline in ethical standard and so forth. These questions became more conspicuous in the later Vedic age and became subjects of principal concern in Buddhism. That is why in the Buddhist tradition the concept of various types of hell and the punishment inflicted therein on the sinners finds greater prominence.

According to Nikāyas,[7] persons who are unbelievers, immoral, indolent and unwise, who are sinful in action, speech and thought, who are miserly and averse to liberality, who indulge in killing, theft, lust, falsehood, consumption of liquor, evil desire, wrong views and who are conceited for their wealth and fame, monks and Brāhmaṇas who are faithless, shameless, reckless, indolent, devoid of insight and who indulge in sensual pleasure, women who are faithless, shameless, unscrupulous, wrathful, grudging, envious, stingy, adulterous, immoral, indolent, muddleheaded and unwise are all liable to suffer in hell. There are seven kinds of torture made successively on the sinners, which comprise the piercing of the hands, feet and chest respectively by five hot iron rods, flaying with hatchets, chopping with knife, dragging the body by fixing it to a chariot, putting on burning coal, casting into a blazing copper cauldron and finally throwing into the Great Hell (Mahāniraya).[8] The Buddhist conception of hell thus reminds us of that of the Purāṇas. In this case a multiplication has only been made in regard to the number of the hells and the technique of punishment. The concepts such as *lohakumbha* or blazing copper cauldron, the Mahāniraya or Great Hell on the other bank of the river Vetaraṇī (Vaitaraṇī), the Roruva (Raurava) etc., appear to have directly borrowed from the Puranic traditions.

Eight major hells are described in Pali Buddhist literature, each of which has four corners and four doors, and are supplemented by sixteen minor hells. The first is Sañjiva meant for those who kill living beings or cause them to be killed. The second is known as Kālasutta and it is meant for the murderers of the great sages, the patricides and those who injure their friends. The third, Saṅghāta is meant for the forgers and slayers of animals. The fourth and the fifth are called Jālaroruva and Dhumraroruva respectively in which flames and smoke enter the body of the sinners. These are meant for the miserly persons, cheats and killers. The sixth, known as Tapana where the sinners are forced to sit upon a burning iron stake, is meant specially for unchaste women. The seventh, Patāpena is meant for the unbelievers and the eight, Avīci for those who injure or slay men of great virtue, the monks, parents and preceptors. Avīci is the most fearful of all the hells. It is also known as the Mahāniraya or the Great Hell.[9] Some important characters mentioned in the Buddhist tradition such as Devadatta, Cunda, Ānanda, Uppavaññā, Sivali, Snuppabuddha, Mallikā, Ciñcā-Mānavikā, Kapila, etc., had to suffer in this hell for committing various types of offences.[10] The Nikāyas describe some hells like Abbuda, Nirabbuda, Ababa, Ataṭa, etc.,[11] but Buddhagoṣa says that these are not separate Nirayas but specified periods of suffering in the Avīci.[12] Adjacent to this Great Hell there are other purgatories known as Gūtha, Kukkula, Simbalivana, Asipattavana and Khārodakanadī where sinners are purified by getting their bodies chopped by sharp weapons or cleansed by fire, steam and caustic water wash.[13] The river Vetaraṇī or Vaitaraṇī which serves as the boundary line of the hell complex is full of spears, razors and swords so that an absconding sinner cannot run away. The

Sarabhaṅga Jātaka[14] mentions another Great Hell called Sunaka where the sinners fall into the jaws of fierce dogs. Besides the eight major hells there are sixteen minor hells or Ussadas. There are also a few subsidiary hells such as Sataporiṣa, Sattisūla, Mahāpariḷāha, Pahāsa, Saṃsavaka, etc.[15] One should not fail to observe in this connection that while describing the hells and the punishment inflicted therein on the sinners the Buddhist authors were absolutely guided by a spirit of violent revenge of the most crude and material type and not by the spirit of the widely proclaimed doctrine of compassion attributed to the Buddha.

Most of the important Vedic gods figure in Buddhist mythology. Indra is represented here as Sakka or Śakra. In the Vedas Indra is the favourite national god as indicated by the fact that about 250 hymns celebrate his greatness, more than those devoted to any other god and very nearly one-fourth of the total number of hymns in the *Ṛgveda*. In Pali literature also Sakka or Indra has been given more prominence than any other god. In the Vedas Indra is primarily the thunder-god. Exhilerated by Soma and generally escorted by Maruts, he kills Vṛtra, the demon of drought or darkness, and liberates the eaters.[16] Owing to the importance of the Vṛtra myth, the chief and specific epithet of Indra is Vṛtrahan, or the Vrtrā-slayer. In Buddhist mythology he is also called Vatrabhū, because he slayed Vatra (Vṛtra) the Asura chief.[17] While in the Vedas Śakra is mentioned as a title of Indra, in Pali literature Indra (Inda) is mentioned as a title of Sakka who is always spoken of as *devānām Indo*, the king of the gods.[18] In the Nikāyas Indra is mentioned along with other Vedic gods, such as Soma, Varuṇa, Īśāna, Vessavana, Prajāpati, Brahmā, Mahiddi and Yama.[19] Elsewhere in the Nikāyas Inda is mentioned with Soma and Varuna as Yakkha.[20] The Jātakas identify Sakka with Inda and also refer to his Vedic association with the thunderbolt for which he is also known as Vajirahattha. His thunderbolt is known as Indavajira, the sound of which surpasses all other sounds by its intensity and volume. It is not stopped by any obstruction and never misses its mark.[21] As in the Vedas, so also in the Bhuddhist texts he is described as Tidivapuravara, i.e. king of the heaven.[22] His Vedic epithet, Pākaśāsana, has also been retained in Buddhist mythology.[23]

Other epithets of the Vedic Indra have been shared by his Buddhist counterpart. One of the names of Sakka is Maghavā. In the Vedas the name Maghavan is attributed to him to describe his bountifulness. Buddhist mythology traces the origin of the name Maghavan to a pious Brāhmaṇa known as Magha who was identified with a Bodhisattva.[24] The Vedic Indra is known as Purandara or destroyer of the forts or towns. In the mythical imagery of the thunderstorm the clouds also very frequently become the fortresses of the aerial demons. These might have been also the strongholds of the non-Vedic tribes which were vanquished by Indra. The epithet 'fort-shatterer' has always been peculiar to Indra. This Purandara (Purindada) also occurs in Buddhist mythology as an epithet of Sakka.[25] Interestingly in Pali literature the speciality of Maghavan as the generous giver has been imposed on Purindada. Vāsava, another epithet of Indra, also applies to Sakka. According to Buddhist mythology, he is so called because he is the chief of the Vasu class of gods.[26] He is also called Vasudevatā[27] which reminds us of the Vedic Vasupati. Like his Vedic counterpart Sakka has one thousand eyes, and hence known as Sahassākkha owing to the fact that he can think of one thousand matters in a moment.[28] The Buddhist authors probably avoided on moral grounds the Puranic legends describing how Indra became possessed of one thousand eyes, but quite in accordance with the Puranic viewpoint they said that very often Sakka used to send heavenly damsels to the earth for destroying the merit of some individuals fearing that they might usurp his position of Sakkahood by means of their virtuous power.[29]

The Vedic Varuṇa also figures in Buddhist mythology. In the *Ṛgveda* the anthropomorphism of Varuṇa's personality is more fully developed on the moral than on the physical side. Varuṇa alone, or conjointly with Mitra, is often called a king.[30] He is the king of all, both gods and men, of the whole world. Varuṇa goes back to the Indo-Iranian period, for the Ahura Mazda of the *Avesta* agrees with him in character, though not in name. His ordinances are fixed, the epithet *dhṛtavrata* being always applicable to him. As a moral governor Varuṇa stands far above any other deity in the *Ṛgveda*. His wrath is roused by sin and he binds the sinners with fetters (*pāśaḥ*).[31] But in the post-Ṛgvedic literature the characteristics of Varuṇa as a sovereign god have become somewhat faded owing to the emergence of new gods sharing his original powers and qualities. In Buddhist mythology although Varuṇa is spoken of as the king of the gods and the gods of the Tāvatiṃsa heaven are asked to look upon the banner of Varuṇa for regaining their courage when they are in combat with the Asuras,[32] he has not been given that exalted position which Sakka was able to acquire. Varuṇa is mentioned with Indra, Soma, Īśāna, Prajāpati, Yama, Soma, Brahmā and other divinities,[33] but no special function has been ascribed to him. The followers of Varuṇa are known as Vāruṇas and his female attendants as Vāruṇis who were efficient in fortune telling. Like Sakka Varuṇa is also described as a Yakkha chief. The decline in the status and position of Varuṇa in the post-Ṛgvedic literature in general and post-Vedic literature in particular must have been the cause of the indifferent attitude shown towards him by the Buddhist authors.

Agni is known in Pali literature by his Vedic appellation Jātaveda. He is also known as Aggideva and Aggi Bhagavā. In the *Ṛgveda* Agni is next to Indra in prominence, celebrated at least in 200 hymns. As his name is the regular designation of fire, the anthropomorphism of his physical appearance is only rudimentary. In consequence of his main function in the Veda of officiating at the Yajñas Agni comes to be celebrated as the divine counterpart of the earthly priesthood. He is the priest, the Brāhmaṇa, the offerer and the spokesman in one.[36] This tradition is also maintained in Buddhist mythology in which it is said that when a king named Mujalinda asked the Brāhmaṇas how to reach heaven he was told that Agni is a Brāhmaṇa god *par excellence* and that he should be worshipped with the offering of clarified butter.[37] In the *Ṛgveda* Agni exclusively bears the epithet Jātavedas which occurs more than 120 times. This epithet is explained as meaning 'he who knows all generations'.[38] The same epithet as a personal name is found in the Buddhist texts.[39] It is said that on the birthday of a man Agni should be invoked by making and maintaining a fire. When the person concerned resolves to renounce the householder's life, that fire should be taken to the forest and especially worshipped.[40] Vaiśvānara, the Vedic appellation of Agni,[41] has also been used by the Buddhist authors to designate Agni.[42]

The Vedic Yama occupies a prominent position in Buddhist mythology. His name occurs about 50 times in the *Ṛgveda* in which he is not expressly called a god, but only a king who rules the dead.[43] His dwelling is in the remote recesses of the sky. The *Vājasaneyi Saṃhita*[44] speaks of him along with Yamī as being in the highest heaven. In their dialogue, as found in the *Ṛgveda*,[45] Yama and Yamī call themselves children of Gandharva and the water nymph. Death is the path of Yama and sometimes Yama is identified with death.[46] In the *Atharvaveda* and the later mythology Yama, being more closely associated with the terrors of death, came to be the god of death. Disease is his messenger.[47] The same is said in the Buddhist texts which describes him as the god of death whose messengers are birth, old age, illness and punishment for crime and death. His assistants are the Nirayāpālas ,who take the sinners and throw them into different hells.[48] Yama's abode is called Ussadaniraya. The river Vetaraṇī forms the boundary of his kingdom.[49] All existence is regarded as subject to Yama's rule, because no one can escape from the cycle of the Saṃsāra. That is why his other name is Vesāyi.[50] Very often he is mentioned with Indra, Varuṇa, Soma, Prajāpati, Kubera, Suyāma, Santusita and other deities as a god to whom Yajñas were offered. The weapon of Yama is his eye (*nayanāyudha*) a glance of which can destroy many thousand of Kumbhaṇḍas.[52] Some Buddhist texts refer to two Yamas (*duve Yamā*).[53] In the Vedic texts the word Yama has also the appellative meaning of 'twin', in which sense it occurs several times in the *Ṛgveda* where Yama is actually a twin with Yamī. The sense of 'twin' also seems to belong to Yama in the *Avesta*.[54] Buddhaghoṣa refers to the Yama-'twin' as *dve Yamakadevatā* and elsewhere he speaks of four Yamas as the guardians of the four gates of the Nirayas.[55] Yama is also described as Vemānika Petarāja, the lord of the ghosts of the atmospheric region who enjoys all the pleasures of heaven being surrounded by the wish-fulfilling trees (*kapparukkhas*).

The various attributes of the sun-god are personified in the Vedic literature in the forms of Mitra, Sūrya, Savitṛ, Puṣan, Viṣṇu, Vivasvat and some deities of the Āditya category. Among them Sūrya and Viṣṇu figure prominently in Buddhist mythology. Ten hymns of the *Ṛgveda* are devoted to the celebration of Sūrya. It is not possible to say how often the name of the god occurs in the *Ṛgveda* because in many cases it is doubtful whether the reference is to natural phenomenon or to its personification. Since his name designates the orb of sun as well, Sūrya is the most concrete among the solar deities. His connection with the luminary is never lost sight of. In Buddhist mythology Sūrya or Suriya is still regarded as the sun-god, but his natural background has not been taken into account. He is one of the Cāturmahārajika-devas because he lives in their world.[56] He is supposed to be seized by Asura Rāhu but when he takes refuge with the Buddha the Rāhu element becomes no factor. In the Vedas Sūrya bears the metronymic Āditya, son of Aditi.[57] The same tradition is maintained in Buddhist mythology in which Suriya is described as Ādicca.[58] According to Buddhaghoṣa[59] he is the son of Aditi. Moreover, Āditya is the general *gotra* name of the Kṣatriyas.[60] In some of the Buddhist texts it is said that Āditya is the *gotra* name of the Sākyas.[61] Elsewhere it is stated that Āditya or the sun belongs to the Gotama *gotra* to which also belongs the Buddha.[62] That is why they are very close to each other and Buddha has been spoken of as Adiccabandhu or friend of Āditya.[63] Both the Buddha and the sun are said to have been born in the *ariya* (Aryan or Noble) family and the latter is also spoken of as the son and disciple of the Buddha. Elsewhere the sun is described as the subject (*pajā, prajā*) of the Buddha[64] and as one who is capable of producing heat.[65] In Buddhist mythology the sun god has become completely anthropomorphised. Even it is said that in one of his previous births he distributed all his wealth, and the merit he thus had acquired caused him to be reborn in heaven.[66]

Viṣṇu is another solar god in the *Ṛgveda*. With his three steps he is described as traversing the earth or the terrestrial spaces. Yāska[67] says that the three steps of Viṣṇu mean the rising, culminating and setting of the sun. Another view interprets the three steps as the course of the solar deity through the three divisions of the universe. The only anthropomorphic traits of Viṣṇu in the *Ṛgveda* are the frequently mentioned strides which he takes and his being a youth in body.[68] In the post-Ṛgvedic literature in which Viṣṇu receives greater prominence he is no longer clearly connected with a natural phenomenon, though in the Brāhmaṇa literature[69] he is still conceived as taking his three steps to cover earth, air and heaven. It is stated in the *Taittirīya Saṃhitā*[70] that Viṣṇu, by assuming the form of dwarf conquered the three worlds. This forms the nucleus of the myth of Viṣṇu's dwarf incarnation in post-Vedic literature in which Viṣṇu appears as a supreme sectarian deity. In Buddhist mythology Viṣṇu is an important god, but no trace of his earlier natural background is found there. In the Nikāyas Veṇhu or Viṣṇu is mostly represented as subordinate to the Buddha, who accompanies the latter with his retinue during his public discourses.[71] Often he is represented as an enquiring god occasionally visiting the Buddha to ask him questions.[72] He is sometimes described as *devaputta*[73] which technically means in Buddhism personal gods holding particular offices and having the colour of lotus.[74]

In Buddhist mythology there are two moon gods—Soma and Candima—both deriving their main impulses from the Vedic tradition. As in the Vedic texts so in Buddhist literature Soma has a dual entity. Since the Soma-Yāgas form the main feature of the *Ṛgvedic* rituals, the god Soma, whose natural background is the terrestrial plant and the intoxicating juice extracted therefrom, is naturally one of the most important deities to whom all the 114 hymns of the ninth, besides 6 in other books, are dedicated. The mysteriously exhilarating and invigorating action of the Soma plant, surpassing that of ordinary food or drink, made its divine prototype a central figure in the Yajña rituals. Buddhist mythology remembers this tradition and accordingly the Buddhist texts record the custom of Soma-Yāgas in which the god is invoked along with Varuṇa, Prajāpati and Yama.[75] He is also mentioned with Dhātā, Vidhātā, Kubera, Suriya and Candima.[76] He is also called a Yakṣa chief in Buddhist literature[77] probably owing to his earlier association with the plants. In post-*Ṛgveda* literature Soma is a name of moon. In the

Brāhmaṇas it is said that the moon is the Soma of gods, that the Soma plant or juice is symbolical of the moon-god and so forth.[78] In the *Atharvaveda*,[79] Soma several times means the moon. The mythology of the Brāhmaṇas explains the phases of the moon as due to the gods drinking its substance which consists of ambrosia. The moon is regarded as being drunk up by the gods and so waning, till it is filled up again by the sun.[80] Soma's association with the moon is recorded also in Buddhist texts. He is regarded as the moon-god and the founder of the lunar dynasty.[81] But the moon-god who has a greater prominence in Buddhist literature is Candima. The Buddhist texts make a difference between the moon and its controller. Moon or Candra is a region or Vimāna which is controlled by the moon god Candima without whose will and permission the moon cannot move in the sky.[82] The moon is described as the abode of various gods[83] and Candima as belonging to the Cātummahārājika group of deities.[84] Candima is also regarded as the protector of children.[85]

The Vedic god who occurs with most of his natural traits in Buddhist mythology is Parjanya (Pajjuna) who is celebrated in three hymns of the *Ṛgveda*. His praises are also sung in one hymn of the *Atharvaveda*.[86] The shedding of rain is his most prominent characteristic. He moves around with a watery car and loosens the rains downwards. Like a charioteer on his horses the Vedic Prajanya displays his rainy messengers. When he sheds rain water, the roar of the lion resounds from every corner. He is besought for rains and is implored to withhold them after shedding. Thundering he strikes down trees, demons and evil doers.[87] The Buddhist Parjanya is also the god of rain, the king of storm-clouds who is often invoked to cause rain to fall. Like his Vedic counterpart, the Buddhist Parjanya is an associate of Śakka or Indra at whose behest he pours down the rains on the earth. A Jātaka story says that when there was a terrible drought in Kosala, the Buddha wished to cause rain out of his characteristic compassion for living beings. In order to honour the desire of the Buddha Sakka summoned Parjanya and asked him to pour down the rains on the Kosala country.[88] Parjanya is described in this connection as the upholder of truth who is dressed in three-piece cloudy garment and appearing in the east. He is also described as Vassavalahaka who dwells in the Cātummahārājika world as well as among the Mahāyakkhas.[89] His absolute anthropomorphised form is found in the company of the Buddha during the latter's preaching of sermons.[90] Two of his daughters—Kokanada and Culla-Kokanada—are mentioned as ardent devotees of the Buddha.[91]

Among the abstract deities of the *Ṛgveda* who received greater prominence in later Vedic literature Prajāpati figures in Buddhist mythology. Prajāpati occurs in one passage of the *Ṛgveda*[92] as an epithet of Savitṛ, who is spoken of as a supporter of heaven and the lord of the dependents of the world. As a distinct god he is invoked to bestow numerous offsprings and cattle.[93] In Brāhmaṇa literature he is recognised as the chief god, the father of the gods, the only existent in the beginning of the universe, the creator and the first sacrificer.[94] In Buddhist mythology Prajāpati is also a king of the gods and often in typical Buddhist style he is described as Mahāyakkha who appears to be a saviour of the followers of the Buddha in times of distress.[96] Here also in certain cases he is equated with Brahmā[97] and mentioned along with Sakka, Īśāna, Varuṇa and Soma.[98] Buddhaghoṣa describes him as almost identical in appearance with Sakka enjoying the same life span of the latter, but in the assembly of the gods his position is second. In the Vedas Dhātṛ is mentioned sometimes as an individual abstract god and sometimes as an epithet of Prajāpati, 'Lord of Creatures.' He has the independent character of god who created sun, moon, heaven, earth and air, and is lord of the world.[99] He is invoked to grant a clear eye, offspring and length of life.[100] In the post-Ṛgvedic period, Dhātṛ is the creator and preserver of the world, being the equivalent of Prajāpati or Brahmā. Likewise Vidhātṛ, the 'Disposer' is sometimes an epithet of Viśvakarman and Indra,[101] but often appears to have an independent character.[102] In later mythology Vidhātṛ has also been identified with Prajāpati. Both of these deities occur in Buddhist mythology with some modifications in their characters. The Vedic background of Vidhātṛ is somehow retained as he is said to have been offered rituals by the people for obtaining happiness. Dhātṛ is regarded in the Buddhist text as a secondary god who in his previous birth offered gifts to the Brāhmaṇas, in consequence of which he was reborn in the world of gods.[103]

The Vedic Viśvakarman is present in Buddhist mythology retaining his original character to a great extent. In the *Ṛgveda*, two whole hymns are dedicated to his praise[104] in which he is described as an establisher and disposer, having produced the earth and disclosed the sky. The name Viśvakarman was at first used as an epithet of sun-god, but later owing to the name itself became suggestive of an architectural deity who was supposed to fashion the heaven and earth with the skill of a joiner and carpenter. In Brāhmaṇa literature Viśvakarman is expressly identified with the creator Prajāpati[105] and in post-Vedic times he was conceived as the chief architect of the gods. In Buddhist mythology also he enjoys the same capacity. At the command of Sakka he built a palace called Dhamma for Mahāsudassana and another for Mahāpanāda.[106] In some Jātakas it is said that he was Ānanda in his previous birth,[107] while according to other sources the architect who helped Magha, and his companions in their pious works on earth was reborn as Viśvakarman in the Tāvatiṃsa heaven.[108] He was sent by Sakka to adorn Temiya on the day he left the kingdom,[109] and also to bathe and clothe the Buddha when the latter renounced the world.[110] He built the residence of the Boddhisattvas like Sumedha, Kuddālapaṇḍita, Hatthipāla, Ayoghara, Jotipāla, Sutosoma, Temiya, Vessantara and others.[111] He also built hermitages for Dukulaka and Pārikā.[112] Apart from the erection of buildings and monasteries he is credited with having excavated ponds.[113] He is also said to have gone with Aśoka to fetch the relics for his Caityas which lay buried in such a way that no one could find them.[114]

The Vedic Rudra-Śiva appears in Buddhist mythology under two names, Śiva and Īśāna. Rudra-Śiva occupies a subordinate position in the Vedas, though in the post-Vedic period he became the supreme being of one of the most powerful sectarian cults of India. The Rudra or fearful concept of the deity is, however, absent in the Buddhist texts. Malevolence is frequently attributed to Rudra in the *Ṛgveda*. The hymns addressed to him chiefly express his terrible shafts and deprecation of his wrath. He is implored not to slay or injure his worshippers, their parents, children, men, cattle or horses, and is besought to avert his bolt when he is incensed and to keep away from them his missiles of destruction.[115] Rudra appears to have originally represented the baleful side in the destructive agency of lightning. But he has some beneficent and healing powers which were based on the fertilising and purifying action of the thunderstorm. Thus the deprecations of his wrath gave rise to the euphemistic epithet Śiva, meaning 'auspicious', which became the regular name of Rudra's historical successor in post-Vedic religion. This Śiva aspect which had received a finality in the *Śvetāśvatara Upaniṣad* is insisted upon in Buddhist mythology which refers to Śiva sometimes as a devaputta or a deity holding a particular office.[116] and sometimes as a full god, though a dependent of the Buddha.[117] His Puranic epithet *Candraśekhara*, the one having moon on his forehead, finds parallel in his Buddhist epithet Candadhara.[118] Also there are references to a particular Śiva cult and the worship of Śivalinga. The *Ṛgvedic* epithet Īśāna, lord of the vast world, attributed to Rudra[120] which became a synonym of Śiva in later mythology was also crystallised in Buddhism as a divine figure. In Buddhist texts he is one of the gods mentioned along with Indra, Soma, Varuṇa, Prajāpati and Brahmā as being invoked by the Brāhmaṇas.[121] When the gods fought against the Asuras, Īśāna was a commander there; his banner indicated fearlessness.[122] Īśāna is equal to Indra in beauty and longevity. In the assembly of the gods he has the fourth seat, next to Varuṇa. Among the Puranic deities associated with Śiva, Kumāra, Skanda and Mahāsena occur in Buddhist mythology in which Kumāra and Skanda are described as identical and associated with Śiva.[123] Mahāsena on the other hand has been described as a separate deity, having no link with Śiva, who lived in the Ketumati palace to the east of Vejayanta and was reborn in the world of men as Nāgasena at the behest of Śakka.[124]

Some Vedic goddesses such as Śrī, Śraddhā, Hrī, etc., lower deities, demi-gods, mythical priests and heroes, deified animals and inanimate objects, demons and fiends occur in Buddhist mythology. In Buddhism Āśā, Śraddhā, Śrī and Hrī are the four daughters of Sakka who are of golden form and who dressed in golden robes look bright and glow like flames.[125] Āśā is the goddess of hope, Śrī of glory, Śraddhā of faith and Hrī of modesty. Among these female deities, Śrī (Siri) or Lakṣmī (Lakkhi) became a prominent figure not only in Buddhist mythology but also in the subsequent Hindu mythology. In Pali literature both the names Śrī and Lakṣmī are often found mentioned together.[126] Śrī-Lakṣmī is regarded as the goddess of beauty and fortune and often as the synonym of the same. In the Jātakas she is also described as the goddess of family property, wisdom and virtue.[128] She lives in four objects—a fowl, a gem, a club and a wife.[129] The Pali literature also knows of a goddess Sarasvatī, a later Jain and Hindu crytalisation of the Vedic Vāk, who seems to have absorbed some qualities of Śrī-Lakṣmī. Mention is found of a Buddhist king who erected a Sarasvatī-maṇḍapa in Ceylon.[130] The popular belief that Lakṣmī and Sarasvatī cannot live together is not, however, supported in the Buddhist tradition which emphasises that a man cannot be favoured by Lakṣmī, i.e. the goddess of wealth, unless he is favoured by Sarasvatī, the goddess of wisdom.[131] The *paññа* (prajñā) element in the mythological concepts of Lakṣmī and Sarasvatī, seems to have contributed a great deal to the Mahayanic crystallisation of deified wisdom in the form of Prajñāpāramitā, while Śrī of the earlier tradition who was in her basic form a Corn Mother (of. Roman Ceres) had her later manifestation in the form of Vasudharā. Side by side with the concept of Lakṣmī, the Buddhist mythology refers to her destructive opposite, the goddess Alakṣmī who is sometimes equated with Kālī.[132] Though in the *Muṇḍakopaniṣad*[133] Kālī is mentioned as one of the seven tongues of Agni, in Buddhist literature she has been referred to as a fierce goddess and equated with Caṇḍī and Kalakanni.[134]

In the Vedas, besides the higher gods, there are a number of mythical beings not regarded as having a completely divine nature. Such beings were not regarded as having been gods from the beginning, but their association with the gods was responsible for endowing them with some sort of divinity. The Ṛbhus, for example, were such beings raised who received an elevated status due to their association with Indra, Agni and the Ādityas. Likewise the Apsarases denoted a kind of nymphs who even in the *Ṛgveda* appear almost completely separated from their physical basis. With the Apsarases were associated a kind of beings named Gandharvas. In the *Ṛgveda* the Gandharvas seem to be localised in the higher region of air or sky and often associated with some form of celestial light, with 'golden-winged bird, the messenger of Varuṇa'[135] with the stars of moon's orbit, especially with Rohinī,[136] with the rainbow[137] and with water.[138] The Gandharvas' love for women and their proficiency in music are prominent in the later texts. The conception of the Gandharvas was somehow related to that of the Yakṣas who gradually acquired prominence in later belief. Apparently, the Vedic idea that the Gandharvas and Apsarases live in the trees might have some bearing on the characteristics of the Yakṣas who were also regarded as tree spirits. Originally both the Gandharvas and the Yakṣas who made their way into Hindu and Buddhist mythology probably belonged to the group of tribal divinities who held power over man's life and death, reputed to be the hoarders of unspent wealth and conceived as having a beautiful and earthly form. Kubera, who is regarded both as the king of the Gandharvas and that of the Yakṣas in Hindu mythology is extolled in Buddhist literature as Vessavana (Vaiśravaṇa). He is one of the four regent gods and rules the northern quarter.[139] He is also mentioned by the name of Kubera and described as the god of wealth who had nine specific treasures.[140] Yakkha Puṇṇaka is his minister.[141] In Buddhist mythology Kubera or Vessavana is the spokesman of the gods, is an expert in conversation, is intimate with the Buddha and is a friend of Sakka.[142] His chariot runs through the space as that of his Hindu counterpart.[143] He is worshipped by those who desire children and is also invoked to avert earthquakes.[144] His association with trees, plants, ponds and lakes is also recorded.[145] The Gandharvas in the Buddhist tradition were led by Dhataratiha (Dhṛtarāṣṭra), the ruler of the eastern quarter,[146] and the Kumbhaṇḍas by Virubha, the regent god of the southern quarter.[147] Virupākkha is one of the gods of the Cātummahārājika heaven who rules the western quarter and is the lord of Nāgas.[148] In the

Atharvaveda and later *Saṃhitās* serpents appear as semi-divine beings, and in the Gṛhyasūtras, Nāgas, called for the first time by this name, are supposed to belong to earth, sky and heaven, as also to the quarters.

According to Buddhist mythology, the Gandharvas dwell in the Cātummahārājika world and are regarded as the lowest of all gods.[149] They dwell in the fragrance of root-wood and sap-wood and in their flowers.[150] Those who practise a little *śīla* are reborn in the Gandharva world.[151] In some texts, the Gandharvas are classed with the Asuras and Nāgas, regarded as heavenly musicians waiting on Sakka and described as beings capable of going through the air.[152] Sometimes they are malevolent causing trouble to monks and nuns. Besides Dhatarattha other important Gandharva chiefs were Panāda, Opamañña, Mātali, Cittasena, Janasabha and Pañcaśikha.[154] Some of them have also been mentioned as Yakṣa chiefs who were invoked by the followers of the Buddha in times of need.[155] Among them Pañcaśikha happens to be a renowned name who was a favourite of the Buddha who liked his music and employed him as a messenger and a reporter of the happenings in the assembly of the gods. The Apsarases are likewise regarded in the Buddhist mythology as female counterparts of the Gandharvas. They are celestial nymphs living in the Nandana, the celestial park in the Tāvatiṃśa heaven where they play the lute and awake the gods and goddesses in the morning and delight them by dancing and singing.[157] The garden of Nandana has also a very important role in the epico-puranic mythology. Like Indra of the Hindu tradition, Sakka often sends them to earth for seducing the ascetics who by virtue of their austerities threaten his suzerainty in heaven.[158] Often they were employed to serve good purposes.[159] Among some important Apsarases mention may be made of Nandā, Sunandā, Sokatiṇṇā, Alambuṣā, Missakesi, Huṇḍarika, Enipassā, Suphassā, Subhaddā, etc. Some of these names are also found in the Hindu mythology.

Closely allied with the Gandharvas and the Apsarases were the Yakṣas and Yakṣiṇīs. In Pali literature they are often described as non-human beings and mentioned along with the Devas. Sometimes they are spoken of as beings belonging to a category which is just in the middle between human beings and the Gandharvas.[161] In other places they are described as humanised Pretas or departed souls.[162] Generally speaking the Yakṣas are semi-divine beings having some supernatural power to cause good or bad to people. Sometimes they are described as equal to gods.[163] But there is no doubt that the Yakṣas were pre-Buddhist divine or semi-divine beings who were objects of an extensive cult. The Buddhist texts record the existence of an elaborate Yakṣa worship and speak of certain important Yakṣas such as Nighaṇḍu, Puṇṇaka, Kāmaseṭṭha, Kinnaghaṇḍu, Korātiya, Gula, Cara, etc. who were also worshipped by the followers of the Buddha.[164] Two kinds of the Yakṣas are frequently mentioned—*rukkha* and *bhauma*—the first associated with the trees and the second with the earth.[165] Although some of the Yakṣas did not believe in the teachings of the Buddha and often molested his followers, most of them, however, were sympathetic.[166] Yakṣas such as Indakuṭa and Suciloma used to put intelligent questions on metaphysics and ethics. Some of them acted as messengers to warn the prospective sinners.[167] They were the guardians of underground riches and hidden treasures.[168] They were of different categories the highest among them being very nearly to the gods while the lowest resembled ghosts.[169] Often they are described as red-eyed and possessing horrific and uncanny qualities.[170] They can assume any form or disguise, are more active at night and are carnivorous at the same time.[171] They neither wink, nor cast a shadow.[172] Though most of them are suspended in the air and dwell in their self-created place in the air, in trees or ponds some of them live on earth and even have cities of their own, such as Alakanandā. The female Yakṣas or Yakṣiṇīs are described as being more fearful, evil-minded and full of spite than the male.[173] Though sexual intercourse with a Yakṣiṇī is generally forbidden, sometimes they were married with human beings. For example, Kuveṇī, the Yakṣa princess of Ceylon married Vijaya and bore him two children.[174] In some cases, the Yakṣas have been identified in the Buddhist texts with Piśācas, Rākṣasas and Asuras and branded as demons while in other cases they are regarded as fallen angels who came eagerly to listen to the discourses of Buddhism. Historically, however, the Yakṣas were primitive popular divinities having a wide following among the masses, the influence of which could not be ignored, and hence, notwithstanding a basic apathy towards the Yakṣa cult, Buddhism had to make a compromise with it by declaring the prominent Yakṣa gods, who also occur in Jainism and Puranic Hinduism, as devout followers of the Buddha.

This ambivalence is also found in Buddhist and Jain mythology in regard to the animistic and zoomorphic cults of the Nāgas, Garuḍas, Kinnaras and others. These beings figure in Hindu mythology as well. The Nāgas play a prominent part in Buddhism. Those who live beneath the surface of the earth are called *sthalaja* Nāgas and those who live in water are called *jalaja* Nāgas.[175] Though often described as snakes, they are believed to be able to assume human form at their will. Four royal families of the Nāgas are mentioned, namely, those of Virupākkha, Erāpathā, Chabyāputtā and Kanhāgotamaka.[176] Several Nāga dwellings are mentioned in the Buddhist texts, such as Mañjerika in Sineru, Darddara under the mountain of the same name, the river Yamunā, the lake Nabhasa and so forth; and there are references to Nāga settlement in Vaisali, Tacchaka and Prayāga.[177] The *Bhuridatta Jātaka* speaks of Nāga woman who married human prince and bore him children.[178] In Hindu mythology also the Nāgas, despite their basic serpentine characteristics, are regarded as having human forms. Historically it appears that the Nāgas were snake-worshipping tribes of ancient India or those who had snake as their totem, and that certain special features of their cults and rituals and some legends pertaining to them had to be accommodated in Vedic, Buddhist, Jain and Puranic mythologies. The story that a Nāga king protected the Buddha from rain by spreading his hood like an umbrella over his head reminds us of the same service done by the serpent-king to the just-born Kṛṣṇa whom his father shifted from the prison of Kaṃsa to the house of Nandagopa in a rainy night. The Nāgas were not only the followers of the Buddha,[179] but the word Nāga was often used as an epithet of the Buddha and the Arhants.[180] The Bodhisattva was born several times as the king of the Nāgas under the names of Atula, Bhūridatta, Mahadaddara and so on. The counterforce of the Nāgas in Buddhist mythology is a kind of heavenly bird known as the Garuḍa who are also sometimes identified with the Suparṇas.[181] While in Puranic mythology Garuḍa and Suparna are proper names with their individual activities in Buddhist mythology they are regarded as a class living in the Simbali grove which is regarded as a special tree of the Garuḍa world.[182] The Garuḍas are described as huge in size, sometimes 150 *Yojanas* from wing to wing, capable of raising a storm and plunging a whole city into darkness.[183] They are the eternal enemies of the Nāgas.[184] They can assume human form, mix with men and even seduce their wives.[185] They are frequently mentioned as devotees of the Buddha.[186]

Compared with the Nāgas and Garuḍas, the Kinnaras of the Buddhist tradition, like their Puranic counterparts are of milder temperament. They are described as human-faced birds, generally found on the mountains and banks of the rivers and often falling in love with human beings.[187] They are devoted to the Buddha; some Bodhisattvas also were born as Kinnaras.[188]

The Asuras are described in Buddhist mythology as a class of evil spirits who are usually in conflict with the Devas.[189] The Buddhist conception of the Asuras is in striking agreement with that of the Vedas. From an historical point of view the Asuras belonged to the earlier Indo-Iranian period of Vedic mythology. Varuṇa and some other powerful Vedic gods were originally Asuras. In the older substratum of the Vedas, the Asuras were highly exalted divine beings, but later the Asura-worshippers, probably owing to their Iranian connection, began to be treated with diminishing importance by the Deva-worshipping Vedic Indians, and subsequently the meaning of the term Asura was changed and the Asuras were described as a class of demons. But even in the Purāṇas and also in the great epics, which give details of the never-ending battles between the Devas and the Asuras, they were held in high exteem. There the Asuras were also stated to be well-versed in the Vedas. They were often favoured by Brahmā who always granted them the boon of invincibility. In military skill they surpassed the Devas in consequence of which they often conquered the heaven and forced Indra and others to take shelter elsewhere. The might, generosity, virtue and other noble qualities of some Asura kings are recognised in the Purāṇas, though the general tendency of the Puranic authors was to defame them by saying that they were hostile to goodness and virtue. The same double-standard in the treatment of the Asuras is found in Buddhist mythology which holds that they were originally Devas because Sakka referred to them as the 'older-Devas' or Pubba-devā.[190] They are also regarded as the brethren of Sakka or Vasava.[191] It is also said that the Asuras dwelt in the Tāvatiṃśa heaven from which they were dislodged by the new-fangled gods.[192] In some texts the Asuras are brought in connection with Surā or wine. When Sakka and his followers were born in the Asura world, the Asuras prepared a drink for them. Sakka and his followers did not drink that preparation but the Asuras drank it in consequence of which they became unconscious and were thrown to the bottom of Sineru. When they gained consciousness they made a vow never to drink wine (Surā) again, and hence they were called Asuras.[193] The story, however, does not end here. The expelled Asuras thereupon made a city of their own at the bottom of Sineru. It was known as Asurabhavana and was 10,000 *Yojanas* in extent.[194] Then they wanted to regain their old region and invaded the Deva kingdom. This is the Buddhist version of the Puranic Deva-Asura conflict. Sakka tried to resist the Asura invasion, but he was worsted in the fight and his Vaijayanta chariot took him to the realm of the Garuḍas. Ultimately he was able to reconquer his heavenly abode from the hands of the Asuras.[195] The Buddhist texts mention a good number of Asura chiefs. Prominent among them was Vipracitti[196] who is mentioned in the Sanskrit Buddhist texts as Vemacitra or Vemacitri.[197] His Puranic counterpart is Vipracitti who was the founder of an Asura lineage. It is also said that the original name of Vepacitti was Sambara, the Asura with Vedic and Puranic fame.[198] In the Vedas and also in the Purāṇas the Asuras are described as having *māyā*, i.e., magical or miraculous power to their credit. The same is echoed in the Buddhist tradition in which it is said that once when Vepacitti was ill on account of a curse of sages, Sakka visited him and offered to cure him if he would teach him Sambarī-māyā or 'magic art of Sambara'.[199] Although Vepacitti was always in conflict with the Devas and was eventually defeated by Sakka,[200] there was a family relationship between the two, since Sakka had married his daughter Sujā.[201] Among other important Asuras, the Buddhist texts mention the Puranic Rāhu who devours the sun and the moon but fails to digest them because they are worshippers of the Buddha. He is described as one of the four 'stains' on the sun and the moon and one of the five causes of drought. He is also associated with the ocean. Originally he was hostile to the Buddha, but later he understood his folly and became his disciple.[202] Prahlāda of the epico-puranic tradition also occurs in the Buddhist mythology as one of the three leaders of the Asuras who visited the Buddha on the day of his enlightenment.[203] In some Buddhist texts the Asuras are called Dānavas because they were supposed to be the descendants of Danu.[204] Virocana and Bali of the Puranic mythology also find mention in the Buddhist literature.

In view of what has been said and cited above it is abundantly clear that the Vedic gods and their Puranic elaborations have a prominent position in Buddhist mythology, and this position was consistently maintained even in the later phases of Buddhism. It should be stated in this connection that the Buddhists tried to introduce a variety of new classes of divinities, the important classes being those of Aruṇā, Ariṭṭhakā, Āpā, Ummāpupphā, Odātagayhā, Khiḍḍāpadosikā, Manopadosika and other thirty-one classes;[205] the Valāhakāyika class comprising Sitavalāhakā, Unhavalāhakā, Abbhavalāhakā and Vātavalāhakā deities including those of the Satullapakāyikā category;[206] the Samacitta class comprising Parisuddhābhā, Saṃkiliṭṭhābhā and Abhibhū deities[207] those belonging to the categories of Pabbata, Sayaṃpabha and Naradā;[208] the Varavāraṇa,[209] Lokavyūha,[210] and Bhavya[211] classes; etc. But interestingly none of these classes of divinities was able to leave any mark, even the faintest, on the subsequent history of Buddhism. They simply evaporated like camphor. But the older Vedic gods and divine beings and their subsequent Puranic forms were never stamped out. Again, the earlier Buddhist concept of the Brahmās and Mahabrahmās in which some of the Puranic Ṛṣis like

Nārada, Hārīta, Sanatkumāra, etc., were inducted and attributed super-godship, did not find favour in later Buddhist tradition.

Coming to the later phases we find that the same Vedic and Puranic deities as well as demi-gods and divine beings also survive in the Mahayanic texts. The Mahāyāna does not possess a canon of its own owing to the fact that it does not represent one unified sect. But the Mahayanic texts represent the same mythology as found in the earlier Buddhist tradition. In Mahāyāna also gods of the Deva and Brahma categories are regarded as inferior to the Buddha. The natural gods of the Vedas recur in later Buddhist mythology and the Vedic tradition of the deification of natural phenomena is recognised in the Sanskrit Buddhist literature, as reflected especially in conception of the Varṣavalāhaka (rain) and Vātavalāhaka (wind) gods.[212] Particular interest attaches to the *Saddharma Laṅkāvatāra Sūtra*, generally known as *Laṅkāvatāra*,[213] in which the deities and personalities pertaining to the Vedic and other forms of Indian systems are attributed to the Buddha. Here the Buddha has countless names such as Śakra, Indra, Tathāgata, Svayambhū, Nāyaka, Vināyaka, Buddha, Ṛṣi, Vṛṣabha, Brāhmaṇa, Viṣṇu, Īśvara, Pradhāna, Kapila, Bhutānta, Ariṣṭanemī, Bhāskara, Rāma, Vyāsa, Śukra, Bali, Varuṇa and others. Elsewhere in the same text another Buddha, a predecessor of Gautama, introduces himself as a Jina belonging to the Kātyāyana-gotra and says that his father is Prajāpati Brahman and mother is Vasumatī.[214] In Puranic style the prophecy about the future is described as follows:

> After my passing away Vyāsa, Kaṇāda, Ṛṣabha, Kapila, the Śākya leader and others will grace the world. A hundred years thereafter will come in succession Vyāsa, famed for the Bhārata, the Pāṇḍavas and Kauravas, Rāma, the Mauryas, Nandas and Guptas, and then the barbarious and total chaos, and then after the end of Kali Yuga true religion will prevail.[215]

The same text also speaks about the arrival of masters like Pāṇini, Akṣapāda, Bṛhaspati, the Lokāyatas, Kātyāyana, Yājñavalkya, Vālmīki, Masuraksa, Kauṭilya, Āśvalāyana and others.[216]

We thus find that in the aforesaid work the entire Indian tradition with all its heterodoxies, as was imperfectly known to its author, has been appropriated. The *Saddharmapuṇḍarika*[217] mentions Sakra, Sūrya, Candra, Vāyu, Maheśvara and Vaisravaṇa as the followers of the Buddha. The spirit of the Purāṇas pervades the entire work and at times the Buddha of the *Saddharmapuṇḍarika* reminds us of the Kṛṣṇa of the

Bhagavadgītā. The *Kāraṇḍavyūha*, the purpose of which is to glorify Avalokiteśvara as the Supreme Being, says that the sun and the moon came forth from his eyes, Maheśvara from his brow, Brahman and other gods from his shoulder, Nārāyaṇa from his heart, Sarasvatī from his teeth, Vāyu from his mouth, the earth from his feet and Varuṇa from his stomach. The *Kāraṇḍavyūha* upholds the cosmogony of the Vedic tradition and views the process of creation as the manifestation of the 'self-existent', Svayambhū, equated with Ādibuddha and Ādinātha. In the *Suvarṇaprabhāsa*[218] which for a great part already bears the stamp of a Tantra, goddesses like Sarasvatī, Śrī-Mahādevī, Harītī, Caṇḍikā, etc. are described. Lakṣmi or Śrī in this text is described as the goddess of fortune in contrast with Alakṣmī as that of misfortune,[219] while Nārāyaṇa is mentioned in the Sanskrit Buddhist literature as a powerful god often equated with the Buddha himself.[220] While in the Hindu mythology Nārāyaṇa is connected with water, in Buddhist mythology he is connected with the concept of physical strength (*bala*) which the Buddha is said to have derived from him. In the *Kāraṇḍavyūha* passage quoted above Nārāyaṇa is, however, described as inferior to the Buddha since he is regarded as being produced from Avalokiteśvara.[221] The *Mahāparinirvāṇa*[222] says that the Buddha possesses the power of many hundred Nārāyaṇas. In the Mahayanic text Śakra and Indra are identical with each other and Varuṇa, Yama, Āditya, Candra, Vāyu and Agni retain their Vedic character in the sense that their natural background has not completely sunk into oblivion. Āditya or the sun god is regarded as a son of Buddha, and Yama is still the lord of death. The same holds good in the case of other older gods such as Viśvakarman, Prajāpati, Soma, Skanda or Kumāra, Śiva, Kubera, Pṛthivi, etc.[223]

The Mahāyāna introduced a new type of divinities comprising a mulitplication of the Dhyānī and Mortal buddhas, their emanations, various Bodhisattvas and host of subordinate deifications in which philosophical dogma, ritualistic literature, abstract ideas, human qualities, even desires such as sleeping, yawning and sneezing were given form of a god. Besides the Hindu deities like Indra, Yama, Varuṇa, Kubera, Īśāna, Agni, Āditya, Nairṛti, Vāyu, Brahmā, Viṣṇu, Maheśvara, Gaṇapati, Kārttikeya, Sarasvatī, Tārā, Vārāhi, Camuṇḍā, Mahakāla and others, the Yakṣas, Kinnaras, Gandharvas and Vidyādharas, mythological beings like Bhriṅgī, Nandikeśvara, etc. and the nine planets and twenty-eight constellation formed an integral part of the Mahāyāna pantheon. The Dhyānī Buddhas and their Bodhisattvas and emanations were mostly the creation of the mind. They lacked the traditional mythological background and popular base. That is why, despite a serious attempt to popularise them by means of an extensive image worship, they evaporated in no time. Some of them were, however, local or traditional deities who were inducted in the Mahayanic scheme. The Dhyānī and Mortal Buddhas, their Bodhisattvas and emanations, containing the term *vajra* as the prefix of their names derived their primary conceptual impulse from Indra. Just as the Vedic pantheon was ruled by the thunderbolt-bearer Indra, so also the Mahāyāna pantheon was headed by Vajradhara who was also the bearer of thunderbolt, and the embodiment of the highest reality, Śūnya. *Vajra* or thunderbolt, however, had acquired a technical and sophisticated significance in Buddhism. Likewise the Dhyānī Buddha Vairocana seems to have been conceptually related to the Asura chief Virocana of the Vedic texts. Nīlakaṇṭha, a form of Bodhisattva Avalokiteśvara is evidently modelled on Śiva who is said to have saved the world from destruction by swallowing the poison that issued from the mounth of Vāsuki, the lord of serpents, while the gods and the demons were churning the ocean together. He kept the poison in his throat and that is why the name Nīlakaṇṭha (one who has a blue throat) was attributed to him. The Buddhist iconological texts describe him purely in terms of the description of Śiva as wearing a tiger's skin, having a blue throat caused by poison and flanked by cobras. In the same way the Hayagrīva or horse-faced form of Viṣṇu was inducted in the Buddhist pantheon in which he is treated as an emanation both of Amitāba and Akṣobhya. Interestingly there is a Hayagrīva Mādhava temple at Hajo in Assam. In the medieval period this place was a well-known centre of horse-trade. Jambhala, who is regarded as emanation of both Akṣobhya and Ratnasambhava, is a Yakṣa which indicates his non-Buddhist origin.

Coming to goddesses we find that Aparājitā,an emanation of Vairocana, is regarded in the Puranic tradition as the wife of Skanda, being identified with Devasenā and Ṣaṣṭhi. Aparājitā is also a name of Durgā. She figures in the Jain pantheon as well, having an additional name Dhāraṇapriyā Vairoti. Vajravārāhī reminds us of Varāhī, one of the traditional seven Mātṛkās who is characterised by two rows of curled locks of hair rising upwards, the *kapāla* in the back left hand, a child on her lap and a buffalo mount. In the Buddhist texts she is often called a Ḍākini, a fiendess. Vasudhārā is a Mahayanic development of the earlier concepts of Śrī or Lakṣmi, thought of as the consort of Jambhala, the lord of wealth and described as carrying corns. Jāṅguli is the Buddhist counterpart of Hindu Manasā who cures snake-bite and even prevents it. Even in the time of the Buddha she was a well known folk goddess which is indicated by the legend that the *mantra* of her worship was imparted to Ānanda by the Buddha himself.[224] Jāṅguli is also a marked epithet of Manasā. Likewise the goddess Parṇaśabarī, whose worship is believed to be effective in preventing outbreaks of epidemics and in assuring safety to the terror-striken, has her Hindu counterpart in Śītalā.[225] Parṇaśabarī might have had her original affiliation with Aparṇā, the goddess 'without her leaf-cloth' who was inducted in the Puranic pantheon from the tribal cults of the 'naked hunters' (Nagna-Śabaras) and 'leaf clad' hunters (Parṇa-Śabaras) and was identified with Vindhyavāsinī and allied goddesses fond of wine and meat.[226]

The followers of the Mahāyāna regarded the Buddha as eternal, without origin and decay, and as such beyond any description whatsoever. They indulged in certain speculations regarding the Buddha's body and gave currency to the *trikāya* conception which was further elaborated with the rise of regular Mahāyāna pantheon. The latter came into being with the five Dhyānī Buddhas who were said to have been issued out of Ādi Buddha (the original Buddha) through contemplation. Each of these Buddhas was associated with a Bodhisattva and a Śakti in the form of a goddess. Of the Bodhisattvas or potential Buddhas, Avalokiteśvara and Mañjuśrī received the highest prominence. The former was associated with the goddess Tārā while the latter with Lakṣmī or Sarasvatī or both. Subsequently Buddhism came completely under the grip of the Tārā. According to the Mahāyāna conception, Tārā is the primordial female energy, the consort of Avalokiteśvara, who enables her devotees to surmount all sorts of dangers and calamities. She is also known as the goddess Prajñāpāramitā, as it is by the fulfilment of this Pāramitā that a Bodhisattva reaches the goal. Sometimes she is conceived as the supreme being, 'the mother of all the Buddhas and Bodhisattvas'. The conception of this goddess is, however, primitive and it is quite possible that in course of her conceptual development she had absorbed within herself a number of divinities representing different aspects of the female principle. The epithets Tārā, Tāriṇī, etc., attributed to the supreme goddess in the *Mahābhārata* and the Purāṇas, may be traced in the *Yajurveda* in which the term *tāra*, meaning 'saviour' is an appellation of the god Śiva. In Sanskrit and other Indian languages Tārā or Tārakā means 'star' (Cf. Persian *sitara*, Greek *aster*, Latin *stella* and English *star* as also the name of such non-Indian goddesses as Ishtar, Astarte, Atargatis, Astaroth) and the name that of a goddess representing a star or dwelling among the stars. In the Buddhist tradition Tārā is also a star-goddess serving as a guide to the navigators. Many streams culminated in the conception of Tārā and a whole cult was established in different parts of India by the sixth century A.D. as is attested by

Subandhu's *Vāsavadattā*. From the seventh century onwards, the influence of Tārā began to be felt upon the religious systems of India and abroad. In Śāktism Tārā was identified with the supreme goddess and her various forms like Ugratārā, Ekajaṭā, Nīla-Sarasvatī, etc., found their parallels in the Buddhist pantheon. In Jainism also Tārā is a popular goddess who often bears the appellation Dhāriṇī.[227]

Tārā passed out of India to Tibet and came to be known as Sgrol-ma or Dol-ma in the Tibetan translation of her name. Like her husband Avalokiteśvara (Spyan-ras-gzing-chen-re-si) she was also conceived under numerous forms. Tārā also went to China as the Śakti of Avalokiteśvara. But in China, Avalokiteśvara was already on way to transformation from a god into a goddess through the influence of the pre-Buddhistic (Taoist and Confucian) Mother Goddess Si-Wang-Mu, the representative of *Yin* or the female principle of creation. This happened in the seventh or eighth century when Tārā became absolutely merged with her husband, who became transformed into the goddess Kuan-yin. This double form of Tārā became very popular in China and brought in with her most of the existing beliefs and rituals, especially those belonging to Taoism.[228] As early as the beginning of this century H.P. Sastri[229] pointed out from Sanskrit texts the connection of the goddess Tārā with Tibet and China. On the basis of the *Tārātantra* Sylvain Levi[230] also came to the conclusion that the worship of Tārā in a new garb and some Tantric practices came from China. P.C. Bagchi[231] brought fresh proofs indicating Chinese and Tibetan influence on the Tārā cult. Tantric texts like the *Mahācīnācārakrama*, *Brahmayāmala*, and even later texts like the *Merutantra*, etc., make categorical statements about the cult and *vāmācāra* practices connected with worship of the goddess Tārā and hold that these came from China being brought from there by the sage Vasiṣṭha who was instructed by the Buddha himself, and who witnessed these practices in China itself.[232] Tārā occurs in her various forms like Bhṛkuṭi, Locanā, Māmakī, Śvetā Pāṇḍaravāsinī, Sutārā etc.[233] She is elevated to the position of the highest deity in *Mahāpratyaṅgirādharaṇī* a fragment of which is found in Central Asia in which she is described as a goddess of white colour, wearing a garland of *vajras* and having the figure of Vairocana on her crown. From the seventh century onwards we find the exuberance of *Tārā-stotras* (cf, the *Sarangdhārā-stotras* composed in praise of Tārā by the eight century Kashmiri poet Sarvajñamitra) and the goddess is raised to the mothership of all the Buddhas. According to the *Sammoha Tantra*, Nīlasarasvatī or Ugratāra was born in a lake called Cola on the western side of the Meru which was included in the Cīnadesa. P.C. Bagchi suggests that Cola is connected with *kul, kol*, the common world for 'lake' which is found in the names of so many lakes to the west of T-ien-shan.[234]

As has been stated above, in the Mahāyāna Sūtras the Buddha is actually nothing less than the highest god, an infinitely exalted being that had lived since countless aeons in the past and will live for ever, the self-existent, the physician and protector of all creatures. In the *Saddharmapuṇḍarīka* which in form, content and style resembles any Hindu Purāṇa we come across a steady growth of the *bhakti* cult. It expressly refers to Buddha-*bhakti* and in this connection emphasises the efficacy of image worship. This *bhakti* cult through image worship was subsequently extended to the new fangled five Dhyāni Buddhas, their Bodhisattvas and various emanations in the forms of numerous gods and goddesses, a considerable number of them being adopted from the traditional and folk divinities also figuring in the wider Hindu context. From an historical point of view various streams of later Buddhism were coming close to the bed of the mainstream. Hindu gods, as we have seen above, were already in the Buddhist pantheon. In the later phases of the history of Buddhism their cults were renovated and fitted into the scheme of Buddhist Maṇḍalas. A perusal of the *Niṣpannayogāvali* shows how the Hindu gods were classified, how directions and colours were assigned to them and how they were incorporated in the Buddhist scheme. Among these Hindu deities, three deities apear to be of great importance. These are Mahakāla, the prototype of Śiva with *triśūla* as his recognition symbol, the elephant-headed Gaṇapati and Sarasvatī with her characteristic *vīṇā*. Two, four, six and sixteen-armed Mahākāla finds description in Buddhist inconological texts.[235] He carries *kartari* and *kapāla*, looks terrible with bare fangs and is decked in ornaments and serpents. The cult of this deity was widespread in Nepal, Tibet and China.[236] Gaṇapati is described as twelve-armed and one-faced, his vehicle being mouse. The description of Gaṇapati as found in the Dharmadhātuvāgīśvara of the *Niṣpannayogāvali* absolutely tallies with that of his Hindu form. Here he is described as white in colour and riding on a mouse. He has an elephant face and snake forms his sacred thread. In his two right hands he carries the *triśūla* (trident) and the *laḍḍuka* (sweetmeat) and in the two left the *paraśu* (axe) and the *mūlaka* (radish).[237]

The Buddhist Sarasvatī deserves special mention. This goddess has a long and chequered history which may be traced as far back as the Vedic age. Originally she appeared as the personalised form of the river Sarasvatī, a river which was considered by the Vedic Indians to be extremely sacred on the banks of which many hymns were composed. But in the *Ṛgveda* she was not the goddess of learning. The latter aspect was presided over by the goddess Vāk, the impersonation of sound and speech which was then considered to be the basis of all knowledge. The identification of Vāk with Sarasvatī took place at a certain unspecified period of Indian history. Sarasvatī subsequently came to be regarded as the spouse of Brahmā and in still later Śākta Purāṇas she was described as a cosmogonic principle. In Vātsyayana's *Kāmasūtra* we come across the fact that during the earlier centuries of the Christian era the image of Sarasvatī was worshipped in various clubs of the aristocrats and she was treated as the goddess of learning, culture and fine arts. The Jains also worship the goddess Sarasvatī though many of her functions and attributes were taken up by the Vidyādevīs. The earlier Buddhist Sarasvatī was somewhat shadowed for a time being by Prajñāpāramitā, the embodiment of the Mahāyāna scripture of the same name which was, according to the Buddhist tradition restored from the nether regions by Nāgārjuna in the second century A.D. Prajñāpāramitā absorbed many features of Sarasvatī and her image worship became very popular among the Buddhists. Ārya Asaṅga is credited with having composed one of the Sādhanas for her worship which is said to confer wisdom and erudition on her devotees. But Sarasvatī, after a temporary eclipse, regained her position and reabsorbed some of the attributes of Prajñāpāramitā. The Buddhist Sarasvatī has at least five varieties—Mahā-Sarasvatī, Vajravīnā-Sarasvatī, Vajraśāradā-Sarasvatī, Ārya-Sarasvatī and Vajra-Sarasvatī. She may have one face with two arms or three faces and six arms. The latter type is represented by Vajra-Sarasvatī alone. All forms of the Buddhist Sarasvatī are white in complexion and represented in the prime of her youth. The distinctive feature of the goddess Mahā-Sarasvatī is that she shows like the ordinary Tārās the *varada mudrā* in the right hand and carries the lotus in the left. She is surrounded by four deities identical in form with herself—Prajñā in front. Medhā to the right, Smṛti to the left and Mati in the back. The distingushing feature of Vajravīnā-Sarasvatī is that she carries in her two hands the *vīṇā* and plays upon it. Vajraśāradā and Ārya Sarasvatīs carry *Prajñāpāramitā* book.[238]

Among the Vedic and Purāṇic deities who enjoyed a special position in the later Buddhist pantheon, Indra is described as a god of the eastern direction who rides on the Airāvata elephant and carries the thunderbolt in his hand.[239] Although he is also known by his other name Śakra, the earlier Buddhist attributes by which he was characterised seems to have sunk into oblivion giving rise to a conception of this god which is more akin to his Puranic personality. The same holds good in the description of Yama, the ancient lord of the dead who is now transformed into one of the eight gods of direction. But his lordship over death is retained. He is described as the guardian of the southern direction who rides on a buffalo, is blue in colour and holds in his two hands the staff of death and spear.[240] But Varuṇa of the later Buddhists has little resemblance with his Vedic or Puranic counterpart. He is described as the lord of western direction. His vehicle is the crocodile. He is white in colour and has seven hoods. He holds in his two hands a noose and conch.[241] The noose reminds us of the *pāśa* which the Vedic Varuṇa used to throw at the sinners. His mount crocodile may have something to do with his Puranic connection with the waters. Kubera, the chief of the Yakṣas and Gandharvas of the earlier tradition who was accorded a high position in the earlier Hindu and Buddhist mythology as the god of wealth has been reduced in later Buddhism into the presiding deity of the northern direction and is described as having a man as his vehicle and complexion of deep yellow colour who holds in his two hands a goad and mace.[242]

Four other presiding deities of direction were adopted by the later Buddhists from the existing Hindu pantheon and they are described in the Dharmadhātu Vagīśvara Maṇḍala and other places of the *Niṣpannayogāvali*.[243] These deities represent the corner regions which are still known as Vāyu (north-west), Īśāna (north-east), Nairṭa (south-west) and Agni (south-east) respectively. The presiding deities are all Vedic gods whose anthropomorphised forms are found in the Purāṇas. In the earler Buddhist pantheon they also occur with distinctive power and position, though subordinated to the Buddha. But in the later Buddhist conception the vesitges of their ealier characteristics are rarely found. Vāyu is described as blue in colour and riding on a deer. His hands contain nothing.[244] Deer may have been a symbol of the swiftness of air, the natural phenomenon which was originally represented by Vāyu. His empty hand may also be suggestive in this respect. Īśāna, however, is the same as the Puranic Śiva, though in the mythology of the later Buddhists Maheśvara, another name of Śiva, is described as a different god who, however, contains all the attributes of Śiva and also of Īśāna who is regarded as the presiding deity of the north-east. Īśāna is described as riding on a bull. He is white in colour and holds in his two hands a trident and skull-cap. On his matted hair appears the half-moon, on his body a sacred thread of'serpent and his throat is blue. This Īśāna is thus absolutely the same as the Puranic Śiva. Nairṛti who is the presiding deity of the south-western corner is a direct adaptation of the Vedic Nairṛti, an abstraction of such forces which work against Ṛta, the moral and rational principle of the law-governed universe, and it was against this force that the Vedic poets raised their voice: 'Save us from the rule of Nirṛti'. In subsequent Indian tradition Nirṛti got crystallised as a goddess representing the dark and anarchic forces, but her tenure was short-lived owing to the fact that her attributes were absorbed by various deities of the terrible category. In later Buddhist mythology Nirṛti is a male deity who is regarded as the lord of the Rākṣasas, blue in colour and sitting on a corpse. In his two hands he holds a sword and a stick. Agni, the god of the south-eastern direction, is described as red in colour and riding on a god. His complexion faintly reminds us of his ancient Vedic conception as the personified form of fire. He holds in his two hands *sruva* (ladle) and *kamaṇḍalu* (water-bowl). The former may be a vestige of his earlier association with the Yajñas and the latter of his Puranic characterisation as a Brahmāṇa.

In later Buddhism we have other Hindu gods with their essential Puranic conceptions and attributes. Foremost among these deities are Brahmā, Viṣṇu and Maheśvara, who form the typical Hindu trinity. The Buddhist garb in which they were presented in Pali literature is no more in their representation in later Buddhism. Now there is no endless series of Brahmas or Mahābrahmas. Instead we have the original Pitāmaha of the Hindu Puranic tradition. In the Dharmadhātu-Vāgīśvara Maṇḍala of the *Niṣpannayogāvali* the Brahmā of the later Buddhists is described as having a swan as his vehicle. He is yellow in colour and has four arms. In his two principal hands he carries the rosary and the lotus. His two other hands carry the staff and the *kamaṇḍalu*. Likewise Viṣṇu is not also the Venhu of the earlier mythology. His Hindu form is pronounced. The usual Garuḍa is his vehicle. With his two principal hands he carries a *cakra* (wheel) and a *śaṅkha* (conch), while his other two hands contain *gadā* (mace) and the bow (instead of the traditional *padma* or lotus). Maheśvara is described as white in clolour and sitting on the bull. His crown of matted hair is beautified by the moon. His two principal hands carry the *triśūla* and *kapāla* respectively. But the later Buddhists graft two other hands which display the *añjali* pose. Among Śiva's children, Kārttikeya is described as red in colour, riding on a peacock and having six faces. With his two right hands he holds the Śakti and the *vajra* and with his two left the hen. Kārttikeya's association with the hen is also attested by the Purāṇas in which he is invoked as *mayura-kukkuṭa-vṛte*. We have already referred to the later Buddhist description of Gaṇapati or Gaṇeśa.[245] Bhṛṅgī and Nandī, attendants of Śiva, as also Mahākāla and Mātṛkas like Vārāhī and Cāmuṇḍā occur in the later Buddhist pantheon. Divinities pertaining to the lower mythologies, as found in the Purāṇas, abound in later Buddhism as well. These include the nine planets, deified human characters like Balabhadra, etc., Yakṣas, Kinnaras, Gandharvas and Vidyādharas, the constellations and so forth.[246]

In view of what has been stated above certain points seem to have become clear. The first and foremost of these is that in the field of lower mythology the deities representing the facts of popular life were common to all forms of Indian systems. These deities were concerned not with any great world force but with the problems of simple day to day life, such as smallpox, snakebite, protection of children, etc. The earth and tree spirits, Mother Goddesses associated with vegetation and fertility, the atmospheric spirits supposed to influence individual destiny in unexpected ways, the stars, planets and aerial bodies possessing mysterious wonder-working power, etc. formed the substratum of this mythology of the masses, the origins of which may be traced to the pre-Vedic period and the elaborations in the Vedas, the epics and Purāṇas, the Buddhist and Jain texts as well as in the medieval Indian regional literature. The second point which one must consider is that though in the Buddhist texts we come across a host of new gods and goddesses—barring such divinities as found close parallels in the Vedic, Puranic and folk tradition—all of them dwindled into nothingness almost in no time even though their cults were attempted to be popularised through the institution of an extensive practice of image worship. Why did they sink into oblivion? It is even more surprising that the gods of the so-called Hīnayāna or early Buddhism as introduced by the Pali Nikāyas have been absolutely negated in the Mahāyāna. In fact the word 'negation' does not suffice. The authors of the Mahāyāna texts seem to have been quite unaware of the deities mentioned in the Pali Nikāyas. And what is worse, in a still later period of the Mahāyāna, the deities introduced by the exponents of Mahayanism were forgotten. But surprisingly, the earlier Vedic and Puranic gods, though they were theoretically subordinated to the all-pervading, omniscient and omnipotent Buddha, could not be dislodged from their seat and position at any period in the history of Buddhism. It seems as if a counter-revolution had taken place which removed the theoretical veneer and its corresponding created set of divine beings and led the older ingredients to come forward and manifest in accordance with the propensities inherent in them. This strange phenomenon requires an explanation. We have no real evidence to prove that the historical Buddha ever tried to set up a new religion. His basic approach was rather philosophical, in the sense that he wanted to understand the science of the general laws of beings, human thinking and the process of knowledge. Like all other schools of Indian thought, the Buddha's own thinking centred round the problems of suffering and its extinction. The Buddha was after a way of life which he thought could develop through discussions of persons who were to a certain extent able to detach themselves from the fetters of worldly life. It was for such persons that the Buddha instituted Saṅgha or monastic organisation, the Order of the Bhikṣus. There is also no real evidence to prove that the Buddha had at all any genuine concern for laymen. A religion is always for the masses, but the teachings of the Buddha were meant only for the monks. With the expansion of the Saṅghas there developed a typical monastic culture which gave the followers of the Buddha a sectarian identity. This monastic or monkish culture tended to develop a near-theistic system projecting the Buddha as the fountainhead of the existing earlier mythology supplementing it with a good number of divine and semi-divine beings, in the manner in which other theistic sectarian systems like Vaiṣṇavism, Śaivism, etc., were formed. But that was not very easy task for the theistic followers of the Buddha because of the wide geographical distribution of the monasteries and various groupings among the monks. Historically it has been admitted that there were at least thirty-two such groups scattered in different parts of the country, some of which preferred to stick to the older viewpoints as outlined by the historical Buddha as far as possible. But the attempt to elevate the Buddha in the position of the supreme being was continued through the ages and eventually the task was accomplished by the Mahayanists who tried to reach the masses and understood at the same time that the supreme being should have a greater following of more powerful and effective gods and divine beings having a functional base in the popular mind. Hence thay retained the gods belonging to the Vedic and Puranic tradition and inducted powerful local and folk deities into their own pantheon. These deities eventually survived owing to their agelong association with the masses. But others, especially those who were products of the earlier Buddhist fanciful innovations or the abstract meditative figurations belonging to the clan of the new-fangled Dhyānī Buddhas and their emanations had a different fate of getting gradually shrunk into the state of non-entity.

NOTES

1. *Dīgha*, I, 82; *Aṅguttara*, II, 226-27, 237; III, 3, 19, 39-40, 103-04, 171, 204, 432; *Saṃyutta*, I, 30, 92; IV, 243-45; V, 366; *Itibuttaka*, 14, 99; *Visuddhimagga*, I, 9, 199, 208-09; *Jātaka*, III, 306, 443. All references to the Buddhist texts, unless otherwise indicated, are from the PTS editions.
2. *Dīgha*, I, 215-223; *Majjhima*, I, 289, III, 100-03, 147; *Aṅguttara*, I, 210, 227-28; III, 287, 332-33; IV, 119, 240 ff.
3. *Dīgha*, II, 207-08, 225, 257-58; III, 194-204; *Majjhima*, III, 100-03; *Aṅguttara*, I, 142-43, 213-14; etc.
4. *Dīgha*, II, 207-12, 268, 296; *Majjhima*, I, 253-54, II, 79; *Aṅguttara*, I, 242; III, 40; IV, 117, 396; *Saṃyutta* I, 5, 234-36; V, 342; *Jātaka*, I, 202-05; II, 189, 312; III, 87; IV, 357; V, 158, 167-68, 392, 400; VI, 126-27, 132, 232 271-72, 278, 289, 333; etc.
5. *Dīgha*, I, 17-18; II, 36, 50-52, 69; III, 28-79, 84-85, 218, 253; *Majjhima*, I, 289, 326-27; II, 194-95; III, 147, 162; *Aṅguttara*, I, 210; II, 127-29; III, 202; IV, 40, 89, 401; V, 59-60, 80; *Saṃyutta* I, 34-35, 141-42, 586; *Jātaka* II, 43, 69, 90; III, 359; VI, 242-243; *Kathāvatthu*, 208, 262; *Vibhaṇga*, 424-26.
6. II. 14.3; V. 19.3; XII .4.34.
7. *Dīgha*, I, 82; *Majjhima*, I, 307-09, III, 179; *Aṅguttara*, I, 292-93; II, 226-31, III, 3, 170, 204, 432; *Saṃyutta*, IV, 240-43; etc.
8. *Aṅguttara*, I, 141; *Majjhima*, III, 178-83; etc.
9. *Jātaka* V, 266-75, VI , 236-39.
10. *Vinaya*, III, 35; *Milinda*, 108, 301, 357; *Jātaka*, IV, 187-88; *Dhammapada Com.* I, 125; II, 49-50; 44-45, 119ff.; 178-79.
11. *Saṃyutta*, I, 149-52; *Aṅguttara*, V, 173; etc.
12. *Aṅguttara, Com.*, V, 61-62.
13. Cf. *Majjhima*, III, 185.
14. *Jātaka*, V, 143-45.
15. *Ibid.*, IV, 307; 143-45 269; *Saṃyutta*, V, 450-52; etc.
16. *RV*, I, 80.11; II.11.9-10; VI.17.9; X.89.7 etc.
17. *Saṃyutta Com.*, (PTS) I, 104, *Jātaka*, V, 153.
18. *Dīgha* I, 216-17; II, 221, 275; *Aṅguttara*, IV, 89; *Saṃyutta*, I, 219.
19. Cf. *Dīgha*, I, 244; II, 274; *Majjhima*, I, 140.
20. *Dīgha*, III, 204.
21. *Jātaka*, III, 146; V, 33, 115, 409-12, 568, VI, 127; *Udāna Com.*, 67; *Vibhaṅga Com.*, 333.
22. Cf. *Dīgha*, III, 176.
23. *Culavaṃsa*, LXXXII.186; *Abhidhānappadīpikā*, 20.
24. *Saṃyutta Com.*, I, 267; *Dīgha Com.*, III, 710 ff; *Dhammapada Com.*, I, 264 f.; *Jātaka*, I, 201 ff.
25. Saṃyutta, I, 230.
26. *Dīgha*, II, 230.

27. *Sum, Vil.* 690.
28. *Ibid.*, I, 230.
29. Cf. *Jātaka*, V, 152.
30. *RV*, I. 24.7-8; II.27.10; VII.87.8; X.132.4; etc.
31. I. 24.15; I.25.21; VI. 74.4; VII 86.3-4; X.85.24.
32. Saṃyutta, I, 219.
33. *Digha* I. 244.
34. *Dīgha*, I, 244, III, 204; *Jātaka*, V, 28; VI, 20.
35. *Ibid.*, III. 204
36. *RV*, III, 5.4; IV.9.4; VI.16.1; VIII.49.1; X.17.3; etc.
37. *Jātaka*, VI, 202.
38. *RV*, VI. 15.13.
39. Cf. *Jātaka*, I, 204, 494; III, 17; V, 452; VI.201; etc.
40. *Ibid.*, I, 285.
41. *RV*, III. 26.2; VI.8.4.
42. *Jātaka*, VI, 203.
43. *RV*, IX. 113.8; X.16.9; etc.
44. XXI. 63.
45. X.10
46. *RV*, I.38.5; I.165.4; *AV*, VI.28.31.
47. *AV*, VI, 29.3.
48. *Majjhima*, III,179 ff.
49. *Jātaka* I, 21; II, 318, III, 472; IV, 273, 405; V, 268, 274, 304.
50. *Ibid.*, II, 318.
51. *Dīgha*, I, 244; *Milinda*, 37.
52. *Suttanipāta Com.*, I, 225.
53. Cf. *Dīgha*, II, 259.
54. *Yasna*, XXX.3.
55. *Dīgha Com.*, II, 690; *Aṅguttara, Com.*, II, 228.
56. *Vibhaṅga Com.*, 519.
57. *RV*, I.50.12; I.191.9; VIII.90.11; X.88.11.
58. *Dīgha*, III, 196.
59. *Dīgha Com.*, III, 963.
60. *Vibhaṅga Com.*, 466.
61. *Suttanipāta*, 423.
62. *Vibhaṅga Com.*, 116.
63. *Dīgha*, III, 197; *Suttanipāta* 1128.
64. *Saṃyutta*, I, 57.
65. *Majjhima Com.*, Aluvihara ed., II, 783.
66. *Jātaka*, IV, 63.
67. *Nirukta*, XII. 19.
68. *RV*, I. 155.5.
69. Cf. *Śatapatha*, I.9.3.9; *Taittirīya*, III.1.2.7.
70. II.1.3.1.
71. *Dīgha*, II, 259.

72. *Saṃyutta* I, 52.
73. *Saṃyutta Com.*, I, 110.
74. *Culavaṃsa*, II, 152.
75. *Dīgha*, I, 244; II, 259.
76. *Jātaka*, VI, 201.
77. Cf. *Dīgha*, III, 204.
78. *Aitareya*,VII.11; *Śatapatha*,I.6.4.5; *Kauṣītaki*, VII.10; etc.
79. VII. 81.3-4; XI.6.7; etc.
80. Cf. *Chāndogya Up.*, V.10.1.
81. Cf. *Culavaṃsa*, LXII.5; LXIII.14.
82. *Dhammapada Com.*, II, 143, 146; III , 97.
83. *Dīgha*, II, 259.
84. *Vibhaṅga Com.*, 519.
85. *Jātaka*, IV. 1.
86. *AV.*, IV.15.
87. *RV.*, V.83.
88. *Jātaka*, I, 329-32.
89. *Dīgha*, III, 205.
90. *Ibid.*, II,260.
91. *Saṃyutta* I, 29-30.
92. IV. 53.2.
93. X.85.43; X.169.4; X.184.1; etc.
94. *Śatapatha*, II. 4.4.1; VI.2.3.1; XI.1.6.14; *Taittirīya*, II.2.3.1; VIII.1.3.4; etc.
95. Cf. *Āśvalāyana* G.S. III. 4; etc.
96. *Dīgha*, III, 204.
97. *Majjhima*, I. 140, 327, 239; *Jātaka*, VI, 568.
98. *Dīgha*, II, 274; *Saṃyutta*, I, 219; *Jātaka*, V, 28; etc.
99. *RV*, X. 128.7; X.190.1.
100. *RV*, X.18.5; X.158.1; X.184.1.
101. *RV*, X.82.2; X.167.2.
102. *RV*, VI.50.12; X.81.13.
103. *Jātaka*, VI.201-02.
104. *RV*, X.81-82.
105. *Ait.Br.* IV.22; *Sat. Br.* VII.2.1.10 etc.
106. *Dīgha*, II.180.
107. Cf. *Jātaka*, IV, 323-25.
108. Cf. *Dhammapada Com.*, I, 272.
109. *Jātaka*, VI, 12.
110. *Ibid.*, I, 60.
111. *Ibid.*, I, 7, 317; IV, 489, 499; V, 132, 190-91; VI, 29, 211, 510-20.
112. *Ibid.*, VI, 72.
113. *Aṅguttara Com.*, 126-27.
114. *Dīgha Com.*, II, 614.
115. *RV*, I.114.7-8; II.33; IV.3.6; VI.28.7; VI. 46.2-4; etc.

116. *Saṃyutta* I, 56.
117. *Culavaṃsa* XCIII, 9-10.
118. *Ibid.*,LXXXIV, 193.
119. *Samantapāsādikā,* III, 606.
120. *RV,* II. 33.9.
121. *Dīgha,* I, 244.
122. *Saṃyutta,* I, 219.
123. *Udāna Com.*, 351.
124. *Milinda,* 6-7.
125. Cf. *Jātaka,* V, 382-412.
126. Ibid., I, 110; II, 39, 176; III, 262, 443; V, 112; etc.
127. Cf. *Abhidhānappadīpikā,* 966.
128. *Jātaka,* III, 306, 443; IV, 281-82; V, 146.
129. *Ibid* II,415.
130. *Culavaṃsa* LCCIII.86.
131. *Jātaka,* VI, 356-62.
132. *Ibid.*, IV, 378.
133. I. 2.4.
134. *Jātaka,* III, 259, 264.
135. *RV*, X.123.6.
136. *VS*, IX.7; *AV*, XIII.1.23.
137. *RV*, X.123.
138. *RV,* IX. 86.36; X.10.4; *AV*, 11.2.3; IV.37.12. In the *Avesta* Gandarewa is a lord of the abyss, who dwells in the waters.
139. Cf. *Dīgha,* II, 207.
140. *Dīgha,* III, 261; *Dīgha Com.*, III, 967; *Suttanipāta Com.*, I, 369; *Jātaka,* VI, 270; *Culavaṃsa,* XXXVII, 31, 105, XXXIX. 5; etc.
141. *Jātaka,* VI, 30,325.
142. *Dīgha,* III, 194; *Dīgha Com.*, III, 962; *Majjhima,* I, 253.
143. *Suttanipāta Com.*, I, 370.
144. *Thera Com.*, I, 149, 409.
145. *Dhammapada Com.*, III, 74; *Jātaka,* I, 128, 328; etc.
146. *Dīgha,* II, 253-62, III, 194ff.; *Jātaka,* II, 257-62.
147. *Dīgha,* II, 207, 221, III, 198.
148. *Dīgha,* II, 207, 221, 258; III, 199; *Jātaka,* III, 257, VI, 186; etc.
149. *Dīgha,* II, 212.
150. *Saṃyutta,* III, 250-51.
151. *Dīgha,* II, 212, 271-74.
152. Cf. *Aṅguttara,* II, 39; IV. 200, 204, 207.
153. *Dīgha,* III. 203-04.
154. *Ibid.*, II, 257-58.
155. *Ibid.*, III, 204.
156. *Ibid.*, II, 220, 263 ff, *Dīgha Com,* II. 640.
157. *Saṃyutta,* I, 33.
158. *Jātaka,* V, 152.

159. *Ibid.*, II, 253.
160. *Vimānavatthu,* 16.
161. *Aṅguttara,* V, 420.
162. *Petavatthu Com.*, II, 38.
163. Cf. *Saṃyutta,* I, 205.
164. *Dīgha,* III, 204-05.
165. *Petavatthu Com.*, II, 5, 55; *Jātaka,* III, 309, 345.
166. *Dīgha,* II, 236, 257; III, 194-95; *Udāna* IV, 4; *Aṅguttara,* IV, 63.
167. *Petavatthu,* 45-46.
168. *Petavatthu Com.*, II, 145, 274.
169. *Jātaka,* IV, 492.
170. *Dīgha,* II, 344-45; *Jātaka,* I, 103; V, 34.
171. *Jātaka,* I, 129; IV, 191; V, 91; VI, 303.
172. *Ibid.*, I, 492; V, 34; VI, 331-37.
173. *Ibid.*,I, 205; II, 15 ff., 128; III, 200; IV, 549; V, 21, 34; VI, 336; etc.
174. *Vinaya* III,27; IV, 20.
175. *Jātaka,* VI, 160.
176. *Vinaya,* II,109.
177. *Dīgha,* II, 258.
178. *Jātaka,* VI, 160.
179. *Mahāvaṃsa,* XXXI 27-28; *Mahābodhivaṃsa,* 153-54.
180. *Mahāniddesa,* 201.
181. Cf. *Vimānavatthu Com.*, 9.
182. *Jātaka,* III, 397; *Visuddhimagga,* I, 206.
183. *Dhammapada Com.*, III, 135; *Jātaka,* III, 188, 397;
184. *Ibid.*, II, 13; III, 103, 187; IV, 177, 463, VI, 178, 184.
185. *Ibid.*, III, 91, 187.
186. *Ibid.*, III, 187, 400; VI, 261-62.
187. *Ibid.*, IV, 106, 254, 262ff., 438; V, 47, 456, VI, 222; *Milinda,* 267.
188. *Apadāna,* I, 165; *Jātaka,* IV, 282 ff.
189. *Aṅguttara,* II, 91.
190. *Saṃyutta,* I, 222; Cf. *Suttanipāta Com.*,II. 484.
191. *Jātaka,* V, 139.
192. *Suttanipāta Com.*, II, 484-85
193. *Saṃyutta Com.*, I, 338.
194. *Suttanipāta Com.*, II, 485.
195. *Loc. cit.*
196. *Saṃyutta,* I, 222; IV, 201ff.; *Jātaka,* I, 205.
197. *Divyāvadāna,* 126-48; *Mahāvastu,* III, 138, 254.
198. *Saṃyutta,* I, 227.
199. *Ibid.*, 237-39.
200. *Ibid.*, 221-25; IV, 201.
201. *Jātaka,* I, 205-06; *Dhammapada Com.*, I,278-79

202. *Aṅguttara*, II, 17, 35, 243, 295, 488; *Dīgha*, II, 259; *Saṃyutta*, I, 225-26; *Majjhima*, I, 87; III, 164; *Jātaka*, III, 365; etc.
203. *Aṅguttara Com.*, II, 758.
204. *Milindapañho*, 153.
205. *Dīgha*, II, 253-62.
206. *Saṃyutta*, I, 16-22; III, 254 ff.; *Milinda*, 191.
207. *Majjhima*, III, 102, 147.
208. *Suttanipāta*, 404, 543; *Ibid, Com.*, II, 435.
209. *Sumaṅgalavilāsinī*, II, 576-77.
210. *Visuddhimagga*, 415-16.
211. *Jātaka*, V, 171.
212. Cf. *Lalitavistara*,ed. S. Lefmann, (Halle, 1902) 273: *Mahāvastu*, ed. E. Senart (Paris, 1882-97), III, 324; *Divyāvadāna*, ed. Cowell and Neil (Cambridge, 1886), 127.
213. ed. B. Nanjio, (Kyoto, 1923), III, X.
214. X.798-99.
215. X.784 ff.
216. X.813 ff.
217. ed. H. Kern and B. Nanjio, (St. Petersbourg, 1908); Eng. trans. H. Kern in *SBE*, XXI, 1884, Ch. I.
218. ed. S.C. Das (Calcutta, 1898), Chs. VIII, IX, XIII.
219. See P.L. Vaidya's ed. (Mithila Institute, 1967), 11, 48, 87.
220. *Lalita*,109-10, 262, 291; *Saddharma*, 42B; *Mahāvyutpatti*, 8214, etc.
221. Cf. P.L. Vaidya, *Mahāyānasutrasaṃgraha*, Pt. I. (Mithila, 1961), 285.
222. ed. E. Waldschmidt, 31.
223. *Lalita*,62-66, *Saddharma*, 69, *Aṣṭasāhasrikā*, 69-73, 95, 112, 140, 190; *Laṅkā*, tr. Suzuki, 216; *Suvarṇa* 87-89; *Dharmasaṃgraha*, Sc. VIII; *Sikṣāsamuccaya*, ed. Bendal, 169. ff.; etc.
224. Cf. *Sādhanamālā*, 248 ff.
225. M.M. Haraprasad Sastri wanted to connect Śītalā with the Buddhist goddess Hārītī. *Discovery of Living Buddhism in Bengal* (Calcutta, 1897), 20.
226. For details see my *Indian Mother Goddess* (New Delhi, 1977), 121, 128.
227. *Ibid.*, 110, 114-15, 136-37, 150, 183-85, 203-11.
228. S.K. Chatterji in *JAS*, 1959, 118.
229. *Notices of Sanskrit MSS*, 2nd series (Calcutta, 1900) I. Pref.
230. *Nepal* (Paris, 1905), I, 346.
231. *IHQ*, 1931, 1-16.
232. B.T. Bhattacharyya, *Buddhist Esoterism* (Oxford, 1932), 155-56. For details see my *IMG*, 201-07.
233. *Mañjuśrīmūlakalpa*, 508, 647-48.
234. *Studies in the Tantras* (Calcutta, 1939), 43-44.

235. *Sādhanamālā,* 585 ff. For iconological description of the Hindu gods in Buddhist pantheon see B.T. Bhattacharyya, *In-lian Buddhist Iconography* (Calcutta, 1968), 344 ff.
236. For details see A. Getty, *Gods of Northern Buddhism* (Oxford, 1928), pl. XLIX; W.E. Clark, *Two Lamaistic Pantheons* (Cambridge, Mass.), 1937. II, 75 ff.; A.K. Gordon, *The Iconography of Tibetan Lamaism* (New York, 1939), 90.
237. *Niṣpanna,* 62.
238. *Sādhana,* 329 ff., See Bhattacharyya, *IBI*, 349-52; Gordon *ITL*, 72, 88; Getty, *GNB*, 127-28; Clark, *TLP,* 173, 181.
239. *Niṣpanna* 61; Clark, *TLP*, II 89, 178.
240. Gordon, *ITL*, 90; Getty, *GNB*, pl. XLVII a-b.
241. Clark, *TLP*, II, 98, 178.
242. Gordon, *ITL*, 90, Getty, *GNB*, pl. LII b.
243. For details see B.T. Bhattacharyya, *IBI*, 352 ff.
244. Clark, *TLP*, II, 181.
245. This deity had a love-hate relationship with the Buddhists, because they insisted more on the *vighnarāja* (trouble-maker) than on the *siddhidātā* (bestower of success) aspect of Gaṇeśa. Thus in the Indian Museum images of Parṇaṣabarī and Aparajitā, and in the Baroda Museum image of Vighnāṭaka, etc. the deities have been represented as trampling Gaṇeśa under their feet. In two Vikrampur images of Parṇaśabarī and in the Dacca Sahitya Pariṡat image of Mahapratisarā, Gaṇeśa appears below the lotus seat lying prostrate on the ground crushed under the weight of Buddhist deities.
246. For Details regarding the mythological characters of the Buddhists see G.P. Malalasekera, *A Dictionary of Pali Proper Names*, 2 Vols. (London, 1937-38); T.O. Ling, *Buddhism and the Mythology of Evil* (London, 1962); J.R. Haldar, *Early Buddhist Mythology* (New Delhi, 1977). For Mahāyāna see the works of A. Getty, W.E. Clark, A.K. Gordon and B.T. Bhattacharyya referred to above.

V

IN NON-BUDDHIST PHILOSOPHICAL PERSPECTIVE: CONVERGENCES AND DIVERGENCES

How Buddhism in its doctrinal aspects was viewed by the followers of the non-Buddhist schools of thought may be exemplified with reference to Mādhava's review of the Buddhist system as found in his *Sarvadarśanasaṃgraha*.[1] It is interesting to note that Mādhava derived his knowledge of the Buddhist doctrines from the philosophical works mostly belonging to the non-Buddhist schools. Mādhava never considered Buddhism to be a separate religion. According to him, it was a philosophical system belonging to the same category of the Vedānta or the Sāṅkhya or the Nyāya-Vaiśeṣika. He discussed at length the Buddhist viewpoints in regard to the cause-effect relations, the law of invariable concomitance, ascertainment of identity and difference as determinants, principles of effectuation, validity of inference as a form of evidence and so forth. He gave what appeared to him to be the most important tenets of Buddhism and the principal arguments by which their followers endeavoured to maintain them. He often displayed some quaint humour as he threw himself for the time into the position of their advocate and held, as it were, a temporary brief on behalf of opinions sometimes entirely at variance of his own. At the same time he was not uncritical. He made his assessment of Buddhism from the point of view of a Vedantin. He reviewed in detail with arguments and counter-arguments the Buddhist concepts of momentariness, pain, thatness and vacuity and explained how these concepts were taken into account by the Vaibhāṣikas who admitted the reality of both mind and external objects, the Sautrāntikas who also admitted the same with the distinction that external objects were not directly known in perception but they could be inferred from their mental pictures or ideas, the

Yogācāras who held that there could be no external reality since the objects perceived were all ideas in the mind, and the Mādhyamikas who insisted that the whole world of experience was an appearance, a mere network of unintelligible relations.

As we have stated above, there is a structural unity in all forms of Indian thought. All schools, barring the Cārvākas, have squarely based themselves on the concept of *duḥkha* or suffering which is the first of the four truths preached by the Buddha. Suffering is due to the failure to obtain what a man wants. In Buddhist terminology the combination of five aggregates (*skandhas*) ends in suffering and is always accompanied with on account of constant change and ultimate decay. By *duḥkha* is therefore meant 'existence in the world with concomitant pain and pleasure' which are without any real substance (*anātma*) and are impermanent (*anitya*).[2] The origin of suffering (*duḥkha-samudaya*) is explained by the Buddha in the light of his special theory of dependent origination (*pratītyasamutpāda*) which traces the source of suffering to ignorance. It is said that suffering in life is due to *jāti* or birth caused by *bhava* or will to be born. This 'will to be born' is caused by *upādāna* or mental clinging to the worldly objects which is due to *tṛṣṇā* or craving to enjoy sense objects. This 'craving' in its turn is caused by *vedanā* or sense-experience which is due to *sparśa* or sense-object-contact. This contact cannot rise unless there is *ṣaḍāyatana* or six organs of cognition, the five senses and mind. These six organs in their turn are dependent for their existence, on *nāma-rūpa* or body-mind organism. This 'body-mind organism' which constitutes the perceptible being of man cannot develop without *vijñāna* or some initial consciousness. The latter comes from *saṃskāra* or the impressions of the experience of past life. The root cause of these impressions or tendencies to cause rebirth is *avidyā* or lack of true knowledge.[3] Absolute ending of suffering is *duḥkha-nirodha* which is the third of the four truths preached by the Buddha. This is the cessation of suffering, complete detachment from desires, relinquishment of all worldly objects and of desire to possess them. In the Pali texts it is described as unborn (*ajātam*) and unoriginated (*abhūtam*), uncreated (*akatam*) and unconstituted (*asamkhaṭam*).

Though there are functional differences among various schools of Indian thought in regard to the specific practical methods of putting an end to all forms of suffering and of achieving liberation, all of them agree on the basic point that the path which leads to the cessation of suffering concern the control of the conditions which cause suffering. The Sāṅkhya philosophy also starts with the concept of suffering and its extinction. According to the Sāṅkhya, there are three kinds of suffering—*ādhyātmika* which is due to the intra-organic causes like bodily disorder, diseases and mental sufferings caused by fear, anger, greed, etc.; *ādhibhautika* which is produced by extra-organic natural causes; and *ādhidaivika* which is caused by extra-organic supernatural conditions.[4] The Yoga, the Nyāya-Vaiśeṣika and the Vedānta also speak of suffering. In line with Buddhism all these schools hold that ignorance (*ajñāna*, *avidyā*, *aviveka*, etc.) is the basic cause of all suffering and bondage. We have seen that, according to Buddhism, human misery and suffering, like all else, depend on certain conditions, there being a chain of cause and effect which leads to suffering in this world. If the transitory, painful nature of the worldly existence is perfectly realised, there cannot arise any *karma* resulting in rebirth. Ignorance or *avidyā* is therefore the root cause of the tendencies that cause rebirth. It is the first constituent of the twelve sources (*dvādaśanidāna*) of the wheel of existence (*bhavacakra*). According to the Sāṅkhya, ignorance or *aviveka* is the cause of suffering. This ignorance is due to the lack of *vivekajñāna* which makes a discrimination between the experiencing subject (*draṣṭā*) and experienced object (*dṛśya*).[5] According to the Yoga, *avidyā*, or ignorance is one of the five *kleśas* or sources of afflictions. It is wrong knowledge of the non-self as the self, of the unpleasant as the pleasant and of the impure as pure. In Vedānta, ignorance (*ajñāna* or *avidyā*) has the double function of concealment (*āvaraṇa*) and distortion (*vikṣepa*) of reality. Illusion is the product of ignorance; it prevents one from seeing the real nature of the thing and makes one see something else in its place.

Another common concept held by all Indian thinkers is that of bondage caused by ignorance. By bondage is commonly meant the process of birth and rebirth and the consequent sufferings to which an individual is subject. The general concept of bondage is interpreted differently by different systems in the light of their ideas of the individual and the world. The term is specially used in Jainism according to which bondage of the soul to matter is due to its bondage to bad dispositions or passions caused by the influx of matter which the Jīva takes up in accordance with its *karma* (*sakaṣā-yalvāj-jīvaḥ karmaṇo yogān pudgalānādatta sa bandhaḥ*).[6] In Buddhism it has been explained in terms of the chain of cause-effect relations. Suffering, like every other thing, depends on some conditions. It is the 'will to become' (*bhava*), the force of the blind tendency or predisposition to be born, which causes bondage. According to the Sāṅkhya, bondage is due to *aviveka* which is the inability to discriminate between self and not-self. It is mind, not the self, that feels pleasure or pain. Thus all moral properties belong to the ego (*ahaṃkāra*) which is the striver and doer of all acts.[7] In the Nyāya-Vaiśeṣika, owing to the body and sense organs the individual has to suffer bondage which has a lot to do with *adṛṣṭa*, the stock of merit and demerit, the unseen principle which sways even over material atoms and brings about objects and events in accordance with moral principles and with the general concept of *karma*. According to the Yoga, the self's bondage is due to its identification with mental modifications caused by the five sources of afflictions (*kleśas*) to which a human being is subject. These are *avidyā* or wrong knowledge, *asmitā* or false notion, *rāga* or desire, *dveṣa* or aversion and *abhiniveśa* or instinctive fear of death.[8] The Advaita Vedāntins hold that bondage is due to the soul's association with body. Out of ignorance it forgets that it is really *brahman*, and this is bondage.

The concepts of suffering, bondage and liberation are inextricably connected with the law of *karma* which has been accepted by most philosophical systems of India. In its simplest form the law of *karma* means that all actions, good or bad, produce their proper consequences. The word *karma* means both this law and also the force generated by an action having the potency of bearing fruit. We have already had the occassion to deal with the origin and development of this concept in the Vedic and post-Vedic literature. The Buddhist law of *karma* is only a special form of the more general law of causation. Since life is thought of as an unbroken stream of successive states which are causally concerned, the present existence of an individual is in accordance with that of *karma*, the effect of the past. Rebirth is, therefore, not transmigration but a continuity in life-series in which process *karma* serves a causal connection. According to the Buddhist view, in the formula of causal sequence, the *saṃskāras* or mental dispositions which arise owing to the non-realisation of truth (*avidyā*) represent the accumulated *karmaic* effects left in a being before its rebirth. The results of acts done in the previous life are transmitted to that consciousness which brings about re-existence (*pratisandhivijñāna*) and this transmission takes place ceaselessly and uninterruptedly (*sanātana*) like water flowing in a stream. In Buddhism *karmas* are divided into three categories : those which yield fruit in this life; in the next life; and in a future life.[9] In Buddhism, as also in the Sāṅkhya and the Mīmāṃsā, the law of *karma* is autonomous and works independently of the will of God. The Mīmāṃsākas hold that the world is always there, neither created nor destroyed, but regulated by *karma*. The law of *karma* is thought to guide the formation of objects. The world is composed of living bodies wherein the souls reap the consequence of their past deeds (*bhogāyatana*), the *indriyas* or organs which are instruments for suffering or enjoying of those consequences (*bhogasādhana*) and the objects which contribute the fruits to be suffered or enjoyed (*bhogaviṣaya*). In Jainism which also holds that the world is eternal, neither created nor destroyed, *karma* is conceived of as being material and permeating the Jīvas, thus weighing them down to the mundane level. The passions of a man act like a viscous substance that attracts the *karma* matter, which thus pours into the soul and sticks to it; gradually it ripens and exhausts itself in accordance with the suffering and enjoyment of the individual. According to the Vedantins *karmas* accumulated in the past lives admit of a twofold division; those still lying accumulated (*sañcita*) and those which are being stored in the present life (*sancīyamāna*). The bondage of the soul to the body is due to its *karma*. The Nyāya-Vaiśeṣikas hold that the law of *karma* is under the guidance and control of God who creates the world in accordance with the law. *Adṛṣṭa*, or the stock of merits and demerits of *karmas* of the individual souls, cannot by itself lead to their proper effects, because it is an unintelligent and unconscious principle. It is therefore God who controls the *adṛṣṭa* and dispenses all the joys and sorrows of human life.

All Indian systems agree that liberation cannot be achieved without knowledge of reality, i.e. the real nature of the world and the self. Liberation is the state of perfection. To denote this state the Buddhists use the term *nirvāṇa*. This particular term is also used by the Jains and the Hindus in the same sense of liberation. *Nirvāṇa* is described as the free state of consciousness, the tranquil state of one's internal nature and the highest emotional state of spirituality and blessedness. It means the annihilation of passions, hatred and delusion.[10] It is like a matchless island which possesses nothing, grasps at nothing and which is the destroyer of decay and death.[11] It is the extinction of five *skandhas*.[12] Its other names are *nirodha*, *nirmokṣa*, *nivṛtti* and *nirveda*.[13] It is uncaused, uncompounded but realisable. From the ethical point of view *nirvāṇa* involves the process of perfect self-examination, self-purification, self-restraint and self-culture. In spite of the inconceivability of *nirvāṇa*, there are passages in the *nikāyas* which give it a mixture of positive and negative attributes.[14] The ethical positive in *nirvāṇa* is perfection in *śīla*, *samādhi* and *prajñā*, in four *smṛtyupasthāna* (mindfulness) practices leading to a state of perfect bliss. The ethical negative is in the eradication of attachment (*rāga*), ill-will (*dveṣa*) and delusion (*moha*), removal of all impurities (*kleśas*, *āsravas*) and ignorance (*avidyā*). Both the positive and the negative attributes lead to the end of desire for worldly objects or existence. Metaphysically, *nirvāṇa* is eternal and fixed, homogeneous beyond the scope of discussive and discriminatory thoughts, having neither origin nor decay, without past, present and future, unlimited and unsurpassable, unfathomable and immeasurable, unconditional and unconstituted (*asaṃskṛta*). According to Nāgārjuna, *saṃsāra* and *nirvāṇa* are two relative ideas. The *pratītyasamutpāda* viewed and interpreted as a law of sequence of causal antecedents and consequents, explains the essential nature of *saṃsāra* or worldly existence. The same, viewed and interpreted as 'mere origination' (*uppādamātta*) without any idea of temporal relation associated with it, expresses the essential nature of *nirvāṇa*.

In Buddhism, the term *nirvāṇa* is thus used instead of *mokṣa* or *mukti* and is cessation of suffering. It is not the extinction of existence, but the extinction of misery and of the causes of rebirth. The Buddha's silence about the condition of the liberated after death may or may not mean his denial of the existence of such a person after death. The real nature of *nirvāṇa* can only be realised; it cannot be described in terms of ordinary experience. According to the Jain ideas when a Jīva is freed from the bondage of *karma* and has passed for ever beyond the possibility of rebirth, it is said to have attained *nirvāṇa* or *mokṣa* or liberation. It is a state of pure happiness (*anantasukha*), pure and infinite knowledge (*anantajñāna*) and infinite perception (*anantadarśana*). Every Jīva has the potentiality for liberation which is achieved by faith, knowledge and conduct.[15] The Nyāya-Vaiśeṣikas hold that *apavarga* or liberation is absolute freedom from suffering which is a state in which the soul is released from its connection with the body and the senses. It is just that unfettered condition of soul which has been variously described as freedom from fear (*abhayam*), freedom from decay and change (*ajaram*), freedom from death (*amṛtyupadam*) and so forth.[16] To attain liberation one should listen to scriptural instructions (*śravaṇa*), understand them by means of reason (*manana*), and meditate on the self in conformity with the principles of Yoga (*nididhyāsana*). According to the Sāṅkhya, the attainment of liberation means just the clear recognition of the self as a reality which is beyond time and space and also of body and mind. It is essentially free, eternal and immortal. The term which the Sāṅkhya uses for liberation is *mukti* which means complete destruction of the three-fold suffering (*duḥkhatraya-bhighāta*). There are two kinds of liberation: *jīvanmukti* and *videhamukti*. The former is liberation within the span of life and the latter after death.[17] In the Yoga liberation consists in restraining the activities of the body, the senses and the mind (*manas*) and in finally suppressing all the mental modifications (*cittavṛtti*).[18] In the Mimāmsā the highest good is the attainment of heaven or a state in which there is absolute bliss. Later Mīṃāmsakas conceived of something like liberation in line with other philosophical systems. According to the Advaita Vedānta realisation of identity between the self and the *brahman* is liberation from bondage. It is not the attainment of something new. It is only recognition of what already exists like the finding of a necklace around the neck after forgetting its existence and searching all over. Bondage is due to illusion.[19]

Another feature common to most philosophical systems of ancient India is the special emphasis on concentration and meditation, the necessity of which led to the development of an elaborate technique of self-control known as the Yoga system. Although Yoga is regarded as a distinct branch of Indian philosophy, it is not confined to that system only. It is found in some form or the other in Buddhism, Jainism, Sāṅkhya, Vedānta and even the Nyāya-Vaiśeṣika system. Buddhism speaks of four stages of concentration : the first is on reasoning and investigation regarding the truth; the second is unruffled meditation free from reasoning etc.; the third is detachment from even the joy of tranquillity; and the fourth is detachment from all sorts of bodily feeling.[20] Buddhghoṣa has often used the two words *citta* and *samādhi* synonymously and interpreted the latter as the act of putting or placing the mind and mental functions evenly and properly on one object.[21] There are various kinds of *samādhi*. The Buddhists use the term *paṭipadā* to mean the way which leads to the disciplining of one's thoughts so as to reach the *upacāra* stage which is the withdrawal of mind from the surrounding objects as also from the characteristics of the subject for mental concentration. According to Buddhaghoṣa there are ten *patibodhas* or hindrances to the practice of concentration.[22] These ten act as obstructions not to all but only to those who have got mental weaknesses.[23] There are forty steps of meditation consisting of ten *kasiṇas* or objects to be conceived of in their entirety; ten *aśubhas* or invariable unpleasant states to confront and overcome; ten *anussatis* or recollections which lead to the quietude of mind and destroy the hindrances; four *brahmavihāras* or states of mental purity; four *āruppas* or *samāpattis* which lead the mind from the limits of mundane existence to the realm of the infinite; one *saññā* or the feeling of non-attachment for the body; and one *vavatthāna* or realisation of voidness of one's self as also of the world.[24] There are successive steps known as *upacāra* or the preparatory conditions to abstraction, *appanā* or abstraction and the four *jhānas* or trances. Like all other systems Buddhism also holds that mere theoretical knowledge is not sufficient, that continued meditation on truths is needed to remove false preoccupations and that self-control is needed to remove passions which obstruct concentration. This self-control implies the bringing of the lower self under the control of the higher by cultivating positive virtues.

Now we shall deal with the convergences and divergences of Buddhism with other systems. The basic theoretical difference between Buddhism and Jainism was on the question of momentariness. The Buddhists regarded all changes as being due to the assemblage of conditions absolutely momentary (*kṣaṇika*) in character and went so far as to deny the existence of any permanent soul. The Jains also believed that changes were produced by the assemblage of conditions and held that, since no ultimate absolute view of things could be logically taken, the reality of the permanence of the world, at least some of the fundamentals must be acknowledged side by side with the question of change. The Buddhists hold that the changing qualities can alone be perceived and that there is no unchanging substance behind them. The common example of clay and jar may be cited here. A thing such as clay is seen to assume various shapes and to undergo diverse changes in the forms of jar, pan, etc. But inspite of these changes the clay itself remains permanent. The changes occur only qualitatively. The Buddhists hold that what we perceive as clay is a specific quality and what we perceive as jar is also another quality. Since we cannot perceive any substance apart from quality, and since all the changes are by nature qualitative, the conception of any permanent and unchangeable substance is mere fiction of ignorance. The Jains on the other hand hold that it is not true as the Buddhists say that there is no permanent substance, but merely the change of passing qualities. By the assemblage of conditions, old qualities in things disappear, new qualities come in, and something remains permanent. Thus in the case of the jar, the clay has become lost in some form, has generated itself in another and remains permanent in another form.

Thus according to the Jains, those who hold that there is nothing really permanent in the universe and that everything changes from moment to moment are one-sided because change and permanence are both real. Reality consists of three factors: permanence, origin and decay—*utpāda-vyaya-drauvyayuktaṃ sat.*[25] As against the doctrine of momentariness the Jains hold that, if everything is taken to be momentary, it will be impossible to explain memory, recognition, the immediate feeling of personal identity, etc. Accordingly the concept of liberation will not be able to stand in the absence of any permanent soul to be liberated. If everything were momentary no moral life would be possible then, since it is impossible for a momentary person, to make any attempt for attaining any end. The consequences of *karma* or one's own action will then have no meaning. Momentariness cannot explain the constitution of any individual series, because without something permanent behind the changing modes (*paryāyas*), the changing states cannot be held together to form a continuity in the individual. The doctrine of momentariness cannot also be proved by perception of inference. These valid sources of knowledge do not reveal the existence of anything in the world in which there is only change and no element of continuity.[26]

So far as the Buddhist theory of knowledge is concerned, the Jains do not contribute to the Buddhist view that all knowledge by perception of external objects is in the first instance indefinite and indeterminate. The main difference of the Jains from Buddhists in the question of perception lies in this that, according to the Jains, perception reveals the external objects just as they are with most of their diverse characteristics of colour, form, etc. Objects are not mere forms of knowledge, as the Vijñānavādin Buddhists think, but actually exist. Ignorance like a veil covers the self, and this veil is removed by perception which is determinate. The Jains, contrary to the Buddhists, deny the existence of any indeterminate (*nirvikalpa*) stage preceding the determinate (*svavikalpa*) stage of perception. The Buddhists on the other hand regard that the first stage consisting of the presentation of indeterminate sense materials is the only valid part of perception and that the determinate stage is the result of the application of mental categories like imagination, memory, etc., not truly revealing the presentative part.[27]

The Jains reject the Buddhist view that reality consists in causal efficiency, i.e. an object is real if it is capable of causing any effect. The Jains reject the approach because, according to it, even an illusory snake must be called real as it can cause effects like fear, etc. In fact production of effect is with the Buddhists the only definition of existence. Each unit of effect is different from any other such unit, but a succession of the different units of effect reveals a succession of new substances every moment, and that is why all things are momentary. The Jains refute this view on the following grounds : We can only assert that thing the existence of which is indicated by a corresponding experience. The Buddhist view that each unit of effect produced is not exactly the same at each new point of time and that therefore all things are momentary is fallacious, because experience shows that not all of an object is found to be changing every moment. To take an example, gold in a gold ornament is found to remain permanent while its form like ear-rings or bangles are seen to undergo change. In the face of such an experience it is impossible to assert that the whole thing vanishes every moment and that new things are being renewed at each succeeding moment. According to the Jains, this analysis has given birth to the curious *arthakriyākāritva* doctrine of Buddhists leading them to unfounded nihilism. Thus if we go by experience we can neither reject the self not the external world. The rise of knowledge through experience can be parallel to certain objective collocation of things.

The Buddhists began with a sense of realism, but the two schools of Mahāyāna, viz. Śūnyavāda and Vijñānavāda, shifted to absolute idealism which considered the empirical world to be a completely unreal, as false as the beauty of the daughter of a barren woman. In course of its philosophical history, Jainism also developed some idealistic tendencies, but the realistic nature of Jain standpoint remained unaltered in essence. It rejects Śūnyavada and Vijñānavada because they do not accept the competence of sense organs. The Buddhist theory of dependent origination conceives in its own distinctive manner the series of qualities and attributes that originate or perish, but it posits no permanent atomic substance in the form of the substrata of these qualities and attributes. But Jainism posits over and above the perceptible world an infinite number of two utterly distinct types of subtle elements, one physical and the other conscious. The gross world is according to it only the effect (*kārya*) or modification (*pariṇāma*) of the subtle physical elements. The concept of Buddhist atomism is also basically different from that of the Jains. It is only in the Sarvāstivāda school of Buddhism that we come across the doctrine of atomism. According to the Jains, the atoms are eternal, but the atoms of Buddhism are not so, because Buddhism dogmatically asserts the impermanence of all things. According to the Buddhists, the atoms have only a functional role which may be compared with a focus of energy.[28] The atoms of the four elements, and also their molecules are related to the five senses. The four elements have distinctive attributes and functions, e.g. solidity and support in the case of earth, moisture and cohesion in that of water, heat and ripening in that of fire, motion and expansion in that of air.[29] The atoms constitute molecules which must include at least one atom of all four elements, and acquire their characteristics according to the atoms predominantly composing them. Such concepts which are basically different from the Jain formulations, are closer rather to those of the Nyāya-Vaiśeṣikas.

On the problems of knowledge in general the Jains are in agreement with the Buddhists belonging to the Vijñānavāda school on the point of the self-revelatory character of cognition, but while the

Vijñānavādins hold that there exist no object apart from cognition, and a particular piece of cognition is possessed of a particular form, the Jains posit the existence of external objects and treat cognition as a general phenomenon. So far as the question of *prāmaṇa*, meaning both valid cognition and the instrument of valid cognition, is concerned, the Buddhist logicians introduced the idea of self-cognition or self-revelatoriness[30] which had influenced the earlier Jain logicians like Siddhasena or Samantabhadra. As to the problem whether the validity or invalidity of a piece of cognition is intrinsic or extrinsic, the Buddhist viewpoint, as upheld by Śāntarakṣita, is that both the validity and the invalidity of a piece of cognition can well be intrinsic in one case and extrinsic in another. Thus in the case of repeated acquaintance (*abhyāsa-daśā*) the validity as well as invalidity of a piece of cognition ought to be treated as intrinsic while in the case of first acquaintance they both ought to be treated as extrinsic. The Jain position also exactly tallies with the Buddhist view as presented by Śāntarakṣita. As to the nature of the effects of a *pramāṇa*, the Buddhist tradition holds two views : (i) that it consists in cognition of an object and (ii) that it consists in self-cognition. According to the Jain tradition, the immediate effect of *pramāṇa* is the removal of ignorance, but the remote effect can possibly be the decision to accept or reject or ignore the object. The Jains consider memory (*smṛti*) to be *prāmaṇa* and class it under non-perceptual knowledge, but the Buddhists do not contribute to this idea.

The first critical evaluation of Buddhism is met with in the *Vedānta-Sūtras* of Bādarāyaṇa,[31] composed not later than A.D. 200, in which attempts have been made to refute the Buddhist doctrines of dependent origination and momentary existence on the ground that *avidyā*, *saṃskāra*, etc., do not stand in the relation of mutual causality and that the Buddhist doctrine of dependent origination itself goes against the doctrine of momentariness because on the origination of subsequent moment the preceding one ceases to be. Bādarāyaṇa says :

> If it is said that (the formation of aggregates may be explained) through (nescience, etc.) standing in the relation of mutual causality, we say 'no' because they merely are efficient causes of the origin (of the immediately subsequent links).
>
> (Nor can there be a causal relation between nescience etc.) because on the origination of the subsequent (moment) the preceding one ceases to be.

> On the supposition that there being no (cause; while yet the effect takes place), there result contradictions of the admitted principle; otherwise simultaneousness (of cause and effect).
> Cessation dependent on a sublative act of the mind, and cessation not so dependent cannot be established, there being no (complete) interruption.
> And the account of the objections presenting themselves in either case.
> And in the case of the space also (the doctrine of its being a non-entity is untenable) on account of its not differing (from two other kinds of non-entity).
> And on account of remembrance.
> (Entity) does not spring from non-entity on account of that not being observed.
> And thus (on that doctrine) there would be an accomplishment (of ends) in the case of non-active people also.
> The non-existence (of external things) cannot be maintained on account of (our) consciousness (of them).
> And on account of their difference of nature (the ideas of the waking state) are not like those of a dream.
> The existence (of mental impressions) is not possible (on the Bauddha view) on account of the absence of perception (of external things).
> And on account of the momentariness (of the *ālaya-vijñāna*, it cannot be the abode of mental impressions).

And on account of its general deficiency in probability.[32]

It should be pointed out in this connection that the said *sūtras* are not by themselves quite intelligible because of which subsequent interpreters of these *sūtras* did not develop the same view. Gauḍapāda, the next important exponent of the Vedānta system depended especially on Buddhism for developing his own ideas. His *Kārikās* on the *Māṇdukyopaniṣad* were evidently inspired by the teachings of the Vijñānavāda and Mādhyamika schools of Buddhism. There are even some who believe that Gauḍapāda was himself a Buddhist by conviction. His views were so much in similarity with the Vijñānavāda and Mādhyamika brands of Buddhist philosophy that he, fully aware of this, had to put it on record, *naitad buddhena bhāṣitam*, i.e. 'not spoken by the Buddha'.[33] This has of course a different implication, as we shall see later. Gauḍapāda welcomed the subjectivism associated with Vijñānavāda[34] and was even ready to declare consciousness or *vijñāna* as unreal in accordance with the Mādhyamika line. Following Nāgārjuna he denied the validity of causation as an empty abstraction[35] and held a world-view very similar to that of the vacuity of the Mādhyamikas. Abundance of Buddhist phraseology, such as *dharma* for entity, *samvṛti* for relative knowledge. *saṃghāta* for objective existence, etc., which are met with in Gauḍapāda *Kārikās*[36] proves that he was familiar not only with the Buddhist doctrines, but at the same time adjusted them to the Advaita design.

Gauḍapāda was the teacher of Śaṅkara's teacher Govinda, and it was therefore natural that Śaṅkara would be influenced by the pro-Buddhist views of Gauḍapāda. The epithet 'crypto-Buddhist' attributed to Śaṅkara by his critics was not without any base. The subjective idealism of the Buddhist Vijñānavāda or Yogācāra school was closely akin to Śaṅkara's conception of pure consciousness. Although in his own commentary on the *Vedānta-sūtras* Śaṅkara did his best to refute Buddhism as a system rival to his own, in his own theory he incorporated Buddhist elements, which did not escape the notice of his contemporaries and later critics. Yāmunacārya in his *Siddhitraya* remarked that the Buddhists and Śaṅkarites declared the distinctions of the knower, the known and the knowledge as unreal, the former tracing them to *buddhi* and the latter to *māyā*. According to Vijñānabhikṣu, the commentator on *Sāṅkhyasūtra*, the *māyā* theory of the Śaṅkarites is nothing but a restatement of the subjective idealism of the Buddhists.[37] This was also the view of Rāmānuja, the theistic interpreter of Vedānta, who held that Śaṅkara was a Buddhist in disguise. As Śaṅkara had a wide range of followers probably on account of his establishment of Vedantic monasticism in the pattern of the Buddhists, and later came to be regarded as an incarnation of Śiva, the propounders of popular theism found it hard to reconcile his original doctrine to his popular image. Thus in the *Padmapurāṇa*,[38] Śiva is made to say to Pārvati that although the theory of *māyā* is a false one, a disguised form of Buddhism, he himself was responsible for preaching it in the *kaliyuga*—something which he did assuming the shape of a Brāhmaṇa.

But in his commentary on the *Vedānta Sūtras* Śaṅkara displayed an attacking mood. According to him three principal schools of Buddhism could be identified : that which maintains the reality of everything (Saravāstivāda); that which maintains the reality of thought only (Vijñānavāda); and that which maintains the voidness of everything (Śūnyavāda). To the Sarvāstivādins what is external is either the elements (*bhūta*, like earth, water, etc.) or the elementary (*bhautika*, like colour, smell, etc.) and what is internal is either mind (*citta*) or mental (*caitta*). The four elements, which are external, arise from the aggregation of four kinds of atoms while the internal consists of the aggregate of five *skandhas* (*rūpa, vedanā, vijñāna, saṃjñā* and *saṃskāra*). These taken together constitute the basis of all personal existence. Having thus put forward this doctrine of the Sarvāstivādins as the viewpoint of the opponent (*pūrvapakṣa*), Śaṅkara says that the aggregate of the elements and elementary things caused by the atoms and that of the five *skandhas* cannot be established since the constituents of the aggregates are devoid of intelligence. Secondly, since the Buddhists do not admit any other permanent intelligent being that could effect the aggregation of the atoms, how could the atoms and the *skandhas* then be supposed to be active on their own account? Nor can it be explained it terms of the *ālayavijñānapravāha* or the train of self-cognitions which, if viewed as permanent, leads to the Vedantic position of the acceptance of an eternal self, and if viewed as momentary, leads to the immobility and non-functionary character of the atoms.[39]

Śaṅkara puts forward the Buddhist position that although there exists no permanent intelligent principle of the nature either of a ruling lord or an enjoying soul, under whose influence the formation of aggregates could take place, the course of mundane existence is rendered possible to the mutual causality of *avidyā* etc. Śaṅkara strikingly says that the chain of causation starting with *avidyā* is not characteristic of the Buddhist systems alone, but is acknowledged by the followers of other systems as well. But he rejects it on the ground that it merely assigns efficient causes for the origination of the members (*saṃskāra, vijñāna*, etc.) of this series, and does not intimate an efficient cause for the formation of the aggregates. Referring to the Nyāya-Vaiśeṣikas Śaṅkara says that the formation of aggregates cannot be accounted for even on the assumption of permanent atoms and individual souls in which the unseen fruits of action (*adṛṣṭa*) reside. How much less then are aggregates possible if there exist only momentary atoms not connected with enjoying souls?[40] There may exist a causal relation between the members of the series consisting of *avidyā*, etc., but they cannot be made to account for the existence of the aggregates and even be considered as efficient causes of the subsequent members of the series to which they belong. On the admission that everything has a momentary existence it is possible to establish between two things the relation of cause and effect, since the former momentary existence which ceases or has ceased to be enters into the state of non-existence, and hence cannot be the cause of the later momentary existence. It is not also possible to hold that the former momentary existence on reaching its full development becomes the cause of the later momentary existence. That the mere existence of an antecedent entity constitute its causal energy is also a fruitless assumption because we cannot conceive of the origination of an effect which is not imbued with the nature of the cause. Nor can it be admitted that the relation of cause and effect holds good without the cause somehow giving its colouring to the effect. Moreover, the origination and cessation of things of which the Buddhists speak must either constitute a thing's own form or another state of it, or an altogether different thing. If origination and cessation constitute the form of a thing, it would follow that the word 'thing' and the words 'origination' and 'cessation' are interchangeable, which is not the case. If the terms 'origination' and 'cessation' denote the initial and final states of an intermediate state called 'thing' in that case the 'thing' will be connected with three moments which will go against the doctrine of momentariness. A third alternative that 'origination' and 'cessation' are altogether different from the 'thing' would lead the invariable conclusion that the 'thing', disconnected with 'origination' and 'cessation', is everlasting. Causality and momentariness are thus incompatible.[41]

In his zeal to refute the Buddhist viewpoint he invokes an imaginary counter argument "if the Buddhists say that an effect may rise even when there is no cause".[42] (No Buddhist, however even for argument's sake, can subscribe to a causeless origination). Then he refers to the Buddhist assumption that, except the triad of space (*ākāśa*), all produced things have cessation either dependent on a sublative act of the mind or not dependent on such an act. According to him, both are impossible 'on account of the absence of interruption'. Both presuppose a reference either to the series of momentary existences or to the single numbers constituting the series. The former alternative is impossible in the series of momentary existences the members stand in an unbroken relation of cause and effect so that the series cannot be interrupted. The latter alternative is also inadmissible because momentary existence cannot undergo complete annihilation because we find that a thing has a connected existence and is recognised in its various states.[43] From the Buddhist standpoint the cessation of *avidyā*, etc., must take place either in consequence of perfect knowledge or of its own accord. The first alternative implies the rejection of the Buddhist doctrine of destruction while the second involves the uselessness of the Buddhist instruction as to the 'path'.[44] With regard to the Buddhist view of space Śaṅkara says that it cannot be maintained that it is non-definable since substantiality can be established also in the case of space which is the substratum of sound and sprung from the self. The Buddhists place themselves by their view of space in opposition to other parts of their system. The Buddha said that on space the air is founded. How can air which is a positive entity have its support in space if the latter be a non-entity?[45]

According to Śaṅkara, the doctrine of momentariness is invalidated by recollection or remembrance. Remembrance can take place only if it belongs to the same person who previously made the perception. There is one thinking subject only to which the original perception as well as the remembrance belongs. This necessarily implies that the doctrine of universal momentariness cannot stand.[46] The Buddhists deny the existence of permanent stable causes and maintain that entity springs from non-entity. From the decomposed seed the young plant springs, from decomposed milk curd is formed or a lump of clay ceases to remain as a lump when it becomes a jar. Young plants, etc., spring from seeds, etc., only after the latter have been merged in non-existence. Its effects spring from changeless or permanent causes, the former should originate from the latter without having any need of specification. Śaṅkara refutes this point saying that if entity springs from non-entity, the assumption of special causes will be purportless, since non-entity is in all cases one and the same. If non-distinguished non-existence be admitted to have causal efficiency, we should also have to assume that sprouts, etc., originate from horns of hares etc.—a thing certainly not actually observed. Since according to the Buddhists all minds and mental modifications spring from the four *skandhas* and all material aggregates from the atoms why then do they stultify their own doctrine by the fanciful assumption of entity springing from non-entity? If it be admitted that entity issues from non-entity purposes should be obtained without endeavour, since non-existence is a thing to be had without much trouble.[47]

Then Śaṅkara goes on to refute the Vijñānavāda or Yogācāra system of Buddhism which holds that external objects do not exist. He describes it as a system according to which all experience, constituted by the act, object and result of knowledge, is internal existing insofar as it is connected with mind (*buddhi*). Even if external things exist they cannot be experienced unless the mind determines their forms. There is no outward thing apart from consciousness. External things are impossible. If external things are admitted, they must either be atoms or aggregates of atoms such as pillars and the like. Since atoms are imperceptible, atoms cannot be apprehended as the aggregate of atoms. Secondly, as the Buddhists argue, the cognitions undergo successive modifications in accordance with the ideas or concepts of different objects, such as pillar, wall, jar and so forth. This is not possible without some distinction on the part of the ideas themselves. It follows that the form of the objects is determined by the ideas. Thirdly, our knowledge of the objects in the form of ideas and of objects themselves being always simultaneously presented, they must in reality be one and the same. Thus the hypothesis of the existence of external things is untenable. Fourthly, perception is to be considered to be similar to a dream and the like. The ideas present to our minds during a dream and the like appear in the twofold form of subject and object, although there is all the while no external object. Thus the experience of our waking may also be independent of external things. Our perceptions of the objects are simply ideas. The variety of ideas is not due to external objects, but to the variety of the impressions left by the previous ideas. In the beginningless *saṃsāra* ideas and mental impressions succeed each other as causes and effects, just as the plant springs from the seed and seeds are again produced from the plant.

Having thus established the Vijñānavāda standpoint, Śaṅkara (though his own views on external objects are more or less similar to it) offers the following counter-arguments. The non-existence of external things cannot be maintained because we are conscious of external things. In every act of perception we are conscious of some external things corresponding to the idea, whether it be a pillar or a wall or a jar. That the outward thing exists apart from consciousness has necessarily to be accepted on the ground of the nature of consciousness itself. The perception of a pillar or a wall is not an individual perception only; so many persons do it as the same object. Even those who contest the existence of external things bear witness to their existence when they say that what is an internal object of cognition appears like something external. No one says that Viṣṇumitra appears like the son of a barren mother. Secondly, possibility and impossibility of things is to be determined only on the ground of the operation and non-operation of the means of right knowledge which are not dependent on preconceived possibilities or impossibilities. The external things are, according to their nature, apprehended by all the instruments of knowledge. Hence non-existence of external objects cannot be maintained on the ground of such idle dilemmas as that about their difference or non-difference from atoms. Thirdly, it is difficult to understand how ideas have the forms of objects. Because the distinction of a thing and an idea is given in consciousness, their invariable concomitance has to be considered as proving only that the thing constitutes the means of the idea, not that the two are identical. That the idea and the object are different and distinct from each other can moreover be shown by reference to the difference between a substance and the attributes belonging to it. The awareness of the idea implies the awareness of the external thing. To say that the 'idea is self-luminous' like a lamp, is an absurdity like saying that 'fire burns itself'. And if the Buddhists hold that by insisting on the concept of the self-luminous idea they subscribe to the position of the Vedantins, since the latter hold that the idea itself implies consciousness, Śaṅkara replies that just as a lamp in order to become manifest requires some other intelligent agent, so also the idea, as equally being a thing to be illuminated, becomes manifest only through an ulterior intelligent principle.[48]

According to Śaṅkara, the Buddhist view that the ideas of waking life are similar to the ideas in a dream is not correct. The things of which we are conscious in a dream are negated by our waking consciousness. Likewise, those things of which we are conscious in our waking state, such as the pillars and the like, are never negated in any state. Moreover, the visions of a dream are acts of remembrance, while the visions of the waking state are acts of immediate consciousness. As the distinction between the two states is evident to everyone, it is impossible to formulate the influence that waking consciousness is as false as the dreaming consciousness.[49] Again, the Buddhist view that the variety of ideas can be explained through the variety of mental impressions and without any reference to the external things is not correct. The variety of mental impressions is caused altogether by the variety of things perceived. How, indeed, could various impressions originate if no external things were perceived? The hypothesis of a beginningless series of mental impressions would lead only to a baseless *regressus ad infinitum*, sublative of the entire phenomenal world. Moreover, an impression is a kind of modification, and modifications cannot take place unless there is some substratum which is modified.[50] Even if the so-called internal cognition (*ālayavijñāna*) is assumed to constitute the abode of mental impressions, that cognition is also admittedly momentary and non-permanent, and hence cannot be the abode of impressions. For unless there exists one continuous principle equally connected with the past, the present and the future or an absolutely unchangeable Self which cognises everything, it is not possible to account for remembrance, recognition and so on, which are subject to mental impressions dependent on place, time and cause.[51]

As was the common practice with the ancient Indian philosophers (including the Buddhist philosophers) the *pūrvapakṣa* or the views of the opponent were to a certain extent tailored for the sake of their refutation. The usual practice was also adopted by Śaṅkara who even transgressed the limits of his own philosophical position in his eagerness to refute the Buddhist views. Both Vijñānavāda (Yogācāra) and Śūnyavāda (Mādhyamika) were akin to the views propounded by Śaṅkara himself. While refuting the Vijñānavāda doctrines in many cases Śaṅkara did not even hesitate to assume the role of a near-materialist, but the influence of the Mādhyamika doctrine was so great on him that he left if unexplained and quietly passed it over saying that it contradicted all means of right knowledge and therefore needed no special refutation. The central point of Mādhyamika philosophy like that of the Advaita Vedānta is substantially the same as that of the Upaniṣadic idealists. The tradition that survived in the country accusing the Advaita Vedantists as being but disguised Buddhists cannot be regarded as baseless. The renowned Buddhist philosopher Śāntarakṣita did not hesitate to give a patronising certificate to the Vedantic idealism. According to him, its defects are slight (*alpāparādha*).[52] Stcherbatsky has made the point quite clear :

> Śaṅkara accuses them (i.e. the Mādhyamikas) of disregarding all logic and refuses to enter in a controversy with them. The position of Śaṅkara is interesting because at heart he is in full agreement with the Mādhyamikas, at least in the main lines, since both maintain the reality of the one-without-a-second, and the mirage of the manifold. But Śaṅkara, as an ardent hater of Buddhism could never confess that. He therefore treats the Mādhyamikas with great contempt ... on the charge that the Mādhyamika denies the possibility of cognizing the absolute by logical methods (*pramāṇa*). Vācaspati Miśra in his *Bhāmati* rightly interprets this point as referring to the option of the Mādhyamikas that logic is incapable to solve the question about what existence or non-existence really are. This opinion Śaṅkara himself, as is well known, shares. He does not accept the authority of logic as a means of cognizing the absolute, but he deems it a privilege of the Vedāntin to fare without logic, since he has Revelation to fall back upon. From all his opponents he requires strict logical methods.[53]

V.A. Sukhtankar[54] has categorically said that Śaṅkara was highly indebted to Nāgārjuna for the formulation of his own views. The theory that the Māyāvāda is a Vedantic adaptation of the Śūnyavāda was first put forward by him. Vallee Poussin,[55] however, thought that conclusions based on philosophical parallels are by no means definitive and that autonomous developments were not at all inadmissible. But at the same time he did not dismiss the elements of commonness existing in both the systems and also their historical suggestivities. According to him, Nāgārjuna, who regarded 'voidness' to be the real nature of things, was not unprepared to distinguish the relative truth (*saṃvṛtisatya*) and the absolute one (*paramārthika*). This is also foreshadowed in the Upaniṣads in which the Absolute is viewed in terms of the two *vidyās*, empiric and intuitive super-empiric. According to Poussin, the conception of the universal void and the intuition of the infinite are convergent in the end. Nāgārjuna's *samvṛti* is the Buddhist counterpart of the Vedantic *māyā*. But more important are the comments of the ancients, which speak of some forms of Vedānta, specially those insisting on *māyāvada*, as 'Buddhism in disguise' (*māyāvādam asat sāstraṃ pracchannaṃ bauddhaṃ eva ca*). Vijñānabhikṣu, author of the *Sāṅkhya-pravacanabhāṣya*,[56] says:

> The theologians who maintain the 'neo-illusionism' (*ādhunika māyāvāda*) and style themselves Vedāntins are in fact Buddhists; more precisely, they belong to that branch of the Buddhist school which is named Vijñānavādins, 'who maintain the sole existence of thought' (*bauddhaprabhedāḥ, vijñānavādyeka-deśitayā*). They assimilate the 'data' of experience, merit and demerit, etc., to the 'data' of a dream, and using the Buddhist phrase *samvṛtika* (erroneous) as the exact connotation of the 'particular', they admit that the world, the whole of the 'knowable' (*prapañca*) is produced by ignorance. Therefore they ought to be styled *nāstikas* (miscreants or Buddhists). Thus Vijñānabhikṣu.[57]

Yāmunācārya, the spiritual grandfather of Rāmānuja, refers to Dharmakīrti in his *Siddhitrayam*[58] when he compares a thesis of the 'avowed-Buddhists' with the formula of the 'crypto-Buddhists'. According to the former : "Although the pure intelligence is free from differences, it is understood by people whose view is troubled as multiple—object of knowledge, subject of knowledge, and knowledge. According to the latter : 'The pure reality is not the cause of the development (of names and forms, of the intellectual contingencies) because it ceases not to be (what it is, pure)—therefore it is an illusion who is the mother of this distinction, knower, knowable'".[59]

The oldest writings on Vedānta philosophy, besides Bādarāyaṇa's *Brahma Sūtras*, are the *Kārikās* on the *Māṇḍukyopaniṣad* by Gauḍapāda.[60] He is the first author who formulated Māyāvāda or the doctrine that everything except *brahman* is an illusion. But one should not fail to recall in this connection that one cannot read the *Kārikās* of Gauḍapāda without being struck by the Buddhist character of the leading ideas found in his work. The author seems to have used Buddhist works or sayings and to have adjusted them to his Vedānta design. As Gauḍapāda was the godgrandfather of Śaṅkara this fact is not insignificant. Gauḍapāda has used the very same arguments as the Buddhists to prove the unreality of the external objects of our perception.[61] The external world has no reality, and yet it appears to be. This appearance demands an explanation which is supplied by the *avidyā* of the Vedantins and the *vāsanā* of the Buddhists; it is *avidyā* or *vāsanā* that changes *vijñāna* into the external phenomena even as happens in illusion, mirage, dream etc. As is said in the *Laṅkāvatāra* : "As appears the castle in the sky, or mirage, so does always the visible; but in transcendental wisdom it does not exist".[62] Gauḍapāda supplements :

> As in a dream owing to illusion, the mind moves having the appearance of the duality (the subject and the object), so does it in the waking state owing to illusion, having the appearance of the duality. There is no doubt that in dream the mind through which without-a-second is with the appearance of duality, so is undoubtedly the mind in the waking state with an appearance of duality, though it is without a second.[63] This duality having the subject and the object (the perceiver and the perceptible) is only the vibration of the *citta*. *Citta* has no object, therefore it is said to be always *asaṅga* (i.e. having no attachment or relation to an object).[64]

In Buddhism *citta, manas, vijñāna* and *vijñapti* are synonymous.[65] That the visible universe is the creation of *vijñāna* or *manas* or *citta* is found also in the *Laṅkāvatāra* :

> There is only *citta* and not the visible. The *citta* comes forth in two ways, in the form of the perceiver as well as the perceptible. It is neither eternal nor has it annihilation.[66] The *citta* of men inclines (towards its objects) in the form of the perceiver as well as of the perceptible. There is no characteristic of the visible, as imagined by fools.[67]

As V. Bhattacharya[68] has shown, the first part of Gauḍapāda's *Kārikās* establishes non-dualism of the Māṇḍukya type; the second and the third part begin with the Vedānta and end with Buddhism, while the fourth part confines itself to the exposition of Mahāyāna Buddhism, mainly of the Vijñānavāda and partly also of the Mādhyamika variety. The gist of the fourth part has been given by Macdonell thus:

> It is entitled Alātaśānti, or 'Extinction of the Firebrand (Circle)' so called from an ingenious comparison made to explain how plurality and genesis seem to exist in the world. If a stick which is glowing at one end is waved about, fiery lines or circles are produced without anything being added to or issuing from the single burning point. The fiery line or circle exists only in the consciousness (*vijñāna*). So, too, many phenomena of the world are merely the vibrations of consciousness, which is one.[69]

To quote from the *Kārikās* of Gauḍapāda :

> As the movements of a fire-brand appear to be straight, or crooked, etc., so the vibrations of the *vijñāna* appear as the perceiver and the perceptible.[70] As a fire-brand when it does not move has no appearance (of its being straight, etc.) and (thus) is not born, so when the *vijñāna* does not vibrate it has no appearance (of the perceiver and the perceptible), and (thus) is not born.[71] When a fire-brand moves the appearances are not produced from anything other than that; and when it is at rest they are not in a place other than that, nor do they enter then into that.[72] When the *vijñāna* vibrates the appearance are not produced from anything other than that and when it is at rest they are not in a place other than that, nor do they enter then at that.[73]

The simile of the fire-brand circle may be traced to the *Laṅkāvatāra* and other Buddhist texts as one of the numerous symbols of unreality. It is also of use in the Sautrāntika school to explain the *quomodo* of the 'compound perceptions'. Nevertheless, the main idea of Gauḍapāda is that there is no birth, production, *jāti*, *utpāda*, etc. Causation is impossible since the cause cannot be identical with, or different from, the effect. Gauḍapāda maintains *ajāti* or *anutpatti* (non-origination) and denies *uccheda* (annihilation) with the same emphasis as found in the *Aṣṭasāhasrikā Prajñāpāramitā* or the *Laṅkāvatāra*, and supports his thesis by Nāgārjuna's or Buddhapālita's favourite arguments such as that 'there is no destruction, no birth, no bondage, no endeavour (for liberation), no desiring release, no released'. It is the *śūnyebhya eva śūnyā dharmāḥ prabhavanti dharmebhyaḥ*, from void things, void things are born.[74]

The last but one *Kārikā* of the fourth part of Gauḍapāda's work[75] says that *kramate na hi buddhasya jñānam dharmeṣu tāyinaḥ/sarva dharmās tathā jñānaṃ naitad buddhena bhāṣitam*. According to Vidhusekhara Bhattacharya,[76] it has been repeatedly shown in his *kārikās*[77] that *jñāna* or knowledge is '*asaṅga*, i.e. 'free from attachment', in other words, 'free from any relation to its objects' as the *dharmas* or objects have no reality. Here Gauḍapāda refers to this and concludes showing the supreme truth that according to the Buddha there is neither *jñāna* nor *dharmas* as he has said neither of them : *naitad buddhena bhāṣitam*. What does the last line mean? In one way it can be said that there are only two things—*jñāna* (knowledge) and *jñeya* ('knowable' or *dharmas*, i.e. 'elements of existence', 'objects'). Here we are told that neither of them is said by the Buddha, and this has been confirmed by the Buddhist authors.[78] Let us now try to understand what it signifies. This statement is based on two grounds : (1) *pratyātmadharmatā*, i.e. the nature of the highest truth that is realised in one's own self, and (2) *paurāṇasthiti-dharmatā*, i.e. the nature of the elements of existence that remains from the past. As regards the first it is held that the transcendental reality *(paramārtha)* springs up only as inward conviction (*pratyātmavedya*), it cannot be attained through instruction from others (*aparapratyaya-paropadeśagamya*), for it cannot be expressed by speech or word. So we are told that for the noble the transcendental truth is silence.[79] This is also well known in the Vedānta.[80] Thus the Buddha did not say anything in fact, yet the people according to their own dispositions think that he did so. The *Laṅkāvatāra*[81] categorically says that one should rest on the meaning or the inner implication and not on only letters, for one who rests on letters not only misguides oneself, but also cannot make others understand. The Buddha has said nothing because what he is reported to have said was from the past. Nothing depends on the birth or absence of birth of the Tathāgata. But the true nature of the elements of existence always remains the same. This is meant by the statement that the speech of the Buddha was no speech.

The commentator on the *Kārikās* of Gauḍapāda concluded that while denying the existence of the external world and supposing the sole existence of knowledge the Buddha came very near the essential non-duality. For in *Kārikā* IV.24, in which the view of the opponent is presented, a realist contends that ideas (*prajñapti*) and feeling would not arise if not caused by external things. *Kārikās* IV.25-27 shows the unreasonableness of the aforesaid view of assuming objects existing beside and independent of ideas (*prajñapti, citta*). This refutation, as the commentator tells us, is 'the argument of the Buddhists of the Vijñānavāda school who combat the opinion of the realists (*bāhyārthavādin*), and the Ācārya agrees with him thus far'. Śaṅkara, as we have seen above, in his attempt to refute the Buddhist Vijñānavāda took the position of a realist, ignoring his own Vedantic convictions. But the closeness of Vedānta to the Vijñānavāda had been demonstrated earlier by Vasubandhu[82] according to whose idealism all appearances are but transformations of the principle of consciousness by its inherent movement and none of our cognitions are produced by external objects which to us seem to be existing outside of us and generating our ideas. All that we know as subjective or objective are mere ideation (*vijñapti*) and there is no substantive reality or entities corresponding to them. Perceptual evidence of the existence of the objective world cannot be trusted, because the objects of the visual perception are one as a whole or many as atoms. In the *Triṃsikā* of Vasubandhu and its commentary by Sthiramati it is said that both the soul (or the knower) and all that it knows as subjective ideas or as external objects are but transformations of pure intelligence (*vijñānapariṇāma*). There is neither externability nor subjectivity in pure intelligence, but they are imposed on it. All erroneous impositions imply that there must be some entity which is mistaken as something else. There cannot be erroneous impositions on mere vacuity; so these erroneous impositions of various kinds of external characteristics, self, etc., have to be admitted to have been made on the transformation of pure intelligence. This is very near to the Vedantic approach which is also attested by the commentator on the *Kārikās* of Gauḍapāda. Vasubhandhu holds that pure consciousness (*vijñaptimātratā*) is the ultimate reality. This ultimate consciousness is a permanent entity which by its inherent power (*śakti*) undergoes a threefold transformation as the inherent indeterminate inner changes (*vipāka*) which again produce the two other kinds of transformation as the inner psychoses of mental operations (*manana*) and as perception of the so-called external sensibles (*viṣayavijñapti*). Thus, according to Vasubandhu, the eternal and unchangeable thought substance undergoes by virtue of its inner dynamics three distinct orders of superficial changes. The first represents the basic changes which later determine all subjective and objective possibilities. The second starts the process of the psychosis by the original ignorance and the false attribution of selfhood to non-self-elements and in the third grade we have all the concrete mental and extra-mental facts. Vasubandhu thinks that an awareness has always a twofold relation with the subject as the knower and with the object which is known and even admits the necessity for projecting a psychological objectivity in regard to the function of determinate thought. But this psychological objectivity does not imply ontological objectivity.[83]

The treatise of Vasubandhu starts with the statement that all the world-show is nothing but a manifestation of consciousness. Things that appear as contents of consciousness are absolutely unreal. The whole world of appearance is no more than an illusion. The Vijñānavādins and their other philosophical counterparts counted much on the evidence of the dreams and sense-illusions to prove the general possibility of something intrinsically mental appearing as objective reality. The process of idealism, of attempting to prove the unreality or the illusory character of the material world, began with the Upaniṣads, and was carried to the extreme by the schools of Mahāyāna Buddhism and by Advaita Vedānta. But there were other schools of Indian thought which were not ready to accept the phenomenal world as utterly unreal. For example, the followers of the Mimāṃsa school had a different approach. They held a realistic view of the world as against the Buddhists and the Vedāntists. According to Kumārila, if everything was unreal, then neither the ritual acts nor the fruits thereof—nothing with which the Mīmāṃsa was basically concerned—could have any meaning. Kumārila has devoted two long chapters of his *Ślokavārtika*[84] exclusively to the refutation of the Vijñānavāda (Yogācāra) and Śūnyavāda (Mādhyamika) schools of Buddhism. Since the Buddhists hold that the experiences of heaven, etc. are similar to those of a dream,[85] Kumārila says that it is for the refutation of this theory that the Mīmāṃsakas seek to establish the reality of the external world.[86] The present form of the *Mīmāṃsā Sūtras* does not help us in understanding Buddhism from the Mīmāṃsaka point of view, but in the Bhāṣya of Śabara[87] we find the problem definitely faced in answer to the charges made by the Mādhyamikas. The doctrine of Nāgārjuna and his paradoxes evoked from other schools elaborate replies. The reply of the Mīmāṃsakas, as found in the *Bhāṣya* of Śabara, are mainly concerned with the validity of working perceptions, the form and continuity of ideas and the reality of the external world.

There were commentators on the *Mīmāṃsā Sūtras* older than Śabara whose views and writings were quoted by the latter. The most notable of them was referred to as a certain Vṛttikāra. According to him, what is perceived cannot be a mere idea, nor can the form perceived be a form of knowledge itself. Besides it is useless to argue that all perceptions are like the dream-experiences or the sense illusions, because dreams are eventually negated by the waking experience. Besides, the normal waking perceptions are characterised by greater clearness and distinctness (*suparinišcaya*) as contrasted with dreams and sense illusions. Vṛttikāra's line of argument was followed by Śabara against the idealism of the Buddhists. But Śabara's argument does not show clearly to which of the schools of Buddhism he has given his attention. The argument as a whole falls in two parts, the first dealing with the contention that ideas have no foundation (*nirālambana*) and the second with the view that the external reality is void (*śūnya*), both reminding us of the two celebrated schools of Mahāyāna. The Buddhist views that idea is momentary although it can and does impress its successor, and that there is no substantial reality like the soul, but a never-ceasing series of momentary ideas, impressed on each by the former, giving man the semblances, regarded in ordinary life as the outer world and soul, have been refuted by Kumārila who emphasises the impossibility of the momentary character of ideas, accepts the reality of the universals and regards them as objects of perception. The Buddhists on the other hand hold that specific individuality alone is real and universality is a product of imagination. The Buddhist view has also been criticised by Pārthasārathi who holds that the universal is an object of perception, since whenever we perceive we do it as belonging to a particular class. According to the Mīmāṃsakas, cognition as a quality belongs to the substance called the soul, and refuting the Buddhist conception of the so-called soul as a series of ideas, each of which gathers from its predecessors the impressions of the past, Kumārila asserts that if the law of *karma* is to have any meaning there must be a common substrata and that the Buddhists are not able to account for the law of retribution or possibility of rebirth.[88]

Kumārila holds that the denial of the external world is common to both the Yogācāra and Mādhyamika schools of Buddhism. The former which holds that ideas are without corresponding supports in the external world is called by him Nirālambanavāda realities.[89] The latter denies the reality of ideas also stressing that inasmuch as the external objects are unreal, no cognition based on them can be real. The Buddhists deny the external world on the ground that neither atoms nor their conglomeration are accountable to the senses.[90] Secondly, perception which is supposed to be produced by the contact of the sense organs with a particular object has no real validity since the relation between the objects and sense-organs cannot be established. An assumed contact is present in dream also, and hence it is impossible to differentiate between cognition produced by such contact and not so produced. There can be no specification in regard to falsity, since whatever is a cognition has always been found to be false.[91] While stating the Buddhist view, Kumārila says that the Buddhists accept the self-cognisability (*svāṃśagrāhya*) of cognition and deny the reality of the external objects of perception.[92] The denial of the external world is introduced by them on a twofold consideration, epistemological (*pramāṇāśrita*) and ontological (*arthaparikṣaṇāśrita*). The epistemological argument, again, is twofold. Kumārila calls the first inferential (*anumāṇāśrita*) and characterises the second as being based on an examination of the faculty of perception (*pratyakṣa-śakti-parikṣaṇāśrita*). The ontological argument is primarily a criticism of the atomic hypothesis, perhaps because most of the opponents of idealism share the atomic hypothesis in their exploration of objective reality.

Kumārila argues that the Buddhist emphasis on the total denial of everything that is cognisable is also a denial of the Buddhist theory itself. 'If the cognition is not a real entity, then in what way do you wish to explain it to us? Or how do you yourself comprehend it? If the cognition of the subject and the predicate, as belonging to the speaker or hearer is without corresponding reality, then both of them stand self-contradicted. That is why we do not admit of any such entity as not having a real corresponding object. There is no such thing as 'mere mind' (*vijñānamātra*) without objects, because such a 'mere ideation' cannot be recognised or specified. (Though for us, the Mīmāṃsakas, there is a specification in the shape of the signification of a word, but such cannot be the case with you.) If you seek to prove the fact of being devoid of a substratum, as universal, then you are open to the faults of having your predicate unrecognised, and that of the absence of an example. If by *nirālambanatā* (*vijñaptimātratā*) you mean that consciousness has no substratum in the external world, as the pole and the like, then this would contradict a visible fact. Your argument that there being no sense organs there can be no other ground for holding cognition having a real substratum is baseless. Moreover, when you do not recognise the reality of any external object how could you have such a minor term as 'cognition appears to be external'? You go on asserting the non-difference between the object of cognition and the cognition itself. There is no denotation without connection, and this connection is impossible without some difference between the word and its denotation, which you do not admit and hence make your argument unintelligible. Further it is impossible to impart any instruction with regard to Dharma and the like without ascertaining, in its reality, *dharma* and *adharma* or between teacher and pupil. In fact, your teacher (the Buddha) made this difference, but by denying the difference between the percipient and the perceptive, the cognition and the cognised, you contradict your own Master.[93]

Kumārila holds that the analogy of dream-cognition is untenable and offers a counter-syllogism against the idealistic one : 'All knowledge of the external objects is true because there is no other knowledge negating it, just as the waking experience that negates the dream experience is true.' If all cognitions were false, there could be no idea of comparative reality or unreality of objects, in regard to the sense organ concerned. It also negates the distinction between the 'bound' and the 'liberated' invalidating the concept of any effort in quest of liberation. "If you urge that even waking-cognitions become invalidated by the contrary cognitions of a Yogin, we reply that such Yogic cognition does not belong to any person in this life; and as for those who have reached the state of a Yogin, we do not know what happens to them".[94] It is interesting to note that the so-called Yoga experience was to Kumārila nothing more than sheer fancy. He says that if one system of philosophy can claim support to its conclusions on the strength of the experience of the mystics belonging to that system, others may as well produce their own Yogis and draw support to their conclusions from the mystic experience gained by them. To quote Stcherbatsky :

> The psychology of trance is indeed a characteristic feature of many Indian systems, not Buddhism alone. It appears almost inevitably in that part of every Indian system which is called 'the path' (*mārga*) in which the means of a transition out of the phenomenal world into the Absolute are considered. With the exception of the orthodox Mīmāṃsakas and the materialists, every system is in this part, but not in others, contain a certain amount of mysticism.... However, just as the European mind is not altogether and always free from mysticism so is the Indian mind not at all necessarily subject to it. Not to speak about numerous materialistic doctrines, the orthodox Mīmāṃsakas themselves held about Yoga an opinion which probably represents, just what all of us, so far we are not mystics, think about it, viz. that Yoga is sheer imagination, just as any other ordinary fanaticism.[95]

But to return to Kumārila's refutation of Buddhist idealism. After dealing with the questions in regard to the denial of the external world, the dream and waking cognitions and allied features he proceeds to refute the Buddhist concept of impression (*vāsanā*) basing his arguments chiefly on the doctrine of momentariness which he describes as *ksaṇabhaṅgavāda*. According to Kumārila the theory of pure idealism is inconsistent with the conception of impression and the Buddhists have failed to specify it. There is no evidence for the existence of impression. Even assuming its existence, it may be said that impression is only able to bring about the differentiation of the apprehender (*grāhaka*). But it cannot explain how the differentiation of the apprehended (*grāhya*) should be brought about. Moreover, the theory of momentariness is contradicted by the theory of impression. Since, according to the former theory, the ideas being momentary there cannot be any association of the impressed and the impressor, of the consequent and antecedent moment, there can be no impression thereby. Since the preceding and following moments cannot operate upon one another, causal relation between ideas is impossible. It is only the permanent entities that can be impressed by other entities which are also permanent. Since every moment is subject to total destruction in succession, how can that which is in the course of destruction be impressed by another which too is undergoing destruction? If the property of the previous cognition persists in the subsequent cognition then the former cannot be said to have been destroyed totally. If the potentiality of the idea to subsist even after its destruction is held, its momentary character would disappear and the Buddhist theory of momentariness would be contradicted.[96]

The Śūnyavāda or Mādhymika position has been outlined by Kumārila as follows : It is not a fact that a cognition is able to function only when such objects as the pillar and the like have an existence in the external world. Rather cognition rests only in itself as the object cognised, and not in any extraneous object. The identity of the cogniser (consciousness) and the cognised (the object) should therefore be admitted and the assumption of externality or internality should be rejected. Though the real character of consciousness is naturally pure, there is an agglomeration of diverse dispositions or impressions born of foregoing cognitions. The reciprocal causality of the seed of the cognition and its faculty in the form of dispositions is not faulty just as the reciprocal causality of the seed and the shoot or tree is not faulty. Thus it is reasonable to postulate the form to belong to the self-luminous cognition itself. Without comprehension of the cognition the object cannot be comprehended. Even in the absence of external objects we have a reminiscence of their forms following upon mere ideas thereof. Thus objects are cognised only after the cognitions have been cognised. Objects are not reflected in the cognition. There can be no mutual contact between the object and the cognition. Such a contact is impossible because of the difference of their locations and because of cognition being incorporeal and the object being corporeal. Such contact cannot be said to consist of the coevality of contemporaneity, for that would apply to the whole universe. If such contact could be held to be universal, then taste would come to be perceived by the eye which is impossible. There is no proof of the existence of an external object independent of the idea, while we have the idea independent of the external object. The contact theory can be maintained only with reference to the impressions. In the final analysis, objects do not exist. For example, the terms 'Nakṣatra', 'Tārā', 'Tiṣya' all signify stars. But if the object star had any real existence in the external world then names of such contradictory genders could not be applied to it. And again in the case of a fair girl, the ascetic looks upon her as a disgusting corpse, the licentious man look upon her as an object of pleasure and a dog looks at her as an article of food, which diversity would not be possible if the fair girl had a real existence. Further, with regard to the same object we have multifarious notions. A jar, for example, is conceived as a jar, being earthly, being a substance and being predictable—all these notions appear simultaneously in the observer. But this could never be the case if there existed any such single object as the jar. The object therefore should be traced to the form that an idea takes and never the vice versa. The form of an object depends on the idea, resting on itself, so that the existence of the external object is not possible.[97]

Having thus presented the Śūnyavāda doctrine as *pūrvapakṣa* or the view of the opponent, Kumārila proceeds to refute the same with the following arguments : The Buddhists of the Śūnyavāda school hold that the idea is both the cogniser and the cognised, but they fail to cite any instance wherein such a duplicate character belongs to a single entity. In no case can the same object be both the cogniser and the cognised. No pure idea would be possible if it were to be non-different from the object. The Buddhists assert that both the idea and the object are identical in form. Therefore, when one is comprehended, the other too is comprehended. But this is proved neither by perception nor by inference. The word *jñāna* when applied to the object would be explained as 'that which is known' and when applied to cognition as 'knowledge' or as 'that which cognises everything'. There is no distinct category of *jñāna* which embraces both the cognition and the cognised.

There can be no causal relation between two ideas even when they appear simultaneously. The mere concomitance of the idea and the object cannot be called a causal relation. The Buddhist example of the lamp and the light emitted by it as an example of the simultaneity of the cause and the effect is unsound, because in this case there is a minute point of time intervening between the appearance of lamp and that of the light. The same applies when the Buddhists assert the simultaneity of the two parts of cognition, the comprehender and the comprehended. What is comprehended by memory is a comprehended object mixed with its past character. Dream consciousness is always false because in dreams what is not present is cognised as present. But this is not so in the case of waking state. The theory that cognition cognises itself is not sound. Though the idea illuminates other things, yet for its own illumination it needs something else. Just as the eye does not see itself, so also the idea cannot know itself. There is no such rule that one object must have one and only one form. It is quite possible for a thing to have different forms. Apart from the form of the object there is no recognition of idea. Idea cannot be the object of cognition because it is like a mirage.[98]

But Prabhākara, the second luminary of the Mīmāṃsā school, was greatly influenced by Buddhism. That is why he has been called by Stcherbatsky 'a real bastard son of Buddhism'. He went against the super-realism of his master Kumārila and denied the latter's thesis that time, space, cosmic ether, motion and non-existence were perceived by the senses. The perception of non-existence which according to Prabhākara was simply the perception of an empty space was in line with the Buddhists. He also agreed with them in the most important problem of illusion as due to a non-perception of difference. He admitted introspection (*sva-saṃvedana)* as an essential character of all consciousness. He admitted the fundamental unity of subject, object and the act of cognition (*tripuṭī*, i.e. *pramātṛ-pramāṇa-prameya*) and many other details in which he opposed his master, agreed with the Buddhists, and thus was led to found a new branch of the realistic school. His theory of tripartite perception (*tripuṭipratyakṣa*) holds that in every perception three factors are that of the object, that of knowledge itself which must be held to be self-luminous and that of the knower. Śrīdhara of the Nyāya-Vaiśeṣika school while dealing with Prabhākara's repudiation of non-existence as a reality openly charged him for defending the Mahāyāna Buddhists who held that cognition had no object support. According to Prabhākara when the non-existence of a jar on the ground is experienced, it is nothing but the experience of the vacant condition of its ground, and not that of a positive reality like the non-existence of a jar. Here the jar is not comprehended, but not its non-existence. The Buddhists also endorse the same view. In connection with Prabhākara's explanation of error as being due to non-discrimination between what is perceived and what is remembered (*akhyātivāda*) Jayanta charged him for stealing from Dharmakīrti's works. Prabhākara's view that an illusion is caused by non-comprehension of the difference between what is directly perceived and what is recollected shows that there is an obvious similarity between the analysis of error made by him, which is based on non-comprehension of distinction (*bhedāgraha*) between the two cognitions, and the analysis of percetive judgement made by the Dignāga school. A perceptive judgement refers to the ultimate particular (*svalakṣaṇa*) as grasped by the sensation and also to the generalised form (*sāmānya-lakṣaṇa*). It thus arises owing to the non-comprehension of the distinction between its two parts. This similarity of approach between the Prabhakāra school and the Buddhists did not escape the notice of the Nyāya-Vaiśeṣika thinkers.[99]

Buddhism had its closest relation with the Nyāya-Vaiśeṣika school of philosophy. The purpose of the Nyāya was to examine critically the objects of knowledge through the canons of logical system. Buddhism was also able to build up a complete and comprehensive logical system, and as such there developed between the Buddhists and the Nyāya-Vaiśeṣikas a special relationship. It is difficult to determine the date of Gautama's *Nyāya Sūtras* which must have gone through several redactions before it assumed its present shape. Its essentials must be of an earlier date than Nāgārjuna, although its present form is later than the Mādhyamika system.[100] Jacobi thinks that the *Nyāya Sūtras* could have been redacted between A.D. 200 and 400 while the *Vaiśeṣika Sūtras* somewhat earlier. Unlike the Sāṅkhya, Mīmāṃsa and Vedānta, the actual origin of the Nyāya-Vaiśeṣikas need not be traced to any great antiquity, for there is no tradition like that. According to Jacobi[101] the Buddhist views criticised in the *Nyāya Sūtra* are those of Śūnyavāda advocated by Nāgārjuna and not the Vijñānavāda of Asaṅga and Vasubandhu. Gautama[102] clearly refers to the view of Nāgārjuna and Āryadeva that the effect before production is neither existent, nor non-existent, nor both; to the doctrine of the former that all things have no real existence, possessing merely an illusory interdependence; to the assertion that a substance has no reality independent of its qualities nor the whole apart from its part; to the denial of the doctrine of atoms; and to the belief that means of proof and their objects are no more that a dream or a mirage, as well as to the less distinctive Buddhist doctrines as the momentary character of existence and the defilements. But a closer inspection seems to reveal that Vijñānavāda is also criticised as is indicated by the categorical statement of Vācaspati Miśra that one passage of the *Sūtra*[103] is directed against the Yogācāra doctrine which accepted ideas alone as real.

In the classic commentary of Vātsyāyana on the *Nyāya Sūtra* the Nyāya attitude towards Buddhism is defined in more clear terms. The Buddhists hold that the preceding cause-moment is annihilated totally without leaving any residue to be transferred to the effect-moment which comes into existence as an altogether new entity. In other words, the Buddhists contend that if the cause is destroyed before the effect comes into existence, it will mean that the effect is produced from the destruction of the cause, that is, from the void. Vātsyāyana refutes this argument saying that when the old arrangement of parts is disturbed and, consequently, the cause-substance which was born of that arrangement disappears, the effect is produced from the new arrangement of parts which comes into being and not from the void.[104] It is important to note that according to this early Nyāya-Vaiśeṣika theory, as interpreted by Vātsyāyana, the effect is not merely a new arrangement of parts but a new substance produced by that new arrangement. The cause-substance is destroyed according to this theory as well. The difference between the two is this that while according to the Buddhists the cause is wholly destroyed without leaving any residue or any kind of continuity, according to the early Nyāya-Vaiśeṣikas although the cause is destroyed, it leaves its part behind. It is not a case of destruction without any kind of continuity. The Mādhyamika school of Buddhism holds that just as an object seen in a dream, magic and mirage are not real though we believe in them, so also neither is our knowledge nor its object real. Vātsyāyana tries to refute this approach saying that if there is proof that nothing exists then this proof sublates its own existence. If there is no proof how can it be established that nothing exists? If it is to be assumed without proof, then the opposite contention is at least legitimate. As regards the argument from the dream state, it is pointed out that no argument is adduced by the nihilists to show that the knowledge we have is really comparable to that of a dream in place of that of our waking experience, nor again it is shown that our dream experience is of non-existing things. In addition Vātsyāyana says that the only ground on which it can be taken that things seen in a dream do not really exist is that they are seen no more in the waking state, which implies that our waking experience is real.

This paved the way for an intellectual campaign of the Nyāya-Vaiśeṣikas against Buddhism and vice versa which lasted for so many centuries. Before dealing with the currents and crosscurrents of this long drawn ideological combat it is necessary to present the main features of the Nyāya Vaiśeṣika approach to the Buddhist challenge. Regarding the real nature of perception as the source of knowledge logicians of the Buddhist and Nyāya school differ widely. The Buddhist views that all knowledge of substances, qualities and actions is false, that the outer objects are momentary and so cannot be known, and that all knowledge is purely mental—are all sharply criticised by Vātsyāyana and other exponents of the Nyāya school who insisted on a realistic structure based on common sense or rather common experience. Starting from the fundamental idea that whatever we experience directly must have an external existence, the Nyāya-Vaiśeṣikas laid down a basic guiding principle that 'experience is the sole criterion of our acceptance of the reality of external objects'. The Buddhist view that all universals are imagined since specific individuals alone exist is rejected by the Naiyāyikas who hold that universals are real as the individuals in which they submit by the relation of inherence. The Nyāya view of *vyāpti* assumes that the universals are factors of reality while the Buddhists regard universal propositions as ideal constructions and not real relations. As regards the doctrine of causation the Nyāya school holds that an effect has nothing in common with the cause and what we call effect is actually a new creation. Every effect thus requires to be effected by an efficient cause, a God. Following almost the same line, the absence of any agreement between cause and effect, the Buddhists, according to their opponents, came to an opposite conclusion that there are no causes; there are only effects coming out from nothing; all phenomena are born out of nothing and are born only for a moment during which they are perceived. The Mādhyamika theory that there is no present time apart from the past and future is rejected by Vātsyāyana who holds that time or *kāla* is not manifested by space but by action. The past and future are devoid of action, but the present apprehends the actual existing connection of the object and the action.[105] He criticises the idea of momentariness on the ground that we cannot be certain that an entity will be replaced by another after the lapse of a moment, and there must be a connecting link between the origination of an entity and its cessation. Momentariness is not perceived in stones, etc.[106] The doctrine of impermanence does not hold good in the case of atoms, time, space, etc. which are neither produced nor destroyed. The Nyāya accepts the metaphysics of the Vaiśesika and regards the world of nature as a composite of eternal, unalterable, causeless atoms existing independently of our thoughts. While the Vaiśeṣikas partially accept the Buddhist view of the sources of knowledge, perception and inference, they argue that souls and substances are real entities. The atomic theory of the Vaiśeṣikas has something in common with that of the Sarvāstivāda schools of Buddhism, but they differ as regards the characteristics of the atoms and the efficient cause controlling them.

Probably at a time after the production of Vātsyāyana's commentary on the *Nyāya Sūtra* need was felt to combat the further development of the nihilism of Nāgārjuna which in the hands of Asaṅga and Vasubandhu led to the doctrine of Vijñānavāda or Yogācāra which denied absolutely the reality of the external things and accepted as the only reality our ideas or mental acts. In their view therefore external things were merely products of our consciousness due to the ideas existing independently of objects. A modified version of this doctrine was presented by Dignāga (fifth century A.D.) who accepted the challenge of Vātsyāyana and criticised his interpretation from the Buddhist point of view. Dignāga is credited to have given logic a well defined form separating it from metaphysics and dialectics. He also evolved a special theory of sense perception based on a strict differentiation of impressions made by the objects from the subjective facts of consciousness and introduced a new doctrine of inference along with a special classification of logical fallacies. He revolutionised Indian philosophy by introducing into it the theory of radical distinction between two mutually exclusive sources of knowledge—'direct sense-apprehension' (*grahaṇa*) and 'intellect' or 'thought' (*vikalpa, adhyavasāya*)—which may be compared to the 'sensibility' and 'understanding' of Kant. Although in the details of their metaphysical analysis Dignāga and Kant naturally differ, the similarities between them also cannot be overlooked. In his principal work entitled *Pramāṇasamuccaya* Dignāga laid down the foundation of his 'realistic-idealistic' epistemology and threw a challenge to the realism of the orthodox schools, especially the early Nyāya-Vaiśeṣika school represented by the naive realism of Vātsyāyana.[107] Dignāga is known to have been a champion of the Vijñānavāda or Yogācāra idealism but he could not give up his original Śarvāstivādin realistic background and that is why his views are described as realist-idealist. He holds that the external reality, which is in the form of unique particulars (*sva-lakṣaṇas*), has no extension in terms of space and no duration in terms of time. It is devoid of all attributes, determinations or relations. The universal (*sāmānya lakṣaṇa*) is only a generalised from imposed by our mind on the data (*sva-lakṣanas* or unique particulars) grasped in pure sensation. All our conscious knowledge is restricted to the generalised form which is the work of intellect. It never touches the reality which is transcendent. The so-called determinate perception (*savikalpa-pratyakṣa*) of the Nyāya-Vaiśeṣikas is thus for Dignāga only a pseudo-perception, because it comprehends a generalised form (which is merely a mental factor) as an external real object. The essence of the doctrine of Dignāga was the exposition of a theory of logic, in modification of the established doctrine of Nyāya, to harmonise with the fundamental idealism of the Vijñānavāda school of Buddhism which held that while there were no realities external to the mind, nevertheless thought itself was not unreal. This thought for them assumed two forms : consciousness proper (*ālaya-vijñāna*) which lasts until the individual reaches salvation and which serves in lieu of the substantial soul, and the thoughts of the individual about things (*pravṛtti-vijñāna*). According to Keith,[108] Dignāga's logic went beyond this standpoint. His doctrine of perception reveals elements which are not always in harmony with the Vijñānavāda view of reality. Whereas on a strict idealistic theory in the last analysis perception should not have remained distinct from other mental processes, Dignāga appears to have held the view that in it man comes into contact with a reality which though lasting but an instant (*kṣaṇa*) is real (*vastu, paramārthasat*), but because of its momentary character never knowable. For Dignāga, therefore, the whole of knowledge, despite its contact at one point with an unknowable reality, is made up of ideas involved in both perception and inference. These ideas are the product of our mental activity and are not created by any external cause. The ideas obey law of connection not imposed by reality, but by the action of our own thought and thus *a priori* in character. The nature of these laws is further made explicit by the division of syllogism on the basis of the relations of identity, cause and negation.

The views of Dignāga were subjected to a sharp criticism by Uddyotakara of the Nyāya-Vaiśeṣika school (sixth century A.D.) whose *Nyāya Vārtika*[109] is a defence of Vātsyāyana against the onslaughts of Dignāga, which was held as a great event in Subandhu's *Vāsavadattā*.[110] Uddyotakara was a writer imbibed with a strong fighting temper and a most voluble style. He did not at all mind distorting the opinion of his adversary and answering him by some bluffing sophistry. Uddyotakara himself is silent as to the name of the logician against whom his polemic is directed, but the omission is supplied by his commentator Vācaspati Miśra. According to the Nyāya-Vaiśeṣikas, there are two chief or unifying principles—the principles of the whole—(*avayavin*) and that of the Universal (*samanya*)—both being objectively real. While the former is mainly ontological, the latter covers a wider aspect and as such has been the target of extensive Buddhist attack. The Buddhists hold that the external objective world consists of discrete and detached bits of reality called moments (*kṣaṇas*). Their synthesis exists only in our thought, and hence it has no objective reality. On the other hand Nyāya-Vaiśeṣikas hold that the universals residing in particulars have their independent reality. External objects exist independently of their cognition. A defence of the Nyāya-Vaiśeṣika theory of the Universal and refutation of the theory of *apoha*, the Buddhist counterpart of the Universal, was emphatically advanced by Uddyotakara who initiated the theory that every object in a determinate perception must appear as qualified by its universal, but since a qualified comprehension (*viśiṣṭa pratīti*) is not possible without a previous knowledge of the qualification, the determinate (*savikalpa*) perception should be preceded by an indeterminate (*nirvikalpa*) perception in which there is the comprehension of an object (e.g. jar) and its universal (e.g. jar-ness) as unrelated to each other.[111] While the Nyāya-Vaiśeṣikas emphatically maintain that determinate perception is a valid perception, and the world presented by it is not a mental construction, but a real objective world, the Buddhists in general and Dignāga in particular hold it as a pseudo-perception. To Dignāga perception always means indeterminate perception which grasps the external reals, the particulars (*svalakṣaṇas*), while the universals (*sāmānya-lakṣaṇas*) are comprehended by inference. His insistence only on two kinds of *pramāṇas* (means of knowledge)—perception and inference—has not become acceptable to Uddyotakara who says: 'we do not accept that there are only two *pramāṇas*, or that there are only two kinds of objects; nor do we accept the view that there is no intermixture of prāmaṇas'. As we have seen, according to Dignāga, a particular can be grasped by perception and not by inference while a universal can be grasped by inference and not by perception. Uddyotakara contradicts it saying that the same object may be comprehended by any means of knowledge. 'We do not hold that an object is comprehended by inference and other *prāmaṇas* in the same way as it is comprehended by perception. By perception it is comprehended through sense-contact; by inference without sense-contact; by *upamāna-pramāṇa* the relation of a word with the object denoted by it is comprehended; and by *śabda-pramāṇa*, the comprehension is by means of words'.[112]

It should be pointed out in this connection that originally the terms *sāmānya* and *viśeṣa* were used by the Nyāya-Vaiśesikas to denote two aspects of an object, the former in the sense of the universal and the latter in that of an individual object in which the universal resided. From an historical point of view, so far as the Vaiśeṣika literature goes, Praśastapāda was the first to hold *sāmānya* to be objectively real eternal. As time went on, general attributes like *dravyatva* (substance-ness) etc., were conceived as only *sāmānyas* which perform both the functions of causing the idea of commonness as well as that of differentiation. It was supposed that they were *sāmānyas* primarily, but they were also called *viśeṣas* in a secondary sense. Originally *viśeṣa* denoted that aspect of an object which caused the notion of its exclusion or differentiation from other objects. When that function was assigned to *sāmānya*, the term *viśeṣa* was restricted to the sense of ultimate particulars residing in atoms and other eternal substances. With the establishment in course of time of the objective reality of the universal, it was not only held to be inferable but also directly perceptible. This viewpoint was naturally opposed by the Buddhists. The view that every attribute which causes the notion of commonness should be considered an objectively real universal became popular among the Nyāya-Vaiśeṣikas, though Uddyotakara had some reservation in this respect.[113] He does not expressly say that a universal is omnipresent or all-pervasive but holds that as a matter of fact it resides only in all particulars.[114] The Buddhist counter-argument is that the universal cannot subsist in its particulars by its parts; nor can it subsist in its parts in entirety; both the positions are impossible. The Nyāya-Vaiśeṣika position with regard to the nature of the universal is that it is one, but it subsists in many. The Buddhist opponent retorts in this connection that if the universal subsists in every individual in entirety, then it will be, like an individual, a different entity in each case and not 'one' common entity residing in 'many' individuals. Again, if it subsists in individual by parts, it will be a case of 'many' subsisting in 'many'. Thus in no case is there a common universal. Meeting this objection Uddyotakara says that the words 'in entirety' or 'by parts' are not applicable in the case of the universal. There can be no such alternatives whether 'cowness' subsists in every individual cow either in its entirety or by parts. The Buddhist counter argument is that there can be no universal like 'cowness' because it can subsist neither in a cow nor in a non-cow. In the former case the cow is already a cow without the subsistence of 'cowness' in it, and therefore the universal is not needed. In the latter case, if it subsists in a non-cow, even a horse may be viewed as that. Therefore 'cowness' cannot be the cause of a common notion. Uddyotakara replies that the alternatives are not valid since prior to the subsistence of 'cowness', an individual is neither a cow nor a non-cow. Both of these are qualified notions which are not possible without the association of the qualifier, that is 'cowness'. An individual cow itself does not exist prior to its association with 'cowness'. A non-existent object cannot be designed as a cow or a non-cow.

Uddyotakara's polemics are sharper in his defence of the Nyāya-Vaiśeṣika's atomism. The Buddhists split reality as conceived by them into *kṣaṇas* or moments—not the smallest unit of time but that of the ultimate reals—coming in continuous succession. According to the Nyāya-Vaiśeṣikas, the world of external objects is made up of the smallest particles called atoms which are the ultimate reals. While the Buddhists do not believe in any principle of synthesis in the external world, the Nyāya-Vaiśeṣikas offer two synthetic principles, namely, 'universal' (*sāmānya* or *jāti*) and 'substance' (*dravya*). We have already had the occasion to see how the former principle was vehemently assailed by the Buddhists of the Dignāga school. They also rejected the second principle saying that there is no separate substance apart from the qualities which alone are presented to us by our senses.[115] The evidence of common experience in favour of the Buddhists appears to be so strong that in the first round Uddyotakara had to accept defeat, tacitly admitting that a substance apart from its qualities cannot be perceived. While the Buddhists bank on the analysis of an experience, the Nyāya-Vaiśeṣikas count only on its external implications. Uddyotakara says that our experience that *sandal* has white colour, pungent taste, etc. shows that qualities like colour, etc. are different from the substance called *sandal*.[116] But when the Buddhists say that there is no separate substance apart from qualities, they mean that colour, etc. are ultimate particulars and that they are real by themselves, there being no substance as their substratum.[117] Uddyotakara holds that a single object is cognised by seeing and touching, and therefore that object must be accepted as one substance as distinguished from the qualities of which it is a common substratum. As to the Buddhist suggestion that qualities arranged in different forms cause merely the notion of substance and not the substance itself, he says that the arrangement itself implies that such forms must exist somewhere as real. If different arrangements are identical with the qualities they cannot account for the difference in cognition. And if different arrangements are different from the qualities it tantamounts to the acceptance of a separate substance by another name. Contradicting the Buddhist position that a substance is not cognised when its qualities are not cognised, Uddyotakara cites the illustration of a white crystal appearing as blue owing to its proximity of a blue object and asserts that though its white colour is not cognised, there is no difficulty in cognising the crystal itself.[118]

The main concept of the Nyāya-Vaiśeṣika atomism is that the atoms of the substances of earth, water, light and air are eternal while the composites made of these are non-eternal. Since atoms are not perceptible their existence is known by inference. Whatever is produced must be made up of parts. Now if we go on separating the parts of a composite thing, we shall pass from larger to smaller, from smaller to still smaller, and from these to the smallest parts which cannot be further divided in any way. These indivisible and minute parts, called atoms, can neither be produced nor be destroyed. Thus being neither produced nor destroyed the atoms are eternal. Objections to this atomic theory came mainly from two sources, namely, the Vedantists and the Buddhists, though the Vaibhāṣika and Sautrāntika schools of the latter contributed to some forms of atomism. The main Buddhist approach in relation to the Nyāya-Vaiśeṣika atomism is that the splitting and further splitting of the atoms will end in annihilation with the disappearance of the last parts. This negates the Nyāya-Vaiśeṣika viewpoint that the smallest parts cannot be further divided by any means. On this point Uddyotakara argues that splitting (*vibhāga*) is a quality which cannot take place without a substratum, i.e. a substance to be split. There cannot be any disconnection (*vibhāga*) without 'something to be disconnected' (*vibhajyamāna*). The Buddhists refuse to accept the Nyāya-Vaiśeṣika stand that splitting of a material object end on reaching a partless atom and hold that an atom must be made up of parts because it has a corporeal form (*mūrti*). Uddyotakara replies that the assertion that parts of the atom are also corporeal but without further parts cannot stand because parts of atom should then also be corporeal and have further parts. He says that if according to the Buddhist theory a corporeal form consists only of colour etc., then the atom cannot possess that kind of corporeal form. Similarly, he says, the argument put forward by the Buddhists (especially Vasubandhu) that an atom is made up of parts because of its connections with other atoms is untenable. Owing to the fact that although the connections of other atoms with the central atom may have the same substratum, the other atoms (six on the six sides of the central one) cannot have the same substratum. No two material substances cannot subsist in the same substratum by inherent relation. Against the Buddhist argument that the atoms are made up of parts because they have a particular shape or form Uddyotakara says that the shape or form does not mean anything different from the parts.[119]

Before dealing with the next round of controversy between Buddhists and the Nyāya-Vaiśeṣikas we ought to say something about the atomism of the Buddhist Vaibhāṣika and Sautrāntika schools which hold a realistic view of the universe maintaining that everything, external as well as internal, is real. Both these schools belong to the Sarvāstivāda branch of Buddhism and they do not differ very much in regard to the basic viewpoints. They admit the reality of the external world and the atomic theory. Both of the schools do not admit of double or triple atoms, though they allow indefinite aggregations. The Sautrāntikas, while insisting on the ideality of the phenomenal objects, accept the independence of the thing-in-itself. They admit the extra-mental existence of the world, but according to them, there is no direct perception of the external objects. They are only known by inference. The Vaibhāṣikas on the other hand appeal to experience by which they mean knowledge produced by direct contact with the object. The external world is open to perception. The substance of things has a permanent existence. The permanent substances are not the transitory phenomena, but the elements which underlie them, though no definite account is given of the relation between the underlying reality and the phenomental manifestations. Objects are distinguished as *bāhya* (external) and *abhyantara* (internal), the former consisting of *bhūta* (elements) and *bhautika* (objects belonging to the experience) and the latter of *citta* (intelligence) and *caitta* (those belonging to intelligence). There are only four elements : earth, water, fire and air. Space or Ākāśā is a non-composite element, free from all distinction and limit, eternal and all-prevading positive substance. All these to a certain extent remind us of the Nyāya-Vaiśeṣikas. The atoms have six sides and can be perceived in a mass though we cannot see them singly. According to Vasubandhu, it is the smallest particle of *rūpa*, indivisible, unanalysable, inaudible, unstable and intangile. The atoms are the same in all the elements possessing the qualities of earth, water, fire and air. The Jains also have an atomic theory according to which the number of the atoms is infinite and their combination is revealed in the *pariṇāma* or transformation into the being of an object. The aggregates come about through different processes of amalgamation. The atoms are arranged in two or in three dimensional order in the circular, orbicular, triangular and square formations, but in the case of linear formation they are arranged in a single dimensional order. There are eight kinds of combination through which substances are shaped. The qualities of touch, smell, taste or colour which characterise the material substance are possessed by the atoms and their compounds. Sound along with light, heat, shadow, darkness, union, disunion, fineness, grossness, shape, etc. are produced by accidental modifications of matter and hence constituted by the atoms. The difference between the Jain and the Nyāya-Vaiśeṣika viewpoints regarding atomism may be summarised as follows. According to the Jains the atoms are all of the same kind while the Nyāya-Vaiśeṣikas hold that they are different in kind. The five substances of ether, time, space, mind and soul do not come within the purview of the atomic theory of the Nyāya-Vaiśeṣikas, but the Jain scheme is more comprehensive which includes many other categories. The Jains as well as the Vaibhāṣikas and Sautrāntikas also differ from the Nyāya-Vaiśeṣikas on the point that all composite objects of the world, framed by the combination of atoms, must have an intelligent maker.

The position of the Nyāya-Vaiśeṣikas as established by Uddyotakara was assailed by Dharmakīrti (seventh century A.D.) who had written seven logical treatises which became the fundamental writing for the study of Buddhist logic. In the Tibetan Buddhist tradition, as has been preserved by Bu-ston, it is said that among his seven works, the *Pramāṇavārtika* is the chief one containing the body of the system. The remaining six are its six feet. The *Pramāṇavārtika* consists of four chapters dealing with inference, validity of knowledge, sense perception and syllogism respectively. It is written in mnemonic verse and contains about 2000 stanzas. The next work *Pramāṇa-viniścaya* is an abridgement of the first. It is written in stanzas and prose. More than the half of the stanzas are borrowed from the principal work. The *Nyāyabindu* is a further abridgement of the same subject which with the commentary of Dharmottara is extant in original Sanskrit and one of our principal sources of information of the school of Dignāga. Another commentary on it was made by Vinītadeva which survives in its Tibetan translation.[120] In the prefatory sentence of his *Nyāyabindu* Dharmakīrti insists on right knowledge—knowledge 'which is not contradicted' (*avisamvādaka*) and 'non-erroneous' (*abhrānta*). His purpose, as stated by his commentators, is to remove misconceptions and contradictory notions (*vipratipatti*) pertaining to different systems of thought, but his views are mostly directed against those of the Nyāya-Vaiśesikas, and especially against those of Uddyotakara.

According to Dharmakīrti, right knowledge is of two kinds—perceptive and inferential. Perceptive knowledge is non-constructive and non-illusive cognition. In other words, perception is that knowledge which is free from 'construction' (*kalpanāpodha*) and 'illusion' (*abhrānta*). The later condition, namely, 'non-illusive' is an addition to Dignāga's definition of right knowledge. Perception is to be classified under four heads, namely, sense-produced (*indriyajñāna*), mentally-produced (*mānasa*), self-cognised (*ātmasaṃvedana*) and intuition of the saints (*yogijñāna*). The object of perception is the 'unique particular' (*svalakṣaṇa*) which means an entity or essence that is unique, a thing-in-itself, shared by nothing else. This unique particular is nothing but the object which produces difference in the reflex relating to a piece of knowledge. As the object is near or remote, it produces a different mental image, making it either vivid or dim. This 'unique particular' is essentially real because of its efficiency, i.e. capability of producing an action in respect of an object. Against those who assume a difference between cognition and its result Dharmakīrti says that the piece of perceptual knowledge alone is the effect produced by the instrument of valid cognition and there is no other effect over and above that piece of perceptual knowledge. There is no difference between the act of perception and the percept. If asked, in what sense then is it a result, the answer is that it has the form of distinct cognition. The result of cognising is but cognition itself. The opponent's next question is : If perception alone is to constitute the effect, what then is actually to be regarded as the instrument of valid cognition? In reply Dharmakīrti says that the instrumentality of a perception consists in the coordination between the constructed image and its real object.

According to Dharmakīrti, the universal is the other kind of object belonging to the province of inference which is of two kinds—*svārtha* (for one's own sake) and *parārtha* (for the sake of others). Inference for one's own sake (*svārtha*) is a cognition produced through a mark (*liṅga*) having three characteristics (*trairūpa*)—its existence in the object cognised by inference; its presence only in similar (*sapakṣa*) cases; and its absolute absence in dissimilar cases. An inferrable entity means a substratum (*dharmin*)—the property of which is sought to be known. There are only three varieties of the three-aspected mark—non-apprehension (*anupalabdhi*), identity (*svabhāva*) and causation (*kārya*).[121] The first is that which does not fulfil the conditions of cognisability; the second is the reason for deducing a property in which the subject alone is sufficient for the deduction; and the third is reason based on causation. While the first aspect establishes negation (*pratiṣedha*) the second and third establish a positive entity (*vastu*). To the opponent's question : How can only two forms of reason prove positive entities? The answer is that the thing offered as the mark can establish the existence of the thing sought to be inferred, when it is found that the two are connected with each other by their own nature. The mark is sometimes identical in nature with the inferrable entity itself; again sometimes it originates from the inferrable entity. Hence it is to be admitted that the invariable connection is established through identity and causation, and not otherwise. As regards the principle of negative judgement various forms of non-apprehension have been mentioned by Dharmakīrti as the cause of successful behaviour in respect of an absence. But all these are to be understood virtually as some particular forms of the non-apprehension of the perceptible because the absence of an effect etc., can be proved only when there is non-apprehension of the same etc., which fulfil the conditions of cognisability, and not otherwise.

Dharmakīrti's *parārthānumana* (syllogism, inference for others) was in principle challenging to the realist schools. For example, as against the Nyāya-Vaiśeṣika theory that concomitance between smoke and fire is established by observing their association in many instances and by the knowledge that the association is not due to some adventitious cause (*upādhi*), Dharmakīrti says that concomitance between the object to be inferred (*sādhya*, e.g. fire) and the inferential mark (*sādhana*, e.g. smoke) is based on the relation between cause and effect or that by identity, and not on the observation of the inferential mark (smoke) as associated with the object to be inferred (fire), and non-existence of the former in the absence of the latter. Apart from outlining the definitions and varieties of syllogism, the principal logical topics dealt with by him are : the method of agreement conducive to negative deduction; analytical deductions which are according to him deductions of coexistence; syllogism of causality in the method of agreement; deduction by the method of difference; whether causation is a necessary member of the syllogism; definition of a thesis, logical fallacies, unreal reason, reason contradicting an admitted principle; what fallacy ensues when both aspects of the reason are uncertain, the counterbalanced reason, the import of examples, positive and negative examples of fallacy, and refutation. According to Dharmakīrti a proper syllogism should consist in communicating the three aspects of the middle term when the reason is set out in words to produce a conviction in others.

The philosophical position of Dharmakīrti is that of an idealist, but it was not the idealism of the Vijñānavāda or of the early Yogācāras. It is indeed difficult to find out his sectarian affiliation. M. Hiriyanna held that both Dignāga and Dharmakīrti were exponents of the Vaibhāṣika views.[122] S.N. Dasgupta also held a similar view.[123] Stcherbatsky on the basis of their theory of transcendental idealism, held that they belonged to a hybrid school of the Sautrāntika-Yogācāras.[124] It is interesting to note that Dharmakīrti never contributed to the theory of *ālayavijñāna* or 'store-house-consciousness'. "The *Pramāṇavārtika* never mentions *ālayavijñāna* doctrine and there is evidence enough to maintain that Dharmakīrti rejected it as a soul-in-disguise".[125] It is to be mentioned in this connection that the original Buddhist doctrine of no-soul found a new dimension in the epistemology of Dignāga and Dharmakīrti. Śrīdhara[126] has quoted a verse from Dharmakīrti's *Pramāṇavārtika* which says that if the theory of self or soul be accepted, there arises the idea of the other and their difference causes attachment and hatred. On the one hand he believed in the reality of external objects on logical grounds and on the other he insisted on the doctrine of *sva-saṃvedana* self-consciousness. The former is suggestive of his Sautrāntika leanings and the latter is that of his Yogācāra-Vijñānavāda affiliation. In the *Pramāṇavārtika* he says that if thought reflects external object then it should be held to have the form of that object. But the external object will necessarily vanish leaving only the concept of its form, since it is never known by itself.[127] Though there is no diversity, the intellect, owing to illusory perceptions, appears to possess a duality of cognition. Perception of an object is impossible if perception itself is unperceived.[128] In the *Nyāyabindu* he states clearly that every conscious and every mental phenomenon are self-conscious. Dharmottara explains this by saying that what we experience is nothing but knowledge. Self-consciousness is essentially a case of knowledge. It makes present to us our own self. It is neither a construction nor an illusion and therefore it is direct knowledge.

Dharmakīrti was followed by his commentators Dharmottara and Vinītadeva and also by Śāntarakṣita, Kamalaśīla and a host of others. On the Nyāya-Vaiśeṣika side Uddyotakara was followed by Vācaspatimiśra, Jayanta, Udayana and Śrīdhara during the ninth and tenth centuries. Vācaspatimiśra, the doyen of logicians, laid the Nyāya-Vaiśeṣika realism on a firm foundation in his *Nyāyavārtikatātparyaṭīkā*. He wrote treatises on all the principal systems of orthodox philosophy. Although he has not written any independent work on Buddhism, his exposition of various Buddhist theories scattered over his works is meticulously faithful and unsurpassed in lucidity. Vācaspatimiśra's insistence on reason rather than on argument for argument's sake may be illustrated with reference on his observation that Uddyotakara's refutation of the Buddhist view that substance does not exist apart from qualities is over-simplified, one-sided and unfair. His scrupulous regard for a faithful representation of the views of the opponent may be exemplified by his presentation of the Buddhist view of perception, as outlined by Dignāga and Dharmakīrti. He says that the main Buddhist argument against determinate perception is that it cannot represent a proper sense-cognition, because it contains an image (*pratibhāṣa*) which can be conveyed through verbal expression (*abhilāpa*). But a piece of cognition originating through the function of a sense-organ and an object does not have the power of uniting the image of the object to a verbal expression. The verbal expressions or words are not contained in the objects, nor are they identical with the objects themselves. An object, for instance, may be endowed with both colour and taste. But its visual perception of the colour can never reveal its taste also. Secondly, if it were possible to express verbally what is exactly perceived one would have known the heat of fire, as one knows it through perception, simply from the words 'fire is hot'. Thirdly, a determinate perception would be a form of 'qualified cognition' (*viśiṣṭa-jñāna*) in which the object (i.e. the unique particular) would be revealed as qualified by an attribute which is the universal. In other words, the object would be qualified (*viśeṣya*) and the universal would be the qualifier (*viśeṣaṇa*). A qualified cognition can be produced only after one has properly understood the relation between the qualifier and the qualified and the 'normal order of things' (*laukika-sthiti*). It is not possible for the sense to perform all such functions merely through its contact with the object. Perception is defined by the Nyāya-Vaiśeṣikas as knowledge resulting from sense-object contact. But there is neither any positive concomitance (*anvaya*) nor any negative concomitance (*vyatireka*) between such a contact and construction. Had the sense-object contact been really the cause of construction, it would have produced the element of construction at the very first moment, and not after the term referring to the object has been remembered. If it is admitted that in the case of determinate perception the sense-cognition stands in need of not only a sense-object contact but also a coalescing with the recollected verbal expression determinate perception itself would be an impossibility.[129]

Vācaspatimiśra's exposition of the Buddhist doctrine of perception is divided into two parts. In the first part a Buddhist leads and makes a statement while the Nyāya-Vaiśeṣika makes passing remarks and is occasionally snubbed by his opponent who frequently quotes Dharmakīrti. In the second part they interchange their functions and the Nyāya-Vaiśeṣika answers all the arguments of the Buddhist and makes a final conclusion. As for the Buddhist objection that there is a contradiction in determinate perception being produced by the power of an object and being an image capable of a relation with verbal expression,

Vācaspatimiśra submits that the contradiction would be there if the unique particular alone were a reality. But it is not so. The object is permanent and is qualified by universals, etc., which are also ultimate realities, and it is capable of relation with verbal expression. There is thus no contradiction in it. Regarding the Buddhist objection to the apparent identity between a word and the object denoted by it, Vācaṣpatimiśra says that an object is not presented by a determinate cognition as identical with the word; but the word, while remaining aloof, indicates the object by means of the relation in the form of the power of the word to denote an object. The recollection of the name of an object does not adulterate perception. It does not produce a break in the operation of the sense and of the external object. The sensory stimulus is lodged in the centre of all the factors which participate in the production of a full percept, and memory plays an important part among them. The present is related to the past and this relation is a reality, and as such the past also must be a reality. Although the past state of an object may not be grasped by the sense, yet that state is comprehended by the perceptive knowledge produced by the sense with the aid of memory or impressions. The qualified percepts are sense perceptions because they are produced by a sensory stimulus with which they are invariably concomitant. The Buddhist view that the attributes are not something apart from substance of a thing constructed as something by productive imagination (suggestive of the fact that synthetic images are not due to a stimulus coming from an object but to imagination) has been contradicted by Vācaspatimiśra who establishes that the attributes and the universals are separate realities connected with the substance of a thing by inherence.

Vācaspatimiśra and also Jayanta and Śrīdhara of the Nyāya-Vaiśeṣika school have refuted the Buddhist theory of evanescence.[130] That reality is evanescent which was an original and basic doctrine of Buddhism, was revived by the exponents of the Dignāga school, especially by Śāntarakṣita (eighth century) in his *Tattvasaṃgraha* and Ratnakīrti in his *Kṣaṇabhaṅgasiddhi*. The Buddhist view is that the same thing cannot be the abode of contradictory attributes at the same time. For example, one thing cannot be hot and cold at the same moment. Existence at one moment implies non-existence at any other moment. All reality is therefore momentary, i.e. evanescent by its very nature. A durable entity cannot be existent because it cannot be the cause of anything. An efficient action can be produced only in two ways, either in succession or simultaneously. Both the alternatives are impossible if the reality of existence which produces efficient action is assumed to have a permanent or enduring nature. Because, if a permanent object is capable of producing an efficient action, it must produce it at once and not in successive stages. If it be said that a permanent or enduring cause does not produce its effects at once because it has to wait for accessories (e.g. earth, water, light, etc. in the case of a seed to produce a sprout) which appear only in successive stages, the question arises whether or not such accessories produce some addition or 'excellence'. If not, the accessories would be useless. But if they do, the question is whether the excellence is different from the cause or is identical with it. If the former approach be taken into account, then 'excellence' alone should be regarded as the cause and the original cause becomes redundant. If, on the other hand, the 'excellence' produced by the accessories is regarded as identical with the cause, it will only mean that the cause remains what it was before, and therefore it should have produced its effect at the very first moment of its existence and not in successive stages. Thus, according to the Buddhist view, the principal cause and its accessories come into existence at one and the same moment, and beyond that moment they do not exist. An enduring object cannot produce its effect by succession; it cannot produce it simultaneously either. And as such the permanent or enduring object must be held as devoid of existence. Evanescence is also proved from the destructibility of objects. The destruction of an object means the imperceptible decay which is supposed to be going on every moment of its existence.

It is interesting to note that the aforesaid account of the Buddhist doctrine of evanescence, as submitted by the Nyāya-Vaiśeṣika writers, is strictly in accordance with the theoretical formulation outlined in Śāntarakṣita's *Tattvasaṃgraha* and Kamalasīla's *Panjikā* on it.[131] Now we shall see how the Nyāya-Vaiśeṣikas tried to refute the Buddhist arguments. Against the Buddhist view that the present, past and future moments, being contradictory to each other cannot refer to the one and the same object and that existence must therefore be different in two different moments, Vācaspatimiśra, Jayanta and Śrīdhara hold that though there may be incompatibility of the present with the past or future times, the relation of an object with the present time is not incompatible with its relation with the past and future times. The Buddhist conception of existence as capability for efficient action is untenable. Causality of an object is not its essence; it is an adventitious attribute. Existence does not prove evanescence. Origination of an effect from its cause is impossible according to the theory of evanescence. With regard to the Buddhist objection that an enduring object can neither produce its effect successively nor simultaneously, the Nyāya-Vaiśeṣika answer is that it produces its effect in succession, at the moment when all the accessory causes come to proximity with the principal cause which alone is incapable of producing its effect. The accessories do not produce any excellence in the nature of the object. According to Vācaspatimiśra, existence in the Buddhist sense must invariably be accompanied either by dependence on accessories or by non-dependence on them. Both these alternatives are impossible in an evanescent object. With regard to the function of accessories he says that the principal cause requires the help of accessories, but it does so for its own production, but not for the production of its effect.

Meeting the Buddhist attack from various corners, Uddyotakara, Vācaspatimiśra and Jayanta evolved many new ideas which were further developed by Śrīdhara, Udayana and other writers of the Nyāya-Vaiśeṣikas till they were crystallised by Gaṅgeśa, the founder of the Navyanyāya school. The dialectics of the Navyanyāya school founded by Gaṅgeśa grew within the framework of the Nyāya-Vaiśeṣika metaphysics. A basic study of the manuals of the metaphysics of the Nyāya-Vaiśeṣika school were always in vogue among the traditional scholars. But these manuals were mere outlines and were studied without much insight into the metaphysical structure of the school or without adequate understanding of the implications of its theories. This stagnant condition was due to the lack of acquaintance with the Buddhist philosophy. The Nyāya-Vaiśeṣika metaphysics developed in conflict with the Dignāga school of Buddhism. In a prolonged controversy lasting over many centuries with the Dignāga school the Nyāya-Vaiśeṣika doctrines received their depth and clarity. But with the sinking of the Dignāga school into oblivion, under diverse historical conditions, studies in Nyāya-Vaiśeṣika metaphysics became crippled. However, resurgence of the study of the Dignāga school began to take place from the last decade of the nineteenth century, especially owing to the efforts of Satis Chandra Vidyābhusana.[132] The text of Dharmakīrti's *Nyayabindu* was discovered by Bhagandas Kevaldas and it was first edited and published by P. Paterson in 1899 as an appendix to Dharmottara's commentary on the text itself. A new dimension in the field of the study on the Dignāga school was created by Stcherbatsky.[133] His contribution to the elucidation of other systems of Buddhist philosophy is by no means negligible, but *Buddhist Logic* (2 Vols. 1930-32) is his *magnum opus* which is a masterly exposition of the Dignāga school. The development of the Nyāya-Vaiśeṣika metaphysics in terms of the corresponding development of the Buddhist Dignāga school has been presented with a refreshingly new approach by Dharmendra Nath Sastri in his *Philosophy of the Nyāya-Vaiśeṣika and Its Conflict with the Buddhist Dignāga School alias Critique of Indian Realism* (1964). This well-documented volume shows that although the Nyāya-Vaiśeṣikas belonged to a different metaphysical background, it was in the course of the philosophical duel sustained for over six centuries with the Dignāga school of Buddhism that many of their basic conceptions such as substance, attribute, universal, inherence, causation, perception, etc., underwent considerable modification and reformulation.

NOTES

1. Ed. Isvaracandra Vidyasagara (Calcutta, 1858); Taranatha Tarkavacaspati (Calcutta, 1872), Eng. trans. by E.B. Cowell and A.E. Gough (London, 1882), 12-35.
2. *Vinaya* I, 10; *Dīgha* II, 305; *Majjhima* III,249 f; *Vibhaṅga* 99. The *Visuddhimagga* 498-99 refers to seven kinds of suffering. Cf. *Abhidharmakośavyākhyā* I, 10.
3. The usual meaning attributed to it in the Buddhist Nikāyas is 'non-comprehension of four truths' while in the Abhidhamma it is non-comprehension of the world-beginning (*pubbānta*) and world-end (*aparānta*), eternalism (*sassata*) and annihilationism (*uccheda*) and of 'this-conditional' nature of objects (*idappaccayatā*).
4. *Kārikā* and *Kaumudī* 44-68; *Sūtra*, *Pravacana-bhāṣya* and *Vṛtti* III, 65-84.
5. *Kārikā* 62; *Pravacana-bhāṣya* III.72.
6. *Tattvārthādhigama* VIII.2.
7. *Sūtra* and *Vṛtti* V,25-26.
8. *Yogasūtra* and *Bhāṣya* I.1-4; I.12-18; I.23; II.1-2; IV.29-34.
9. *Aṅguttara* I, 134, 223; *Mahāvastu* III, 63; *Suttanipāta* 653-54; etc.
10. *Majjhima* I, 160 ff; *Kuddhakapāṭha*, Ratna 12; *Dhammapada* 21.
11. *Suttanipāta* 215.
12. *Visuddhimagga* II, 611.
13. *Saundarānanda* V.15; VIII.62; XVI.19, 44.
14. *Saṃyutta* II, 124-26; III, 143; IV.372; *Majjhima* I, 509; *Itivuttaka* 37.
15. *Dravyasaṃgraha* 39-40; *Pañcāstikāyasamayasāra* 28.
16. *Nyāyabhāṣya* I.1.22.
17. *Sūtra* I.56; III.66.75; V.74 ff ; VI.20; *Kārikā* 59-68.
18. *Yogasūtra* I, 5-11; II.3.9.
19. Śaṅkara on *Brahmasūtra* I.1.4. etc.
20. See Rhys Davids, *Dialogues*, I, 245-46.
21. *Visuddhimagga* 84.

22. *āvāso ca kulaṃ lābho gaṇo kammañ ca pañcaman addhānam nāti ābādho gantho iddhi ti te dasā ti.*
23. Cf. *Milinda* 365-99; *Yogasūtra* I.30.
24. *Visuddhimagga* 170 ff.
25. *Tattvārthādhigama* V, 30.
26. Guṇaratna on *Ṣaḍdarśanasamuccaya*, 52.
27. *Prameyakamalamārtaṇḍa* 8-11.
28. A.B. Keith, *Buddhist Philosophy* (Oxford, 1923), 161.
29. W.M. McGovern, *A Manual of Buddhist Philosophy* (London, 1923), I.115.
30. *Prāmaṇasamuccaya* I.10; *Pramāṇavārtika* II.1; Th. Stcherbatsky, *Buddhist Logic* (Leningrad, 1932), I,12.
31. II.2.19-32.
32. Thibaut's trans. in *SBE*, XXXIV, 404-27.
33. Gauḍapāda IV.99. Cf. infra.
34. IV. 24-29.
35. II.32; IV.4 ff.
36. III.10; IV.72; etc.
37. On *Sūtra* I.22.
38. I.14.
39. Com. on *Ved. Sūt.* II. 2.18.
40. Com. on II.2.19.
41. Com. on II.2.20.
42. Com. on II.2.21.
43. Com. on II. 2.22.
45. Com. on II.2.24.
46. Com. on II.2.25.
47. Com. on II.2.26-27.
48. Com. on II.2.28.
49. Com. on II.2.29.
50. Com on. II.2.30.
51. Com. on II.2.31.
52. *Tattvasaṃgraha* V.330.
53. *The Central Conception of Buddhism* (London, 1922), 22.
54. *The Teachings of Vedānta according to Rāmānuja* (Bonn, 1908), 13 ff.
55. *JRAS*, 1910, 129-40.
56. Ed. R. Garbe.
57. Poussin, 132.
58. Chowkhamba Sanskrit Series (No. 36), 19.
59. Poussin 133.
60. Anandasrama Series No. 10.
61. *Kārikā* II. 24; II.31.
62. X.69; Nanjio, 272.
63. *Kārikā*, III. 29-30.

64. Ibid., IV.72.
65. *Abhidharmakośa*, ed. Poussin II 34; *Mādhyamikavṛtti*, ed. Poussin 203.
66. III.65; Nanjio 181.
67. X.58; Nanjio 272.
68. 'The Gauḍapāda Kārikās on the Māṇḍukya Upaniṣad' in *Proc. Sec. Or. Con.* 439 ff.
69. *Sanskrit Literature* 242.
70. IV.47.
71. IV.48.
72. IV.49.
73. IV.51.
74. For parallels of the *Kārikās* of Gauḍapāda with passages from various Buddhist texts, see Poussin in *JRAS*, 1910, 135-40.
75. IV.99.
76. *IHQ*, XIV, 1938.
77. especially IV.96.
78. Cf. *Madhyamakārikā*, XX.25; *Mādhyamakavṛtti* 264. 539; *Laṅkāvatāra*, Nanjio, 142-44; *Vajracchedikā* ed. Max Müller, 24; etc.
79. *Mādhyamakavṛtti* 493.
80. *Taittirīya Up.* II.4.1; *Katha*, II.3; *Brahma Sūtras* with Śaṅkara's Com. III.2-17.
81. Nanjio 194-95.
82. *Vijñaptimatratāsiddhi* containing his two treatises of *Viṃśatikā* and *Triṃsikā*, ed. S. Levi (Paris, 1925).
83. See S.N. Dasgupta in *IHQ*, IV, 1928.
84. Eng. Trans. by M.M. Ganganatha Jha (Asiatic Society : Calcutta, 1909), 217-345.
85. Vasubandhu's *Viṃśatikā* 3-4.
86. *Ślokavārtika* (abb. SV, Nirālambanavāda sec.) 12-13; Jha 120.
87. I.1.5.
88. A.B. Keith, *The Karma Mīmāṃsa* (London, 1921), 44 ff.
89. *Ślokavārtika* 5-10; Jha 119-120.
90. *ŚV*, 14-18; Jha 120-21.
91. *ŚV*, 19-23; Jha 121-22.
92. *ŚV*, 25, Jha 122.
93. *ŚV* 32-74; Jha 123-30.
94. *ŚV* 79-95; Jha 132-33.
95. Stcherbatsky, *The Conception of Buddhist Nirvāna* (Leningrad, 1927), 19.
96. *ŚV*, 113-199; Jha 137-47.
97. *ŚV*, (Śūnyavāda sec.) 1-63; Jha 148-54.
98. *ŚV*, 64-246; Jha 155-79.
99. See Stcherbatsky, *Buddhist Logic* I, 51 ff.; G.N. Jha, *The Prabhākara School of Pūrva Mimāṃsā* (Allahabad, 1911). Apart

from commenting on the *Śabarabhāṣya*, Prabhākara composed two important works, *Bṛhati* and *Laghvi*. The celebrated commentator on Prabhākara was Sālikanātha who wrote *Prakaraṇapañcikā*, *Ṛjuvimala* and *Dīpaśikhā* explaining the contents of Prabhākara's works.

100. See S.C. Vidyabhushana, *History of Indian Logic* (Calcutta, 1921), 49-50.
101. *JAOS*, XXXI, 1 ff.
102. *NS* IV.1.48.
103. IV.2.26.
104. *Nyāya-Bhāṣya* IV.1.18.
105. *Ibid.* II.1.39-40.
106. *Ibid.* III.2.11-13.
107. The original is lost, but fortunately a Tibetan translation is preserved from which S.C. Vidyabhusana has given a brief synopsis of its matter in his *History of Indian Logic*. Stcherbatsky's *Buddhist Logic* is also an excellent guide to the proper understanding of the epistemology and logic of Dignāga. Besides, there are copious extracts from Dignāga scattered in Sanskrit philosophical treatises. See Randle's *Fragments from Dignaga*, RAS (London, 1926).
108. *Indian Logic and Atomism* (Oxford, 1919), pp. 100-10.
109. *Nyāyadarśana* with *Vātsyāyana-bhāṣya* (Containing Uddyotakara's *Vārtika*, Vacaspati Miśra's *Tātparyaṭīkā* and Viśvanātha's *Vṛtti*), 2 Vols. (Calcutta Sanskrit Series 1936, 1944).
110. Hall's ed. 235; *nyāya-sthitiṃ iva uddotakara-svarūpām*.
111. *Nyāyavārtika* 669-89.
112. *Ibid.*, 13-14.
113. *Ibid.*, 668 : *na punaḥ sarvo'nuvṛtti-pratyayaḥ sāmānyād eva bhavati*.
114. *Ibid.*, 667.
115. Cf. *Mādhyamakavṛtti* 64, 71.
116. *Nyāyavārtika* 210.
117. The idea of a substratum, however, made its way in Buddhist metaphysics. Stcherbatsky observes : "Although emphatically banned from the dwelling of Buddhist philosophy and replaced by the laws of interconnection, the conceptions of substance and quality seem to have found a backdoor through which partly to re-enter in their usual position. For the division of the elements of matter into primary and secondary (*bhūta* and *bhautika*) and of the mental elements into fundamental and derivative (*citta* and *caitta*) approach very nearly the relation of substance and quality". *Central Conception* 35-6.
118. *Nyāyavārtika* 204-13.
119. *Ibid*, 1067-72.

120. *Nyāyabindu* with Dharmottara's commentary ed. Paterson, (Calcutta, 1889), Stcherbatsky, Leningrad, 1918); Eng. trans. with notes in Stcherbatsky's *Buddhist Logic*, II; Tibtan Version with Vinitadeva's com., ed. Poussin (Calcutta, 1907). Its Sanskrit reconstruction with Eng. trans. and notes by M.K. Gangopadhyaya (Calcutta, 1971). Our exposition of Dharmakīrti is based on Stcherbatsky and Gangopadhyaya.
121. As against the three essential characteristics of a valid mark admitted by the Buddhists, the Naiyāyikas consider them to be five. The additional two are 'absence of contradictions with *pramāṇa* (*abādhitatva*) and 'having no counter-reason' (*asatprati-pakṣitatva*). The Buddhists reject the first addtion saying that 'absence of contradiction' cannot be the essential characteristic of valid mark because 'contradiction' (*bādha*) and 'invariable concomitance' (*avinābhāva*) are mutually opposed.
122. *Outlines of Indian Philosophy* (London, 1932), 198.
123. *Indian Philosophy* I. 120.
124. *Buddhist Logic* I, 529.
125. *Ibid.*, II, 328-29.
126. *Nyāyakandalī* (Banaras, 1895), 279.
127. R. Sankrityayana, *Pramāṇavārtikabhāṣyam* (Patna, 1953), 388.
128. *Ibid.*, 427.
129. *Nyāyavārtikatātparyaṭikā* included in *Nyāyadarsana* (Calcutta Sanskrit Series, 1944), 115 ff; Cf. *Nyāyamañjarī* (Varanasi, 1936), I, 86-87; M.K. Gangopadhyaya, Vinitadeva's *Nyāya-binduṭīkā* (Calcutta, 1971), 239-40.
130. *Ibid.*, 435 ff., 823 ff.; *Nyāyamañjarī* II, 17 ff.; *Nyāyakandalī* 73 ff.
131. Śāntarakṣita's special philosophical affiliation is not very clear. According to T.R.V. Murti (*The Central Philosophy of Buddhism*, London 1955, 102) the structure of the *Tattvasaṃgraha* indicates its Mādhyamika character. The *TS* and its *Pañjikā* (see G. Jha's tr. Baroda 1937-39, 949-54), however, lay emphasis on the doctrine of *sva-saṃvedana* indicating the Vijñānavāda influence. According to the Tibetan tradition (Bu-ston, II.135ff) he synthesised the tenents of Mādhyamika, Yogācāra and Sautrāntika doctrines. By nature the *TS* is interpretative and at the same time polemical. It is in *Kārikās* on memorial verses numbering 3646, divided into 26 chapters. Apart from the Buddhist doctrines it makes a critical review of the six orthodox systems of Indian thought, the grammatical school of philosophy, the materialistic school and Jainism. So far as the essentials of Buddhism are concerned, the *TS* lays special emphasis on the doctrine of momentariness, *apohavāda* or doctrine of 'meaning', doctrine of causation, doctrine of consciousness and the omniscience of the Buddha. Śāntarakṣita and his commentator Kamalaśīla accept at many places the views of Dignāga and

Dharmakīrti concerning the self-cognisability of consciousness. Both of them hold consciousness to be real, but at the same time maintain that it is not the one and only reality.

132. See Ch. I. Vidyābhusana wrote a considerable number of articles on Buddhist logic before the publication of his monographs. Thus in the *JASB*—Dignāga and His *Pramāṇasamuccaya* (1905), Indian Logic as preserved in Tibet (1907), The *Nyāyabindu* (1907), *Hetucakradamaru* of Dignāga (1907); in the *JBTS*—The Philosopher Dignāga (1896), Influence of Buddhism on the Development of the Nyāya Philosophy (1898), The Buddhist Version of the Nyāya Philosophy (1900); in *Journal of the Mahabodhi Society*—Life of Dignāga (1890), Influence of Buddhism, On the development of Hindu Nyāya Philosophy, (1902), etc.

133. Apart from his *Theory of Knowledge and Logic according to the Later Buddhists* (2 Vols. 1903-1909) he edited Dharmakīrti's *Nyāyabindu* with Dharmottara's commentary (1918) and with the sub-commentary of Mallavādin (1909) and published its translation in Russian (1903) and in English (in *Buddhist Logic*, II, 1930).

VI

THE CHANGING PHASES

Buddhism, since its inception has passed through several vicissitudes with the inevitable result that its original structure has been changed to a considerable extent in matter, form and spirit. The Buddha did not form a religion meant for the masses, but he did form a spiritual community meant exclusively for the monks (in which nuns also were admitted later). Proliferation of this spiritual community was made possible through the extension of monasteries and the development of a monastic culture in which a layman had practically nothing to do. In the earlier phases of the history of Buddhism laymen appeared more as supporters of the Saṅgha than as actual adherents of Buddhism. They revered the Buddha and his disciples, donated money or property to the Saṅgha, heard the teachings and often uttered *triśasaṇa*. This, however, did not affect their social status and their traditional religious or cultic obligations, which in India had always been associated with caste, culture and occupation. The Buddha's insistence on a spiritual community desirous of having liberation from worldly fetters rather than on a broad-based religious community is also attested to by fact that he did not prescribe any Dharmaśāstra comprising the codes of individual and social behaviour, civil and criminal laws, rules relating to marriage, divorce, inheritance, etc., for the lay devotees, though for the monks he did make elaborate rules and regulations prepared meticulously, which were later crystallised in the *Vinaya Piṭaka*.

This does not, however, mean that in the long history of Buddhism in India there has never been any attempt to give the doctrines of the Buddha a mass-oriented religious form and content. Undoubtedly there were many such attempts as a result of which Buddhism tailored as a distinct religion was preached in countries outside India.[1] But in India it had no possibility of acquiring a complete religious character owing to the fact that the Buddha's difference with traditional wisdom lay not in its contents but in the field of interpretation. And this interpretational difference pertains to other systems as well. The Buddhist thought-complex was, however, appreciated by a section of the intelligentsia and eventually it came to be looked upon as a *mokṣa-śāstra* or science of liberation in the same way as the Sāṅkhya or the Mīmāṃsā or the Vedānta was treated in the Indian tradition. Moreover, the strictly monkish and monastic veneer of Buddhism prevented its involvement with the masses. The monks were honoured and socially respected for their character, conduct and learning; kings, landlords and merchants donated liberally to the monasteries; some of these monasteries eventually became great seats of learning in which non-Buddhists were also admitted as students and where apart from the Buddhist doctrines other systems including secular sciences were taught. Of course there were occasional attempts to reach the masses. The earlier attempt to create a mythology projecting the Buddha on the top of the traditional and innovatory gods failed to make any impact on the popular imagination. An artificial Śakra endowed with endless noble qualities could hardly be a proper match for his vigorous and lively Puranic counterpart. The deified abstractions of the Mahāyānists presented with the abundance of sculptural wealth undoubtedly roused curiosity and feeling of admiration amongst the masses but failed to capture their hearts.

Another important point was the development of factionalism leading to doctrinal centrifugality. This factionalism which stood in the way of the original doctrines becoming well-defined and integrated in form was mostly due to the monastic culture introduced by the historical Buddha himself. Since there were personality clashes among the learned monks who had their individual views on different issues—doctrinal as well as managerial—and who wanted to have their own views accepted, dissension, clique, quarrel and politics could be the only natural outcome. This egoism of the elders was the real cause of *saṅghabheda* or division of the order and the emergence of countless sects, though the sectarian leaders and their cronies were never tired of saying that their difference was purely ideological. When the Buddha had established the community of brethren he thought that the combined wisdom of the learned monks would lead it in the right direction during his physical non-existence. This was due to the fact that the historical Buddha was basically a tribal and as such acquainted with the functioning of tribal council after which the Buddhist Saṅgha was modelled.[2] But even during the lifetime of the Buddha there were severe personality clashes within the Saṅgha. From the *Sutta* and *Vinaya Piṭaka* it is known that many monks left the order because it did not suit their personal ambitions. Certain monks like Sunokkhata, Ariṭṭha, Sāti, etc. misunderstood and misrepresented the Buddha's teaching and very often put the Master in great trouble. At Kausambi a very serious dissension is recorded to have ensued from a dispute between the followers of two teachers, one well-versed in the Vinaya and other in Dhamma. The most important was the revolt of Devadatta who was opposed to the lenient rules in the Order and pleaded strongly for a more stringent life for the monks. The Buddha refused to accept the suggestions of Devadatta. The latter thereupon left the Saṅgha with a good following. The existence of the Devadattakas in later times proves that Devadatta was able to inflict a crushing blow upon the Buddhist order during its formative period. Fa-hien noticed the existence of the followers of Devadatta in Śrāvastī who made offerings to the three past Buddhas except Śākyamuni. According to Rhys Davids, the Gotamaka monks mentioned in the Buddhist literature might have been the followers of Devadatta.[3]

There were two types of disciples of the Buddha, one belonging to the clan of the Master himself, such as Ānanda, Upāli, Anuruddha, Devadatta, etc., and the other comprising the intellectually superior Brāhmaṇas such as Sāriputta, Moggalāna, Mahākassapa, Mahākaccāyana, Piṇḍola Bhāradvāja and so forth. The Brāhmaṇa group played a much more important role than the Śākya faction during and after the lifetime of the Buddha. Piṇḍola Bhāradvāja was eulogised by the Master himself as the greatest of the lion-roarers. The same was true in the case of Mahākassapa who had the honour of exchanging his robes with the Master. Moggalāna's contribution to the cause of Buddhism is well known. Sāriputta was known as Dhammasenāpati or commander of the order and was looked upon almost as the second Buddha. Famous for his lion-roar, Sāriputta delivered sermons in the absence of the Buddha and conducted the business of the Saṅgha. He effectively defended the Buddha during the rebellion of Devadatta.[4] Despite the invaluable services rendered by the Brāhmaṇas, the Śākya faction was not favourably disposed to them. The anti-Brahmanical passages of the *Sutta Piṭaka* derived their main impulses not from the 'misdeeds' of the Brāhmaṇas or from the so-called 'ideological bankruptcy of Brahmanism' but from the inferiority complex of the Buddha's clansmen. It was also a fact that the Śākyas and other tribes who lived outside the limit of Madhyadeśa or Aryāvarta, the land inhabited by the *śiṣṭas* or culturally superior people, were looked down upon by the

Brāhmaṇas. This is attested by the evidence of the *Ambaṭṭha Sutta* in which the Śākyas have been described by the Brāhmaṇa Ambaṭṭha as uncivilised, arrogant, low-born and dark-complexioned. The Buddha, who had a somewaht grudging respect for the knowledge and austere life of the Brāhmaṇas, however, is made in this Sutta to defend the position of his own clan by claiming its Kṣatriya origin and suggesting that the Kṣatriyas are superior to the Brāhmaṇas because they never acknowledge any Brāhmaṇa-Kṣatriya hybrid, either in the mother's line or in the father's line, as true Kṣatriyas and that the forefathers of the Śākyas maintained the purity of their Kṣatriya blood by marrying their own sisters. Ānanda, to whom the Buddhist tradition ascribes the compilation of the *Sutta Piṭaka*, had reasons to be more anti-Brahmanical than the Buddha himself for he was severely rebuked by Mahākassapa for his bad conduct who publicly charged him for moral lapses. He was reproached by the Buddha himself because he secretly cherished ill-will and was mischievous to others. He could not free himself from lust, hatred and ignorance.[5]

The first council which was convened by Mahākassapa shortly after the Buddha's death to check the unseemly behaviour of the monks heralded the voice of dissent.[6] According to the *Cullavagga* the council was held at Rājagṛha in which Mahākassapa questioned Upāli on the Vinaya and Ānanda on the Dhamma, and in this process the *Vinaya* and *Sutta Piṭakas* were recited. When Ānanda informed the councillors about Buddha's instruction that minor rules of discipline could be abolished by the Order, there was a stirring controversy as to which rules should be taken as the minor ones. Ānanda was also admonished for his bad deeds and there was some rift among the members about the admission of Ānanda to the council.[7] At the end of the Council when Mahākassapa sought the approval of senior monks of the texts settled by the Council, Gavāmpati preferred to remain netural. Another senior monk, Purāṇa or Dakkhinagiri refused to accept the recited text as the word of the Buddha saying that he preferred to bear in his mind the law as he had himself heard and learnt from the Buddha's own mouth. He also insisted that seven rules relating to food should be incorporated into the Vinaya, but his proposal was rejected.[8] According to Przyluski the episode of Purāṇa in the account of the First Council had a far-reaching consequence. The Mahīśāsaka Vinaya attaches special importance to the person of Purāṇa who insisted on a second rehearsal which, according to this school, was complied with by Mahākassapa. This shows that Purāṇa and his followers formed a group by themselves, though probably it was not yet known by the designation Mahīśāsaka. The difference of the latter with Theravāda was thus heralded in the First Council. In course of time that group of monks who held Purāṇa in high esteem, formed the Mahīśāsaka school by including his seven rules not accepted by Mahākassapa in his Vinaya Code.[9]

The most significant schism in Buddhism took place in connection with the Second Council held at Vaisali about a century after the Buddha's death in consequence of which the Mahāsaṅghikas seceded from the main body and asserted their independent entity. There are two sets of mutually disagreeing traditions regarding the split. According to the Pali tradition, monks belonging to the eastern provinces, mostly the Vajjians, demanded laxity of certain disciplinary rules, which the westerners were not ready to grant. Hence the easterners broke away, convened another council, adopted their own modification of the Vinaya rules as valid and came to be known as the Mahāsaṅghikaṣ. The second set of tradition as found in the treatises of Bhavya, Vasumitra and Vinītadeva and some other later sources, including Hiuen Tsang's account, ascribes the cause of division to the five doctrinal propositions of Mahādeva, a celebrated monk of Pāṭaliputra which were outvoted by the elders.[10] It should be remembered in this connection that by this time, a century or more after the demise of the Buddha, there was a regrouping of factions. On the one hand there were some forms of regional grouping like the easterners and westerners, as we find in the first account of the schism,[11] and on the other, emergence of a protestant group that was unlikely to submit to the exclusive powers and privileges of the elders who proclaimed themselves as Arhants, as we find in the propositions of Mahādeva, which clearly state that the Arhants are subject to temptation, ignorance, doubt and dependence. According to Mrs Rhys Davids, the point of issue was the rights of individual as well as those of the provincial communities as against the prescriptions of centralised hierarchy.[12] According to the first set of traditions, Yaśa, a senior monk from Kausāmbī, having found that the Vajjian monks allowed ten rules which were against the Vinaya as lawful started mobilising opinion against them and was able to secure support of the elders such as Sambhūta Sānavāsī, Revata, Sumana, Sāḷha and Sabbakāmī. They all assembled at Vaiśālī, to hold a council for settling the points under dispute. A select body of referees formed under the chairmanship of the venerable Ajita voiced against the ten points of the Vajjians or the easterners. The latter did not accept the resolution and held a separate council called Mahāsangiti and got their own views approved by this council. As a result of this, the order became divided into two sections.

The Eastern monks having their stronghold at Vaiśālī and Pāṭaliputra came to be known as the Mahāsaṅghikas, while the Westerners, those stationed at Kausāmbī, Mathura and Avantī, were known as Sthaviravādins or Theravādins.

Division or dissension in most cases is primarily due to personality clash and quarrel over comparatively minor things or demands. After the split, each unit upholds lofty cause for its separation. The rude feelings and events are smoothed out and ideological differences are emphasised. The Mahāsaṅghikas tried to suggest that their separation was not due to any breach of disciplinary rules but to an ideological difference as outlined in the five propositions of Mahādeva. Not all the separate groups which thus come into existence as a result of the split can survive for long. Some of them come into prominence, acquire functional efficiency, grow in size also with the propensity of further subdivisions, while other sink into oblivion or survive merely in name. This universal law also held good in the case of Buddhism. The traditional accounts would have us believe that eleven sects originated from the Sthaviravāda and seven from the Māhasaṅghika.[13] The real conditions leading to the splitting of Buddhism into numerous sects will never be known because they are not recorded. We have on record only the ideological points of difference among various sects. The human or personality factor and special events which worked behind the schisms subsequent to the Second Council are not very clearly known to us. The genesis of the later sects, their interrelation, affiliation and stratification are almost impossible to work out. Different traditions preserved in the literature of the Theravādins, the Sāmmitīyas and the Mahāsaṅghikas as also in the subsequent Chinese and Tibetan works and translations give divergent accounts about the origin, name and order of secession of these factions.

Our purpose is not to deal with the history of the Buddhist sects. That history only pertains to their regional distribution, doctrinal peculiarities and scriptural works. Here we want only to outline various traditions on the basis of which scholars tried to make their stratification and find out their affiliation with one another. According to the *Dīpavaṃsa*[14] of the Theravāda tradition, from the original Theravāda arose the Mahīśāsaka and the Vajjiputtakas. The Mahīśāsaka was subsequently divided into Sarvāstivāda and Dharmaguptaka; the former, in its turn, yielded the Kāśyapīya, Saṅkrāntivāda and Sūtravāda. From the Vajjiputtaka arose the Dharmottarīya, Bhadrayāṇika, Sannagarika and Sammitīya. The Mahasaṅghika which was the first to secede from the main body was divided into Gokulika and Ekavyavahārika. From the

Gokulika sprang Bahuśrutīya and Prajñaptivāda.[15] The *Dīpavaṃsa*[16] also refers to the Haimavata, Rājagirika, Siddhārthika, Pūrvaśaila and Aparaśaila. The *Kathāvatthu-Aṭṭhakathā* of Buddhaghoṣa, besides the names enumerated in the *Dīpavaṃsa*, adds Vajjriya (Vajra), Uttarāpathaka, Hetuvāda and Vetulyaka. These names also occur in the *Mahāvaṃsa*.[17] According to the Sarvāstivāda tradition as preserved in the *Samayabhedoparacanacakra* of Vasumitra,[18] the first schools to originate were the Sthaviravāda and the Mahāsaṅghika. From Sthaviravāda evolved Sarvāstivāda and Haimavata; Vātsiputrīya, Mahīśāsaka, Suvarṣaka (Kāśyapīya) and Sautrāntika (Saṅkārntīya, Uttarīya); from Vātsiputriya Dharmottarīya, Bhadrayanīya, Sammitīya and Sannagarika. From the Mahāsaṅghika sprang Ekavyavahārika, Lokottaravāda, Kukkuṭika, Bahuśrutīya, Prajñaptivāda, Caitika, Aparaśaila and Uttaraśaila. I-tsing, who represents the Mūla-sarvāstivāda tradition, says that the first division gave rise to the Mahāsaṅghika, Sthavira, Mula-sarvāstivāda and Sammitīya schools. From Mūla-sarvāstivāda sprang forth Dharmaguptaka, Mahiśāsaka and Kāsyapīya.[19] According to the *Sāriputraparipṛcchā* of the Mahāsaṅghika tradition Therravāda gave rise to the Vātsiputrīya. Kāśyapīya, Sūtravāda (Saṅkrāntika) and Sarvāstivāda; from Vātsiputrīya emerged Dharmopaka, Bhadrayānika, Sammitīya and Sannagarika; and from Sarvāstivāda came into existence Mahīśāsaka, Dharmaguptaka and Suvarṣaka. From the Mahāsaṅghika came Ekavyavahārika, Lokottaravāda, Bahuśrūtika and Prajñaptivāda.[20]

Apart from the Sthaviravāda-Mahāsaṅghika basic division, the divergent traditions mentioned above present only names of various sects, but fail to provide any correct idea as to what really happened after the first great split. These traditions offer no chronological stratification of the sects; nor do they throw any light on their mutual affiliations. Which of these sects was the first to get separated from its Sthaviravāda or Mahāsaṅghika genre, what was the reason of its separation, why and how further subdivisions and fragmentations took place and other relevant facts are mostly unknown at the present state of our knowledge. The groupings of the sects and subsects are also imaginary. Very often a sect with Mahayanic leaning is grouped with those belonging to the Hīnayāna category and vice versa. There are some cases in which one particular sect has been called under different names. Lama Tāranātha equates Kāśyapīya with Suvarṣaka, Saṅkrāntivāda with Uttarīya and Tāmrasāṭīya, Caityaka with Pūrvaśaila and schools of Mahādeva, Lokottaravāda with Kaukkuṭika, Ekavyavahārika with Mahāsaṅghika and Kaurukullaka with Vātsiputrīya, Dharmottarīya, Bhadrayāṇīya and Channagarika.[21] In some cases sects have been designated after the venue of their original establishment. They differ form other in name only. Again, some sects have been recorded in the lists which should not be called sects in the real sense of the term. This may be demonstrated with reference to the Vibhajyavāda, which was originally a term to designate genuine Buddhists.[22] An alternative name of Sthaviravāda is also given as Vibhajyavāda, but it is doubtful whether Vibhajyavāda was an independent sect. The term Vibhajyavāda was sometimes affixed to the name of a sect. It perphaps denoted a dissident group differing in minor points from the principal doctrine of a particular sect with which it did not sever its bond but preferred to maintain a distinction. Bhavya and Vinītadeva regard Vibhajyavāda as an offshoot of the Sarvāstivāda. Vallee Poussin traced in the Chinese commentary of the *Vijñapti-mātratāsiddhi* a passage in which the Vibhajyvādins are identified with the Prajñaptivadins.[23] According to N. Dutt it apparently refers to the Bahuśrutīya-Vibhajyavādins by which name the Prajñaptivādins distinguished themselves from the Bahuśrutīyas. The position of the Vibhajyavādins cannot clearly be made out as their doctrines have much in common with those of the Sarvāstivādins, Mahāsaṅghikas, Sammitīyas and others.[24]

According to both Pali and Sanskrit traditions, the original school, which the Ceylonese chronicles do not count as schismatic,[25] was called Theravāda or Sthaviravāda. The Tibetan traditions ascribe the foundation of this school to Mahākaccāyana. Moggaliputta Tissa, the key figure of the Third Council seems to have been instrumental in the development of this school. The Theravāda seems to have been originally based on Pāṭaliputra. Later it became popular in the Western countries making Ujjayinī its second centre, and then it gradually made its headway towards the South, settling in and around Kāñchi, and migrated ultimately to Ceylon, Burma, Siam, Cambodia and Laos. Three sects of Ceylonese Theravāda are known, viz., the Jetavanīya, Abhayagirivāsins and Mahavihāravāsins. It is difficult to say whether the Mahīśāsakas or the Sarvāstivāda was the first to secede from the Sthaviravāda. The Mahīśāsakas were originally associated with Mahiṣamaṇḍala or Māhiṣmatī, modern Maheswara on the bank of the Narmada.[26] Reference to them occurs in the inscriptions found at Nagarjunikonda and Vanavasi.[27] The Sarvastivāda, which like the Theravāda had ground under its feet, was centred in Mathura whence it spread over Gandhara and Kashmir, besides its strongholds at Kanauj, Sarnath, Śrāvastī and Rājagṛha, as is attested by inscriptional evidence.[28] Hiuen Tsang found its existence in Kashgar, Koucha,

Tamasavana (Sialkot) and several places of Northern frontier and Western India while I-tsing found it in Lāṭa, Sindhu, southern and eastern India, Sumatra, Java, Central Asia, China and Cochin-China. In the first list of Bhavya, Sarvāstivāda has been identified with Hetuvāda, but this identification does not seem tenable. The Dharmaguptaka sect which had a Vinaya of its own had its centre in the North-west. Hiuen Tsang and I-tsing noted its existence in Uḍḍiyana and Central Asia but not in the mainland of India. The Kāśyapīya which was also known as Sthavīrīya, Saddharma-varṣaka and Suvarṣaka had its centres in the north-west, in and around the Taxila region as also in Uḍḍiyana, Kharachara and Khotan.[29] No special centre of the Sautrāntika sect, also known as Saṅkrāntika or Sūtravāda, is mentioned, though a few inscriptions from Sanchi and Bharhut refer to Sutaṃtika, Sutatika and Sutatikini.[30] Almost all traditions derive Sautrāntika from Sarvāstivāda. Sautrāntika appears more to be the name of a particular type of the Sarvastivāda doctrine—which is confirmed in the Indian philosophical tradition—rather than a simple sect. The Haimavata sect should be associated with the Himalayan region, but epigraphical evidence locates this sect in Central India, especially in the region around Sanchi.[31] Przylusky identifies the Haimavatas with the Kāśyapīyas, though this identification is not generally accepted.[32] The precise area of influence of the Uttarāpathaka sect is not known to us. Like the Uttarāpathakas the Tāmraśāṭīyas had no distinct identity. Tāranātha considered the Tāmraśāṭīyas as identical with the Saṅkrāntivādins, Uttarīyas, Sautrāntikas and Dārṣṭāntikas.

Apart from the Sthavira or Theravāda, other sects mentioned have somehow been placed by authorities, ancient and modern, in the Sarvāstivāda group. The principal point of difference between the Theravāda and the Sarvāstivāda is that the Sarvāstivādins maintain the existence of five *dharmas* in their subtlest states at all times—whether in the past, present or future—while the Thervādins deny any such existence. According to the Sarvāstivādins, the past and the future as usually understood, do not exist, though they are perceptible in the present. They accept the doctrines of non-substantiality and impermanence of worldly objects. But they hold that though the things constituted out of the *dharmas* are subject to disintegration, the *dharmas* themselves are not. They contend that the *dharmas* (or *bhāvas*) of past are transmitted into the present and likewise the *dharmas* of the future are latent in the present. An object may lose its pastness, presentness or futurity, but not its objectness.[33] The Mahīśāsakas hold that the present alone exists and that all *saṃskāras* perish at every moment. The material constituents of the sense organs as also *citta* and *caitasikas* (mind and mental states) are subject to change. The Kāśyapīyas hold that the *saṃskāras* perish every moment and that the past which has not produced its fruit exists, the present exists and some of the future exists. According to Vasumitra the views of the Dharmaguptakas agree with those of the Mahāsaṅghikas though they were a branch of the Sarvāstivādins. The Saṅkrāntivādins or Sautrāntikas believed in the transmigration (*saṅkrānti*) of a substance from one life to another. According to them, out of the five *skandhas* of an individual there is one subtle *skandha* which transmigrates, as against the whole of the *pudgala* of the Vātsiputrīyas and Sammitīyas. In course of time the Sautrāntikas evolved into a distinct philosophical school. In the *Abhidharmakośa*[34] this school is described as the upholder of the *Vinaya piṭaka* and also as Dārṣṭāntika because it admitted examples as proofs for a thesis. It admitted that the external objects were appearances (*prajñapti*) and their existence could be proved only by inference. The unconstituted (*asaṃskṛta*, e.g. *ākāśa* or *nirvāṇa*) is not a real object (*dravya*). It is only absence (*abhāva*) of all objective element. There is no substance (*anātma*), no duration (*anitya*) and no bliss (*duḥkha*) except *nirvāṇa* (*sukha*).[35]

There are also many points of divergences in regard to the Buddhas, Bodhisattvas, Arhats, gods and individuals. The Theravāda viewpoint that the Buddhas possess *rūpakāya* and worldly attributes and are subject to all physical frailties of human being is accepted by most sects of the category mentioned above. The Sarvāstivādins in consonance with the Theravādins regard the Buddha as a human being, but they attribute to him divine, sometimes superdivine, powers. The Mahīśāsakas add that though the Buddha is included in the Saṅgha, a gift made to the Buddha is more meritorious than that to the Saṅgha. The Dharmaguptakas had just the opposite view: gifts to the Saṅgha are more meritorious than those to the Buddha.[36] According to the Uttarāpathakas it is the attainment of *bodhi* alone that makes a Buddha and that the Buddhas are above *maitri* and *karuṇā*.[37] The Sautrāntikas hold that there may be many Buddhas simultaneously. The Theravāda view that the Bodhisattvas are average beings, not self-born and subject to the *kleśas* or afflictions is also shared by others. But in regard to the Arhats there are differences of opinion. According to the Theravāda, Arhats are perfect and hence they cannot have a fall from Arhathood. The Mahīśāsakas hold that while a Srotāpanna has a chance of retrogression an Arhat has not and that the Arhats do not perform meritorious deeds. Both of these opinions are directly opposed to those of the Sarvastivādins and are partly in agreement with those of the Theravādins. The Sarvāstivādins like the Mahāsaṅghikas assume the existence of two classes of Arhats with different degrees of attainments.[38] Not all Arhats are perfect. All of them may have *kṣayajñāna* (knowledge of the extinction of all impurities) but only a few can gain the *anutpādajñāna* (knowledge of the cessation of rebirth). The Arhats are governed by the limbs of the causal law and are not free from the influence of past *karma*. Some of them perform meritorious deeds. They gain four fundamental *dhyānas* but cannot realise their fruits. Some and not all Arhats attain *nirvāṇa*. The Dharmaguptas hold that the body of the Arhat is pure (*anāsrava*). According to the Kāśyapīyas, Arhats have both *kṣayajñana* and *anutpādajñāna* and are not subject to passions. The Haimavatas hold that Arhats have ignorance and doubt; they are subject to temptation; they gain spiritual perception with the help of others; and the path is attained by an exclamation. This is an agreement with the Mahāsaṅghika view. The Uttarāpathakas admit that there may be persons claiming Arhathood falsely, but all *dharmas* possessed by an Arhat are pure. The Arhats are able to end their lives in the same way as the Buddha did.[39] Other points of convergences and divergences in regard to doctrinal matters such as those pertaining to the concepts of *pudgala, antarābhava, anuśaya, paryāvasthāna, vijñāna, asaṃskṛta*, etc., will be discussed in connection with other groups.

The next group comprised the Vajjiputtakas or Vātsiputrīyas, Dharmottarīyas, Bhadrayāṇikas, Sannagarikas and Sammitīya. Among these the Vātsiputrīyas, later known as Vātsiputrīya-Sammitīyas, became most prominent.[40] The earliest evidence to the existence of this sect is furnished by two inscriptions recovered from Mathura and Sarnath belonging respectively to the second and fourth centuries A.D.[41] The Dharmottarīyas, Bhadrayāṇikas and Sannagarikas, according to most traditions, originated from the Vātsiputrīyas. References to the first two sects occur in inscriptions, datable to the second and third centuries A.D., recovered from places like Karle, Sopara, Junar, Nasik and Kanheri.[42] Vasumitra skips over the special doctrines of these three schools mentioning that they differed regarding the attainments of an Arhat and the consequent chances of his fall from Arhathood. In other matters these sects agreed with the views of the Vāstiputriya-Sammitīyas. The most remarkable doctrine of this group is that, besides the elements constituting a being, there is a *pudgala* (approximating self or soul) which persists through all the existences. This *pudgalavāda* was almost heretical since it was a negation of the *anātmavāda* of the Buddha and as such it evoked bitter criticism from outstanding Buddhist philosophers like Vasubandhu,[43] Nāgārjuna,[44] Śāntideva[45] and others. This issue forms the subject matter of the first controversy in the *Kathāvatthu*,[46] which says that according to the Pudgalavādins, the term *pudgala*, used by the Buddha in different contexts, suggests something positive. It is neither an unconstituted reality like *nirvāṇa* or *ākāśa* nor a constituent material element like *rūpa*, etc. Though *pudgala* is not apart from the constituents of a being (*khaṇḍas*), its relation with the latter is not like that between the container and the contained. The concept of *pudgala* is variously interpreted in the Buddhist texts. In the *Abhidharmakośa* and its commentary, the relation between the *pudgala* and the *skandhas* is explained by the simile of fire and fuel. According to the *Kathāvatthu* version, the Sammitīyas hold that their *pudgala* has a material form. It corresponds to the entity called a being (*sattva*) and also to the vital force (*jīva*) of the living being, but at the same time it is neither identical with nor different from the body (*kāya*). It is thus something like a soul which is transmigratory as well. It passes from one existence to another, though the *pudgala* of two existences is neither the same nor different. In support of this contention the Sammitīyas refer to some utterances of the Buddha which are indirectly suggestive of the transmigration of soul. They state that their *pudgala* is the percepient but it is different from mind. According to them the soul is actually existent though not eternal. If the soul be wholly non-existent there would be neither killing of beings nor a killer, neither the attainment of fruits of sanctification nor a saint, consequently, neither Buddha nor his teachings.[47]

The Mahāsaṅghikas who were the first seceders from the Order established their centres at Pāṭaliputra and Vaiśālī whence they spread towards the north and the south. The earliest epigraphic evidence about this sect is found in the Mathura Lion Capital inscription of the time of the Śaka Kṣatrapa Soḍāsa. Other inscriptions recovered from Mathura, Nagarjunikonda and the cave temples of Karle refer to the wide geographical distribution of this sect.[48] I-tsing found the Mahāsaṅghikas in Magadha, Lāṭa and Sindhu as also in northern, southern and eastern India.[49] The earlier offshoots of the Mahāsaṅghikas seem to have been the Ekavyavahārikas and the Gokulikas or the Kaukkuṭikas. The latter sect derived its name probably owing to its association with the Kukkuṭārāma monastery of Paṭaliputra. Another offshoot was Lokottaravāda about which the Theravāda tradition is silent. The Sammitīya tradition does not distinguish between the doctrines of Lokottaravāda and Ekavyavahārikas. Tāranātha identifies Lokottaravāda with the Ekavyavahārikas and Kaukkuṭikas. A close examination of the doctrines of all these sects suggests that these sects acquired separate denominations owing to geographical reasons; the Mahāsaṅghikas themselves came to be known subsequently as Ekavyavahārikas and Lokottaravādins. Among other offshoots of the Mahāsaṅghikas the Bahuśrutīyas are referred to in the inscriptions from Gandhara and Andhra.[50] The Prajñapativādins were probably a dissident group of the Bahuśrutīyas and preferred to be known as Bahuśrutīya-Vibhajyavādins. The Caitikas, mentioned in inscriptions from Amaravati and adjoining regions,[51] have been included by Buddhaghoṣa among the Andhakas or Andhrakas whose name seems to have gained currency owing to their stronghold at Amaravati in Andhra. The Pūrvaśailas and Aparaśailas also mentioned in the inscriptions from Alluru, Nagarjunikonda, Ghantasala, Kanheri and Amaravati,[52] seem to have been the names of the two branches of the Caitikas. Buddhaghoṣa has put the Rājagirikas, the Siddhārthikas, the Pūrvaśailas and Aparaśailas under the category of Andhaka sects. Another offshoot of the Mahāsaṅghikas was the Vetulyakas who had their stronghold in the Abhayagiri monastery of Ceylon.

While the Theravādins and the Sarvāstivādins along with their ofshoots conceived of the Buddha as a human being, the Mahāsaṅghikas attributed to him not only supramundane existence but also all perfections and omniscience. His material body is unlimited; so also his length of life and divine power. He is never tired of enlightening sentient beings and awakening pure faith in them. He never sleeps, nor has any dream since his mind is always in meditation. He can comprehend everything in one moment (*ekakṣaṇikacitta*). He has no impurities.[53] According to the Theravāda and other kindred sects the Bodhisattvas are not self-born, and they are average beings subject to *kleśas* (impurities). According to the Mahāsaṅghikas the Bodhisattvas do not pass through the embryoinc stages. They assume the form of white elephants when they enter their mother's womb and come out of the same by the right side. They take birth out of their own free will in any form for imparting *dharma* to the sentient beings.[54] According to the Theravādins, Arhats are perfect and as such they cannot have a fall from Arhathood. They possess both *kṣayajñāna* (knowledge that they have no impurities) and *anutpādajñāna* (knowledge that they will have no rebirths). The Mahāsaṅghikas could not agree to the high spiritual status attributed to the Arhats by the Theravādins for they argued that Arhats could realise only half-truth, namely, absence of the individual soul (*pudgalaśūnyatā*) and not the absence of both the individual soul and the worldly objects (*dharmaśūnyatā*). The high spiritual status of the Arhats was first challenged by Mahādeva in the Pāṭaliputra council. Even according to certain factions of the Sarvāstivādin and the Sammitīyas the Arhats are subject to retrogression. The Uttarāpathakas regarded some Arhats as imposters. In the commentary on the *Kathāvatthu* Buddhaghoṣa says that a section of the Mahāsaṅghikas and their offshoots asserted on the basis of the first four propositions of Mahādeva that the Arhats may have imperfections.[55] A section of the Mahāsaṅghikas, however, held that Arhats have no chance of retrogression.[56]

According to the Theravāda the five Vijñānas (perception derived by the organs of sense) conduce to attachment to the objects as also to detachment from the same. The Mahīśāsakas are in agreement with this view, but the Sarvāstivādins state that the five *vijñānas* engender *rāga* or *sarāga* (attachment) but no *virāga* (detachment). The Vātsiputrīya-Sāmmitīyas hold that the five *vijñānas* conduce neither to *sarāga* nor to *virāga*. The Mahāsaṅghikas supports the Theravāda viewpoint in regard to the five *vijñānas*. It has also a *ṣaḍ-vijñāna* concept according to which beings of Rūpa and Arūpa *dhātus* possess all the six sense-perceptions. Regarding the *asaṃskṛtas* or the unconstituted (that which has neither origin, nor decay nor any change in) the Sthaviravāda admits three—*ākāśa* (uncovered space), *pratisaṃkhyānirodha* (liberation by means of knowledge) and *apratisaṃkhyānirodha* (emancipation by meditational practices).[57] According to the Mahīśāsakas and the Sarvāstivādins there are nine *asaṃskṛta dharmas*, but there is difference in their lists. But according to the Sautrāntikas, the *asaṃskṛtas* have no real existence.[58] The Andhakas also postulate nine *asaṃskṛtas* adding to the Sthavira list four *āruppas* and *āryamārgāṅgikatva*.[59] The Theravādins do not recognise the Mahāsaṅghika categories of the *asaṃskṛtas* except the two *nirodhas*. The Mahāsaṅghikas hold that the *asaṃskṛtas* are unchangeable—the unchangeable nature of *dharmas* and undisturbed by appearance or non-appearance or continuity. As for the *āryamārgāṅgikatva* the *Kathāvatthu* explains that the Puravaśailas regard as *asaṃskṛtas* the fact of attainment (*patti*) of a *magga* or *phala* by the removal of certain mental impurities and not the *maggas* or *phalas* by themselves.[60] According to the Theravāda there is no intermediate stage of existence (*antarābhava*) in the *kāma* and *rūpa* Dhātus. This is contradicted by the Sarvāstivādins who hold that only in *kāma* and *rūpa* Dhātus there is an intermediate state of existence. The Mahīśāsakas on the other hand suppport the Theravāda standpoint. The Vātsiputrīya-Sammitīyas follow the line of the Sarvāstivādins and hold that every being, whether destined for Kāmaloka or Rūpaloka by his *karma* remains for some time in an intermediate state of existence. At that time the body takes no material form, not even the *skandhas*. It is not an independent state of existence but just a waiting stage preliminary to its existence in one of the two Lokas. The Sammitīyas add that those beings who are destined for hells or *asañña* (non-conscious) sphere or *arūpa* Loka have no *antarābhava*. The Mahāsaṅghika group is in accord with the Theravādins regarding the question of *antarābhava*.[61] According to the Theravāda, *anusayas* (dormant passions) and *paryavasthānas* (pervading passions) are mental states and are associated with mind and have objects of thought. The Sarvāstivādins also hold the same view. But the Mahīśāsakas are directly opposed to this thesis and hold that the *anusayas* are neither *citta* (mind) nor *caitasika* (mental). The Theravādins and Sarvāstivādins hold that all the *anuśayas* can be included in the *paryavasthānas*, but all *paryavasthānas* are not *anuśayas*. But the Mahīśāsakas hold that *anuśaya* (dormant passion) is different from *paryavasthāna* (pervading passion). The former is never an object of thought (*analambana*) and is dissociated from mind (*citta-visamprayukta*). But *paryavasthāna* is associated with mind. The Mahīśāsaka view is in agreement with that of the Mahāsaṅghikas.

Philosophically there was not much difference between the Mahāsaṅghikas and the Theravādins. The main deviation made by the Mahāsaṅghikas was to deify the Buddha, and to assert that he was superamundane (*lokottara*), so that what passed for the Buddha in this world was an apparition. Along with this deviation they maintained that the Arhathood was not the highest or the fully emancipated state. According to the Vetulyakas, a Mahāsaṅghika subsect, the Buddha does not live in the mortal world; neither should he be located anywhere. He is made of *anāsrava-dharmas* (pure objects) and is without sleep or dream. The Buddhas have unlimited *rūpa-kāyas* (material bodies), *balas* (power) and *āyu* (length of life).[62] As we have stated above, according to Tāranātha, Caitakyas and Purvaśailas were but the names of the same sect. From them branched off the Siddhārthakas and Rājagirikas. The Lokottaravādins and the Kaukkuṭikas were the same. The Ekavyavahārika was another name of the Mahāsaṅghikas.[63] Paramārtha in his translation of Vasumitra's *Samayabhedoparacanacakra*[64] gave literal meanings and special views of the subsects of the Mahāsaṅghikas. According to Paramārtha the Ekavyavahārikas held all *dharmas* as conventional and unreal and fictitious while the absolute was contingent, i.e. dependent on some thing else. The Lokottaravādins held that all mundane *dharmas* were unreal and the supramundane *dharmas* are real. Paramārtha explains it as the view that stands between *śūnyatā* (the transcendental reality), *tathatā* (thatness) and *amalavijñāna* (pure knowledge). The Bahuśrutiyas preferred a syncretism of Hinayāna and Mahāyāna. They affiliated themselves with the Satyasiddhi school[65] and attributed two meanings *nitārtha* (direct) and *neyārtha* (indirect)—to the teachings of the Buddha. Though belonged to the Mahāsaṅghika group, the Bahuśrutīyas accepted, according to Vasumitra, many views of the Sarvāstivādins. The Prajñaptivādins, as Paramārtha tells us, appeared some time after the Bahuśrutīyas and distinguished themselves as Bahuśrutīya-Vibhajyavādins. The main difference between the Prajñaptivādins and the Bahuśrutīyas is that the former held the view that the Buddha's teachings as embodied in the Piṭaka should be distinguished as nominal (*prajñapti*), conventional (*saṃvṛti*) and causal (*hetuphala*).[66] According to Vasumitra the Prajñaptivādins held that *skandhas* and *duḥkha* were not concomitant, that the twelve *āyatanas* were not real and that either attainment of *āryamārga* or death was dependent on *karma*. The Rājagirikas and Siddhārthakas hold that mind (*citta*) only functions and there are no other mental states associated with it.[67]

The period between c. 350 and 100 B.C. witnessed a rat-race of various Buddhist sects in course of which the Theravādins, the Sarvāstivādins and Mahāsaṅghikas were able to outrun others. The Theravādins remained in the central belt of India making their position stronger in Avanti. The Sarvāstivādins were also in the central belt with their centres of activity in Mathura and Kashmir whence the doctrine spread widely all over northern India including Tukhāra in the north-west, Malāva on the west and Oḍiviśa and Kāmarūpa on the east. The Mahāsaṅghikas established themselves at Vesāli and had followers scattered all over northern India, but they became more popular in the South. However nowithstanding sectarian differences the general background of the monastic culture remained the same. Monks belonging to different sects often lived in the same monastery observing the same monastic rules. Even in a later period when the Mahāyāna assumed a distinct character, monks belonging to the new order observed the same monastic rules as those of the earlier sects, because the Mahāyānists had no monastic code of their own. The relation of the laity to the Buddhist Saṅgha also did not undergo a material change. But there were some attempts to reach the masses. Following the example of the Purāṇas, the Jātakas and the Avadānas were composed. Great spiritual merit was attached to reading, writing, painting and carving them. This caught the fancy of the laity as a means of earning religious merit. The depiction of Jātaka stories and scenes from the Buddha's life at Sanchi, Bharhut and other places bear testimony to this. Those who were engaged in such activities were not necessarily Buddhists by conviction. As we have stated above, the formation of an organised religion in the modern or Western sense was outside the purview of the great teachers of Buddhism because that would entail the structuring of a Budddhist way of social life which they did not care to do. The laity was allowed to follow the social norms and injunctions as prescribed by the traditional Dharmaśāstras. Each Buddhist sect, prior to the development of Mahāyāna, viewed its own doctrine as a *mokṣa-śāstra* or science of liberation, exclusively meant for the individual. The goal of life remained Arhathood and Pratyekabuddhahood with the Theravādins while the Sarvāstivādins added to them the goal of Samyaksambuddhahood.

After the appearance of the Mahāyāna as a new phase of Buddhism about the second-first century B.C. the earlier sects came to be viewed as belonging to the Hīnayāna category. From a functional point of view a two-fold division of the Hīnayāna was suggested—Śrāvakayāna and Pratyekabuddhayāna. The Śrāvakas were supposed to enrich themselves by the teachings of Buddha. They could impart those teachings to others till the advent of another Buddha. But they could neither attain *nirvāṇa* themselves nor help others to do so. The Pratyekas claimed themselves as belonging to a rather superior rank because they were supposed to possess the capability of attaining *nirvāṇa* by their own efforts without the help of a Buddha. But they had not the capability of helping others to achieve *nirvāṇa*. The third *yāna*, Bodhisattvayāna, claimed that its followers could not only attain *nirvāṇa*—nay even Buddhahood—with their own unaided efforts, but also could help others to attain these ideals.

But though Mahāyānism was evolved as a distinct stage in the process of the constant metamorphosis which characterised the history of Buddhism from the very beginning, it was not a single system. It was a conglomeration of heterogeneous doctrines, having various schools and sects of its own, though their adherents, unlike the sectarian constituents of the Hīnayāna, preferred to designate themselves after the generic name and not after the brand names. Some of the Mahayanic ideas may very well be traced to the earlier sources.[68] The deification of the Buddha is said to be the innovation of the Mahāsaṅghikas and allied sects while others insisted on his human character. But this human Buddha, as we have seen while dealing with the Buddhist mythology, was no less than any supreme being. The *Majjhima Nikāyas* says that all gods, such as Indra, Brahmā, Prajāpati, etc., are unable to trace the mind of the Tathāgata as it is unknowable and unfathomable. The Tathāgata is composed of *saṃkhāras* (constituent of worldly being) and when the *saṃkhāras* are eschewed by him he disappears in unfathomable infinity. Those who have attained mental freedom (*vimuttacitta*) and highest knowledge and insight (*anuttariyadassanena*) are capable of devoting themselves to the worship of the Tathāgata.[69] The Mādhyamika Śūnyavāda is also foreshadowed in the Pali texts.[70] In the *Saṃyutta Nikāya*[71] the following is said: Śūnya is the world. People say, O Lord, how does this saying do? Because the world is void of the self, Ānanda, of what belongs to the self is unreal. Likewise aspects of the Yogācāra-Vijñānavāda is foreshadowed in the *Dīgha Nikāya*.[72] Although the Mahāsaṅghikas are generally regarded as the precursors of Mahāyānism, the role of the Sarvāstivādins was also by no means insignificant. The Mahāyānists incorporated the Sarvāstivādin interpretations of the concepts such as *dhātus, skandhas, āyatanas, āryasatyas, aṅgas* of the *pratityasamutpāda* and so forth in their own system in toto. This is also attested by the Prajñāpāramitā literature which contains numerous Sarvāstivādin terms. The Sarvāstivādins were responsible for the addition of the term *śūnya* to the usual trio comprising *duḥkha, anitya* and *anātma*. Moreover, the Sarvāstivādins had developed two *kāya* concepts—*rūpakāya* and *dharmakāya*—which acquired a new dimension in Mahayanism. Again, negatively, it was the realism of the Sarvāstivādins which evoked sharp criticism from Nāgārjuna and other Mahāyānist writers. The *dharmaśūnyatā* (non-existence of everything whatever) doctrine of the Mahayanists was just the alter ego of the *astitvavāda* (reality of the existence of the elements composing a being) of the Sarvāstivādins. The adoption of the *Lalitavistara* by the Mahayanists as the authentic biography of the Buddha is also suggestive of the Sarvāstivāda influence on Mahayanism. Whether the concept of the Bodhisattva and the practice of six *pāramitās* were introduced for the first time by the Mahāsaṅghikas or by the Sarvāstivādins is uncertain. The mention of the six *pāramitās*, the fulfilment of which is compulsory for the Bodhisattvas, is frequently found in the works of both the Sarvāstivādins and Mahāsaṅghikas, and both were responsible for the growth of the large mass of the Avadāna literature, the central theme of which is the fulfilment of the *pāramitās*.

It is difficult to assign any particular date to the rise of the Mahāyāna, though from circumstantial evidence it appears that the Mahāyāna originated about the first century B.C. in the Andhra country where the Mahāsaṅghikas had their centre. The first Prajñāparamitā[73] was composed about the same time when we come across the following tenets of Mahayanism—*dharmaśūnyatā* (non-reality of phenomenal objects) besides *pudgalaśūnyatā* (absence of any substance such as soul); conception of countless Buddhas and Bodhisattvas; worship of gods and goddesses; use of *mantras* for attaining emancipation; and so forth. These ideas did not spring up all of a sudden. In connection with the Sarvāstivādins Vasumitra has referred to the sameness of the *vimutti* of the Buddhas, Śrāvakas and Pratyekabuddhas, to the three Yānas and to the Bodhisattvas continuing to be average beings (*pṛthagjana*) till they step into the path leading to the right knowledge (*samyaktva-nyārna*).[74] While the Jātakas are confined to the previous lives of the Buddha, the Avadānas introduced the Bodhisattva concept. The *Mahāvastu* refers to devotees developing *bodhicitta* and aspiring to Buddhahood. It mentions the four *caryās* of Bodhisattva and the ten *bhūmis*.[75] In the Jātakas the Buddha in his former existences has been described as Bodhisattva and in later Buddhist literature the term Bodhisattva has been used in various senses but there is reason to hold that at a certain stage in the history of Buddhism the term Bodhisattva denoted no more than a class of monks. This is evident from the fact that Tāranātha[76] says that five hundred Bodhisattvas took part in the Jālandhara council of Kaṇiṣka. The *Divyāvadāna*[77] speaks of the existence of a class of monks called Bodhisattvajātika. The Avadānas, which are primarily the production of the Sarvāstivādins, clearly show a new phase of development of a form of Bodhisattvayāna which had a multi-streamed culmination in the Mahāyāna. The Lokottaravādin offshoot of the Mahāsaṅghikas shows a little more development than the Sarvāstivādins by defining the four *caryās*, the first referring to the preliminary practices of a Bodhisattva while he is still an average person, the second to the development of *bodhicitta*, the third to the gradual progress made by a Boddhisattva up to the sixth *bhūmi* and the fourth to the practice of the last four *bhūmis*, from which a Bodhisattva can never retrocede but must ultimately attain *bodhi*.[78]

The origins of Mahāyānism lay to a greater extent outside the sectarian history of Buddhism than inside it. Although in the spiritual community established by the Buddha there was no room for the common people, still there were stray attempts from time to time to reach the masses. One of the main reasons why Buddhism did not serve the purpose of a religion was its inherent atheism. It has also to be remembered in this connection that, except the Nyāya-Vaiśeṣikas, most of the schools of Indian philosophy like the Buddhists, Jains,

Sāṅkhyas, Mīmāṃsakas, etc., were basically *atheistic*. Their argument was that every real entity was a cause as also an effect, but the first cause (God) as an effect had no cause and as such it was no effect. They held that if God might be regarded as a free agent he could not have the desire to create, and if taken as an agent under bondage he could not have the capacity to create. The non-theistic Vedānta held that the cause alone was real and its apparent transformation in the form of the effect was only an illusion. Atheism may attract intellectuals but not an average person who wants a God as the supreme being who is all-powerful and all-merciful. This was understood at least by a section of the monks even during the earliest period of the history of Buddhism. And these people, nowithstanding their theoretical affiliation with the one or the other of the so-called Hīnayāna sects,were the forerunners of Mahāyānism. Even from the earliest times they tried to deify the Buddha. While dealing with the early mythology of the Buddhists we have seen that in the Pali texts the Buddha had already been conceived of as the supreme being heading a pantheon of such Vedic gods as Indra, Varuṇa, Prajāpati, etc. But this projection of Buddha failed to evoke public interest because of conceptual drawbacks. His human form did not still then sink into oblivion. Though he was held in high esteem as one of the greatest of the saints, even having omniscience, his basic human character was inconsistent with the personality of the supreme being attributed to him, especially when his dependents were no other than the powerful Vedic gods. On the other hand, the Buddhist form attributed to the Vedic deities like Indra, etc., was also inconsistent with traditionally established mythological forms crystallised by means of popular narratives dealing with their legendary exploits. Next time the Buddhists were more careful and systematic in projecting an eternal and all-pervading body of the Buddha, the existence of which was viewed on different planes. This ultimately gave rise to the *trikāya* theory according to which the Buddha as the ultimate principle representing the totality of things or the cosmic unity, has three aspects known as *kāyas* or bodies which are the *Dharmakāya*, the *Sambhogākāya* and *Nirmāṇkāya*. This *trikāya* theory is a restatement of the traditional Hindu concept of the tripartite divinity—the supreme *brahman* beyond all attributes, the limited *saguṇa brahman* or Īśvara and his *avatāra* or incarnation.

By the Dharma-kāya is meant the unqualified permanent reality underlying the things (*dharma*) or in other words, the uncharacterised pure consciousness (*vijñaptimātratā*) which was foreshadowed in the Upaniṣadic concept of the *brahman*. In the Mahāyāna terminology the word *dharma* denotes the sense of 'entity' and as such the Dharma-kāya means *tathatā-rūpa* or the 'thatness' of all entities, the primordial element (*dharma-dhātu*) underlying all that exists. That is why it is also called Svabhāva-kāya, that is, the body of the ultimate nature. According to the *Avataṃsaka*,[79] the *dharma-kāya* which manifests itself in the triple world is neither an individual reality nor a false existence. It is universal, free from all impurities, non-assertive, undecaying, ever serene and eternal and the one devoid of all determination. It has no boundary, no quarters, its freedom or spontaneity being incomprehensible. But it is in everything. There is no place in the universe where this body does not prevail.

The Sambhoga-kāya is explained in the Prajñāpāramitās[80] as an exceedingly refulgent body which emits countless brilliant rays of light and illuminates the *lokadhātus*. On each ray of light is found a lotus with thousand petals on which is seated a *tathāgata* preaching to the Bodhisattvas, householders, recluses and others the doctrine of the six *pāramitās*. The Sambhoga-kāya usually means the subtle body of the eternal Buddha which manifests itself in the various conditions of bliss. It should be mentioned in this connection that the concept of the Sambhoga-kāya did not mature completely in the early Mahayanic works. The *Suvarṇaprabhāśa* and the *Abhisamayālaṅkāra-kārikā* tell us that the Sambhoga-kāya is a very subtle body of the Buddha, endowed with all the *mahāpuruṣa* signs and is generally assumed by the Buddhas for imparting the higher and metaphysical truths to the advanced Bodhisattvas.[81] While the Dharma-kāya corresponds to the impersonal Absolute of the Vedānta, the *brahman*, the Saṃbhoga-kāya corresponds to the Īśvara when *brahman* assumes name and form. Every Buddha has his own Sambhoga-kāya but all the Buddhas have one and the same Dharma-kāya.

The Nirmāṇa-kāya or Rūpa-kāya is the body of transformation, the human incarnation of the eternal Budha, such as our known Śākyasiṃha. The *Sutrālaṅkāra* refers to those forms which are assumed by the Buddhas to render service to beings of various worlds. It generally refers to the human form that the Buddha takes in order to make a show of his acquiring the functional role of an average man, living a family life and then retiring from it and ultimately attaining *nirvāṇa* by recourse to ascetic practices.[82]

Outside the Buddhist church and discipline the *bhakti* concept was replacing the older religious ideas. Thinking of this particular popular emotion the Mahāyānists, in order to reach the masses, also introduced a typical cult of the Buddha by making him the highest god and allowing his worship in images. In order to reach the masses Mahāyāna also had to make a compromise with the local cults and rituals, just as Christianity did in Europe by conferring sainthood on the pagan deities. Once this process started in Mahāyāna it multiplied.

Side by side with the *trikāya* concept arose that of the incarnations of the human Buddha, the Buddhas of the past, present and future. Legendary careers and achievements were ascribed to each of these Buddhas. Five Dhyāni Buddhas were also conceived, each symbolising one of the five *skandhas* or elements. They were Vairocana, Akṣobhya, Ratnasmbhava, Amitābha and Amoghasidhi supposed to have sprung from one Ādi Buddha. Each of these Buddhas had a Bodhisattva and a goddess as female consort. Originally Bodhisattvahood was an ideal as opposed to Arhathood. One who actively endeavoured for the development and upliftment of intellect and mind (*bodhi-citta*) with the purpose of the attainment of Buddhahood was a Bodhisattva. From a theoretical viewpoint every Mahayanist should be a potential Bodhisattva. But in reality the Bodhisattvas emerged as a class of gods having an intermediary position between the Buddhas and their devotees. They came to be regarded as powerful deities who could grant desired effects to their worshippers. Of such Bodhisattvas the important ones were Avalokiteśvara, Mañjuśrī, Vajrapāṇi, Samantabhadra, Ākāśagarbha, Maitreya, etc. Avalokiteśvara was the god of compassion whose female consort Tārā represented *prajñā* or wisdom. She was the saviour of mankind in distress. Mañjuśrī was ever young, the god of knowledge and teacher of the future Buddha Maitreya. Besides, there were other deities collected mostly from the surviving popular cults and regarded as emanations of the Dhyānī Buddhas and the Bodhisattvas.

The source of the philosophical idealism of the Mahāyāna were also extra-Buddhist. The philosophical controversies dealt with in the preceding chapter bear testimony to this. From an historical point of view, while the central doctrine of Buddhism—that of *anātma*—is conceived in Hīnāyana as the conglomeration of five elements (*skandhas*) which are constantly changing (*anitya*) and momentary (*kṣaṇika*), in Mahāyāna they are regarded as actually non-existent. For example, it may be said that the Hinayanist does not recognise the existence of any eternal inner reality or self of an earthen pot because it may also be given the shape of a horse. But the existence of the element, that is clay, of which the earthen pot or horse is made, is not denied. But the Mahayanist denies even the existence of clay. Just as the pothood or horsehood of clay, is false, so also the clay itself is false.

The first is *pudgalaśūnyatā* and the second *dharmaśūnyatā*. The essence of the Mahāyāna teaching is that the worldly person travels in the world of false notions. These false notions are created by six imperfect sense organs. According to the Mahayanic Yogācāra or VIjñānavāda, pure consciousness or Vijñāna is self-effective and is the ultimate reality beyond which nothing exists. This consciousness constitutes the world of apparent existence. This doctrine, as is well-known, has its root in the Upaniṣads which had the potentials of a philosophical outlook which reflected the reality of the world. Regarding the idealism of the Upaniṣads Deussen wrote :

> It was negative in so far as no experimental knowledge led to a knowledge of *brahman*; and it was positive in so far as the consciousness was aroused that the knowledge of empirical reality was an actual hindrance to the knowledge of *brahman*. The conception of *avidyā* was developed from the negative idea of mere ignorance to the positive idea of false knowledge. The experimental knowledge which reveals to us a world of plurality, where in reality only *brahman* exists, and a body where in reality there is only the soul, must be a mistaken knowledge, a delusion, a *māyā*. This is very noteworthy step in advance. It is the same which Parmenides and Plato took when they affirmed that the knowledge of the world of sense was mere deception, which Kant took when he showed that the entire reality of experience is only apparition and not reality. It is of the greatest interest to follow up the earliest foreshadowings of this thought in India, and to trace how the term *avidyā* passed from the negative idea of ignorance to the positive idea of false knowledge.[83]

The philosophical idealism of the Mahāyāna Buddhists and the Advaita Vedāntists was mostly derived from the Upaniṣadic sources. The followers of the Vijñānavāda or Yogācāra divide the basic ingredients of existence into two categories—constituted and unconstituted. These ingredients are not *rūpa* or matter; they are produced from *citta* or mind. The external objects have no real existence, because we can have no medium outside consciousness which can distinguish between the knower and the knowledge. An apparently visible pillar is nothing but a mental form. While the Yogācāra thus declares everything to be the creation of mind the Mādhyamika or Śūnyavāda goes a step further and declares that even what is called conciousness is false. The central point of the Mādhyamika philosophy is also substantially the same as that of the Upaniṣadic idealism. Objects are neither momentary nor eternal, neither produced nor destroyed, neither composite nor separate. What is produced by concurrent causes is not produced by itself and hence does not exist in itself.[84] The Upanisadic idealists denied the empirical world and gave to the ultimate reality the name *brahman*. The Mādhyamikas, proceeding on similar lines, called the ultimate reality the *śūnya*. But, unlike the *vijñāna* of the Yogācārins, the *śūnya*, in the last analysis, could not have been more than a mere mystical concept. It was no thesis to be established or refuted by means of formal logic. The Mādhyamikas also did not lay any stress on the importance of formal logic.[85]

Besides the cult of the Buddha, the Bodhisattvas and their emanations as well as a philosophy of pure idealism, the Mahāyānists offered other methods for attaining liberation such as psychic exercises, meditation, mystic experience and so forth. All these were not typically Buddhist and their sources lay elsewhere. The Mahāyānists frequently resorted to the *haṭha-yoga*, the Indian traditional Yogic system, as a basic feature of their spiritual exercise. The name Yogācāra which has been attributed to the followers of Vijñānavāda is suggestive of their emphasis on Yogic practices. Yoga has been the principal subject matter of the *Guhyasamāja* which insists on the six traditional limbs of the Yoga.[86] Psychic exercise, meditation, rituals and other performing aspects on which the Mahāyāna lays so much emphasis have been ancient practices common to all forms of Indian systems. A class of Mahāyānic literature which was composed between the fourth and eighth centuries is known as Dhāraṇi which refers to *mantra, mudrā, maṇḍala, kriyā, caryā,* etc., by which the Tantric cults are characterised. Occasional references to this kind of literature are found in early Mahāyāna texts.[87] The spell *om maṇipadme hum* occurs in the *Divyāvadāna*.[88] The *Bodhisattvabhūmi* also contains numerous spells and deals with the mystic aspect of the syllables.[89] The Prajñāpāramitā Sūtras lay emphasis on the cult of the Female Principle. The Kāraṇḍavyuha contains not only Tantric terminology and rituals as well as the concept of the Female Principle, but also cults of some eminent Purāṇic deities. Its prose version refers to a rudimentary concept of Avalokiteśvara as emanating from an Ādi Buddha-like entity.[90] The *Bhaiṣajya-guruvaidurya-prabharāja* shows remarkable Tantric influence. It specially mentions rituals of *ugra* of dreadful type.[91]

As we have mentioned out earlier, as regards the Mahāyāna we have no clear sectarian accounts. The *Tattvaratnāvalī* of Advayavajra,[92] however, provides some sectarian information. It affiliates both the

Śrāvakayāna and the Pratyekabuddhayāna to the Vaibhāṣika school. The Sautrāntikas, Yogācāras, and Mādhyamikas are all said to belong to Mahāyāna. The Yogācāras have been subdivided into Sākāravāda and Nirākāravāda while the Mādhyamika into Māyopamadravyavāda and Sarvadharmāpratiṣṭhānavāda. A general division of the Mahāyāna has also been made under two categories known as the Paramitānaya and Mantranaya.[93] In the former insistence was laid upon the cult of ten *pāramitās*, namely, Dāna (charity), Śīla (good conduct), kṣānti (forebearance), Vīrya (energy), Dhyāna (meditation), Prajñā (wisdom), Upāya (means), Praṇidhi (concentration), Bala (strength) and Jñāna (knowledge). In the *Vimalaprabhā* we find that the doctrines of the Pāramitānaya are written wholly in Sanskrit while those of the Mantranaya are explained in Sanskrit, Prakrit, Apabhraṃśa, etc., The principles of Mantranaya are said to be very deep and subtle and inaccessible to ordinary men. Though the ultimate purpose of the Mantra-śāstra is the same as that of the other Sāstras, it is regarded as distinctly superior to them. It is said to be free from delusions and accessible only to persons of higher intellectual calibre. This Mantranaya or Mantrayāna school of the Mahāyāna seems to be the introductory stage of the so-called Tantric Buddhism from which other offshoots such as Vajrayāna, Kālacakrayāna, Sahajayāna, etc. arose in later times.[94] The Tibetan tradition, however, makes no distinction between Mahāyānism and Tantrism. The great exponents of Mahāyānism have been described in the Tibetan tradition also as experts in Tantric lore. The Tibetan writers confused the great Mādhyamika teacher Nāgārjuna with the alchemist of the same name, and connected teachers like Asaṅga and Maitreyanātha with Tantric ideas and practices. It is possible that because these teachers enjoyed great fame and prestige, the Tibetan writers wanted to associate Tantrism with them. At the same time it is not impossible that these teachers might have also contributed in some way or other to the growth of certain ideas and practices from which the existing form of Tantrism drew much inspiration.[95]

Two contradictory sets of elements were amalgamated in the Mahāyāna. One was the set of popular elements which was directly connected with the cultic and ritualistic requirements of the people whom the Mahāyānists wanted to reach. The other was the idealistic viewpoint, an acute form of idealism, which regarded the world as a false or void entity. A pure devotional cult with the Buddha as the highest god who is eternal, without any origin or decay, and the ultimate reality which is beyond any sort of description, was grafted onto the frame of the Śūnya doctrine of Mahāyāna. This Buddha was also regarded as the head of a pantheon, the members of which came from a variety of sources with their typical cults and rituals. A regular pantheon comprising a hierarchy or innumerable deities is also met with in the Vajrayāna ramification of Mahāyānism which later dominated the field. Many of the later Vajrayāna elements are foreshadowed in the Mahāyānic texts such as the *Saddharmapuṇḍarīka*, *Sukhāvativyūha*, etc. The *Dharmasaṃgraha*, attributed to Nāgārjuna, knows of five Dhyāni Buddhas and their female consorts and also of the eighteen Lokapālas, six Yoginīs and eight Bodhisattvas.[96] The same holds good in the case of the *Suvarṇaprabhāśa* which is to a great extent Tantric in contents, formulae and rites. It mentions four Dhyāni Buddhas, a few Bodhisattvas and goddesses. A rudimentary form of the doctrine of Ādi Buddha is indicated in the *Mahāyānasutrālaṅkāra*.[97] In Śāntideva's *Śikṣāsamuccaya* mention is made of a number of deities who become prominent figures in the Vajrayāna.

The second important achievement of the Mahāyāna was to bring the doctrine of universal vacuity or Śūnyatā in relation to that of universal compassion or Karuṇā. The principle of Karuṇā or universal compassion is closely associated with the Bodhisattva ideal according to which a Bodhisattva deliberately postpones his own salvation until the whole world of suffering beings is saved. The *Kāraṇḍavyūha* describes how Bodhisattva Avalokiteśvara renounced *nirvāṇa* in favour of suffering humanity. In Śāntideva's *Bodhicaryāvatāra*[98] we find the Bodhisattva saying that he is eager to renounce all he has achieved for the sake of the welfare of beings and urging others to do the same. Thus the Bodhisattvas are those who dedicate their lives to the service of others. According to the Mahāyāna, Śūnyatā and Karuṇā, on being combined, develop *bodhicitta* (etymologically, intellectual and mental faculties) which helps an individual to obtain *bodhi* or the highest knowledge. This *bodhicitta* is achieved through ten stages or *bhūmis*. The stages are *pramuditā* (of delight or joy), *vimalā* (free from defilement), *prabhākari* (brightening), *arciṣmati* (full of flames that burn all passion and ignorance), *sudurjayā* (far above evil passion or temptation), *abhimukhī* (face to face with highest knowledge), *duraṅgamā* (knowledge of expedience), *acalā* (immovable), *sādhumatī* (sentience) and *dharmamegha* (perfect knowledge and great compassion).[99] *Bodhi*, as we have already seen, is perfect knowledge and *citta* is the mind bent on attaining perfect enlightment. It is in the latter that a perfect harmony of Śūnyatā and Karuṇā takes place. This view is maintained in Vajrayāna and in other schools of Tantric Buddhism which hold that *bodhicitta* is a state of supreme realisation transcending both *bhava* (existence) and *nirvāṇa* (extinction). It is without beginning or end, quiescent, immutable in existence as also in non-existence, the non-duality of Śūnyatā and Karuṇā.[100]

We have seen that in the *Tattvaratnāvalī* collected in the *Advayavajrasṃgraha* Mahāyāna is subdivided into two schools—Pāramitānaya and Mantranaya. The latter, also styled Mantrayāna, 'the way of the *mantras*', is regarded as the precursor of Vajrayāna and its offshoots. Vajrayāna has no clear-cut definition in the Buddhist texts. The Tibetans do not differentiate between Mahāyāna and Vajrayāna. They equate the Mahāyāna Sūtras (mDo) with Tantra (rGyud).[101] In the *Guhyasamāja*[102] it is described as the cult of the five *kulas* or families of the Bodhisattvas, each representing a distinct mental state of the aspirant. In the *Sādhanamālā*[103] it is described as the path of transcendental perfect enlightenment, to be achieved through different rites and ceremonies, *mantras* and meditation. Elsewhere Vajrayāna is compared to a raft on which one can cross the ocean of existence.[104] Vajrayāna literally means the adamantine path or vehicle, but its special meaning is the 'Śūnya vehicle'. But the Śūnyatā of the Vajrayāna is not the Śūnyatā of the Mādhyamikas. According to Vajrayāna Śūnyatā is a positive principle designated as Vajra (thunderbolt) because it is firm and sound and cannot be changed, pierced, penetrated, burnt and destroyed.[105] Among the many innovations Vajrayāna had introduced the following may be noted: theory of the five Dhyāni Buddhas as embodiment of the five *skandhas*; theory of the *kulas* or clans of the Dhyāni Buddhas from which deities emerge; worship of *prajñā* or *śakti*; inconological forms of the deities for meditation; *mantras, yantras, mudrās, maṇḍalas*, etc., psychic exercise; and mystic realisation.

According to the *Guhyasiddhi* of Padmavajra and the *Jñānasiddhi* of Indrabhūti, it was the *Guhyasamāja*[106] which was the first authoritative work on Vajrayāna. It is believed to have been introduced in an Assembly of the Faithful by lord Buddha who is known as Sarva-Tathāgata-Kāya-Vāk-Citta. The earliest work dealing with the tenets of Vajrayāna is said to have been the *Vidyādharapiṭaka* described by Hiuen Tsang as belonging to the canonical literature of the Mahāsaṅghikas. But this work is not available in original Sanskrit, and it is not possible to say anything with regard to the contents of the text. The next important work is the *Mañjuśrīmūlakalpa*[107] which is written in the Saṅgīti style in prose and in verse in mixed Sanskrit. It deals with the formulae and practices which lead both to material prosperity and spiritual regeneration, and belongs to the early centuries of the

Christian era, but decidedly after the time of the composition of the *Amitāyus Sūtra* or the *Sukhāvati Vyūha* which ushered in the conception of Amitābha and Avalokiteśvara for the first time in the Mahāyāna.[108] It should be mentioned in this connection that the *Mañjuśrīmūlakalpa* does not refer to Vajrayāna directly, but it speaks of Mantrayāna. The doctrine of the five Dhyāni Buddhas, their names, *mudrās, mantras, kulas, śaktis,* etc., are all absent in the *Mañjuśrīmūlakalpa*. So it may be called as a work of Mahāyana Sūtra type containing certain tenets which were further elaborated in the Vajrayāna.

The word *vajra* which means thunderbolt denoted the real nature of things which is Śūnyatā. The Vajrayāna considers Śūnya as a positive entity and the ultimate reality. Gods and goddesses are the manifestations of this Śūnya. They have no real existence; they are born of the mind, issuing from the *vijamantras* uttered by the worshipper. The Śūnya takes the form of divinity in accordance with the germ-syllable uttered and exists only as a positive idea in the mind of the aspirant. It takes different forms according to the different functions it has to discharge, for instance, the form of Siṃhanāda when a disease is to be cured, that of Jāṅguli when there is a snake-bite, that of Kurukullā when there is a love affair, and so on. The number of gods and goddesses increases when Śūnya manifests itself in different forms; since the inspirations of these manifestations are innumerable, the deities can also be innumerable. But all these are creations of mind and basically symbolic. The cosmic concept of Śūnya is naturally equated with *bodhicitta* which has been defined as the mind bent on attaining perfect enlightenment. The weapons and emblems by which the deities of Vajrayāna are characterised are nothing but the weapons needed by *bodhicitta* to fight against the elements obstructing the path of knowledge. For instance, when the darkness of ignorance is to be dispelled the *bodhicitta* becomes a sword, when the heart of the wicked is to be pierced it becomes the *aṅkuśa* or goad, when a bad element is to be cut away it becomes a *kartari* or knife and so on. The *mudrās* also serve the same purpose. When protection is needed the *bodhicitta* becomes *abhaya*; when a boon is desired it becomes *varada*; when instruction is required it becomes *dharmacakra*.

To the concepts of *vajra* or *śūnyatā* was added the term *sattva* which implied pure knowledge.[109] The combination of these two principles was crystallised in the form of a personal god, the supreme being, Lord Vajrasattva or Vajradhara, regarded as the essence of Śūnyatā—transcending all imagination, omniscient, embodiment of pure wisdom, abode of all merits and so on.[110] With the development of the idea of Vajrasattva or Vajradhara as the supreme being and also as the Ādi Buddha or the Primal Enlightened One, there evolved a new pantheon in the Vajrayāna—five Dhyāni Buddhas emanating from him and representing the five *skandhas*, namely, *rūpa* (material element), *vedanā* (feeling), *saṃjñā* (conceptual knowledge), *saṃskāra* (mental states) and *vijñāna* (consciousness). Each of the Dhyāni Buddhas has a Śakti, a Bodhisattva, and a number of emanations, male and female. By far the most ancient among the Dhyāni Buddhas is Amitābha who resides in Sukhāvati heaven in peaceful meditation. He belongs to the lotus family and is of the nature of the cosmic element called *saṃjña*. His consort or Śakti is Paṇḍarā or Pāṇḍaravāsinī and Bodhisattva Padmapāni who later became celebrated as Avalokiteśvara. Akṣobhya belongs to the Vajra family and represents the cosmic element *vijñāna* or consciousness. His consort is Māmakī or Māmakā and Bodhisattva Vajrapāṇi. Vairocana represents the cosmic element *rūpa* (form) and belongs to the family of Tathāgata. His consort is Locanā and Bodhisattva Samantabhadra. Amoghasiddhi represents the cosmic element of *saṃskāra* (mental states) and belongs to the family of *karma*. His consort is Tārā who was destined to play a greater role in subsequent religious history and Bodhisattva Viśvapāṇi. Finally, Ratnasambhava represents the cosmic element of *vedanā* (sensation) and belongs to the family of *ratna*. His consort is Vajradhātvīsvarī and Bodhisattva Ratnapāni.[111]

Besides the five major Bodhisattvas deriving their origins from the five Dhyāni Buddhas there are other representing different aspects of life and universe.[112] Among the Bodhisattvas Avalokiteśvara and Mañjuśrī became the most popular. In the *Mahāvastu* we come across Avalokita Bodhisattva whose duty was to instruct new adherents of the faith. In the *Kāraṇḍavyūha* he is said to manifest himself in countless forms of godhead for the welfare of mankind. This explains why his forms have multiplied. No less than 108 forms have been attributed to him which include almost all the Bodhisattvas and other Buddhist gods as Lokeśvaras. "He soon became the most popular of the northern Buddhist gods, being looked upon as a representative of the Buddha, the guardian of the Buddhist faith until Maitreya should appear on earth as Mānuṣī Buddha."[113] He is embodiment of universal compassion. Mañjuśrī is mentioned in the Buddhist texts as one of the greatest Bodhisattvas who confers upon his devotees wisdom, retentive memory, intelligence and eloquence. According to Nepalese tradition, as preserved in the *Svayambhū Purāṇa*, he was originally a human being who performed many pious deeds and subsequently came to be deified as Bodhisattva.

Each of the Dhyāni Buddhas has in addition a number of emanations, gods and goddesses. Mahāvala, Saptaśatika Hayagrīva, Kurukullā, Bhṛkuṭi and Mahāsitavati are emanations of Amitābha; Jambhala, Caṇḍaroṣaṇa, Heruka-Hevajra, Buddhakapāla, Śambara, Saptākṣara, Mahāmāyā, Raktayamāri, Kṛṣṇayamāri, Kālacakra, Jāṅguli, Mahācīnatārā, Ekajaṭā, Parṇaśabarī, Prajñāpāramitā, Vasudhārā, Nairātmā, etc. are emanations of Akṣobhya; to Vairocana belong Nāmsaṅgīti, Mārīcī, Uṣṇīṣavijayā, Aparājitā, Vajravārāhī, Cundā, etc.; Amoghasiddhi's emanations are Vajrāmṛta, various forms of Tārā, Mahāmāyūrī, etc., Ratnasambhava has Jambhala, Vajratārā, Mahapratisarā, Vasudhārā, Aparajitā, Vajrayoginī and Prasanna Tārā. Beside these emanations there are many other deities in the Vajrayāna pantheon—ten gods and six goddesses of direction, eight Uṣṇīsa gods, five protectresses, four door goddesses, four Ḍakinis, twelve Pāramitās, twelve Vasita goddesses, twelve Dhāriṇīs, four Pratisaṃvits and Tārās of five colours . Many of these deities have been adopted from popular cults and some of them have very interesting history, as we shall see later. Quite a good number of Vajrayanic deities are well represented in sculpture. This will be dealt with in our note on iconography. Some Hindu gods and goddesses have also been incorporated in Vajrayāna pantheon such as Mahākāla, Gaṇapati, Sarasvatī, Indra, Yama, Varuṇa, Kubera, Īśāna, Agni, Nairṛti, Vāyu, Brahmā, Viṣṇu, Maheśvara, Kārttikeya, Vārāhī, Camuṇḍā etc.

NOTES

1. It is interesting to note that in many a country of South-East Asia where people followed Buddhism the civil and criminal codes meant for the masses were designated after Manu. See J. Jolly *Recht und Sitte* (1896), Eng. tr. *Hindu Law and Custom,* by B.K. Ghosh, Calcutta 1928, rep. Delhi, 1975, 86ff.
2. R.C Majumdar, *Corporate Life in Ancient India* (Calcutta, 1919), 286 ff., D.P. Chattopadhyaya, *Lokāyata* (Delhi, 1959), 468 ff., N.N. Bhattacharyya, *Ancient Indian Rituals and Their Social Contents* (New Delhi, 1975), 79-80.
3. See S.N. Dube, *Cross Currents in Early Buddhism* (New Delhi, 1980), 37ff. This work elucidates the controversies presented in the *Kathāvatthu* in the light of historical development of Buddhist thought in a wider milieu. The English translation of the

Kathāvatthu was published in 1915 by S.Z Aung and C.A.F. Rhys Davids under the title *Points of Controversy* and that of its commentary by B.C Law in 1940. Treatises of Vasumitra, Bhavya and Vinītadeva (trans. J. Masuda in *Asia Major* II), the Chinese travellers accounts, etc., also throw light on Buddhist factionalism. Vasumitra's treatise has one Tibetan and three Chinese translations by Kumārajīva (402-12), Paramārtha (557-69) and Hiuen Tsang (662). Koue-ki and Ki-tsang wrote commentaries on Paramārtha. Prior to S.N. Dube, N. Dutt utilised the *Kathāvatthu* evidence in his *Buddhist Sects* (Calcutta, 1970).

4. For detailed account in regard to these personalities see G.P. Malalasekera, *Dictionary of Pali Proper Names*, 2 Vols. (London, 1937-38).
5. Some of the guilts of Ānanda were discussed in the First Council. See M. Suzuki, 'The First Buddhist Council' in *Monist*, XIV, 1904, 252-83; Vallee Poussin, *The Buddhist Councils* (Calcutta, 1976), 4ff. (Originally published in French in *Museon*, 1905 and in English in *Indian Antiquary*,1908).
6. On the First Council see Franke in *JPTS*, 1908, 1-80; Jacobi in *ZDMG*, 1880, 184ff.; Poussin in *Ind. Ant.*, XXXVII, 1908, 1-18; W.W. Rockhill, *The Life of Buddha* (London, 1907), 148ff.; T. Watters, *On Yuan Chwang's Travels*, II, 159-61, J. Przyluski, *Le Concile de Rajagṛha* (Paris, 1926-28); etc. See Ch. I.
7. Another monk named Channa was excommunicated. According to the tradition of the Chinese Vinaya at the time of the First Council Channa created at Kausambi a division among the monks and Ānanda was sent to settle scores with him.
8. *Cullavagga*, XI; *SBE*, XX. 370 ff.
9. Przyluski, *op. cit.*, 319 ff.
10. *Cullavagga*, XII; also *Mahāvaṃsa*, IV, *Dīpavaṃsa*, IV-V. Other sources of the Second Council, besides the commentarial literature, are the Sanskrit *Mañjuśrīmūlakalpa*, Tibetan *Dul-va*, XI, 323-30; Bu-ston's and Tāranatha's *History*, works of Hiuen Tsang, and the Chinese *Vinaya* pertaining to different sects. For Vasumitta et al. see Masuda, *op. cit.* And also works of Vasilev, Walleser, Höfinger, Bareau, Frawwallner, Lamotte, Dutt and Dube mentioned in Ch. I.
11. It appears that in contrast to the Westerners who maintained a rural and conservative character the Easterners were more urbanised and prone to hedonistic habits, as is evident from their greed for gold and silver (*jālarūparajatam*) or fondness of drinking (*jalogiṃ pātam*). The latter according to the *Cullavagga* means that form of wine which has not yet attained the quality of intoxication. According to the *Dul-va* it means 'drinking like leech intoxicating liquor while making excuse of sickness'. Vallee Poussin, *op. cit.*, 50-51.

12. *Śākya*, 355.
13. *Dīpavaṃsa*, V. 39-54; Masuda, *op. cit.*, 14-17; Bareau, *Les Sectes Bouddhiques du Petit Vehicule*, 27-29; etc.
14. V. 39-48, 51.
15. The list of Bhavya (third list) which belongs to the Sammitīya tradition agree with the *Dīpavaṃsa* as regards the Mahāsaṅghika group. The Sthaviravāda yielded Mulasthavira and Haimavata; from Mūlasthavira Sarvāstivāda and Vāṣtiputrīya; from Sarvāsti-vāda Vibhajyavāda and Saṅkrāntivāda; from Vibhajyavāda; Mahīśāsaka, Dharmaguptaka, Tāmrasāṭīya and Kāśyapīya; from Vātsiputrīya Mahāgirika and Sammitīya; from Mahagirika Dharmottara, Bhadrayānīya and Sannagarika.
16. V. 54.
17. V. 12-13.
18. Texts available in the Tibetan and Chinese translation out of which Bhavya in his first list confirms the classification of Vasumitra and mentions some new sects of the Theravāda such as the Murantaka, Avantika and Kurukullaka. He omits the Gokulika sect of the Mahāsaṅghika group which seems to have been referred to by Vasumitra as the Kukkutika.
19. Takakusu, *I-tsing*, intro XXII-XXIV. Vinītadeva gives the same list adding Bahuśrutīya, Tāmraśāṭīya and Vibhajyavāda as emanating from Sarvāstivāda; Jetavaniya, Abhayagirivāsin and Mahāvihāravasin as emanating from the Sthaviravāda; and Kurukullaka, Āvantaka and Vātisputrīya as emanating from the Sammitīya. The Māhasaṅghika gave rise to Pūrvaśaila, Aparaśaila, Haimavata, Lokottaravāda and Prajñaptivāda.
20. The second list of Bhavya has substantial agreement with the *Sāriputraparipṛcchā* list save for the insertion of some new names in the case of the Mahāsaṅghika group. According to this tradition the original Order was divided into three schools—Sthaviravāda, Mahāsaṅghika and Vibhajyavāda. From Vibhajyavāda originated the Mahīśāsaka, Kāśyapīya, Dharmaguptaka and Tāmraśāṭīya. See A. Bareau, *Les Sectes Bouddhiques*, 16-18; N. Dutt, *Buddhist Sects*, 51-55; S.N. Dube, *Cross Currents*, 55-60.
21. Lama Chimpa and Alaka Chattopadhyaya, *Tāranātha's History of Buddhism*, (Calcutta 1970), 339-42. Tāranātha tells us further that during the reign of the Pāla kings only seven schools were known. They were Sammitīya comprising Vātsiputrīya and Kaurukullaka; Mahāsaṅghika comprising Prajñaptivāda and Lokottaravāda; Sarvāstivāda comprising Mūla-Sarvāstivāda and Tāmraśāṭīya. Tāranātha says that "the sect earlier known as the *Dārṣṭāntikas* was that of the Sautrāntikas which branched off from the Tāmraśāṭīyas. Hence it is not to be separately counted among the eighteen." According to N. Dutt, this corroborates Masuda's remark as against

that of Vallee Poussin that the Dārṣṭāntikas preceded the Sautrāntikas. *Asia Major*, II, 67; *Buddhist Sects*, 53.

22. *Mahāvaṃsa*, V. 272.
23. *Abhidharmakośavyākhyā*, intro. LV.
24. Dutt, *op. cit.*, 224.
25. *Dīpavaṃsa*, V. 51 : *sttarasa bhinnavādāeko vādo abhinnako.*
26. N. Dutt refers to two sects of the Mahīśāsakas, one earlier and the other later. *Buddhist Sects*, 124-34.
27. *Ep. Ind.*, XX. 24-25; A ref. to them is found in the Kura Pillar (Salt Range) of the time of Toranāna. *Ep. Ind.*, I. 238.
28. See Konow, *CII*, II 48, 137, 145, 155,176; Lüders, *List*, Nos. 125. 918-19, 929; *Ep. Ind.* II, 212; VIII, 111, 172; IX, 29, 135.
29. Konow, *CII*, II, 63, 86ff.; Watters, I, 226; Takakusu, *I-tsing*, 20.
30. Lüders, *List*, 319, 352, 635, 797.
31. *Ibid.*, 156, 158, 655.
32. *Le Concile de Rājagṛha*, 317-18.
33. For the *Kathāvatthu* account on the points to controversy between Theravāda and Sarvāstivāda see Dube, *op. cit.*, 265 ff.
34. ed. Poussin, VIII. 32.
35. J. Takakusu, *Essentials of Buddhist Philosophy*, ed. W.T. Chan and C.A. Moore (Honolulu, 1947), 74.
36. Przyluski, *op. cit.*, 325-26.
37. *Kathāvatthu* IV, 6; XVIII. 3-4.
38. Six kinds of Arhats are described in the *Kośa* VI. 56 ff.
39. *Kathāvatthu* IV.3; XXII.3; XXIII.2.
40. *Vātsiputrīya* may be a mis-Sanskritisation of Vajjiputtaka. This sect arose either among the Vajjis or in the Vatsa country.
41. *Ep. Ind.* VIII, 172; XIX, 67; Lüders, *List* 923. According to Hiuen Tsang (Watters I, 227 ff; II, 47 ff. and I-tsing; Takakusu XXIV) the Sammitīyas were the most prominent sect in the Vātsiputrīya group. According to Vinītadeva the Sammitīyas were subdivided into three sects—Kurukullakas, Āvantakas and Vātsiputrīyas. See Bu-ston II, 99-100.
42. Lüders, *List* 987, 1018, 1094-95, 1123-24, 1152.
43. *Abhidharmakośa* IX; see Poussin's preliminary notes in the *Kośa* IX, Fr. trans. 227-28.
44. *Mādhyamikavṛtti*, 275.
45. *Bodhicaryāvatāra* IX. 60.
46. See Dube, *op. cit.*, 229-60.
47. Vasubandhu asks whether the Vātsiputrīya-Sammitīyas can be regarded as Buddhist and whether they are entitled to attain liberation. His impression is that the Sammitīyas hold *pudgala* as real (*dravya*) and not nominal (*prajñapati*). Candrakīrti (*Mādhyamikavṛtti* 148, 192, 276,) however, does not dismiss the *pudgalavāda* of the Sammitīyas as wholly untenable. He even admits

that the Buddha as an expedient taught the *pudgalavāda* as he propounded the idealistic doctrine later. The *Sāmmitīya-nikaya-śāstra* (Venkataraman's trans. 21 ff) establishes that the Buddha did not fully explain many of his deeper ideas and the existence of soul or *pudgala* is one of them. The Vātsiputrīya-Sammitīya viewpoint as summarised by Vasumitra is that the *pudgala* is neither the same as the *skandhas* nor different from them. The name *pudgala* is provisionally given to an aggregate of *skandhas, āyatanas* and *dhātus*. Dharmas cannot transmigrate from one existence to another apart from the *pudgala*.

48. *CII*. II (1) 48, 170; *Ep. Ind.* VIII, 71 XXX, 183-84, Lüders, *List*, 1106.
49. Takakusu XXIII f. cf. Watters, I, 269.
50. *Ep. Ind.* XX. 24; XXI 62-63.
51. Lüders, *List*, 1130, 1171, 1223, 1230, 1244, 1248, 1250, 1263, 1270, 1272.
52. *Ep. Ind.* XX. 17-21, 214-15; XXIV, 259; XXVII, 4; *ASIAR*, 1923-24, 93; *IHQ*, XVIII, 60; Lüders, *List* 1020, 1250.
53. For the *Kathāvatthu* account of the deification of the Buddha see Dube, *op. cit.*, 120-44. Also see *Mahāvastu*, I, 167-70, *Kośa* (Poussin) III. 200; IX.254 : For Vasumitra, et al. see Masuda, *op. cit.*, 19ff.
54. Bareau, *op.cit.*, 58f., 261.
55. Dutt, *op.cit.*, 87-89, Dube, *op.cit.*, 90-119.
56. Bareau, *op. cit.*, 28.
57. *Aṅguttara* I, 152; *Dhammasaṅgaṇi* 583, 983, 1086; *Kośa* (Poussin) I.5ff. II. 45ff.
58. There is a long controversy in the *Kośa*, II. 55 between the Sarvāstivādins and the Sautrāntikas as to whether the *asaṃskṛtas* have any cause or fruits.
59. cf. *Kośa* III, 77.
60. Dutt, *op.cit.*, 121-22; *Masuda*, op. cit., 40.
61. Dutt, *op.cit.*, 122, 133, 223.
62. *Kathāvatthu*, XVII, 1-2, 6-10; XVIII. 1.
63. Chimpa and Chattopadhyaya, *op.cit.*, 341.
64. Paul Demieville, 'L' origine des sectes bouddhiques d'apres Paramārtha' in *Mélanges chinois et bouddhiques*, I, 1931-32, 42ff.
65. Sogen, *op.cit.*, 178-80.
66. Demieville, *op.cit.*, 49-50.
67. *Kathāvatthu*, VII. 3.
68. See N. Dutt, *Mahāyāna Buddhism* (Calcutta, 1976), 73-80.
69. *Majjhima* I, 140-42, 235, 488; cf. *Saṃyutta* III, 142.
70. *Dīgha* III, 219; *Majjhima* III, 104, 109. The *Mādhyamikāvatāra* cannot help admitting that the Hīnayānists also teach Śūnyatā as much as the Mahāyānists do.

71. IV. 34. Cf. *Suttanipāta* 1119.
72. I. 223.
73. The first Chinese translation of the text was made in A.D. 148 by Lokarakṣa and so we can assume that the original was in existence by the first century A.D. There are several Prajñāpāramitā texts of different dates of which the oldest is *Aṣṭasāhasrikā*.
74. Masuda, *op. cit.*, 49.
75. Ed. Senart (Paris, 1882-97), II, 362ff.
76. Chimpa and Chattopadhyaya, *op. cit.*, 93.
77. Ed. E.B. Cowell and R.A. Neil (Cambridge, 1886), 261.
78. Cf. *Mahāvastu* II, 46; *Lalitavistara* 35.
79. Suzuki, *Outlines of Mahāyāna Buddhism*, 223-24.
80. Dutt, *Mahāyāna Buddhism*, 163-64.
81. Suzuki, *op. cit.*, 257.
82. Vallee Poussin tried to explain the non-metaphysical incipient stage of the concept of *trikāya* in *JRAS*, 1906, 945-46. According to him originally *Dharma-kāya* was the *samādhi-kāya* of the Buddha in *nirvāṇa*. *Sambhoga-kāya* was the state before his attainment of the *nirvāṇa* in which he possessed and enjoyed the fruit of his activities as a Bodhisattva while *Nirmāṇa-kāya* was his physical form.
83. Deussen, *Philosophy of the Upaniṣads*, 74-75. "It is clear that originally Vijñānavāda is based on a number of Upaniṣadic passages containing the word jñāna and vijñāna referring to the *ātman* (self) or *brahman* (the absolute) in their Vedantic interpretation." V. Bhattacharya in *History of Philosophy : Eastern and Western*, I. 180.
84. *Tat tat prāpya yat utpannam na utpannam tat svabhāvataḥ* (Nāgarjuna). Here the original doctrine of the *pratītyasamutpāda* has been twisted to mean that everything that has a cause is bound to be unreal. cf. *Vigrahavyāvartanī*, (tr. S. Mookherjee) XXII.
85. It has been held by Candrakīrti that all the attempts of Bhāvaviveka (an earlier commentator on Nāgārjuna) to adduce formal reasons in his favour only bespeaks his own love of formal logic, but the Mādhyamikas did not require any formal logic at all, as all realities were absolutely denied by them. The Yogācārins, however, banked on the logical approach of the Sautrāntikas, though in regards to metaphysics they were Vijñānavādins.
86. XVIII, 163.
87. Cf. *Lalitavistara* I, 1; *Samādhirāja* II, 250; *Saddharmapuṇḍarika* IV, 234-35; *Laṅkāvatāra* III, 9; *Kāraṇḍavyūha* XVII, 301 etc. All from BST ed.
88. ed. Cowell and Neil, 218.
89. ed. U. Wogihara, 273-74.
90. BST, XVIII, 262-63, 292-304.

91. *Gilgit Mss* I, 13-24.
92. Collected in the *Advayavajrasaṃgraha*, ed. by MM. H.P. Sastri, GOS, XL.
93. *Ibid*., 21.
94. S.B. Dasgupta, *An Introduction to Tantric Buddhism* (Calcutta, 1950), rep. 1974, 52-53.
95. N.N. Bhattacharyya, *History of the Tantric Religion* (New Delhi, 1982), 223.
96. BST, XVII, 319.
97. IX. 77.
98. III. 4-6, 10-11, 13-15.
99. Dutt, *Mahayāna Buddhism*, 86-140.
100. *Jñānasiddhi* (GOS), 72-73.
101. G.N. Roerich, *The Blue Annals* (tr. of *Deb-ther-sñon-po*) 2 parts, (Calcutta, 1949, 1953), II.102.
102. GOS, 154.
103. I, 225; II, 421.
104. *Jñānasiddhi* 31.
105. *Advayavajrasmgraha* 23.
106. ed. B.T. Bhattacharyya, GOS, 53 (Baroda, 1931).
107. ed. T. Ganapati Sastri in *TSS*, 3 Vols. 1920-22. See also J. Przyluski, in *Bulletin de l'ecole Francaise d'Extreme Orient*, XXIII, 1923, 301ff.
108. The *Amitāyus Sūtra* was first translated into Chinese in a period between A.D. 148-70 and hence the time of its composition may be fixed at about A.D. 100.
109. *Advayavajrasaṃgraha* 24.
110. *Prajñopāya* III. 9; V. 45.
111. The conceptual descriptions of the Dhyānī Buddhas are to be found in the *Advayavajrasaṃgraha*, 40-41.
112. *Niṣpannayogāvali*, 50ff.
113. A. Getty, *Gods of Northern Buddhism*, Oxford, 1928, 58.

VII

THE FINAL TRANSFORMATION

The innovations of Vajrayāna were mostly in accordance with the existing Hindu cultic theories and practices. We have already had the occasion to refer to the popular Hindu gods such as Indra, Agni, Varuṇa, Viṣṇu, Śiva, Gaṇapati, etc., figuring in the Vajrayāna pantheon.[1] We have also seen that by postulating the *trikāya* theory the Mahayanists tried to introduce a form of *bhakti* cult among the Buddhists. This theory was evidently modelled on the traditional threefold approach of the Hindu sects towards the divine : *Brahman* or *para* (the Absolute, corresponding to the Dharmakāya of the Buddha), Īśvara or Antaryāmī (the *saguṇa brahman* corresponding to the Sambhoga-kāya of the Buddha) and Avatāra or Vibhava (incarnation, corresponding to the Rūpa or Nirmāṇa-kāya of the Buddha). Moreover, the Hindu concept of Arcā or cult-images formed an essential feature of the Mahayanic cults. The Mahāyāna insistence on *bhakti* is amply demonstrated in the *Saddharmapuṇḍarīka* which was to a great extent modelled on the *Bhagavadgītā*.[2] The germs of the Mahāyāna concept of *bhakti* are also to be found in the Hīnayāna concept of *śraddhā*. Both in the Mahāyāna and in the Vajrayāna (the two are same according to the Tibetan tradition) the word *sādhana* is especially used to mean the invocation of the deity by meditating of his/her form or symbol. The Yoga of Mahāyāna-Vajrayāna are of two kinds—general and specific. The former consists of the feeling of vacuity (*śunyatā*), its transformation into the form of a seed (*bīja*), conception of the seed in the form of a deity (*vimba*) and the feeling of deity in different parts of the body (*nyāsa*), and the latter of the six Yogic practices—control of sense organs (*pratyāhāra*), meditation (*dhyāna*), breath control (*prāṇāyāma*), concentration on *mantra* (*dhāraṇa*), remembrance (*anusmṛti*) and obtaining perfect wisdom (*samādhi*). These practices show that in regard to functional aspects there was no difference between Mahāyāna-Vajrayāna and other Hindu sects. The importance of *guru* or preceptor as the spiritual guide is stressed in Vajrayāna and its ramifications. The *guru* is expected to have complete grasp of the mystic and confidential practices; he should be reverenced even as the Lord. Without his guidance salvation is impossible to achieve and hence he should never be offended.[3] As in the Hindu Tantras, great importance is also attached to the *mantras* or spells. In fact Naropā and Advayavajra were inclined to use the term Mantranaya to designate the transitory stage of Mahayanism.[4] The concept of *maṇḍala* is also the same in the Hindu and Buddhist Tantras.

We have previously remarked that Mahāyāna Buddhism in order to reach the masses made a compromise with the existing local cults and rituals as a result of which numerous local, regional and tribal deities came within the fold of Mahayanism. In the agrarian societies of India the cults and rituals of the Mother Goddess were a very powerful force. This female-oriented religious phenomenon assumed a distinct shape later in the Śākta religion. The cult of the Female Principle and the sexual rites involved therein formed the substrata of a primitive Tantrism which was neither Buddhist nor non-Buddhist. It was a very ancient way of life, an undercurrent which influenced all forms of Indian religious systems in one way or the other. The concept of the primitive Mother Goddess of the agricultural societies contributed to the growth of that of Prakṛti as the embodiment of all the reproductive forces of nature and subsequently to that of Śakti as the only principle responsible for the functioning of these forces. In Vaiṣṇavism this Śakti has been deified as Lakṣmī, the consort of Viṣṇu, or Rādhā, the consort of Kṛṣṇa; in Śaivism this Śakti is Devī, the consort of Śiva; and in Buddhism it was conceived of in the forms of different goddesses associated with the Buddhas and the Bodhisattvas and at the philosophical level it has been conceived of as Prajñā or Śūnyatā. While the master logicians like Dignāga, Dharmakīrti, Śāntideva and others were devising hair-splitting arguments on the question of the valid sources of knowledge and philosophers like Asaṅga, Nāgārjuna and others were formulating the means to interpret the world as a void entity, as some form of nothingness like the beauty of the daughter of a barren woman, how Tantric ideas captured the heart of Buddhism through the backdoor, makes a very interesting historical topic. With the influence of the concept of Śakti, the primitive Tantric rituals, basically sexual in character, made their way into various spiritual disciplines. The Buddhists could not remain impervious to this trend; thus woman, flesh and sexual intercourse came to be regarded as essential preconditions for the attainment of liberation. The idea of *yuganaddha*, i.e. god-in-sexual-union-with-the-goddess, in icognological form by which the Buddhas and Bodhisattvas were frequently represented, show to what a great extent the Buddhists were influenced by the Tantric way of life.[5]

The central theme of the *Mañjuśrīmūlakalpa* and the *Guhyasamāja* deals with the *mudrās* and *maṇḍalas* connected with goddesses and spiritually-oriented women who can come from any class of people. The aspirant has to understand that woman, or her generative organ, is the source of existence and that sexual functioning is the imitation of the process of creation. By this process, from Ādi Buddha and his Śakti emanated the goddess Locanā, Māmakī, Pāṇḍarā and Śyāmatārā who represent respectively form, sound, smell and touch (*dveṣarati*, *moharati*, *rāgarati* and *vajrarati*), the four elements (earth, water, fire and air) and four *skandhas* (*vedanā*, *saṃskāra saṃjñā* and *vijñāna*). Locanā is earth, Māmakī water, Pāṇḍarā fire and Tārā air. According to the Tantric view, the act of creation is due to the union of the Female and Male Principles, the former being the more important functionary. In Buddhist Tantras these two principles are known as Prajñā and Upāya or as Śūnyatā and Karuṇā respectively. The union of Prajñā and Upāya is *yuganaddha* or *samarasa*. One who can unite these two principles in oneself can have the highest knowledge and supreme bliss and become free from the fetters of birth and death. This is the real Buddhahood. In order to have this spiritual experience man and woman should first realise that they are representatives of Upāya and Prajñā respectively and that their physical, mental and intellectual union alone can bring the experience of the highest truth. Accordingly, men and women should jointly strive for this secret knowledge and culture. Prajñā is the Female Principle and as such she is Bhagavatī or the goddess herself. She is also known as Vajrakanyā and Yuvati. The woman who is to impersonate Prajñā should preferably be a beautiful maiden of sixteen years. Prajñā also denotes the female sexual organ which is the seat of all happiness. Upāya, the male principle, is also known as Vajra, which means the male generative organ. The union of man and woman, of Upāya and Prajñā, brings the maximum pleasure in which all mental action is lost and the world around forgotten; only a pleasing experience of non-duality prevails. This is known as *mahāsukha*, the greatest pleasure, or *nirvāṇa*, the *summum bonum*, the real manifestation of Bodhicitta.

The introduction of this cult of the Female Principle in Buddhism which rationalised the successive thought-complexes starting from the primitive association of earth and woman based on the analogical identity of natural and human fecundity and cultimating in the Tantric cosmogony viewing the whole affair of creation in terms of a procreative process under the garb of a cute metaphysics was not a sudden development. We have seen that the Prajñāpāramitā Sūtras lay greater emphasis on the cult of the Female Principle. In these texts, the goddess Prajñāpāramitā is conceived of as the supreme being and the mother of all Tathāgatas. This cult, along with the sex rites associated with it was probably popularised by the Andhra Vetulyakas as is hinted in a passage of the *Kathāvatthu*.[6] The *Kāraṇḍavyūha* contains Tantric terminology and rituals as well as the concept of the Female Principle. The *Suvarṇaprabhāṣa* also mentions a number of goddesses. The *Dharma-saṅgraha* knows of the consorts of the Dhyānī Buddhas and six Yoginīs. In the *Mañjuśrīmūlakalpa*[7] we come across the goddess Tārā with the epithet Vidyārājñī and her various forms like Locanā, Māmakī, Pāṇḍarā, Bhṛkutī, Śvetā, Sutārā, etc. The *Guhyasamāja*[8] describes Locanā, Māmakī, Pāṇḍarā and Śyāmatārā as emanations of the original Buddha Vairocana. The concept of Tārā as the highest goddess is found in the *Mahāpratyaṅgirādharaṇī* in which she has been described as having a white complexion, carrying thunderbolt in her hand and as having the effigy of Vairocana on the crown. In the Indian tradition, the name is a modification of the word *tāra* signifying protection, and this tradition is reflected in the conception of her as the saviour. In the Buddhist texts she is described as the goddess who saves or protects her devotees from eight great fears (*aṣṭamahābhaya*). By the eighth century A.D. the cult of Tārā had become immensely popular. Tārā is also an emanation of the Dhyānī Buddha Akṣobhya. Of all the goddesses of the Vajrayāna pantheon Tārā became the most celebrated as the consort of Avalokiteśvara. In practice most of the Buddhist goddesses came under the general name Tārā.[9]

The story of Tārā is highly interesting since she is also an important Śākta goddess and is equated with Kālī. It is interesting to note that the *dhyānā* of Tārā, as found in the *Tantrasāra* of Kṛṣṇānanda Āgamavāgīśa is the same as that found in the *Sādhanamālā*. It is remarkable that even the association of Akṣobhya with Tārā is maintained in the Śākta Tantras according to which she is youthful, fierce, short-statured and big-bellied; she stands in *pratyālīḍha* pose and wears a garland of skulls; has a rolling tongue; in her right arms she holds a sword and knife and a garland of lotus in the left; her head adorned by the Dhyānī Buddha Akṣobhya.[10] As early as 1874 Rasik Mohan Chatterjee brought out a series of Hindu Tantric texts from Bengal Mss, and published them in Bengali script. Among the works he brought out were Brahmānanda's *Tārārahasya*, the *Rudrayāmala* and the *Mahācīnācārakrama* all of which refer to the Vāmācāra practices connected with the worship of Tārā as being brought by the sage Vasiṣṭha who was instructed by the Buddha himself. The *Tārātantra*[11] opens with the following question of Devī Tārā or Mahānīlasarasvatī: 'Thou didst speak of the two Kula-Bhairavas—Buddha and Vasiṣṭha. Tell me by what *mantra* they became Siddha'. The same Tantra defines a Bhairava as follows : 'He who purifies these five (Ms) and after offering the same (to the god) partakes thereof is a Bhairava'. The Buddha then is said to be a Kula-Bhairava. According to the *Rudrayāmala*[12] the sage Vasiṣṭha practised severe austerities when the goddess appeared to him and pointed out that he had not taken the right mode of *sādhāna*. She advised him to go to Mahācīna, the country of the *Bauddhas*. So he went to Mahācīna, but having observed the Buddhist rituals his mind was disturbed. He met the Buddha and said to him :

> Protect me, O Mahādeva, the imperishable one, in the form of the Buddha. I am humble Vasiṣṭha, son of Brahmā. For my perturbed mind I have come here for the *sādhāna* of the Mahādevī.... But doubts assail my mind (*bhayāni santi me hṛdi*) having seen the methods (*ācāra*). Remove them, and also the weakness of my mind which is inclined to the Vedic way (*vedagāminī*). O Lord, here I find rites which are outside the Veda (*vedavahiṣkṛta*). How is that wine drunk, meat eaten and women enjoyed by Siddhas who are naked (*digambara*), high (*vara*) and about to drink blood (*raktopānodyata*). They drink constantly and enjoy beautiful women (*muhurmuhu prapivanti ramayanti varāṅganām*)....They are beyond the Vedas and always indulged in wine and woman.... How can inclinations to such things purify mind? How can there be *siddhi* without Vedic rites?

The Buddha was not perturbed at these direct questions, but delivered a lecture on the duties of the Kaulas and explained to him their mysteries and utility. Vasiṣṭha was fully convinced, followed the way of the Buddha and eventually attained final liberation. In the *Brahmayāmala*[13] the same story is repeated but with a slight modification. Here, Vasiṣṭha was practising austerities on the Blue Mountain (Nīlacala), the site of the celebrated goddess Kāmākhyā of Kāmarūpa, and he was asked by the Devī to go to Mahācīna and get himself initiated into Cīnācāra. Vasiṣṭha went there to see a land inhabited by great *sādhakas* and thousands of beautiful and youthful women, full of mirth by the inspiration of wine and doing sexploiting gestures. He was surprised to see the Buddha with eyes drooping from wine. He asked himself : 'What is Viṣṇu doing in his Buddha form? This way is opposed to the Veda (*vedavādaviruddha*). I do not approve of it.' At once he heard a voice coming from air telling him not to think in this way. Being afraid he sought refuge with the Buddha who explained to him the mysteries of the Tārā cult which involved five *makāras* known as *Cīnācāra*. The Buddha explained the principal features of this cult, namely, its freedom from the rules of ordinary worship, from bathing, purification, *japa*, etc. It was nothing but worship in the mind. There were no rules as to auspicious and inauspicious times, or as to what should be done by day and by night, what is pure and impure, and so on. The goddess should be worshipped even though the place and worshipper be unclean. Women should be considered her manifestation and be worshipped for they are objects of veneration.

The peculiar features of the Tārā-Vasiṣṭha legends to be noted are these : The Buddha is regarded as another form of Mahādeva (Śiva) or Viṣṇu. The Hindu Tantric tradition did not consider the Buddha to be an outsider. Rather it traced the origin of its special doctrine *vāmācāra* to the teachings of the Buddha. The Hindu Tantric tradition was quite aware of the popularity of the Buddha-based culture of Tibet and China which it did not consider alien to its own. Secondly, Vasiṣṭha is described as basically a follower of the Vedic way. He was surprised to see the *cīnācāra* rites and disapproved of them at the first sight. He spoke of them as 'outside Veda' (*vedavahiṣkṛta*) and even opposed to Veda (*Vedavāda-viruddha*). Thirdly, it is also to be marked that Vasiṣṭha had done austerities and performed the Tārā rituals at Nīlācala, which is even today the seat of the goddess Kāmākhyā worshipped in the form of a Yoni or the female organ. There is still a place called Vasiṣṭhāśrama near Gauhati where the shrine of Kāmākhyā is situated which is largely visited by the pilgrims. Lastly, there are clear indications which point out that quite a good number of rituals and mystic practices of Chinese origin crept into the Indian theories and practices. The *Tārātantra* specifically states that Vasiṣṭha not only received instructions from the Buddha in Mahācīna, but brought from there the cult known as Mahācīnakramācāra. We have already had the occasion to refer to the view of M.M. Haraprasad Sastri[14] Sylvain Levi,[15] Sir John Woodroffe[16] and others who after analysing the Tārā-Vasiṣṭha legends as found in various Hindu Tantras came to the conclusion that many of the rituals of the goddess Tārā which were known as Cinācāra were of Chinese origin. It is also noteworthy that the flower of the goddess is *jabā*, the scarlet hibiscus or Chinese rose. We shall see later that Taoist and Tantric principles have much in common and that Chinese Taoism and Indian Tantrism have a genetic and historical relationship. In the establishment of this relationship, Buddhism evidently played a significant part.

Initially the cult of Tārā passed from India to Tibet where she came to be known as Sgrol-ma or Dol-ma in the Tibetan translation of her name. Like her husband Avalokiteśvara she was also conceived of under numerous forms. The Tārā cult, with the goddess in her various forms, also went to China as the Śakti of Avalokiteśvara. A number of countries beyond India are enumerated in the *Sammohatantra* as the centres of Tantric culture. These are Bāhlika (Balkh), Kirāta (hill tribes of the Himalayan zone), Bhoṭa (Tibet), Cīna (China), Mahācīna (greater China including parts of Tibet and Mongolia), Maida (Media?), Parśvakika (Parasika, Persia?), Airaka (Iraq?), Kamboja, Huṇa, Yavana, Gandhāra, and Nepal. It is not impossible that some Tantric schools associated themselves with these countries either through tradition or through the community of some mystic believers of which the history is not clearly known. The same Tantra holds that China alone possessed a hundred primary and seven subsidiary Tantras (*śatam tantrāṇi cine tu upatantrāṇi sapta ca*). While dealing with Buddhist mythology we have seen that in China Avalokiteśvara was already on the way to transformation from a god to a goddess in the seventh and eighth centuries A.D. when Tārā became absolutely merged with him and came to be known as the goddess KuanYin. This renovated form of Tārā became very popular in China and brought about her connection with most of the existing beliefs and rituals, especially those belonging to Taoism. The Taoist rituals which thus came into the fold of the Tārā cult in China as well as Yinism or Exaltation of the Female Principle in Taoism, which developed in that system as a corollary of the aforesaid Chinese Buddhist cult of the Female Principle, were also able to exert counter-influence upon the development of the Indian *vāmācāra* rites of both the Buddhist and non-Buddhist Tantras.[17] The identification of Mahācīnatārā with Ekajaṭā seems likely whose cult is said to have been recovered by Siddha Nāgarjuna from Bhoṭadesa or Tibet.[18] The description of Ekajaṭā, found in the *Sādhanamālā*, [19] agrees closely with that of Mahācīnakramatārā.[20] Corresponding to these goddesses we find in the Hindu pantheon Tārā, Ugratārā, Ekajaṭā and Mahānīlasarasvatī. The *dhyānas* of these goddesses as found in the Hindu Tantras literally correspond to those found in the Buddhist sādhanas. For example, a comparison of the *dhyāna* of Mahācīnatārā, which has been quoted in the *Sādhanamāla* and attributed to Sāsvatamitra with the description of Tārā as recorded in Brahmānanda's *Taārārahasya* and Kṛṣṇānanda's *Tantrasāra* shows that the Hindu Tantric authors had not only copied from the Buddhist Sādhanas but also made grammatical corrections. Even the Hindu Tārā bears the miniature figure of the Dhyani Buddha Akṣobhya on her crown. While Śāsvatamitra writes *piṅgograi-kajaṭām dhyāyāt maulāv-Akṣobhya-bhuṣitam*, Kṛṣṇānanda writes *pingograi-kajaṭām dhyāyemmaulāv-Akṣobhyabhuṣitam*. According to the *Sammohatantra*, Nīlasarasvatī or Ugratārā was born in a lake called *Cola* on the western side of the Meru which was included in the Cīnadeśa. Mention has already been made of Bagchi's suggestion that *Cola* is probably to be connected with the common word for *Kul* or *Col* which is found in the names of so many lakes to the west or north of T'ien-shan, that is to say, the pure Mongolian zone. It should also be remembered that of the earlier Śakti Piṭhas—Kāmarūpa, Purṇagiri, Oḍḍiyāna and Jālandhara—three were situated on the high roads leading to countries outside India. Oḍḍiyāna was situated on the high road that connected the upper valley of the Indus with Balkh, Samarkand, etc., on the one hand and the Pamirs, Khotan, Kashgarh, etc., on the other. Jālandhara was situated on another highway that connected Tibet with India through the Shipki pass and Kāmarūpa had been a great centre of activities of foreign people since very ancient times.

In China, although Taoism began and expanded as a philosophical movement in course of time it took the form of a distinct religion. This was probably due to the influence of Buddhism. From its very inception Taoism advocated certain esoteric rituals and practices derived from the ideals of primitive community life, a return to which was always urged by the earlier exponents of Taoism who were opposed to domination and oppression of all types, particularly social and political. However, with its growth as a specialised religion, Taosim developed an elaborate pantheon of its own. Some of the Taoist deities were natural and astral beings, others were adopted from Buddhism or invented by imagination. A few of them were deified human beings. Lao-tzu himself was elevated to the rank of a deity. At the head of the pantheon was triad of Three Pure Ones, evidently formed in imitation of the three Kāyas of the Buddha. They consisted of (i) Yuan Shih T'ien Tsun (or Yuan Shih Tien Wang, later merged with Yu Huang Shang Ti), the First Principle; (ii) Tao Chen, the controller of the opposite principles of *Yin* and *Yang* (the female negative and the male positive power); and (iii) Lao-tzu, who expounded the doctrine emanating from Honourable Tao. The extent of the influence which Buddhism exerted on Taoism can be estimated if we take into account the following criticism of the Neo-Confucianist Chu-hsi (A.D. 1130-1202) offered against Buddhism and Taoism. Chu-hsi wrote :

> Taoism was at first confined to purity of life and to inaction. These were associated with long life and immortality, which by and by became the sole objects of the cult. Nowadays they have thought it advisable to adopt a system of magical incantations, and chiefly occupy themselves with exorcism and prayers for blessings. Thus, two radical changes have been made. The Taoists have the writings of Lao-tzu and Chuang-tzu. They neglected these, and the Buddhists stole them for their own purposes; whereupon the Taoists went off and imitated the Sūtras of Buddhism. This is just as the scions of some wealthy house should be robbed of all their valuables and then go off and gather up the old pots and pans belonging to the thieves. Buddhist books are full of what Buddha said and Taoist books are similarly full of what Tao said. Now Buddha was a man, but how does Tao manage to talk? This belief; however, has prevailed for eight or nine centuries past. Taoism began with Lao-tzu. Its Trinity of the Three Pure ones is copied from the Trinity of the three persons as taught by Buddhism. By their Trinity the Buddhists mean (1) the spiritual body (of the Buddha); (2) his joyful body (showing the Buddha rewarded for his virtues); (3) his fleshly body under which the Buddha appears on earth as a man. The modern schools of Buddhism have divided their Trinity under three images which are placed side by side, thus completely missing the true signification (which is Trinity in Unity), and the adherents of Taoism wishing to imitate the Buddhists in this particular worship Lao-tzu under (another version of) the Three Pure Ones, namely, (1) as the original revered God, (2) the supreme ruler Tao, and (3) the supreme ruler Lao-tzu. Almighty God (T'ien) is ranked below these three, which is nothing sort of an outrageous usurpation. Moreover, the first two do not represent the spiritual and joyous bodies of Lao-tzu and the two images set up cannot form a unity with him; while the introduction of the third is an aggravated copy of the mistakes made by the Buddhists. Chuang-tzu has told us in plain language the death of Lao-tzu, who must now be a spirit; how then can he usurp the place of Almighty God?[21]

In this connection the following observation of S.K. Chatterji is significant :

> Just as certain schools of Buddhism like Dhyāna Buddhism of Bodhidharma became an important factor in Chinese Buddhist religious thought and practice, so it is believed that some later Taoist ideas and practices which are partly religious, partly magical, partly scientific and partly also on the plane of an erotic or sexual ritualism with mystic and philosophical implications came to India from China. The sudden and widespread development of Tantric doctrines and practices, both among the Buddhists and the Brahmanists, from the second half of the first millennium after the Christ, is rather significant in India.[22]

Reference has already been made to the very ancient Chinese concept of the Male and Female Principle—*yang* or the male positive power of light and heat and *yin* or the female negative power of darkness and cold—as working through everything in life and being. The proper harmonisation of these two opposite principles is regarded in Taoism as the aim for the purpose of making man transcend his physical limitations by acquiring supernatural powers and even immortality in his physical body. This harmonisation of the Male-Female Principles evidently leads us to the question of sexual rites and techniques inherent in practical Taoism. The achievement of material immortality is known as *hsien* which can be attained through the discipline of certain techniques of living like (1) respiratory techniques, (2) heliotherapeutic techniques, (3) gymnastic techniques, (4) sexual techniques, (5) alchemical and pharmaceutical techniques and (6) dietary techniques.[23] The respiratory technique is analogous to Indian *prāṇayāma*. The heliotherapeutic technique has its analogue in many a solar ritual of India. The gymnastic technique reminds us of *haṭhayoga* and *kāyasādhana*. The dietary technique also has an Indian parallel.

But more important are the two remaining techniques, the alchemical-pharmaceutical technique, and the sexual technique. These two are also fundamentals of Indian Tantrism, Buddhist and non-Buddhist.[24] Nāgārjuna's *Rasaratnākara* is a celebrated Tantric treatise on alchemy. This Nāgārjuna who was also the reputed author of *Kakṣapuṭatantra* and *Ārogyamañjarī* and the redactor of the *Susrutasaṃhitā*, is dated to eighth century AD and is different from the famous exponent of the Mādhyamika system. But he was also a Buddhist and his *Rasaratnākara* bears the stamp of Mahāyāna Buddhism. It contains methods for the purification of important minerals—crude copper by means of 'poling'. extractions of the essence of minerals, liquefaction of mica, fixation of mercury, a recipe of Aethiops mineral, 'killing' of mercury, and also description of the nature of apparatuses. Two other treatises by Nāgārjuna have also been recorded in the Nepal collection of manuscripts.[25] One is *Yogasāra* which contains recipes for improving the physical body, and the other is known as *Yogāṣṭaka* which contains recipes for cosmetics and for the cure of diseases of the hair. Three other Tantric texts of Buddhist origin should also be noted. These are Bhikṣu Govinda's *Rasahṛdaya*, Somadeva's *Rasendracuḍāmaṇi* and Yaśodhara's *Rasaprakāśa-sudhākara*. These texts were composed between the eleventh and thirteenth centuries A.D. and drew heavily upon Nāgārjuna. But Yaśodhara made some substantial contribution to the metallurgy of zinc. In the Tibetan Tanjur and Kanjur collections we have a number of Tantric treatises on alchemy and medicine. In 1932, M.M. Vidhusekhara Sastri referred to four Sanskrit treatises on alchemy as translated into Tibetan which were *Rasasiddhisāra*, *Dhātuvādaśāstra*, *Sarveśvararasāyana* and *Dhātuvāda*.[26]

The study of alchemy however was not the exclusive affair of the Buddhists. Other sects with or without Tantric affiliation were also interested in alchemy. Especially interested in this branch of science were the Nātha Siddhas and the Śaivas. The physicians who depended mostly on chemical drugs were known as Rasavaidyas who formed a sect of their own. They used drugs produced from mercury, sulpher, iron, mica, gold and silver. In the field of mercurial drugs particularly the Rasa sect made wonderful progress. It devised a philosophy of the body in terms of its chemical reactions known as Raśesvara-darśana or Kāyatattva. The Nātha Siddhas, whose Buddhist background will be shown later, were closely allied with the Raśesvara Siddhas. Each of the nine Nātha Siddhas was generally held to stand at the head of a community of expert alchemists who were masters in the preparation of antidotes against old age, diseases and poisons. The Siddhas (Sittars) of the South who also depended on the mercurial drugs were known as Māhesvara Siddhas of the Śuddhamārga. Their works

> ...deal either with alchemy by itself, alchemy and Yoga, alchemy and medicine, or medicine pure and simple. They were written in verse, using easy colloquial and ungrammatical words and often hiding the names of the herbs or minerals in big phrases and metaphors. Detailed instructions are given for the apparatus and processes. There are many *nigaṇṭus* or lexicons of these works

> which give the names of herbs and minerals which are synonymous.[27]

Although according to Tamil tradition the origin of the Sittars is traced to the mythical Agastya, they actually belonged to the tenth century A.D. and after. They had as the founder of one of their seven subsects a Chinese Taoist named Bhoga (Bogar in Tamil). He is said to have come to India in the third century (the date is doubtful) and got some of his pupils initiated in Chinese mechanical and alchemical arts. Tamil works also mention the name of his disciple Pulipani who came with him and settled in South India.

As regards the Chinese sexual techniques and their impact on the Buddhist and non-Buddhist Tantras the following observation of K.H. Van Gulik, as presented to us by H. Goetz, is important:

> This (sexual) practice again, has been the starting point of a secret Tantric-Taoist ritual intended not only to increase the length of life but even to win immortality for the adepts....This ritual sheds a most important light on certain obscure doctrines and practices of Indian and Tibetan mysticism, especially on Yoga, the Buddhist Siddhācāryas and the Kaulacakra of the Vāmācara Śāktas.[28]

And Joseph Needhem writes in this connection:

> It is then of great interest to find that just as ancient or early medieval Taoism was deeply interested in the phenomena of sex, so also this was central to Tantrism. The *vajra* (thunderbolt or lightning flash) was identified with the male external generative organ, the *lingam* (*seng chih*), while the lotus, *padma* (*lien*)—so characteristic of Buddhist iconography—was identified with that of the female, the *Yoni* (*nuken*). Essentially the theological doctrine was that the mystical or divine energy of a god (or of a Buddha) resided in his female counterpart, from which he received it in an eternal embrace. There had to be one of these *śaktis*, therefore, for each god or Buddha. The logical conclusion followed that the earthly Yogī seeking for perfection must also embrace his Yoginī, in a sexual union (*maithuna*) prepared for and conducted with special rites and ceremonies (*cakra*). There followed also the worship of women (*strī-pūjā*) as a preliminary to *maithuna*. The whole forms a remarkable parallel to early medieval Taoism,

though Buddhism seems to have come a long way from its origin when we find the phrase *buddhatvaṃ yoṣid-yoni samāśritam.*[29]

The ideas and beliefs behind the Chinese sex rites have been described by Needham with reference to practices like the *kulacakras* of Indian Tantras.[30] One should not forget that the Buddhist Sūtras containing the nucleus of Tantrism began to be translated as early as the fourth century A.D. The contributions to this field by Chu-fa-hu (Dharmarakṣa) and others are well known. The Buddhist *Dhāraṇis* contained methods of rain-making, getting water from rocks, finding springs and sources, stopping storms, etc. The Buddhist Tantric ideas were popularised in China by three celebrated Indian monks—Subhākara-siṃha (Shan-Wu-Wei, A.D. 636-735) who came to China in A.D. 716, Vajrabodhi (Chin-Kang-Chin, d. A.D. 732) and Amoghavajra (A mou-ka or Pu-Khung, d. A.D. 774). The Chinese also had celebrated Tantric teachers. Chih-thung wrote much on Tantrism. I-ching translated a Tantric work under the title *Ta-Khung-Chhüeh-Chow-Wang-Ching*. I-hsing (A.D. 673-713), the great Chinese astronomer and mathematician of his time was also a reputed Tantric. It should also be noted that in A.D. 520 Song Yun, the Chinese traveller, during a short visit he paid to northern India, lectured on the *Tao-te-king* of Lao-Tzu before the king of Udyāna in the north western frontier of India. When the Chinese envoy Li-Yi-Piao was in India about A.D. 646, he went to Kāmarūpa where he talked with the king, Kumāra Bhāskara, about the *Tao-te-king*, and the Indian prince was eager to have this work translated into Sanskrit, and also wished to have an image of Lao-tzu. In view of all these Needham observes :

> At the first sight, then Tantrism appears to have been an Indian importation to China. But closer inspection to the dates leads to a consideration, at least, of the possibility that the whole thing was really Taoist.... We saw that Taoist sexual theories and practices were flourishing between the second and the sixth centuries in China definitely before the rise of the cult in India, and its reimportation (if it was a reimportation) by the Buddhists. Bhattacharyya (B.T.) significantly tells us here that the principal localities associated with Buddhist Tantrism were in Assam. This reminds us that one of Pelliot's most remarkable memoirs concerned a Sanskrit translation of *Tao-te-king*. It was made for Bhāskara Kumāra, king of Kāmarūpa (Assam) who had asked Wang-hsuan-tshe for it in 644. A very living account of the work

> being done, with all difficulties which the translation involved, exists in *Chi-Ku-Chin-Fo-Tao-Lun-Hêng* (Critical Collection of Discourses of Buddhist Doctrine in Various Ages) under date 647. Pelliot translated this. In Tantric literature, moreover, China (Māhacīna) occupies a very important place as being the seat of a cult *cīna-caryā* which worshipped a goddess Mahācīna-tārā. Sages such as Vasiṣṭha were said to have travelled there to gain initiation into this cult, in which women played a very prominent part. Possibly, therefore, Tantrism was another instance of foreigners amiably instructing Chinese in matters with which the Chinese were already quite familiar. However, the sexual element in Indian religion had from ancient times been so marked that Buddhist Tantrism may, actually, be considered a kind of hybrid of Buddhism and Hinduism. The *śakti* idea is certainly ancient.[31]

To this observation of Needham, Chatterji adds :

> Buddhists brought in India certain new things no doubt, and was welcomed by the deeper spirit of quest in Chinese mind which sought to transcend life and nature. But the acceptance of Nature as such and the logical termination of the line of argument in which Nature, conceived as the result of the eternal play of *yang* and *yin* which were living forces, led Taoism to the idea of *hsien*-ship and the possibility of its attainment, and this proved to be an attractive ideology and discipline for those who in their mental composition or temperament were, to speak in the Indian way, inclined towards the full and free play of *pravṛtti* or natural inclination and did not feel happy with the spirit of *nivṛtti* which led to abstinence and asceticism. It was in this way that when they came close to the atmosphere of later Taoism from the early centuries of the Christian era, that some Buddhists from India also found in it an alluring doctrine, which was sublimated and philosophised in the Indian way. In place of the Chinese *hsien* or immortal, in India we have Siddha or Avadhuta, the adept with miraculous power (*siddhis*) which he can attain through Tantric practices, preferably of the Vāmācāra school. This would appear to come to India with Tantric Buddhism sometimes after the middle of the first millennium A.D. and then joined forces with Indian naturism and eroticism, mysticism and magic, and was established as Vāmācāra or the leftist way, as opposed to Dakṣiṇācāra or the rightist way. In Brahmanical Tantra, it associ-

ated itself with Śiva and Umā, and acquired a kind of spiritual or mythological imprimatur in later Hindu thought in general.[32]

There is a popular view that the so-called decline and downfall of Buddhism was due to its Tantric associations. L.M. Joshi,[33] an exponent of this line of approach, holds that among the internal factors in the decay of Buddhism in India the abuses of Tantrism occupy the foremost place. In later Buddhism the world of senses which in earlier Buddhism was regarded as the cause of evil was considered as the venue of spiritual progress. Instead of cultivating *śīla*, *samādhi* and *prajñā* as the means of the attainment of *nirvāṇa*, the mystic union of the spiritual aspirant and his female partner was considered to be the means of the attainment of *mahāsukha* or eternal bliss conducive to absolute non-duality. But the so called Tantric elements which are supposed to have vulgarised the pristine purity of Buddhism were not a sudden development at any given point of time; these elements were associated with all forms of Indian spiritual systems since times immemorial, and if they did not vulgarise other systems surviving in the fold of Hinduism, there is no reason why they should have vulgarised Buddhism specially. Alex Wayman seems right when he says that "the Buddhist Tantras do not appear to have fostered Buddhism's success in India, nor really in any observably significant degree to have caused Buddhism's decline".[34] Apart from its association with Tantrism, Buddhism, since its inception had an admixture with various heterogeneous ideas and elements as a result of which it acquired a new form and content at every stage of its development. Like its own basic doctrine, the history of Buddhism was also in a perpetual flux, nothing but that of metamorphoses of ideas, each stage of its transformation being marked by a qualitative change. And at each turning point of its historical development, Buddhism had acquired new dimensions and new suggestivities, no matter whether in this process the name of Buddha became redundant or not.

Overlooking this basic feature of transformation by which the history of Buddhism has been characterised through the ages the question of its decline and extinction at a given period of its multifarious channelisation becomes irrelevant. Various causes have been attributed by scholars for its so-called decline such as exhaustion, internal corruption, sectarianism, social failure of Buddhism, withdrawal of royal partronage, Muslim invasion and so forth.[35] According to Conze[36] "what Buddhism in India died from was just old age or sheer exhaustion". K.W. Morgan[37] and many others thought that the decline was due to moral decadence of the Buddhists. Edkins[38] postulated a theory according to which the departure of the Buddhist scholars *en masse* to China caused brain drain contributing to the decline of Buddhism in India. None of these views should be taken seriously. The corruption theory cannot stand because corruption is a part and parcel of human existence. Even in the Buddha's time there was corruption in the Sangha. The social failure of Buddhism or the insufficient cultivation of the laity, as stressed by G.C. Pande[39] and others is also not tenable because Buddhism had nothing to do with lay persons and it was never a social movement. Only at its later phases did it try to reach people with some ideological approaches without providing a proper sociocultural infrastructure for their survival. The theory of Brahmanical hostility has also no historical basis. The common belief, shared by a lot of historians, that it was the Muslim invasion which delivered the final blow to Buddhism is also untenable. How can a religion disappear owing to the destruction of a few monasteries? Moreover, scholars are not at all unanimous in regard to the time of the so-called decline of Buddhism. Some think that it was in the thirteenth century; some want to go back to the seventh century; some still earlier.[40] What is the harm in accepting U. Misra's contention that "both the rise and decline of Buddhism began almost simultaneously"?[41] Interestingly it was in the supposed period of its decline that Buddhism went in a renovated vigour in South-East Asia; it was in the eleventh century that Atīśa went to Tibet. Was he a product of decadence?

Another set of scholars holds that the most important factor in the decline of Buddhism in India was really a gradual assimilation of Buddhism into Hinduism.[42] According to L.M. Joshi, "the Great Vehicle laid emphasis on the image worship, prayers and incantations, pompous ceremonies and rituals; it incorporated many folk-belief, and made room for the emotional demands of the laity, and in doing so, the Buddhists made a near and clear approach to Hinduism; this process ultimately led to the abolition of and distinction between the two faiths. The laymen and lay-women of India found no difference between the worship of Viṣṇu and Buddha, of Śiva and Avalokita, and of Tārā and Pārvatī".[43] S.R. Goyal adds :

> The acceptance of the Buddha as an incarnation of Viṣṇu by Hinduism, though only as the beguiler of the demons, cut the ground from under the feet of Buddhism. The disapproval of animal sacrifice, the relaxation of caste rules and the organisation of monastic community on the lines of Buddhist Saṅgha by Śaṅkara, further helped the merger of Buddhism into Hinduism.[44]

> Common patronage of Buddhism and Hinduism by kings of the Gupta, Vardhana (Puṣyabhuti), Maitraka and Pāla dynastics also made it possible for both the Buddhists and the Hindus to borrow heavily from each other.... The acceptance of the Buddha as an incarnation of Viṣṇu had been accomplished probably in the sixth century A.D., perhaps first in the *Matsyapurāṇa*. A *Matsyapurāṇa* verse is found engraved on a Pallava monument of c. A.D. 700 at Mahabalipuram in which the Buddha is mentioned as the ninth *avatāra* of Viṣṇu. The *Bhāgavatapurāṇa* mentions the Buddha as a deity and also as a god who deluded the demons....In the post-Gupta period the Tantra practices harmonised the two systems so completely that Buddhism's independent existence might have appeared needless or even impossible. In spite of their being 'proclaimed by the Buddha' the Buddhist Tantras are almost identical with the Śaiva and Śākta Tantras. A large number of gods and goddesses became common to the pantheon of Hinduism and Buddhism. The Śākta Pīṭhas became equally important and holy for Hindu and Buddhist Tantrikists.[45]

The flaw in this line of reasoning is not in the conclusion but in the major premise itself. And this is due to the 'Viśiṣṭādvaitavāda' approach of our scholars towards Buddhism. Here we are using the term 'Viśiṣṭādvaitavāda' or 'qualified monism' not in the philosophical sense, but for the sake of comparison. According to this theory, although *brahman* and the universe are absolutely identical (*abheda*) from the theoretical point of view, we should imagine a little difference (*bheda*) between the two for practical expediency. Likewise, most scholars though they understood the identity of Hinduism and Buddhism, imagined a difference between the two and counted the latter as a different form of religion. T.W. Rhys Davids frankly admitted that "Gotama was born, brought up and lived and died as a Hindu" and that "Buddhism grew and flourished within the fold of orthodox belief".[46] Mrs. C.A.F. Rhys Davids held that the Tripiṭaka did not show any rupture with Brāhmaṇas and the preachings of the Buddha agreed with those of Brahmanism.[47] R.G. Basak maintained that Buddhism was another phase of Hinduism and not a heterodox system of Indian philosophy.[48] According to Radhakrishnan, "the Buddha did not feel that he was announcing a new religion. He was born, grew up and died a Hindu. He was restating with a new emphasis the ancient ideals of Indo-Aryan civilization".[49] K.N. Upadhyaya maintained that Buddhism was a departure from the orthodoxy of tradition, though not from the tradition as a whole.[50] According to Coomaraswamy, "the more profound is one's study of Hinduism and Buddhism, more difficult it becomes for him to distinguish between the two".[51]

But while dealing with Buddhism scholars generally use a different standard. A distinction is generally made between Hinduism and Buddhism. This artificial distinction, as we have pointed out earlier, was due to the early European contact with the Buddhist countries, the Christian missionaries and traders being responsible for popularising the idea that in the Eastern countries people practised a cult of Buddha. Thus the term Buddhism was coined at a period when its intimate relation with Hinduism was not known. Subsequently when this relation was discovered, the Western scholars who made pioneering researches on Buddhism admitted it without any hesitation, but they preferred to maintain a distinction between the two. Because Buddhism went to many countries outside India and acquired functional significance of religious character, its separate identity was stressed. There might have been some political motivation also for introducing this separatism. Although the relation between Hinduism and Buddhism was thought of in terms of identity-in-difference, this principle was not boldly used to explain the Indian situation of Buddhism. Had it been done the question of the so-called decline and extinction of Buddhism could never have arisen. And a basic point which is generally missed is that Buddhism has always been a thought complex of the type of the Sāṅkhya or Vedānta or Nyāya-Vaiśeṣika or Mimāṃsā, and as such it was not a religion in the real sense. It may be asked: If Buddhism was no more than a thought complex serving as a crucible responsible for the generation of various philosophical views how should one then account for the concept of divinities, the system of worship, the practice of meditation, the observance of rituals, the performance of austerities and so forth associated with it? The answer is simple. In the Indian tradition, philosophical systems are always regarded as the sciences of salvation; *darśanaśāstras* are also *mokṣaśāstras*.[52] If Vedanta could be a *mokṣaśātra*, why not Buddhism? And the traditional practical methods of spiritual quest could as well be practised by the followers of any school including those of Buddhism.

In order to explain the real functional position of Buddhism as a crucible which generated numerous unrelated and contradictory forms, we need to compare the process with a parallel thought-complex which like its collateral was also in a state of flux and served as a crucible for generating quite a good number of spiritual systems. It is the Vedānta which is based upon the *Brahmasūtra* of *Bādarāyaṇa*. Its absolute non-dualistic intereptation made by Śaṅkara, as we have seen above, regards *brahman* as the only reality and the world of experience as an illusion, the cognition of which is as false as that of a snake in a rope. But a theistic interpretation of the same Vedānta gave rise to various new schools of thought and formation of new sects and subsects within Vaiṣṇavism, Śaivism, Śāktism and other spiritual systems. Rāmānuja propagated the theory of Viśiṣṭādvaitavāda or qualified monism and founded the Śrī-Vaiṣṇava sect which was later subdivided into two subsects—Vaḍakalai and Tenkalaī. The philosophy of Nimbārka is known as Dvaitādvaitavāda or doctrine of identity-in-difference and the sect founded by him is known as the Sanaka sect. Madhva, the expounder of the Dvaita or dualistic school, founded the Brahma sect which was later subdivided into two groups—Vyāsakūṭa and Dāsakūṭa. The Śuddhādvaita school of Vallabha was known as the Rudra sect while the Acintyabhedābheda school of Śrī-Caitanya as the Gauḍīya sect. All these schools and sects were based on varying theistic interpretations of the Vedānta which also formed the basis of different Śaiva schools and sect like Śaiva Siddhānta, Vīra Śaivism, Kashmir Śaivism, etc., as well as that of various Śākta schools.[53] The role of Buddhism as a thought-complex was similar to, if not the same as that of the Vedānta in generating multifarious spiritual systems, and as such its decline and extinction became meaningless, since there was a difference between generated objects and the generating principle.

Also, from the tenth century onwards all the religious systems and spiritual disciplines received a uniform character and sameness in form and content owing to the Tantric influence. In fact one system could hardly be distinguished from another. Like Buddhism, the earlier forms of Vaiṣṇavism and Śaivism, such as the Vyūhavāda or the Pāśupata system, went out of vogue. The concept of the Śakti of Viṣṇu or Kṛṣṇa, like that of the Ādi-Buddha, the Dhyānī Buddhas or the Boddhisattvas, was obviously influenced by Tantric ideas. In the *Lakṣmītantra*,[54] a Vaiṣṇava Tantric text composed between the 9th-12th centuries A.D., the doctrine of Śakti is accorded such a high place that even the Śāktas regarded this text as a scripture of their own. This Śakti was conceived by Rāmānuja and Madhva to be Lakṣmī and by Nimbārka, Vallabha and Śrī-Caitanya as Rādhā. The doctrine of Rādhā found its first expression in the poems of the Āḷvar poetess Āṇḍal. Kṛṣṇa's sport with the Gopīs was foreshadowed in the *Bhāgavatapurāṇa* (9th-10th century A.D.). The relation between Rādhā and Kṛṣṇa has been viewed from a special angle in Jayadeva's *Gītagovinda* (12th century), the *Brahmavaivartapurāṇa* (13th century) and in the poems of Vidyāpati and Caṇḍīdāsa. This special angle is the Sahajiyā viewpoint popularised by the later Buddhists. The union of Kṛṣṇa and Rādhā, like that of the Buddhist Karuṇā and Śunyatā or Upāya and Prajñā, symbolises the union of the Male and Female Principles. Jayadeva described himself as a follower of the Sahajiyā tradition. The Parakīyā theory of Vaiṣṇavism, evidently derived its main impulses from the Sahajayāna of the Buddhists. Jayadeva, Vidyāpati, Caṇḍidāsa, Rūpa, Sanātana, Jīva Gosvāmin and others are reported to have followed the Sahajiyā way. Even Śri-Caitanya himself is said to have practised the Sahajiyā discipline with a female partner. In the *Vivartavilāsa* of Akiñcana Dāsa there is a list of female partners of the celebrated Vaisnava aspirants. The same process also held good in the case of Śaivism.

The theoretical aspects of the ancient Pāśupata doctrine were almost the same as those of early Buddhism. The first category of the Pāśupata doctrine is known as *kārya* or effect, by which is meant all the problems and conditions of worldly existence. This is the same as the *duḥkha* concept of Buddhism. The second category is known as *kāraṇa*. Existence and suffering are produced by concurrent causes. This idea is shared equally by the Buddhists and the Pāśupatas; both trace the cause of suffering to false knowledge. The third and fourth Pāśupata categories are *yoga* and *vidhi* respectively and their features correspond mostly to those of the Buddhist *magga*. The fifth category is *dukhānta* which is the cessation of all suffering. Thus Saivism started with the same or similar ideas as those of early Buddhism. Its later ramifications also correspond to the Tantric spirit which characterised the later forms of Buddhism.

From about the tenth century A.D. the heterogeneous elements of spiritual disciplines scattered all over the country began to be integrated. The Buddhist ideas contributed a lot to this process of integration. Among such contributions mention should be made of the introduction of the concept of Guru or preceptor as the supreme being, special forms of initiation, the Nivṛttimārga or the way of abstinence and renunciation characterised by a deep-rooted apathy towards women, Yogic discipline of body, meditation and concentration, monasticism, the attainment of miraculous powers, and so forth. The concept of Guru as the omniscient principle, far above the gods, like the Buddha himself was accepted by most of the sectarian creeds. Just as the Buddha was regarded as an incarnation of the earlier Buddhas so also each of the sectarian founders was regarded as an incarnation of the deity projected by the sect concerned as the supreme being.[55] Not only with the founders but sectarian leaders of lesser ranks as well were elevated to the position of the highest being, of Brahmā, Viṣṇu and Maheśvara. In the Tantric cults of the five major Hindu sects, in the various offsnoots of later Buddhism such as the Sahajiyās, the Siddhācaryas, the Nāthapanthīs and so forth, in the Sant tradition of medieval India and even in the Muslim Sufi tradition this Guruvāda had a predominant role. The concept of initiation which was a modification of the primitive tribal puberty rites[56] was a practice of general application among the Vedic Indians through which members of all three higher *varṇas* were elevated to the rank of the twice-born. The Buddha made a special application of the concept of initiation in regard to the admission into the monastic order and the sample of the Buddha was followed by the upholders of most subsequent spiritual disciplines. Of course there were some differences in the approach towards initiation. While the Buddhist initiation was an affair of the community of brethren which would decide whether a person was eligible for admission into the Saṅgha either by a general consensus or by majority vote, in the spiritual discipline of the later period it was solely the affair of the Guru. Secondly, while the Buddha prescribed a twofold initiation—lower (*pravrajyā*) and higher (*upasampadā*), later sects insisted on a manifold initiation, each under different names, in accordance with the various stages of spiritual progress of the disciple in an ascending order.

Not all aspects of the Buddhist contribution to the integration of the spiritual disciplines of India need to be discussed. Here we shall confine ourselves to the Nivṛttimārga or the way of abstinence and renunciation stressed so much by the Buddha and followed zealously by most religious leaders. Abstinence from the pleasure of all sensual objects and especially from the sight and touch of woman which originally characterised the Vedic ethics of the first *āśrama* or student life was prescribed by the Buddha as the most effective means of attaining salvation, and this attitude was subscribed to down to the medieval period by subsequent sectarian preceptors whose careers even resembled that of the Buddha who was frankly a misogynist.[57] In the *Mahāvagga*, the Buddha says that one should not see a woman; if seeing cannot be avoided one should not speak with her; if speaking becomes imperative one should speak cautiously. In the *Cullavagga* the Buddha holds that the character of woman cannot be fathomed; they are like robbers with many artifices, with whom truth is hard to find, to whom untruth is the same as truth; no heed should be paid to their likes or dislikes. In the *Milindapañho* the same attitude is reflected. Aśvaghoṣa in his *Saundarānanda* makes the Buddha say that women are like envenomed creepers, like unseathed swords and like the dens of horrible reptiles; an indignant serpent can be appeased but not a woman.[58] This misogynist approach was shared by a good number of subsequent teachers who held that woman was the gateway to hell. It is not proper to generalise, but in many cases the wives were the first victims of the spiritual quest of the celebrated teachers. Like the Buddha, Śrī-Caitanya also left his wife, and so misogynistic he was that he did not hesitate to shun one of his ardent disciples because the latter used to have food—and not sex—from an old lady. Rāmakṛṣṇa Paramahaṃsa did not leave his wife, but he had no marital life. He had a great respect for an idealised womanhood as the manifestation of Śakti, but his apathy towards mortal women is well known. Sri Aurobindo also shunned his wife; he might have deemed a wife with human faculties unfit for his spiritual progress. Whether or not they were justified in their actions and opinions, is not the question of our concern. What we want to say is that consciously or unconsciously they were influenced by the traditional Nivṛttimārga or the doctrine of abstinence from all sensual objects including women, and this doctrine owed much to the teachings of the Buddha.

This evasion of worldly desire and obliteration of sex yielded a counterforce on the spiritual plane which may not only account for the conceptual transformation of the Buddha in the later streams of Mahāyāna but also for the change of approach according to which the means are many and the end not difficult of attainment by men whose senses are sharpened to the highest degree. The earlier concept of Nirvāṇa was replaced by that of Mahāsukha or eternal bliss. In the *Mahāsukhaprakāśa*[59] Mahāsukha is described as Varjasattva of the nature of the unity of Prajñā and Upāya, the non-dual quintenssence of all the entities, the perfect wisdom itself of the nature of bliss. But *sukha* or bliss is not possible without the body. According to the *Hevajratantra*,[60] Mahāsukha is the ultimate reality and it can only be realised through the medium of the body. Everything in the world of objects is of the nature of eternal bliss. It is both the pervader (*vyāpaka*) as well as the pervaded (*vyāpya*). (*Vyāpya-vyāpaka rupeṇa sukhena vyāpitam jagat*). But as the smell of a flower cannot be perceived without the flower; so also bliss as the quintessence of all that is originated can never be realised without the world of originated objects (*yathā puṣpā-śritaṃ gandhaṃ puṣpa-bhāva na gamyate/tathā utpannā-dy-abhāvena saukhyaṃ naivo' palabhyate*). Here arises the question of the body. How can at all the *sukha* or bliss transpire without the body (*dehābhāve kutaḥ saukhyam*)? In the Vajrayāna, very often the concept of Mahāsukha has been solidified into that of an all-powerful supreme deity, Lord Śrī Mahāsukha, who is presented as being deeply embraced by the goddess Śūnyatā or Nairātmā (Vārāhī).[61] The female organ is described as Sukhāvati where Lord Mahāsukha dwells in his own nature as supreme bliss. In the *Hevajratantra* we find that the Lord (Bhagavān) while explaining his own nature to the Boddhisattva Vajragarbha says that he dwells in the Sukhāvati of the generative organ of the female in the form of semen (*yoṣit-bhage sukhāvatyāṃ sukranamnā vyavasthitaḥ*). And without the semen there is no bliss and without bliss he is not (*vinā tena na saukhyaṃ syāt sukhaṃ hitvā bhaven na saḥ*). The lord is the form of the seed while its pleasure is called the girl (*śukrākāro bhavet bhagavān tat-sukhaṃ kāmini smṛtam*).

Thus we find that within a system in which the woman was originally regarded almost as a taboo and the virtues of *brahmacarya* or celibacy were highly extolled, a parallel counterforce insisting on the esoteric spiritual apprehensions of corporeality steadily gathered momentum and reversed the earlier dispensation. In later Buddhism, the concept of Boddhicitta acquired a changed significance; its funciton here is to create Mahāsukha or great bliss through sexual union between man and woman. The motivating force behind this sole emphasis upon the physical union of men and women is the ancient Tantric maxim: 'that which is not in the body is not in the world'. The human body is the abode of all truth and therefore all the mysteries of the world should be explained in terms of those of the human body. We have already had the occasion to mention how the concepts of Upāya and Prajñā began to change with the corresponding transformation of Mahayanism. Prajñā was variously designated as a goddess (*bhagavatī*),[62] a woman to be adopted for *sādhanā* (Mudrā, Mahāmudrā, Vajrakanyā), a young woman (Yuvatī),[63] and also as the femate organ.[64] In the *Hevajratntra*,[65] Prajñā is called *jananī* (mother), *bhaginī* (sister), *rajakī* (washer-woman), *nartakī* (dancing girl), *duhitā* (daughter), *ḍombi* (Doma girl), as also the female organ, the seat of great pleasure (*mahāsukha)*. Likewise Upāya is the male organ. Prajñā and Upāya are also called Lalanā and Rasanā which are also names of the two nerves *iḍā* and *piṅgalā* which are said to carry seed and ovum respectively.[66] Prajñā and Upāya as Lalanā and Rasanā respectively, have also been associated with the moon and the sun (*lalanā rasanā raviśaśī tuḍia veṇṇa vi pāse*).[67] In some Buddhist Tantras such as the *Nirṇāda* or *Ucchuṣma*, Prajñā and Upāya have been identified respectively with Śakti and Śiva (*Śiva-śakti-samā yogāt sat-sukhaṃ param advayam/na śivo nāpi śaktiśca ratnāntargata-saṃsthitam*).[68]

According to the Hindu Tantras the ultimate truth is the union of Śakti and Śiva, the former representing the world force—the kinetic energy—and the latter, pure consciousness which is inactive and static. With the conception of Prajñā and Upāya as the female and male principles corresponds that of Śakti and Śiva and the non-duality produced from their union (Śiva-Śakti-*mithunapiṇḍa*). Śiva is said to be the *bindu* of white colour suggestive of the seed or semen while the emission of Śakti is the procreative red. The principle of the union of Prajñā and Upāya is known as Yuganaddha. In the *Pañcakrama*, Yuganaddha is technically defined as a state of absolute non-duality marked by the absence of notions like *saṃsāra* (worldly process) and *nivṛtti* (cessation of that process), *saṃkleśa* (adherence) and *vyavadhāna* (distinction), *grāhya* (perceivable) and *grāhaka* (perceiver), etc.[69] It is also described as the non-dual state and identified with the Bodhicitta.[70] In other texts this principle is equated with the *dharma-kāya* of the Buddha.[71] In the Vajrayāna pantheon this principle is represented by the deity embracing his consort closely in the act of sexual union.[72] In the *Sādhanamālā*[73] we find descriptions of the major deities, including the Dhyānī Buddhas, who are to be meditated on, as being in union with their female consorts. In the *Herukatantra*,[74] Heruka is represented in the sexual union with Vajravairocanī, a depiction of which is frequently found in sculpture. The union of Prajñā and Upāya through the principle of Yuganaddha for the purpose of the realisation of the non-dual state, symbolised by the physical union of the adept and his female partner, brings in succession, *rāga* and *mahārāga* (emotion and intense emotion), *sāmarasa* (oneness of emotion in which there is no cognition of Prajñā and Upāya) and finally the Mahāsukha or great bliss.[75]

That the universe (*brahmāṇḍa*) is in the body (*bhāṇḍa*), the macrocosm in the microcosm, is evidently an ancient idea, the root of which is to be found in the Upaniṣadic identification of the universal and individual self. This idea worked behind the concept of *kāyasādhana* so much emphasised in the Śākta and the Buddhist Tantras. According to the Śākta scheme there are six nerve-cycles (*Ṣaṭcakras*) within the human body and these are in the *mūlādhāra* (rectal region), *svādhiṣṭhāna* (the region around the generative organ), *maṇipura* (the region of the navel), *anāhata* (region around the heart), *visuddha* (the region connecting the spinal cord and the lower portion of the medulla oblongata) and *ājñā* (the region between the brows). The highest cerebral region is known as *sahasrāra*. The *kuṇḍalinī-śakti*, i.e. Śakti as serpent power, remains latent in the *mūlādhāra*. By yogic exercises this *kuṇḍalinī-śakti* has to be pushed up through the two main nerves, *iḍā* and *piṅgalā*, so that it may reach the *sahasrāra* or the highest cerebral region where it should meet its source. Likewise the Buddhist Tantras speak of nerve-cycles symbolising the three bodies of the Buddha—*dharma*, *sambhoga* and *rūpa* or *nirmāṇa*. They also speak of an additional nerve-cycle which is *uṣṇīṣakamala* in the central cerebral region which is the symbol of the Buddha's *vajrakāya* or *sahajakāya* and which corresponds to the Śākta concept of *sahasrāra*. Below this, around the neck is *sambhogacakra*, near the heart *dharmacakra*, and near the navel *nirmāṇacakra*. There are innumerable nerves within the body, of which thirty-two are vital. Of these, three are most important—the two symbolising Prajñā and Upāya are on either side of the spinal cord and, in between them, into which both these are combined, is one which is known as *sahaja* or *avadhutī*. Like the *kuṇḍalinī-śakti* of the Śākta Tantras, the Buddhist Tantras speak of a female energy having the force of fire which resides in the *nirmāṇacakra* and is known as Caṇḍāli. This Caṇḍali, being accelerated, kindles the *dharma* and *sambhoga* cakras and ultimately reaches the *uṣṇīṣakamala*, the highest cerebral region, and then returns to its own place.

Kazi Dawa Samdup[76] has divided Vajrayāna into six sects. According to him, the earlier schools of Śrāvakayāna, Pratyekabuddhayāna and Bodhisattvayāna gave rise to Mantrayāna or Vajrayāna which was divided into three states, namely, Kriyatantrayāna, (Byavhi-rGyud-kyi-thegpa); Caryā or Upāyatantrayāna (Spyod-pahi-rGyud-kyi-thegpa; and Yogatantrayāna (rNal-hbyor-rg). The latter is again subdivided into three, namely Mahāyogatantrayāna, Anuttarayogatantrayāna and Atiyogatantrayāna. The general practice is, however, to divide Vajrayāna into four classes, namely Kriyātantra, Caryātantra, Yogatantra and Anuttaratantra. Waddell[77] described the first two divisions as the 'lower-Tantras' and the last two as 'upper-Tantras'. Vallee Poussin[78] held that these divisions were modelled after the Vaiṣṇava Tantras as classified in the *Padmatantra* under the titles Jñānapāda, Yoga-pāda, Kriyā-pāda, and Caryā-pāda. The Kriyā and Caryā Tantras were concerned with the rituals, ceremonies, worship of gods and goddesses and so forth, and were meant for the beginners for whom worship and rituals were necessary. But the Yoga and Anuttara Tantras are of higher standard containing the yogic processes for the realisation of the ultimate truth and a discussion on the nature of the ultimate truth. But, as S.B. Dasgupta has rightly observed :

> As a matter of fact, if we go through the Buddhist Tantric texts, we shall find that some of the texts contain nothing but the detailed description of the gods and goddesses and elaborate systems of worship and chantings—without having any element of Yoga

or philosophy in them. It is for this reason that to study the essentials of the Buddhist Tantras we should concentrate our attention more on the Yoga-tantras and the Anuttara-tantras. But the fact is that it is often very difficult to arrange the Buddhist Tantras under the heading of these four classes—for many of the Tantras contain a mixture of the different elements.[79]

One of the offshoots of Vajrayāna is Kālacakrayāna. There is a Buddhist Tantra called *Kālacakratantra* which introduces the cult of Kālacakra. The cult of Kālacakra came into vogue in the tenth century and also became popular in Tibet and China.[80] He is considered to be the principal deity of the Kālacakramaṇḍala of the *Niṣpannayogāvali*. He is conceived of as dancing in *ālidha* attitude on the bodies of Anaṅga and Rudra lying on the back. He is blue in colour, wears a tiger-skin and has twelve eyes, four faces and twelve principal hands on each side. His subsidiary hands, evidently symbolic, are twenty-four thousand. In the four blue right hands are held *vajra*, sword, *triśūla* and *kartari*, in the four red hands shown fire, arrow, *vajra* and *aṅkuśa*, and in the four white hands discus, knife, rod and axe. In the four blue left hands are shown *vajra*-marked bell, the plate, the *khaṭvāṅga* with the gaping mouth, and *kapāla* full of blood. In the four red hands can be seen bow, noose, jewel and lotus. The four white hands hold a mirror, *vajra*, chain and the severed head of Brahmā.[81] However, the description of this god is insufficient to explain the creed. The *Niṣpannayogāvali* refers to *Vimalaprabhā*, the commentary on the *Kālacakratantra* according to which the cult was given the name Adibuddhayāna or Ādiyāna. About Kālacakrayāna Waddell wrote:

> In the tenth century A.D. the Tantric phase developed in Northern India, Kashmir and Nepal, into a monstrous and poly-demonist doctrine, the Kālacakra, with its demoniacal Buddhas, which incorporated the Mantrayāna practices, and called itself Vajrayāna or 'followers of the thunderbolt Vehicle', and its followers were named Vajrācāryas or followers of the thunderbolt....The extreme development of the Tantric phase was reached with the Kālacakra which, although unworthy of being considered as a philosophy, must be referred to here as a doctrinal basis. It is merely a coarse Tantric development of the Ādi Buddha theory combined with the puerile mysticism of Mantrayāna, and it attempts to explain creation and the secret powers of nature, by the union of the terrible Kāli, not only with the Dhyānī Buddhas, but even with the

> Buddha himself. In this way Ādi Buddha, by meditation evolves a procreative energy by which the aweful Sambharā and other dreadful Dakini fiendesses, all of the Kāli type, obtain spouses as fearful as themselves, yet spouses who are reflected as reflexes of the Ādi Buddha and the Dhyānī Buddhas. And these demoniacal 'Buddhas' under the name of Kālacakra, Heruka, Acala, Vajrabhairava, etc., are credited with powers not inferior to those of the celestial Buddhas themselves, and withal ferocious and blood-thirsty; and only to be conciliated by constant worship of themselves and their female energies, with offerings and sacrifices, magic circles, special *mantra*-charms, etc.[82]

Waddell's Christian outlook did not go beyond a cult of savage demoniacal beings with ghastly rites. But a thorough perusal of the *Śrī Kālacakratantra*[83] by S.B. Dasgupta reveals the following:

> A study of the text does not confirm the statement that Kalacakrayāna is not that school of Tantric Buddhism which introduced the demoniacal Buddhas in its province—at least it is not the main characteristic through which the school should be recognised.... It is a system of Yoga which, with all its accessories of *maṇḍala* (magic circle) and concentration (*abhiṣeka*) is explained with this very body... how all the universe with all its objects and localities are situated in the body and how time and all its varieties (viz. day, night, fortnight, month, year, etc.) are within the body in its process of the vital wind. In the body of the text Sahaja has been fully explained and the details of the sexo-yogic practices for the attainment of the Sahaja have also been described.[84]

The word Kālacakra means the wheel of time. Its Tibetan synonym *dus-kyi-k'or-lo* also means the same. The theoretical aspect of Kālacakra is rooted in the *Atharvaveda* in which Kāla occurs as a cosmogonic principle. Its elevation to the First Principle is found in the *Śvetāśvatara Upaniṣad*. In Jainism Kāla or time has been classed as *anastikāya* or non-extended eternal substance. It appears that the followers of the Kālacakrayāna were more interested in the traditional concept of Mahākāla as the source and spring of everything that exists, the ultimate immutable substance, than the original Buddhist doctrine of momentariness. The theory of Kālacakra has also been explained by Abhinavagupta in terms of the wheel of time. The process of controlling the time is possible, according to this authority, by controlling the vital winds in the nerves through Yogic practices.[85] From the *Sekoddeśaṭikā*[86] which is a commentary on the *Sekoddeśa* section of the *Kālacakratantra*, it is known that by *kāla* is denoted the 'ultimate immutable' and unchanging reality remaining in all kinds the elements and by *cakra* is meant the unity of the three kinds of existence, and as such Kālacakra is the same as the unity of Prajñā and Upāya. In principle there is therefore no difference between Vajrayāna and Kālacakryāna. Lord Śrī Kālacakra is not basically different from Ādi Buddha or Vajrasatta-Vajradhara. In the *Laghu-Kālacakraṭīkā*, entitled the *Vimalaprabhā*,[87] Kālacakra is conceived of as the nature of Śunyatā and Karuṇā. He is the source of the Buddha, possessing the three *kāyas*, symbolical of the three times—past, present and future. He is the Boddhicitta, the ultimate immutable substance, and is embraced by the goddess Prajñā in the absolute non-dual state.[88]

Another offshoot of Vajrayāna is Sahajayāna. The word *sahaja* means 'easy'. In philosophy the term *sahaja* denotes the ultimate inner nature of beings and elements; and in a spiritual sense it denotes the easiest or the most natural way by which human nature itself will lead the aspirant to realise the truth. Instead of suppressing, and thereby inflicting undue strain on human nature Sahajayāna holds that truth is something which can never be found through the prescribed codes of study, discipline, conduct, worship and ritual. What is natural is the easiest, and hence there is no need for religious formalities, austere practices of disciplines, reading and philosophising, fasting, constructing temples and images, and so on. This distinguishes Sahajayāna from Vajrayāna, although the exponents of the former recognise the well-known texts of the latter as their authority. The Sahajayāna considers the human body itself as the seat of all human experience including that of *sahaja-mahāsukha* which is the peaceful, blissful, radiant and waveless experience of the *sahaja*. According to them, everything lies within the human frame; the human body is the microcosm of the universe. In the matter of sexo-yogic practices, the Sahajiya Buddhists go further than the Vajrayanists by laying greater emphasis on two points: the imparative necessity of making the body sufficiently strong and fit before starting with the Yogic processes, and the conception of an internal female force in the *nirmāṇa-cakra* (the navel region) corresponding to that of the *kuṇḍalinī-śakti* of the non-Buddhist Tantras. In this system, the identification of Upāya with the male and Prajñā with the female principle has caused the transformation of the character of physical discipline into a kind of sexo-yogic practice, thus introducing an external element into it in the form of a woman.[89]

The *caryā* poems deal with the subtle philosophical questions from the viewpoint of Sahajayāna under the garb of the facts of real life; the pursuits, hopes and aspirations of the common persons; love, hatred and emotion; the beauty of nature and of women; the social classes, conflicts and amalgamations; technical and manual labour; and a variety of other things. The followers of Sahajayāna do not insist on external formalities so far as the spiritual question is concerned, nor believe in any god apart from the self which is regarded as the Buddha or Boddhisattva. Their aim is to realise the Sahaja, the ultimate nature of beings, with the help of the Guru or the preceptor. The realisation of Sahaja, is in fact the realisation of Śūnyatā or vacuity, as the only reality leading one to Mahāsukha or great bliss. Tillopāda says: "Myself is vacuity, all that moves is vacuity, the three worlds are vacuity. There is no sin or merit in pure Sahaja. Let the mind go wherever it likes to go." Mind is solely responsible for the creation of the illusory world. The notion of difference or duality proceeds from the notion of existence. Bhusukupāda, in a song, compares the mind to a fickle rat: "Dark is the night and the play of the rat begins. Kill, O Yogin, this rat of the vital wind, whereby you will escape coming and going. The rat causes existence and makes holes; this fickle rat remains inactive only when skilful devices are employed." Due to *vāsana* or root-instincts man falsely conceives the notion of existence and gets fettered. When mind is conditioned by the realisation of Śūnyatā, the questions of birth and death, of suffering and non-suffering, of bondage and liberation, cease to exist. Luipāda says: "Incomprehensible indeed is the nature of pure consciousness. How can the Āgamas and Vedas explain that whose colour, sign and form are not known? By speaking of what, should I give an exposition of truth? Just like the moon in water it is neither real nor unreal." Although emphasis is laid on the illusory nature of the world, the Sahajayāna insists on the *pravṛtti-mārga* or following the path along which the human nature itself leads the individual. Not only are worship, muttering of *mantras* and performing penances and rituals are worthless, so also is that found in the scriptures and in the sayings and interpretations of the so-called learned persons. The polemics of Saraha are more aggressive :

> If a man becomes a Brahmin by reciting the Vedas, let the people of the lower classes also recite the Vedas and they will also become Brahmins. In vain do they offer *ghee* to the fire, for thereby

> their eyes will only be affected....The devotees of Lord (Īśvara), again, anoint the whole body with ashes...they whisper (religious doctrines) into the ears (of credulous people) and deceive them thereby. The widows, the Muṇḍis (women taking the vow of fasting for the whole month) and others taking different vows, get themselves initiated by these devotees who do it only in greed of money... [Against the Jain Kṣapanaka Yogis it is said] if only the naked attain liberation, the dog and the fox would also attain it; if liberation is attained by tearing of hairs, the hips of young women would also attain it.... The Celas, the Bhikṣus and the Sthaviras take the vow of *pravrajyā*; some of them are lost in explaining the Sūtras, some again in strenuous thinking and reading. Others rush into the Mahāyāna fold, but none of them get the ultimate truth....What will one do with lamps, offerings, *mantras* and services? What is the good in going to holy places or to the hermitage? Can liberation be attained only by bathing in holy waters?[90]

This is, indeed, a qualitative change in spiritual approach. The followers of the Sahajayāna were critical of all elitest approaches found in the scriptures of various sects. They did not even spare the Buddhist scholastic tradition. To them the Buddha meant an altogether different principle. Tillopāda speaks of that essential truth which is to be fully known by the self. The state of communion of the mind with vacuity is pure and without any positive and negative character. In his own words: 'I am the universe; I am the Buddha; I am free from impurity; I am the mental inaction; I am the killer of the cycle of existence.' Saraha says: 'The Paṇḍitas pose to interpret the scriptures. But they do not know that the Buddha is residing in their own body.' Such ideas were preached not by the Brāhmaṇa or upper class elitists who were so long at the helm of all the ideological formulations pertaining to almost each and every sect of spiritual discipline including Buddhism and Jainism, but by persons belonging to the lower strata of society. Most of the Siddhācāryas who were exponents of Sahajayāna and allied systems came from the lower castes. As is apparent from the names like Ḍombi, Śabarī, Tānti, Cāmari, Khaḍga, Tilo, Śāli, Dhobi, Kambala, Kuṭhāri, Karmāra, Jālandhari, Bāguri, Teli, Kumāri, etc., they belonged to the castes of corpse carriers, leather-workers, washermen, oilmen, tailors, fishermen, wood-cutters, and the like. The Siddhācāryas did not care for social distinctions and the caste system. Saraha, who was a Brāhmaṇa, became a voluntary outcaste and ridiculed the Brāhmaṇas and the

Brahmanical way openly. He married a woman of low caste. In his very first *dohā* he attacked Brahmanism. The followers of the *Hevajra-Yoga* regarded everyone as the Buddha and did not differentiate between high and low. They used a special language and secret signs.[91]

In the *caryās* and *dohās* we come across a goddess variously known as Nairātmā, Ḍombī, Caṇḍāli, Śabarī, etc. This female principle is the same as Śūnyatā or Prajñā, conceived of in other systems as Śakti. We find the goddess singing and dancing with the aspirant; sometimes she is conceived as a Ḍombi constantly engaged with him in sexual union; sometimes she is rebuked by the aspirant as *kāmacaṇḍāli* for her excessive passion and harlot-like gestures; sometimes she is a Caṇḍāli who has become a typical housewife; sometimes she is Mātaṅgi, a boat-woman, helping the Yogī to cross the river; sometimes she is a Bediya girl selling bamboo products; sometimes she is a Śabarī having a domestic life with a hunter. Her names are suggestive of untouchable castes and lower professions, the symbolism being that her true nature cannot be realised by sophisticated persons. Her hut is outside the city, i.e. outside the world of senses. Men of sophistication pass by the hut but they cannot enter it and enjoy her company. She is available only to the unprejudiced, to one who can give up all feelings of egoism, disobey scriptural injunctions and disregard public scandal.[92] She is Sahajasvarūpā or of the same nature of Sahaja residing in the *nirmāṇacakra* as Caṇḍāli, in the *dharmacakra* as Ḍombi, in the *sambhogacakra* as Nairāmaṇi and in *Uṣṇīṣakamala* as Sahaja-sundarī. In the form of woman she is present everywhere and that is why sexual union with a partner or *mudrā* is necessary as a means to realise the great bliss of non-duality.[93] At the first stage, the *mudrā* is simply used as *karma*, i.e., plain sexual union yielding only transient pleasures, and the word *karmamudrā* may be applied to any woman. But the higher grades like *jñānamudrā*, *mahāmudrā* and *phalamudrā*[94] are subtle principles, personified in the forms of spiritually advanced women and it is only through union with them that an individual can realise the ture nature of his self and have what is known as Sahaja-Mahāsukha.

Thus in the Sahajayāna a significant change may also be observed in regard to the concept of the Female Principle which in accordance to the Śākta-Tantric spirit regarded all women as manifestations of Mahāśakti, the supreme energy. According to Sahajayāna, this Female Principle is not outside the human body. According to H.V. Guenther, the symbolic *yuganaddha* points to the unique harmony and interpenetration of masculinity and femininity. Bi-sexuality is inherent in all beings and this aspect has to be exercised in order to understand the truth of one's own nature. Sexual partnership is therefore the best expression for the most intimate relations between the two opposites. For the man, woman is the natural object of concentration, a goddess for meditation and a symbolic truth for comprehension.[95]

The Sahajayāna concept of the Female Principle was adopted by a section of the followers of Vaiṣṇavism. The Vaiṣṇava Sahajiyā cult has a considerable literature to its credit. This tradition considered all the major Vaiṣṇava poets and apostles to be exponents of Sahajiyā practice. Śrī-Caitanya, Śrī-Rūpa, Bhaṭṭa Raghunātha, Sanātana, Lokanātha, Śrījīva, Gopālabhaṭṭa, etc., are said to have practised Sahaja-sādhanā with female companions.[96] In the literature of the Vaiṣṇava Sahajiyās we find references not only to the sexo-Yogic practices of the Tantras, but also to the Nātha practice of drinking nectar oozing from the moon situated beneath the Sahasrāra.[97] In the Śaiva and Śākta Tantras, the ultimate reality is the non-dual state of unity of Śiva and Śakti. In Buddhist Tantras it is the unity of Prajñā and Upāya. The realisation of this unity in one's own self is the state of Mahāsukha. The Vaiṣṇava conception of Kṛṣṇa and Rādhā is interpreted by the Sahajiyās in the same sense as that of Śiva and Śakti or of Upāya and Prajñā. All men and women are thought of as physical manifestations of Kṛṣṇa and Rādhā. The love between man and woman may be conjugal (*svakīyā*) but preferably it should be unconventional (*parakīyā*). The Sahajiyā Vaiṣṇavas also insist on the Tantric mode of *kāyasādhana* and the upward march of Śakti through the nerve channels. The body itself is conceived of as Vṛndāvana where reisdes Sahaja in the nature of pure love which flows between Rādhā and Kṛṣṇa.[98] In texts such as *Rativilāsapaddhati*,[99] *Rāgamayī-kanyā*,[100] *Sahaja-upāsanā-tattva*,[101] etc., man and woman as the representatives of the two streams of love are described respectively as *rasa* and *rati*, or as *kāma* and *madana*. The realisation of the true nature of man as Kṛṣṇa and that of woman as Rādhā is known as the principle of Āropa.[102]

The Siddhācārya tradition also derived its main impulses from later Buddhism. According to this tradition there were 84 Siddhas who were endowed with supernatural powers which they achieved through meditation and physical exercises. Their names are mentioned in Jyotirīśvara's *Varṇaratnākara* and they are well known in the literature of medieval Indian alchemy. Their biographies are preserved in the Tibetan canon and in the histories of Bu-ston, Gos-lo-tsa-la, Tāranātha, Sumpa-Khan-po and others. They are also known from medieval Nepalese tradition, from the Caryās and Dohās composed by some of them as also from a few inscriptions.[103] Their basic Buddhist background is attested to by the fact that quite a good number of them are celebrated as composers of the well known Buddhist Tantras. Other spiritual disciplines also claim some of these Siddhas to be their own. The Nātha Siddhas are included in the Buddhist lists and we find such names as Minanātha, Gorakṣanātha, Jālandharī and so on. We have already observed that many of the Siddhācāryas came from the lower ranks of society. There are five *kulas* or brands of the Siddha culture—Ḍombī, Naṭī, Rajakī, Caṇḍālī and Brāhmaṇī. These are symbols of five female forms of Śakti. The way of the Siddhācāryas is basically that of Kāyasādhana or the way of the body. There are 32 nerves through which Śakti flows from its main centre below the navel region. The highest resort of Śakti is the cerebral region known as *mahāsukhasthāna* or the place of greatest bliss. Śakti reaches this point after crossing some important stations within the body named after Tantric Pīṭhas such as Uḍḍiyāna, Jālandhara, Pūrṇagiri, Kāmarūpa, etc. The aim is the realisation of Sahaja. Liberation is *jīvanmukti*, the attainment of immortality which is possible by Kāyasādhana or disciplining the body. Semen is the source of life and that is why it is *bodhicitta*. Immortality is possible by adopting the method of *parāvṛtti* or the opposite way by giving the semen an upward motion which is possible through Yoga. The culture of *bodhicitta* is connected with alchemy and that is why the use of chemical drugs is also desirable. The *aśuddha-māyā* or impure elements of which the body is made should be transformed into pure elements through certain processes. This transformation is *jīvanmukti*, immortality or liberation within the span of life.

In the Siddha culture the concept of Śiva-Śakti has been harmonised with that of the Buddhist *bodhicitta*. The Siddhas believe that the body is the microcosm of universe. Mountain, sea, moon, sun—all that of which the world is composed—are within the human body. The Nātha Siddhas had a general predilection towards occult practices and acquisition of supernatural powers. Nathism is a composite system, but its Buddhist ingredients are by no means insignificant. Mīnanātha, one of the exponents of Nathism is identified in the Buddhist tradition with Luipāda.[104] Mīna or Matsyendra is also mentioned in the Tibetan Buddhist lists of Siddhas. In Nepal he is identified with Boddhisattva Avalokiteśvara. Even today a cart festival is celebrated in his honour. Among the Muslims of Bengal he is known as Mechandali or Mochra Pir. In Munidatta's *Caryāgītikośa* a few verses have been ascribed to him. In the texts of Vajrayāna Matsyendra and Gorakṣa are regarded as Siddhas. A few Tantric texts such as the *Gorakṣasaṃhitā* have been associated with the name of Gorakṣanātha. In north India Gorakṣanthā is regarded as an esoteric system connected with Tantra and Yoga.[105] Hāḍi-pa, another exponent of Nathism is also known by the name Jālandhari. In the Tibetan lists a few Buddhist Tantras such as the *Vajrayoginīsādhana*, *Śuddhivajrapradīpa* *Śricakrasaṃvaragar-bhatattva-nidhi* and *Huṃkāracittavindubhāvanākrama* are ascribed to him. There are a few *dohās* in Apabhraṃśa composed by Kānu-pa or Kṛṣṇapāda. In the Tibetan lists we have references to *Vāyutattvopadeśa* ascribed to Cauraṅgīnātha. The works of Siddha Kānari or Kaneri are mentioned in the Tanjur catalogue.

As has been stated above, Nathism is a composite system consisting of numerous traditions coming from a variety of sources. An historical study of this system should bring to light many hitherto unknown facts and explain many obscure problems. Here we are more concerned with the Buddhist contents of Nathism. The Nātha Siddhas believe that Ādinātha is the first Nātha, the founder of all esoteric sciences. He is very often equated with Śiva and Vajrasattva. The Hara-Gaurī conception of Nathism is an adaptation of both the Mahayanic Karuṇā and Śūnyatā and the Vajrayanic Upāya and Prajñā. The Śūnyavāda of the Mādhyamika system is also accepted in Nathism. According to Nāgārjuna Śūnya or vacuity is of four kinds—Śūnya, Atiśūnya, Mahāśūnya and Sarvaśunyā. The followers of Natbism believe in three kinds of Śūnya—Ādiśūnya, Madhyaśūnya and Antaḥśūnya. This Śūnya is to be realised through Yoga. The process has been described in a text called *Hāḍamālā*[106] which says that by the Yogic control of breath the thirty knots in the spinal cord can be loosened, as a result of which the two vital winds—*prāṇa* and *apāna*—can enter the spinal cord and move upwards as Haṃsa through six nerve plexuses and on reaching the *sahasrāra* region assume the nature of Śūnya. In the *Yogacintāmaṇi* section of the *Gorakṣavijaya*[107] we have the conception *navacakra* which is the addition of three extra stages to the Tantric *ṣaṭcakra*. These extra stages are the three forms of Śūnya—Ādi, Madhya and Antaḥ.

The concept of Sahaja was a characteristic common to all spiritual disciplines of the medieval age. Etymologically it is *sahajāta* (*sahajāyate iti sahaja*), that which is the same as the human instinct itself. The realisation of the highest spiritual principle (Mahāsukha) as identical with one's own self is the basis of all forms of Sahajiyā cult. This realisation is called by the Sahajiyānī Buddhists as Mahāsukha which is possible through the union of Śūnyatā and Karuṇā, or Upāya and Prajñā. The Nāthapanthīs understand Mahāsukha in terms of immortality which is possible through Kāyasādhana. All forms of

Tantric teachings insist the symbolical union of the Male and Female Principle—the efficient and material causes of creation—within the body and this concept has influenced all types of medieval religious ideas. For example, in the *Adi-granth* of the Sikhs, the realisation of *Sach* or *Sahaja*, which is the fifth category (*khand*) of the Sikh way of life, is described as the fourth state (*cauṭhā-pad*) beyond the three qualities of *sattva*, *rajas* and *tamas*. Sahaj-pad is also called *Param-pad*, *Turiya-pad* and *Amar-pad* which is of eternal bliss and contentment. It is unchangeable because it is beyond the cycle of birth and death and beyond the tenth door (cf. the Nātha concept of the tenth door). It is the source of eternal light which causes the light of the individual soul to merge into that of god in the same way as a drop of water merges into the sea. It is that state in which the individual soul merges into the universal soul where there is an end to all sorts of dualism. Nanak called this state Jīvanmukti or Suni (Śūnya) samādhi, Sahaj-samādhi and Sahaj-Yog and its experience as Maha-sukh, Param-sukh or Param-anand. In fact Sahaja is not only the ultimate realty, it is Īśvara or Lord, the last resort, full of love, into which the self merges completely : *jākahi antar vasai prabhu api nanak le jan sahaji samai*. The concept of Sahaja occurs in the teachings of other medieval saints also.

In conclusion we like to emphasise that it is absolutely unnecessary from an historical point of view to suggest a phase of decaying Buddhism and to trace its relics in various Hindu ideas and practices. We are not at all concerned with the so-called 'influences' or 'relics'. We think in terms of the basic ingredients which characterise all the spiritual disciplines of India, Buddhism being no exception. An integrated study of the Indian religio-philosophical ideas and practices clearly reveals that some key-concepts in this field were formulated in space and time under diverse historical circumstances, and these key-concepts were adopted by most spiritual disciplines including Buddhism. The differences were in the case of interpretation and emphasis. And in this criss-cross process of the multi-angled interpretations every spiritual discipline was in a state of flux. This happened not only to Buddhism but to other systems as well. Notwithstanding differences in interpretational points of view, the systems stood in reciprocal relation to one another and the metamorphoses through which they had to pass created new groupings and realignments among them in different ages. One should not fail to recall here that the period which has been stigmatised by most historians as that of the decline and disappearnce of Buddhism was in reality the only period in its long history in India in which it was able to come out of its dry academic shell and renovate all the existing traditional and popular spiritual disciplines by its own spirit.

NOTES

1. Among important gods of Vajrayāna, Hayagrīva is a form of Viṣṇu. Jambhala is the Buddhist counterpart of Kubera. His consort Vasundhārā corresponds to the Hindu conception of Earth and Corn Mother represented by Śrī-Lakṣmi. Jāṅguli is worshipped as the goddess who cures snake-bite and even prevents it. She corresponds to the Hindu goddess Manasā or Viṣahari. In the Purāṇas and Tantras Jāṅguli is an epithet of Manasā, Parṇaśabarī is the goddess who prevents the outbreak of epidemics. She is closely akin to the Hindu goddess Śītalā. Such examples can be multiplied.
2. K.N. Upadhyaya, *Early Buddhism and the Bhagavadgītā,* (Delhi, 1971), 354-55. See also his 'Impact of the Bhakti Movement on the Development of Mahāyāna Buddhism' in *Studies in History of Buddhism,* ed. A.K. Narain (Delhi, 1980), 352.
3. Cf. *Guhyasamāja* 20; *Jñānasiddhi* 12, 33, 71-72; *Sādhanamālā* II, 586; etc.
4. *Advayavajrasaṃgraha* 14, *Sekoddeśaṭīkā* 2-5.
5. In Anaṅgavajra's *Prajñopāyaviniścayasiddhi* V, 25ff. it is stated that for the experience of *mahāmudrā* sex is an important factor. The efficacy of wine, flesh, woman and sexual intercourse amounting even to incest is stressed in *Guhyasamāja* 20, 120, *Jñānasiddhi* I, 80-82; etc.
6. XXIII. 219.
7. Ed. G. Sastri, 504, 647-48.
8. Ed. B.T. Bhattacharyya, 2.
9. To the red Tārā group belongs Kurukullā; to the blue Ekajaṭā and Mahācīnatārā; to the yellow Vajratārā, Jāṅguli, Parṇaśabarī and Bhṛkutī; to the white Aṣṭamahābhaya, Mṛtyuvañcana, Caturbhūjā and Ṣaḍbhūjā Tārās; to the green Khadiravani, Vaśya, Arya, Mahattarī, Varada, Durgottarinī and Dhanada Tārās.
10. Cf. *Nīlatantra*, Paṭala III.
11. I.2; IV.10.
12. Ch. XVII.
13. *Paṭala* I.
14. *Notices of Sanskrit Mss*, Second Series, I (Calcutta, 1900), pref. XXXII and 152.
15. *Nepal* (Paris, 1905), I, 346.
16. *Śakti and Sākta*, 8th Edn., (Madras, 1975), 123.
17. S.K. Chatterji in *JAS*, I, 1959, 118.

18. *Studies in the Tantras* (Calcutta, 1939), 42ff.
19. Nos. 123-28.
20. Nos. 100-101.
21. Bruce, *Chu Hsi and His Masters*, 237-39.
22. Chatterji, *op.cit.*, 104.
23. J. Needham, *Science and Civilization in China* (Cambridge, 1956), II, 33ff.
24. For Tantric texts on chemical sciences see P.C. Ray, *History of Hindu Chemistry*, 2 Vols. (Calcutta, 1902), 1908; enlarged and revised ed. by Priyadaranjan Ray under the title *History of Chemistry in Ancient and Medieval India* (Calcutta, 1956).
25. H.P. Sastri, *Nepal Catalogue* (Calcutta, 1905), 1915, I.135; II, 75.
26. The first of these works is lost. Others have been translated into English and published along with original Tibetan texts (reproduced in Ray's *magnum opus* which also contains the text and translation of another Tibetan treatise called *Rasāyanaśāstroddhṛti* by S.K. Pathak) in Roman script. See also Vidusekhar Bhattacharya, 'Sanskrit Treatises on Alchemy' in *Acharya Ray Commemoration Volume* (Calcutta, 1932), 121ff.
27. K.C. Viraraghava in *ibid.*, 460. Most of their works are scattered as manuscripts. In 1951, D.V. Subba Reddy published a list of 27 works indicating the nature of their contents, originally prepared by W. Ainslie in *Madras Medical Journal*, II, No. 2 adding an extra list of 38 Tamil books composed by the Sittars.
28. A condensed account of Gulik's 'Erotic Colour-prints of the Ming Period, with an Essay on Chinese Sex Life from the Han to the Ch'ing Dynasty' has been given by Goetz in *ABORI*, XXXVI, 1955, 133ff.
29. Needham, *op.cit.* 425-26.
30. *Ibid.*, 149-51.
31. *Ibid.*, 427-28.
32. *JAS*, I, 1959, 113.
33. *Studies in the Buddhistic Culture of India* (Delhi, 1967), 391-94; Cf. C. Eliot, *Hinduism and Buddhism* (London, 1921), II, 6.
34. 'Observations on the History and Influence of the Buddhist Tantra in India and Tibet' in *Studies in History of Buddhism*, ed. A.K. Narain (Delhi, 1980), 360-61.
35. R.C. Mitra, *The Decline of Buddhism in India*, (Visvabharati, 1954). Various theories regarding the so-called decline have been summarised by S.R. Goyal, *A History of Indian Buddhism* (Meerut, 1987), 383-404. Also see L.M. Joshi, *op.cit.*, 379-411; P.V. Kane, *History of Dharmaśāstra*, V(2) (Poona, 1962), 1003-30.
36. *A Short History of Buddhism* (London, 1960), 86.
37. *The Path of the Buddha* (New York, 1956), 48.
38. *Chinese Buddhism*, 99.

39. *Bauddha Dharma ke Vikās kā Itihās* (Lucknow, 1963), 491-92.
40. R.C. Mitra, *op.cit.*, 2; P.C. Bagchi in *Asutosh Mukherjee Silver Jubilee Volume* III, 412; L.M. Joshi, *op.cit.* 302.
41. *Journal of G.N. Jha Research Institute*, IX (1), 111-12.
42. V.A. Smith, *Early History of India*, fourth ed. (Oxford, 1962), 368; S. Radhakrishnan, *Indian Philosophy* (London, 1923), I, 609; B.M. Barua, *Prolegomena to the History of Buddhist Philosophy* (Calcutta, 1918); P.V. Kane, *op.cit.* V(2), 1004-05; P.C. Bagchi, *Asutosh Mukerjee* Vol. III, 4-20; S. Levi, *Le Nepal*, II.317; R.C. Majumdar, *Cultural Heritage of India*, IV, 47-48; R.C. Mitra, *op.cit.*, 150-55.
43. Joshi, *op.cit.*, 379.
44. Śaṅkara did not relax caste rules. Regarding social relations he was a follower of Manu.
45. S.R. Goyal, *op.cit.*, 397-98.
46. *Buddhism* (London, 1926), 83, 85.
47. *IHQ*, X, 276-84.
48. *Bulletin of the RKM Institute of Culture*, XIV, 333-34.
49. Foreword to *2500 Years of Buddhism*, ed. P.V. Bapat (Delhi, 1959), IX.
50. *Early Buddhism and the Bhagavadgītā* (Delhi, 1971), 105.
51. *Hinduism and Buddhism*, 452.
52. In all the philosophical systems of India transcendental perception was added to empirical perception which opened the door for idealism. The earlier empirical basis of philosophy was clearly found in the expression *darśana* which literally meant 'the act of perception' derived from the root *dṛś* 'to see'. But the meaning and significance of the word *darśana* was changed, and it was argued that perception should not be physical. It must be intuitional, for the direct realization of the Self which was conducive to liberation, *mokṣa*. Accordingly *darśana-śāstra* (science of perception) came to be defined as *mokṣa-śāstra* (science of liberation).
53. For details see my *History of the Tantric Religion*, 248-75.
54. Sanskrit edn. by Krishnamacharya, Adyar Library Series, No. 87. Eng. edn. with translation, introduction and notes by Sanjukta Gupta (Leiden, 1972).
55. For example, according to the Pāśupata tradition, as preserved in different Purāṇas, when Vāsudeva Kṛṣṇa, the best of the Yadu family, appeared on the earth at the time of the twenty-eighth repetition of the Yugas, Maheśvara also incarnated himself as a Brahmacārin with the name of Lakulīśa. Cf. *Vāyu* XXIII; *Liṅga* XXIV; *Kūrma* LII; *Śiva* V.
56. See my *Indian Puberty Rites*, second ed. (New Delhi, 1982).
57. The Buddha was not at all in favour of admitting women in the Saṅgha, but did so reluctantly only after the repeated requests of his

foster-mother Mahāprajāvatī. But he laid down eight special rules which were highly insulting for women. For the rules see I.B. Horner, *Woman under Primitive Buddhism* (Delhi, 1975), 119-20; H. Chakraborty, *Asceticism in Ancient India* (Calcutta, 1973), 221. The first of these rules is: A nun, even of a hundred years standing, must make salutation to and bow down before a monk if only just initiated. Other rules are more insulting.

58. Cf. Goyal, *op.cit.*, 297-98.
59. Collected in the *Advayavajrasaṃgraha*, 50.
60. Ed. and trans. by D.L. Snellgrove (Oxford, 1959).
61. *Vārāhy-āliṅgita-mahā-saukhyam. Sādhanamālā* II, 491; Cf. *Ananta-sukha-rūpatvāt śrī-mahāsukha samjñitam. Prajñopaya* 6.
62. *Advayavajrasaṃgraha* 62; *Sādhanamālā* 321, 329 etc.
63. *Guhyasamāja* 19; *Śrīcakrasambhāra* 25; *Dākārnava*, Sahitya Parisat, ed. 157; etc.
64. *Guhyasamāja* 153, *Prajñapāya* 42; *Jñānasiddhi* II, 11.
65. Snellgrove's ed. I, 90 ff.
66. *Sādhanamālā* 448.
67. *Dohākoṣa* of Kāṇhapada, verse 5.
68. *Advayavajrasaṃgraha* 28ff.
69. *Pañcakrama* V.
70. *Sādhanamālā* 17.
71. Cf. *Sekoddeśa-ṭīkā* (GOS)57.
72. *Śrī Cakrasambhāra* 27, 29.
73. II, 491 ff.
74. ABS, Mss 31.
75. *Advayavajrasaṃgraha* 50.
76. *Śricakrasambhāratantra* (Calcutta, 1919), intro.
77. *Lamaism*, 152.
78. *JRAS*, 1901, 900.
79. *An Introduction to Tantric Buddhism*, 64.
80. W.E. Clark, *Two Lamaistic Pantheon* (Cambridge Mass, 1937), II, 49, 233; A. Getty, *The Gods of Northern Buddhism* (Oxford, 1914), 146; A.K. Gordon, *The Iconography of Tibetan Lamaism* (New York, 1939), 84-85.
81. *Niṣpannayogāvali*, 83-84.
82. *Lamaism* 15, 131.
83. Cambridge Ms. Add. No. 1364.
84. S.B. Dasgupta, *op.cit.*, 66.
85. *Tantrāloka* VI.
86. Ed. M.E. Carelli, GOS.
87. Ed. B. Banerjee, ASB.
88. Cf. R. Banerjee, 'Śūnyata as viewed by the Kālacakra School' in *POC* II, Gauhati session, 147-49. N.N. Upadyaya, *Tantrika Sadhanā aur Sāhitya* (Kasi, V.S. 2015), 155ff.

89. There is no exclusive literature beloning to Sahajayāna except the Dohās and songs which have been the main source of inspiration of the regional literature of Eastern India. In 1907, M.M. Haraprasad Sastri discovered as many as fifty songs composed by different Siddhācāryas belonging to the Sahajayāna and these were published in 1916 under the caption *Bauddha Gān O Dohā*. Subsequently P.C. Bagchi discovered from the Tanjur collection the Tibetan translation of all these songs and published many more Dohās of Sarahapāda, Kānhapāda and Tillopāda. *Dohākoṣa*, CSS, 1938; *Journal of the Dept. of Letters*, CU, XXVIII, 1-180; XXX, 1-156. The songs of Kānha and Saraha were translated with interpretations and comments by M. Shahidullah in his *Les Chants Mystiques de Kanha et de Saraha* (Paris, 1928). Rahula Sankrityayana had discovered and published many more Dohās of Sarahapāda. *Dohākoṣa* with Hindi trans (Patna, 1957). The *Caryāgītikoṣa*, edited and annotated by P.C. Bagchi in collaboration with Sānti Bhiksu Sāstri (1956) is an edition of the obscure Bengali *Caryā* songs and the Sanskrit commentary thereon discovered by H.P. Sastri from Nepal. Both the text and the commentary are edited in the light of Tibetan translations previously discovered by Bagchi.
90. P.C. Bagchi in *JDL*, XXVIII, 1-180 (Tillopāda 1-4, 41-45, 139-75; Sarahapāda 5-23, 28-31, 52-120, 176-180; Kānhapāda 24-27, 121-138); XXX, 1-106 (Tibetan), 107-56 (Bengali). Also S.B. Dasgupta, *Obscure Religious Cults*, 35-122, esp. 55-56.
91. Snellgrove, *op.cit.*, I, 54ff.
92. Songs No. 4, 10, 14, 17-18, 28, 49; Dasgupta, *ORC*, 103ff.
93. Cf. *Prajñopāya* III, 20; V.22-23.
94. *Sekoddeśaṭīkā*, 56ff.
95. H.V. Guenther, *Yuganaddha: The Tantric View of Life*, second ed., (Varanasi, 1964).
96. *Śricaitanyacaritāmṛta*, Madhyalīlā, XV; *Vivartavilāsa* of Akiñcana Dāsa, Vanga Sahitya Paricaya II, 1650.
97. See *Anandabhairava* in M.M. Bose's *Sahajiyā Sāhitya*, 132-33.
98. *Brahmasaṃhitā* V.2-20. Also see *Hayaśīrṣapāñcarātra* quoted in the *Bhagavatsandarbha* of the *Ṣaṭ-sandharva* of *Jīva Gosvāmī*.
99. Cal. Univ. Ms. No. 572.
100. *Ibid.*, No. 581.
101. *Vaṅgiya Sāhitya Pariṣat Patrikā*, 1355 BS, No. 4.
102. For details see M.M. Bose, 'An Introduction to post-Caitanya Sahajiyā Cult' in *JDL*, XVI, 1927, 1-162; *Post-Caitanya Sahajiya Cults of Bengal* (Calcutta, 1930).
103. Alaka Chattopadhyaya, *Catalogue of the Tanjur and Kanjur* (Calcutta, 1972); *Tāranātha's History of Buddhism*, tr. Alaka Chattopadhyaya and Lama Chimpa (Simla, 1970); B.N. Dutt, *Mystic Tales of Lama Tāranātha* (Calcutta, 1944), 8-11; Kazi Dawa

Samdup, *Śrīcakrasambhāra* (Calcutta, 1919), intro XXXV; G.N. Roerich, *The Blue Annals*, II, Calcutta, 1953, 753-55, 867-69; *JASB* XXVI, 1930, 132; *IHQ*, 1929, 14-30; *Ep. Ind.* XXVI, 247-48.

104. P.C. Bagchi, *Kaulajñānanirṇaya*, intro. XXXIII.

105. G.W. Briggs, *Gorakhnath and the Kanphata Yogis* (Calcutta, 1913). For a better understanding of Nathism see Kalyani Mallik, *Nātha Sampradāyer Itihās*, in Bengali (Calcutta, 1950); Hazari Prasad Drivedi, *Nātha Sampradāya*, in Hindi, 1966.

106. Ed. Rajmohan Nath, verses 153ff.

107. Ed. Panchanan Mandal, 72ff, 218ff.

APPENDIX

A NOTE ON BUDDHIST ICONOGRAPHY

The railings (*vedikā*) with gateways (*toraṇa*) attached to them which encircled the Stūpas or funerary structures of Sanchi, Bharhut, Bodh-Gaya, Amaravati and other places of the Śuṅga and post-Śuṅga period were adorned with bas-reliefs intimately associated with the episodes pertaining to the achievements of the Buddha during the various states of his incarnatory existence in which neither the present Buddha Śākyamuni nor his predecessors are represented in iconic form. The Buddha's presence in most of these depictions is invariably indicated by means of various symbols, such as the *bodhi* tree, the umbrella, the elephant, the wheel or *dharmacakra*, the Stūpa and so forth. For example, the story of the Buddha's birth as presented in a relief on a sandstone railing-post from Bharhut belonging to the second century B.C. (now in the Indian Museum) depicts the Buddha as an elephant approaching the sleeping figure of queen Māyā. Again, on the dexter of the relief on a limestone casing slab from Nāgarjunikonda (now in the National Museum) the queen is shown grasping the bough of a tree, while the Buddha's presence is indicated by a parasol flanked by two fly-whisks. On the western gateway of Stūpa I at Sanchi in which the story of the shielding of the Buddha during a heavy shower by the Nāga king Mucilinda is depicted, the lord is represented by his seat under a tree over which is an umbrella. On the eastern gateway of Stūpa I at Sanchi in which the stories of the Buddha's victory over a venomous serpent and also over a devastating flood are narrated in the language of art, the Master is represented in both cases in the form of a vacant throne. A seat below a tree has been the symbol of the Buddha also in the northern gateway reliefs which depict the miracle of Vaisali and Sankasya. Such examples can be multiplied. This symbolic or aniconic method, which was at one time universal, constituted by itself, in the words of Coomaraswamy "a complete artistic vocabulary and an iconography without icons". None of these symbols—though most of them were used by the Buddhists and the Jains—is by itself any more Buddhist or Jain than it is Brahmanical or Hindu or simply Indian.[1]

But this aniconic tradition was shortly to disappear and the iconic types of the Buddha made their sudden appearance apparently simultaneously in the so-called Hellenic school of Gandhāra and the Indian school of Mathura. Most western art historians, especially Foucher, floated the idea that the creative genius of Greece had provided a model for the Buddha image which had later been barbarized and degraded by the Indians. The hollowness of this theory has been demonstrated by Coomaraswamy and his arguments are quite well known. The standing Buddha is derived from the standing Yakṣa primitives of the type of Parkham, Patna and Deoriya of a date earlier than that of the Gandhara and Mathura images.[2] The seated image had its prototype in the Yogi-like figures in some Bharhut reliefs as well as the simple effigies found on some early coins. All the images of Gandhara and Mathura and also of Amravati, Sarnath and other places are based on a common iconological tradition, though there are some differences in style. For example, the halo in the Gandhara images is plain while it is scalloped at the edge in the Mathura images. The Gandhara Buddha is occasionally moustached while he never appears with moustaches in the Mathura images. His seat in Gandhara is a lotus, and it is a lion-throne in Mathura.[3] The early Mathura-type differs from Gandhara in the treatment of hair which is indicated by a raised plane above the forehead and a thick single spiral coil on the top centre turned from left to right. The inscribed images of Mathura are sometimes described in their pedestal inscriptions either as Bodhisattva or as Buddha which is suggestive of the fact that the sculptors did not attach much importance to the difference in meaning between the two terms. But the Gandhara artists illustrated in detail the incidents of the Buddha's life and depicted him in several ways as the particular occasions in the narratives demanded. The Gandhara type is eclectic and makes the Buddha an ordinary human being of a rather artificial stature—whereas the Mathura type is characterised by a heavy earthiness of forms and imparts a dignity underlying the idea of a *cakravartin* or universal spiritual monarch. While the influence of the Gandhara school was greater on the Buddhist art of Afghanistan and Central Asia, the trend set by the Mathura school was followed with some modifications by most schools of Indian art.[4]

The Buddhas are innumerable and have a hierarchy among them, the different orders being Pratyeka, Śrāvaka, Samyak-Sambuddha, Jina, Arhat, Tathāgata and the like. The Hinayanists recognise twenty-four mortal Buddhas while the Mahayanists record thirty-two. Prominent among them are the last seven Tathāgatas known as Vipaśyin, Śikhi, Viśvabhū, Krākucuhanda, Kaṇakamuni, Kāśyapa and Sākyasiṃha or Gautama. When represented in sculpture, they appear all alike in colour and form, usually sitting crosslegged with the right hand in *bhūmisparśa mudrā* (gesture of earth-touching with the third finger of the right palm). Standing images of mortal Buddhas are also found in which they are distinguished by the *bodhi* tree at their back and with their individual hand poses. A favourite theme of the Gandhara sculptors is to show eight figures (the seven Buddhas including Gautama and the future Buddha Maitreya) standing side by side with halos behind their heads, the first seven clad in a monk's garment, and the eighth wearing secular dress with a nectar flask in its hand.

Of all the mortal Buddhas, Gautama has a special position whose numerous images are found in India and elsewhere in different attitudes and expressions. In standing images his right hand is generally raised in *abhaya mudrā* (gesture of assurance shown by the right hand raised at the level with chest) while the left holds the fold of the robe which normally covers the left shoulder. But there are instances in which it covers both the shoulders as we find in the Buddha of Mardan belonging to the mature phase of the Gandhara art and other specimens belonging to different schools. The folds of the robe are schematised on the body and indicated vertically. Normally he is represented in monastic robes. Sometimes the drapery is transparent intended to show the physical strength of the disciplined luminous body in transparence. A nice illustration of this type is found in an image of the Buddha from Mathura belonging to the Gupta period, now displayed in the Rashtrapati Bhawan, New Delhi. In most seated images the garment usually covers the left shoulder, a typical example of which is found in an image from Ahicchatra belonging to the Kuṣāṇa period, now in the National Museum, New Delhi. Sometimes the Buddha is shown crowned which variety probably results from his conception as a *cakravartin* or sovereign of the spiritual world. A beautiful illustration of the crowned Buddha comes from Bihar, which is now the Indian Museum, Calcutta. It belongs to the Pāla period. The resplendent figure is bejewelled in a highly embellished crown, a broad necklace and *kuṇḍala*. A good number of crowned images have been found from Kurkihar and Bodh-gaya. These crowned Buddhas were assumed by some to stand for the later concept of Ādi-Buddha. But this view is hardly tenable, for most if not all of them are associated with the incidents of the life story of Gautama Buddha.[5] Seated images are generally in *dhyānāsana* or *vajrāsana* (attitude of sitting in deep meditation in which legs are crossed with soles upturned), the right hand disposed in *bhūmisparśa-mudrā*. Other hand poses like *varada*, *abhaya*, *dharmacakra* and *samādhi* are also common. The palms of the hand and the soles of the feet are sometimes marked by symbols. The ears are elongated and there is a tuft of fine hair (*ūrṇā*) between the brows. There is *uṣṇīṣa* or a protuberance on the middle head. The hair around the central *uṣṇīṣa* are represented by short curls, forming smaller protuberances which cover the whole of the head. In some images the mass of hair is gathered on the crown in the shape of a snail-shell (*kaparda*).

Very often the Buddha is represented in terms of myths and legends associated with him. We have already had the occasion to refer to the Bharhut relief depicting the event of his birth. A sculpture stylistically belonging to the early Gupta period extracted from an ancient sanctuary and now fixed to the back wall of a modern shrine at Lumbini shows Māyādevī, nearly life-sized, standing under a tree grasping its branch with her right hand, her left hand resting on her hip. Mahāprajāvati is shown supporting her and behind her is the slightly bent figure of Śakra in the attitude of receiving the new-born child. The small figure of Gautama with a halo round his head stands below.[6] In a bronze image from Nalanda, which is now in the Nalanda Museum, Māyādevī is shown as standing, holding the branch of a tree by her right hand and the scarf of the upper garment by her left. Indra is also shown supporting the child Buddha on his joined palm. Among the foliage of the tree above is seen a palm, perhaps symbolising the strewing of flowers from heaven at this auspicious event. The composition which is surrounded by an oval flame aureole belongs to c. tenth century A.D. Another images of Māyādevī with the newly born baby Gautama along with the nun Somā standing on a pedestal bedecked with *vajras* and reclining elephants at four corners is also from Nalanda.[7] The Great Departure (*mahābhiniṣkramaṇa*) is depicted on a schist slab found in Loriyan Tangai which is now the Indian Museum. In it the Buddha is seen on his horse Kaṇṭhaka whose hoofs are upheld by Yakṣas. Other characters of the occasion are on his front while behind the horse is Chandaka holding aloft an umbrella over his head. The reduction of the Buddha's body into a skeleton owing to his severe austerities is represented by his emaciated figure, belonging to the Gandhara school, found at Sikri and now in the Central Museum, Lahore. On the wall of Cave 26 at Ajanta and on a slab from Ghantasala, now in the Musee Guimet, Paris, the temptation and assault of Māra have been depicted. The Indian

Museum contains a slab from Jamalgarhi depicting how the gang of assassins hired by Devadatta was subdued in front of the Buddha.

The *dharmacakra-mudrā* in itself symbolises the first preaching of the Law at Sarnath, which is counted as one of the eight great miracles. Numerous images of the seated Buddha representing him setting the Wheel of Law in motion are found in this particular hand pose. In such images the actual wheel is generally represented below the seat of the Buddha. Often the slab contains, besides the central figure, two recumbent deer indicating the venue (*Mrgadāva*), monkish figures flanking the wheel and so forth. A good many medieval compositions have been found in eastern India which show the Buddha seated in a similar manner with his hands in same *mudrā*, but we do not find the wheel and deer indicative of the locality of Sarnath on the pedestal, in place of which are shown Nanda and Upananda on either side of the lotus stalk. A standing image in the same *mudrā* is also found. Mention may be made in this connection of one made of chlorite found at Ratnagiri.[8] Likewise the *bhūmisparśa-mudrā* illustrates the story of the Buddha's calling the earth as his witness for testifying to his right to sit on the Vajrāsana under the *bodhi* tree which was challenged by Māra, just on the eve of his enlightenment. This enlightenment theme in which the cross-legged seated Buddha touches the earth is the most common form of the Buddha image. Among numerous specimens belonging to this type we may refer to two interesting stone images one from Ratnagiri in Orissa belonging to the tenth century and the other from Ujani in Faridpur district, now in the Dacca Museum, Bangladesh. A bronze image from Nalanda, now in the Indian Museum, which depicts the enlightenment theme shows the Buddha in *vajrāsana* and *bhūmisparśa mudrā* against the background of a foliage symbolising the *bodhi* tree. A special form of this enlightenment (as also of the preaching of Law theme symbolised by the *dharmacakra mudrā* mentioned above) is often sculpturally represented in terms of the eight Great Miracles. The principal image is that of the Buddha seated under the *bodhi* tree in *bhūmisparśa-mudrā*. The treatment of the seven other incidents is condensed. Starting from the bottom left corner and proceeding clockwise we find : the birth (the Buddha is seen coming out of the right side of the body of Māyā holding the branch of a tree); the Descent at Sankaṣya (the Buddha is seen standing below an umbrella held by a god); the Miracle of Sravasti (the Buddha in the *dharmacakrapravartana-mudrā* with a tiny figure near the seat probably representing a heretical teacher); the Great Decease (reclining figure on the top with two persons, one near the feet and the other near the head, the former presumably Mahākassapa and the the latter Ānanda); the First Sermon at Mṛgadāva (two dear flanking the wheel indicates the venue); the Subjugation of Nālāgiri (suggested by the attitude of the Buddha's right hand as also by the figure of an elephant lying down near his feet); and the presentation of Honey (in which the Buddha holds a bowl in his hands while the monkey is seen below his seat). A nice example of this type of image found at Nalanda and belonging to the Pāla period is in the Indian Museum which alone possesses numerous such specimens mostly hailing from Bihar and Bengal. The Patna Museum contains one such in bronze with a long inscription on its back.[9] The much mutilated figure in the collection of the Vaṅgīya Sāhitya Pariṣat Museum, Calcutta, shows the Buddha in the *samapādasthānaka* attitude on a double-petalled lotus below which is written the Buddhist formula in a ninth century script. It is flanked on either side by three parallel rows of two scenes each with that of the *mahāparinirvāṇa* just on the top. Many hundreds of images in stone and metal representing the Buddha in *bhūmisparśa mudrā*, symbolising the enlightenment theme, have been found all over India.

Miracle-themes are also represented singly. For example, the Miracle of Sravasti is depicted on a sandstone slab from Sarnath, belonging to the Gupta period which is now in the Indian Museum. The sculpture presents fourteen figures of the Buddha, indicative of his multiplication which he demonstrated in order to prove his superiority over the six heretical teachers, in all the five *mudrās*, both standing and seated in lotuses issuing from the different shoots of a common stem.[10] The Aurangabad cave no. 2 contains a seventh century rock-cut in which the Buddha is depicted as the central figure within two panels containing identical smaller images suggestive of his proliferation. Likewise, the northern gateway of Stūpa I at Sanchi has relief depicting the Buddha's descent from the Trayatriṃśa heaven to earth at Sankasya. The top part of the panel shows the heaven with gods seated by the side of the Buddha represented by a seat below a tree at the head of a ladder. The ladder flanked by rows of gods signifies the Buddha's descent. At the foot of the ladder is a seat again below a tree, suggesting his landing at Sankasya.[11] The Miracle of Sankasya is also depicted in a metal representation from Kurkihar, now in the Patna Museum, which shows the Buddha standing on a lotus, pedestal on a lion-throne, robes covering both the shoulders, the right hand in *varada* with palm marked by a lotus wheel and the left upholding the end of his garment. To his right stands three-headed Brahmā and to his left Indra holding in his two hands a bowl full of contents.[12] This reminds us of a nice piece of stone image from Kirtail, depicting the same theme belonging to c. eleventh century, which is now in the Rajshahi Museum.[13] Many standing images which do not contain illustrations of the stereotyped set of miracles fall either under the Devāvatāra or Nālāgiri-taming types. The first of the two is more common and is often shown attended on either side by Indra and Brahmā. In order to emphasise the act of descent the artists sometimes indicate stairs beneath the feet of the three. This reminds us of the early Buddhist convention of showing the same scene with three stairs side by side, the middle one having one foot mark on its topmost rung and another on its lowermost one.[14] The Miracle of Vaisali which is depicted on the northern gateway of Stūpa I at Sanchi shows a monkey approaching the Buddha (represented by a seat below a tree) with a begging bowl which has been filled up with honey. There is a second monkey behind. There are also a few persons representing the crowd which witnessed the miracle of honey offering to the Buddha by a monkey.[15] (This miracle is often represented by a type of seated Buddha with an alms bowl in hand and a monkey carved on the pedestal or by his side.) An interesting relief in the collection of the Asutosh Museum depicting this variety of the seated Buddha shows the monkey climbing a tree for bringing down the honey to be offered to the Buddha. A limestone relief of the second century A.D. on a cross-bar of a railing from Amaravati (now in the Government Museum, Madras), depicts the Miracle of Rājagṛha. It is the taming of Nālāgiri, a fierce elephant which was maddened and let loose at the instance of Devadatta in order to kill the Buddha. The elephant is shown twice, once in its furious mood running wild on the street of Rājagṛha and the second time submissively kneeling before the Buddha. The calm serenity of the Buddha and his disciples has been delineated in effective contrast to the panic-stricken crowd on the street.[16] The Indian Museum contains a sculptured slab depicting the theme of the Great Decease, the last of the Great Miracles. Here the Buddha is seen lying on his right side on a couch spread between two trees. One tree exists on the slab. The other was presumably carved on another slab which depicted the continuation of the scene. The grief-stricken figures behind the Buddha represent the Mallas. Below the tree are two monks. The one near the feet is probably Mahākassapa. The nude figure behind him is generally considered as an Ājīvika ascetic from whom Mahākassapa received the news of the Buddha's decease. Below the couch is the mourning Vajrapāni. On his left side is Subhadra in meditation.[17] Independent recumbent figure of this type representing the *mahāparinirvāṇa* of the Buddha is extremely rare.

According to the *Sādhanamālā* the Buddha should be represented with Maitreya on the right side and Avalokiteśvara on the left, which is illustrated in a few Nalanda bronzes, now in the Indian Museum, in the famous trio displayed in the Patna Museum[18] and in the staircase leading up to the temple of Bodh-Gaya on the northern side.[19] A dual personality in Buddhist mythology and pantheon, Maitreya is represented in the Buddhist art as the Buddha-to-be and also as a Bodhisattva. Before his descent on earth as the future Buddha he is believed to have been residing in the Tuṣita heaven where many Buddhist Arhats like Asaṅga are said to have had discussions with him on spiritual problems. The special cognizance of Maitreya is a bunch of Nāgakesara flowers placed in one of his hands in place of the earlier nectar-flask. Another distinctive mark is a miniature *stūpa* placed in his crown or by its side.[20] Maitreya is the only Bodhisattva who is worshipped alike by the Hinayanists and the Mahayanists, and his images can be traced from the Gandhara school to the present time. We have already had the occasion to refer to the Gandhara Maitreya in secular dress and a nectar flask in hand as the future Buddha in the company of seven Mānuṣī Buddhas. At Sopara eight bronze images representing seven Mānuṣī Buddhas and Maitreya as the future eighth have been found. A beautiful gold-plated bronze image of this god has been found from Melayur in Thanjavur district, Tamil Nadu and another from Nagapattinam. Both of these are now in the Government Museum, Madras. A good number of stone and bronze images have been found in Amravati. Rock-cut standing images of Maitreya belonging to the seventh century are found in Ellora cave no. VII. They have two hands, the right near the breast holding a flower and the left on the knot of scarf tied near the heap. They contain *stūpas* on *jaṭāmukuṭa* (matted crest). A similar rock-cut Maitreya occurs in an Aurangabad cave.[21] From Nālanda a number of Maitreya images have been discovered. The one in stone, now in the Indian Museum shows *varada-mudrā* (gesture of offering boon shown by right hand hanging down with palm outward) in right hand, *nāgakeśara* in the broken left and *stūpa* on *jaṭāmukuṭa*. Here the god is shown standing with two four-handed female companions. This image belongs to c. ninth century. The Nalanda site museum preserves a number of bronze images of Maitreya of which four deserve special mention. All of them are seated on a lotus pedestal, one of them in *bhadrāsana* (in which the feet dangle down from the seat) and others in *lalitāsana* (an attitude of ease). All of them have *stūpa* on matted crest. The one in *bhadrāsana* shows *vyākhyāna mudrā* (gesture of the exposition of the Law) by his two hands, with the stalk of flower rising up along the left arm and the others carry the stalk of flower (*nāgakeśara*) in their left hands. One of the other images shows *abhaya mudrā* in the right hand while the other two show *varada mudrā*.[22] Of the standing bronze images of Maitreya, we may refer to one from the Kurkihar hoard in which he stands with *nāgakeśara* in left hand, the right hand pedant with *varada mudrā* and *stūpa* in *jaṭamukuṭa* (matted crest). A seated bronze of the same stock depicts him with right leg pendant on a single lotus throne on which rests the left hand with the stalk of a four-petalled flower. The right hand rests on the right knee with a ball-shaped object in it. The *jaṭamukuṭa* is on the apex of the head with screw curls.[23] Mention may also be made of a beautiful bronze image of Maitreya from Baudh in Orissa which follows the major iconographical characteristics. The richly ornamented figure is seated gracefully in *lalita* pose on a throne, holding in the left hand a bunch of *nāgakeśara* and in the right a nectar vase. Maitreya images have also been found from Ratnagiri and Chandraketugarh. Very often Maitreya appears in manuscript paintings.[24] Images of Maitreya have also been found in Tibet and China.[25]

The earlier Buddhist concepts of the five *skandhas* were deified in later Buddhism in the form of five Dhyānī Buddhas known respectively as Amitābha, Akṣobhya, Vairocana, Amoghasiddhi and Ratnasambhava. Each of them has a Śakti, a Bodhisattva, a number of emanations, male and female, and a recognition symbol. They are always represented as seated on a full blown lotus in *dhyānāsana*. The hand resting on the lap is sometimes empty, but in most cases it holds a bowl. The head is bare with thick clustering curls of hair. The eyes are half-closed. Their images are generally depicted in miniature forms on the head of their emanations. They are also represented on the four sides of a *stūpa*—Amitābha facing the west, Akṣobhya the east, Amoghasiddhi the north and Ratnasambhava the south. Vairocana's place is in the sanctum of the *stūpa* and that is why he is not represented on its body. The National Museum contains a *stūpa* from Chitorgarh which depicts on its four sides four Dhyānī Buddhas. Individual images are not rare, but they are more frequent in Nepal and Tibet. There is a unique stone image of Ratnasambhava (c. eleventh century) hailing from Vikrampur and now in the collection of the Rajshahi Museum.[26] The figure is shown inside a temple, the superstructure of which rises up in a number of tiered stages capped by an *āmalaka* and *stūpa* finial. The Buddha is seated in *vajraparyaṅka* on a lotus over a high pedestal which shows representations of jewels (*ratna*) as well as figures of Jambhala and Vasudhārā.[27] The Orissa State Museum contains a small image of Amoghasiddhi against the background of a seven-hooded snake forming his umbrella. Another snake with its hood raised is seen on the lotus pedestal. A life-size image of this Dhyānī Buddha from Udayagiri in Phulbani is also found in the same museum.[28]

Vajradhara, also called Ādi-Buddha, to whom the Dhyānī Buddhas are supposed to owe their origin, is conceived in two forms, single and *yuganaddha* (in union with a female partner). In individual conception he is bedecked in jewels and ornaments sitting in *vajrāsana* carrying *vajra* (diamond, i.e., thunderbolt) in right hand and *ghaṇṭā* (bell) in the left. In *yuganaddha* form, he is locked in close embrace with his Śakti who appears to be Prajñāpāramitā. He is of reddish-white colour, three-faced and six-armed standing in *ardhaparyaṅka*. With two principal hands carrying *vajra* and *ghaṇṭā*, he embraces Prajñā. His other two right hands contain sword and *aṅkuśa* (elephant goad) and his left hands *kapāla* (skull cup) and *pāśa* (noose).[29]

Vajrasattva is sometimes regarded as the sixth Dhyānī Buddha and sometimes as their priest. His Śakti is Vajrasattvātmikā and his Bodhisattva is Ghaṇṭāpāṇi. His worship is performed in secret and like Vajradhara he is represented in two forms, single and *yuganaddha*.[30] In fact, the conceptions of Vajradhara and Vajrasattva are sometimes inextricably mixed up. The National Museum contains a bronze image of Vajradhara which is four-faced, two-handed, crowned and ornamented. It is from Nalanda and belongs to the tenth century A.D. The god is seated in *vajrāsana* (adamantine attitude of sitting in which two legs are firmly crossed and the soles turned upward) on a lotus supported by four lions. Two hands, joined near the chest, seem to balance a *vajra*. A headless stone image with jewelled ornaments (c. twelfth century) found at Bharson which is now in the Rajshahi Museum, has been identified by some scholars with Ādi-Buddha belonging to the Vajradhara thought-complex on the basis of the *vajra* in the centre of the lotus seat. The image is in *bhūmisparśa mudrā*. A diaphanous drapery with folds covers the body, but leaves the right shoulder bare. The Sukhabalpur (Dacca) image of Vajrasattva, with the Buddhist creed inscribed on its back in the script of tenth century, shows that the concept of this god as the sixth Dhyānī Buddha had already been introduced in Bengal.[31] The Indian Museum contains two stone Vajrasattva images from Nalanda and two from Salimpur, Orissa, which correspond to the iconographical descriptions found in the texts. A stone image of Vajrasattva with companions, now in the Nalanda Museum deserves special mention. The god is as usual seated in *padmāsana* (attitude of sitting in which legs are crossed on the lotus seat with soles upturned) with two hands bearing *vajra* in the right hand against the chest and *ghaṇṭā* in the left resting on the thigh. On its four sides in separate aureoles appear four female figures in *padmāsana*. Two of these four figures bear garlands. One of the remaining two has both the hands placed on the thighs while the other shows *añjali* (gesture of adoration shown by two hands joined palm to palm near breast) by two hands. The Banpur hoard, now in the Orissa State Museum, contains five bronze images of Vajrasattva. Seated in *vajrāsana*, they look fierce, all two-handed, the right holding the *vajra* against the chest and the left the *ghaṇṭā* resting on the thigh. Two of them have the figures of Akṣobhya on the crest.[32] A temple in the Monastery 2 complex of Ratnagiri contains on its wall a stone image of Vajrasattva. A fragmentary image of Vajrasattva which came from Chandiasal is now in the Khiching Museum.

Among the Bodhisattvas, the concept of Avalokiteśvara, as we have seen above, is very popular in Buddhist mythology. In the *Māhāvastu* we come across Avalokita Bodhisattva whose duty was to look around (*avalokana*) for the sake of instructing people. His name appears in the *Suvarṇaprabhāśa* and the *Sukhāvativyūha*. In the *Kāraṇḍavyūha* he is said to manifest himself in countless forms for the welfare of mankind. No less than 108 forms have been attributed to him and he is "looked upon as a representative of the Buddha, the guardian of the Buddhist faith until Maitreya should appear on earth as the Mānuṣī Buddha".[33] The *Sādhanamālā* gives 38 *sādhanas* which describe a variety of his forms.[34] A standing rock-cut image of Avalokiteśvara belonging to the seventh century found in Aurangabad cave VII shows the Dhyānī Buddha Amitābha on the crest. The right hand is in *abhaya mudrā* and the left hanging down holding a half-blown lotus by stalk. On either side four registers represent persons in distress seeking aid. Above the shoulders on two sides are two Dhyānī Buddhas. An identical scene is also found in Kanheri cave no. 56 ascribed to the sixth century.[35] A good number of seated Avalokiteśvara images from Nalanda are preserved in the Indian Museum. Among these, one interesting variety shows the god seated in *lalitāsana* on lotus in mountain grotto flanked by Tārā and Bhṛkuti on both sides. Two hands are in *dharmacakra-mudrā*. A lotus stalk with blossom above the shoulder passes under the left armpit. The Dhayāni Buddha Amitābha is on the matted crest. The arched facade of the grotto is topped in the centre by a *stūpa* replica, and flanked by worshippers, ascetics and garland-bearing figures. On the top the stela has five Dhyānī Buddhas, each in a niche, with Vairocana in the middle. A similar image, though the upper left portion of the stela is broken, is found among the numerous Avalokiteśvara specimens preserved in the Nalanda Museum.[36]

Of all the Avalokiteśvara images Padmapāṇi is the most common. He is the spiritual son of the Dhyānī Buddha Amitābha. He is generally one-faced and two armed, and represented as displaying the *varada* pose with the right hand and holding a stem of lotus in the left hand. Individual Padmapāṇi images as well as his representations in the company of the Buddha are frequent. Mention may be made of his bronze image from Sirpur in Madhya Pradesh, the stone image from Pandrethan in Kashmir, cave No. 2 image from Karla in the accompaniment of Tārā, Kondivte image in association of the Buddha, the stone image of Kanhari, Nasik image in the company of colossal Buddha, Ajanta image on the door-frame of cave 6, Aurangabad cave image in company of the Buddha and six goddesses, Ellora Cave 11 image with the Buddha and other Bodhisattvas, the stone image in the Monastery 1 of Ratnagiri, single stone images from Ratnagiri in Orissa, the bronze image from south Jolaibari in Tripura, the bronze image from Mainamati and so forth. The Indian Museum has a good number of Padmapāṇi images in bronze. A bronze image of Padmapāṇi from Nalanda, now in the Patna Museum, deserves special mention. It is in *lalitāsana*, holding an unidentified object in the right hand raised up to the breast and with a stalk of lotus, now missing, in the left.[37] The Banpur hoard of Orissa contains fifteen Padmapāṇi images; one of the images is in *vajrāsana* with Amitābha on the crest and the left hand holding a lotus stalk and the right in *varada*; one is in *mahārājalīlā* (an attitude of kingly comfort in which one leg is raised up on the seat) pose; and others are in *lalita* pose with the right hand folded and the left hanging gracefully from the seat and resting on a lotus.[38] The Asutosh Museum of the Calcutta University contains a stone image of Avalokiteśvara (eleventh century) from Bhadrakali standing in *tribhaṅga*. The broken right hand is in *varada* and the left holds a lotus. To the left is a tree issuing from a vase. Its trunk is clasped by a Yakṣa. Its branches hang down to the right. To proper right appear three figures kneeling Sucīmukha and two others. This also belongs to the Padmapāṇi category.

Among other varieties of Avalokiteśvara Ṣaḍakṣarī Lokeśvara is four-armed, four hands being in *namaskāra-mudrā* (gesture of paying homage; sometimes also used to mean *añjali*) and the back ones holding a rosary and a lotus, and having a smaller male replica of him to his right and another similar but female one to the left. These two are none other than Maṇidhara and Ṣaḍakṣarī Mahāvidyā, the representative male and female attendants of Avalokiteśvara. Images representative of this Ṣaḍakṣarī group correspond mostly to the iconographical description mentioned above. Monastery 2 of Ratnagiri contains image of this god on a temple wall. Two tenth century stone images, one from Sarnath and the other from Kahalgaon, now respectively in the Sarnath and Patna Museums, show the four-handed god seating in *vajraparyaṅka* on a lotus seat; the main pair of hands are in *añjalimudrā*, the upper right containing a rosary and the upper left a lotus; to the right and left of the main image are four-handed Maṇidhara and Ṣaḍakṣarī Mahāvidyā respectively in the same hand poses and with the same articles as shown and held by the principal image. The Patna specimen is heavily damaged.[39] The one hailing from Ranipur is now in the Maldah Museum. This stone image comes from Bamangola and belongs to the eleventh century. It corresponds in every detail to the iconographical features found in the two other images mentioned above.[40] The same holds good also in the case of an eleventh century stone image from Rajshahi now in the Rajshahi Museum. It is also badly damaged. The upper stele contains five Dhyānī Buddhas with Amitābha in the top centre. A bronze image of this deity is found at Nagapattinam. There are also a few bronze images of this deity, one of which is now preserved in the Baroda Museum.

Siṃhanāda Lokeśvara is of white complexion with three eyes and *jaṭāmukuṭa*. He is without ornaments, clad in tiger-skin and sits on a lion in *mahārājalīlā* pose. His symbols are a sword on a lotus and a *triśūla* entwined by a snake. Images of Siṃhanāda Lokeśvara are fairly common of which reference may be made to the well-known specimens from Mahoba and Magadha now preserved in the Lucknow Museum and also a small bronze from Nepal which does not, however, contain the lion.[41] Images of this deity have also been recovered from Sarnath and Sravasti. The Kurkihar hoard contains a bronze image of Siṃhanāda seated on a lion, left hand stretched downwards with lotus stalks while the right hand is pendant on the right leg. Amitābha is in front of the flat, high *jaṭāmukuṭa*. The third eye is marked on the forehead. The image is placed on a oval single lotus pedestal on a *triratha* base.[42]

Khaṣarpaṇa is accompanied by Tārā and Sudhanakumāra to his right and Bhṛkuṭi and Hayagrīva to the left. Sometimes Sucīmukha is also represented on the pedestal. The deity is named after a village of East Bengal. But Hiuen Tsang says that the Potalaka mountain to the east of the Malaya hill in the Pāndya country was the resort of Khaṣarpaṇa. According to the iconological descriptions, he is of white colour, wears *jaṭāmukuta*, holds the image of Amitābha on his head and sits in *ardhaparyaṅka* or *lalita* attitude on a double lotus. His right hand exhibits the *varada* pose and the left holds a lotus stem.[43] The popularity of Khaṣarpaṇa is proved by a number of images of this god discovered in different parts of Bihar and Bengal. The Dacca Museum contains two stone images of Khaṣarpaṇa, seated in *lalitāsana* on a lotus seat, the right hand in *varada* and the left holding a stalk of lotus, with Tārā, Sudhanakumāra, Bhṛkuṭi and Hayagrīva as companions.[44] The Rajshahi Museum contains a stone image on Khaṣarpaṇa which was found at Mulchar in Vikrampur, which corresponds to the iconographical details mentioned above. The same holds good in the case of two stone images of Khaṣarpaṇa from Nalanda, belonging to the eleventh-twelfth century, now in the Indian Museum.[45] The Patna Museum contains two images of this god, one of which found somewhere in Bihar shows the lower portion with Bhṛkuṭi and Hayagrīva. The other from Udayagiri in Cuttack district shows the god in *lalitāsana*, the right hand with *varada mudrā* on the right knee, the left hand resting on the seat holding a long lotus stalk, Sudhanakumāra kneeling with *añjalimudrā* to the right and the four armed Bhṛkuṭi to the left. The Orissan image belongs to the eighth century, while the rest may be placed between tenth and eleventh centuries.[46]

Many standing images of Avalokiteśvara endowed with four and sometimes with six hands have been found in different parts of India and usually described as Lokanātha. A seated variety of this god is also found. The four-armed figures show *vara*, *akṣamālā* (rosary), *bhṛṅgāra* (horn-like pot of drinking) and *padma* (lotus) in the lower right, upper right, lower left and upper left hands respectively. Sucīmukha and Hayagrīva to the right and the left are the usual attendants in these cases. The six-armed standing figures on the other hand have *vara*, *mātuluṅga* and *akṣamālā* in the right hands and *bhṛṅgāra*, *pāśa* and *padma* in the left ones. Here both the attendant figures are females, Tārā and Bhṛkuṭi. There was a Vihara of Lokanātha is Kashmir near Srinagar and Lokanātha Caityas in different parts of Maharashtra. The Mūlavāsa Lokanātha of Dakṣiṇāpaṭha is illustrated on a Cambridge Manuscript (no. add. 1643). The seventh century seated rock-cut image of Lokanātha in Ellora cave IV shows in its right hand *abhaya mudrā* with a rosary; the left is placed on the knee. Flanked by two female companions, Tārā and Bhṛkuṭi, it has Amitābha on the crest. On the upper section there are two Dhyānī Buddha images. Cave VIII contains a standing two-handed Lokanātha image. The right hand is broken; the left holds a lotus but by a long stalk with a *ghaṭa* placed on stem. The figure of Amitābha is on the matted crest. The left upper section is occupied by a figure in *dhyānāsana* while the lower shows a kneeling female figure.[47] A most artistic image of Lokanātha has been found from Mahoba.[48] The

Indian Museum contains a stone image from Sarnath belonging to the seventh century, standing in *bhaṅga* position, arms broken, which shows the miniature figure of Amitābha on the crown.[49] The National Museum contains two stone images, one standing and the other seated, belonging to the seventh and ninth century respectively. The images are two-armed with *varada mudrā* and holding the stalk of lotus. They have Amitābha on the crest. The Patna Museum contains a tenth century stone image from Bishenpur which corresponds to the aforesaid description of the two-armed variety. This also holds good in the case of a ninth century stone image now in the Nalanda Museum.[50] Metal images of Lokanātha are also abundant. One in the Baroda Museum deserves special mention.[51] The Nalanda Museum contains a number of bronze images, most of them seated in *vajraparyaṅka*, with hands in *varada* and lotus or in *vyākhyāna* or *vitaraka mudrā* (gesture of argumentation), having Amitābha on the crest. The Indian Museum bronze images of Lokanātha are mainly from Nalanda.[52] The Patna Museum contains two crowned images of Lokanātha from Nalanda and more than twenty from Kurkihar, all in bronze, standing as well as seated, containing Amitābha in the *jaṭāmukuṭa* and the usual symbols.[53] The already noted Cambridge manuscript contains painted illustrations of the two-armed standing Champitalā Lokanātha and the two-armed seated Jayatuṅga Lokanātha of Samataṭa as well as the six-armed standing Sila-Lokanātha of Harikela.

Another form of Avalokiteśvara, known as Jaṭāmukuṭa Lokeśvara is four-armed, one-faced, the head on the top representing that of Amitābha. Two right hands show the rosary and *varada* pose while the two left hold the lotus and the waterpot.[54] Standing stone images of this deity, belonging to the ninth-tenth century, have been found from Ratnagiri, Udayagiri, Kurkihar and Nalanda. Besides the general correspondence to the iconographical description mentioned above, they have companion images of Sucīmukha and Hayagrīva on both sides. The one from Kurkihar has Tārā and Bhṛkuṭi.[55] The Patna Museum contains a tenth-century seated image of Jaṭāmukuṭa Lokeśvara. Its upper right hand contains rosary, the lower right in *varada* pose, the upper left holds a lotus by stalk and the lower left is on the seat. The absence of water pot is to be noted. The National Museum contains a tenth-century bronze image of Jaṭāmukuṭa Lokeśvara standing in *samapādasthānaka* (straight and erect attitude of standing) pose (legs broken) with four hands, having *akṣamālā* in the upper right, *varada* in the upper left, lotus supporting *vajra* in the lower right and water pot in the lower left.

The Indian Museum contains a bronze image of this god. Its left hand is broken, but the other three hands contain the usual symbols.[56]

The Sugatisandarśana form of Avalokiteśvara has been described as of white complexion with six hands showing *varada*, *abhaya* and *akṣamāla* in the right hands and *padma*, *kuṇḍi* (small water vessel, usually with a spout) and *tridaṇḍī* (a staff with three forks or branches) in the left.[57] The Asutosh Museum has a tenth-century stone image from Bihar Sharif, having most of the aforesaid emblems in the six hands, with Tārā and Bhṛkuṭi as companions and Sucīmukha on the pedestal. A tenth-century standing stone image from Gaya, now in the National Museum, a ninth-century seated stone image from Kurkihar, now in the Patna Museum, and a tenth-century seated stone image from Nalanda, now in the Indian Museum, present the nearest approximation of the Sugatisandarśana form.[58] A rare image of Sugatisandarśana of the eleventh or twelfth century is in the Rajshahi Museum. It is six-handed, fives of which hold a manuscript, *pāśa* (noose), *tridaṇḍī*, *akṣamālā* and *kamaṇḍalu* and the remaining one shows the *varada* pose. Four of these emblems correspond to the aforesaid iconographical description in which the manuscript and *pāśa* are substituted by lotus and *abhaya-mudrā*.[59] The Indian Museum has a metal image, belonging to c. eleventh century from Nalanda, standing in *samapādasthānaka* on lotus, right hands showing *akṣamālā*, *abhaya* and *varada* and the left hands a manuscript, a lotus and a waterpot. Companions and Tārā and Bhṛkuṭi to the left and right respectively. This image may be identified with Sugatisandarśana Lokeśvara.[60]

Nīlakaṇṭha Lokeśvara is described as of yellow colour wearing *jaṭāmukuṭa* adorned with crescent and the effigy of Amitābha, seated in *vajraparyaṅka* on a red lotus and exhibiting *samādhi-mudrā*, with his two hands carrying a *kapāla* filled with a variety of gems. His two sides are occupied by two snakes.[61] A Nīlakaṇṭha image hailing from the monastery of Sarnath is now in the National Museum. In this sculptures two tiny figures carrying bowls are seen instead of two serpents on either side, which is the usual symbol of this god. Another stone image of Nīlakaṇṭha is in the Nalanda Museum which belongs to c. eleventh century. It is seated in *vajraparyaṅka* on lotus with two hands holding a vase near the breast. The effigy of the Dhyānī Buddha Amitābha is on the matted crest. A round aureole edged with flames is at the back.[62] A confusion is likely to arise in the identification of the images of Nīlakaṇṭha and Vajrarāga, a variety of Mañjuśrī.[63]

In sculptural representations Avalokiteśvara is often flanked by goddesses, very often by Tārā, occasionally with a child on her left thigh. Besides the common variety of Avalokiteśvara images, seated or standing, which are abundantly found in metal and stone, we have a few other types which are worthy of mention. One such variety is Vajradharma, the distinguishing trait of which is that the god is to open the blossom of a lotus by his right hand near the breast with its stalk held in the left hand. The distinguishing feature of this god is that he rides a peacock.[64] Two stone images from Nalanda, belonging to the tenth century, illustrate this type. One of these is in the Indian Museum and the other in the Nalanda Museum. Both the figures are seated in *padmāsana* with hands near the breast in the mood of opening something. The Indian Museum image has on either side of the pedestal two peacocks in the middle of a pot-bellied female figure in *ālīḍha* with the right hand holding an upraised sword and the left held near the breast. In the recess of a temple wall in front of the Monastery 2 of Ratnagiri there is a stone image of Vajradharma.

A tenth-century stone image is in the Rajshahi Museum. Pot-bellied and dwarfish in appearance it stands on a lotus with three faces each with a fierce mien and six hands. Two of the right hands contain rosary and arrow while the third is broken. Of the three left hands, only one is intact and it carries a *kapāla*. This image to a great extent corresponds to Halāhala Lokeśvara.[65] Another variety of Avalokiteśvara is Trailokyavasaṅkara, also known as Uḍḍiyāna Lokeśvara. This form of Lokeśvara does not seem to have been widely represented. He is one-faced, two-armed and three-eyed and is seated in *vajraparyaṅka*. He wears a crown of matted hair, and carries in his two hands a noose and a goad stamped with the *vajra*.[66] The Nalanda collection of Patna Museum contains a bronze image of this god, seated on a platform in the *vajraparyaṅka* with upraised hands holding indistinct objects. He has matted hair arranged like a crown.[67]

A bronze image of Śaṅkhanātha Lokeśvara now in Bhuvaneswar, was found at Baudh in Orissa. Although in *lalita* attitude this image—four-armed, one-faced and richly ornamented—is erect on a lotus throne placing its right foot on a footstool. It carries in its upper right hand a conch-shell and in the upper left hand a lotus, while the lower right is in *varada* pose and the lower left is placed on a throne. The Indian Museum contains a bronze image of Ārogyaśalī Lokeśvara, evidently a god of healing, who is known to be a deity of Siṃhaladeśa. He is seated in *lalitāsana* on a lotus pedestal with the right hand in *abhayamudrā* and the left resting on the pedestal. He has a *stūpa* on the crest and has on his two sides decorative herbal plants. The identification of this image, in the absence of any given *sādhana*, has been possible on the basis of manuscript paintings of two Nepalese *Aṣṭasāhasrikā Prajñāpāramitā*, one in the Cambridge University Library[68] and the other in the Asiatic Society.[69]

Mañjuśrī is mentioned in the *Āryamañjuśrīmūlakalpa*, the *Guhyasamāja*, the *Sukhāvativyūha* and other Buddhist texts. The *Gaṇḍavyūha* records that he came out of Pratiṣṭhānakūṭanagara and made a journey to Dakṣiṇāpatha and that he participated in the assembly of five thousand Bodhisattvas. According to the Nepalese tradition, as preserved in the *Svayambhū Purāṇa*, he was originally a human being who performed many pious deeds and was subsequently deified as a Bodhisattva. The *Mañjuśrīmūlakalpa* contains the earliest iconological description of Mañjuśrī.[70] Forty-one *sādhanas* are attributed to him in the *Sādhanamālā*. He is three-faced and six-armed. In his three right hands he exhibits a sword, *varada-mudrā*, and an arrow and in three left hands he has the Prajñāpāramitā manuscript, a blue lotus and a bow.[71] In sculptural representations he is generally one-faced and carries a sword in his right hand for destroying ignorance, and a manuscript in his left hand for transcendental wisdom. These symbols are often placed on lotuses. A very interesting gold-plated bronze figure of Mañjuśrī, belonging to the sixth century was found in the Balaidhap mound near Mahasthan. It is now in the Rajshahi Museum. In *dvibhaṅga* pose, the figure is fully in the round. The image of Akṣobhya is on the *jaṭāmukuṭa*. The right forearm is broken and the left is shown in *vyākhyāna mudrā*. The upper part of the body is covered by a scarf, worn in *upavīti* fashion, the lower half in a *dhoti* (?). The *ūrṇā*, the distended ear lobes, the *trivalī* marks on the front-neck, etc., are all present in this figure.[72] Other interesting bronze images come from Sirpur in Madhya Pradesh, Nalanda and other sites. Stone images of Mañjuśrī have been found in Lumbini, Sanchi, Sirpur, Amaravati, Salihundam, Ratnagiri and other places. The one in the Sanchi Museum is seated on a lotus in *lalitāsana*. Its right hand is in *varada* and the left holds a lotus by its long stalk. There is a peacock on the pedestal. The Rajshahi Museum contains a standing image (legs broken). Its two hands are in *dharmacakrapravartana-mudrā* with a stalk of lotus passing between the left forearm and the upper arm. Mañjuśrī also occurs in the cave reliefs of Ellora and other sites.

Vajrarāga Mañjuśrī, also known as Vāk or Amitābha Mañjuśrī is characterised by one face and two arms in *samādhi mudrā*. He is affiliated with Amitābha whose image he bears on his tongue.[73] He is described as the lord of speech. A stone image of Vajrarāga occurs on the recess of a wall in a temple in front of Monastery 2 at Ratnagiri.

The National Museum has a tenth-century stone stone image of Vajrarāga or Vāk from Nalanda, seated in *vajraparyaṅka* with two hands in *samādhi-mudrā*, *jaṭāmukuṭa* with curls gathered by a band, and an oval aureole edged with flames. A metal image of the god is in the Baroda Museum.[74] The Indian Museum contains a bronze image in *vajrāsana* and *samādhi mudrā* (the upper left hand is broken). With the effigy of Amitābha on the crown, he is decked in ornaments on hands and breasts.

The Siddhaikavīra form of Mañjuśrī is very common. According to one of his descriptions, he bears the image of Akṣobhya on the crown. He is two-armed, one-faced and of white colour. He sits in *vajraparyaṅka* with a lotus in his left hand and *varada-mudrā* in the right.[75] He is accompanied by four subsidiary deities—Jāliniprabha, Candraprabha, Keśinī and Upakeśinī. If represented without companions and without the figure of the paternal Dhyānī Buddha on their crown, a confusion is likely to arise between the forms of Lokanātha and Siddhaikavīra, because both of them have the same symbol (lotus) and the same *mudrā* (*varada*). It is only by the ornaments and the treatment of hair that the two forms may be distinguished.[76] It is said that Mañjuśrī should be decked in ornaments befitting a Kumāra, a boy or youth, wearing particularly a necklace of tiger-claws with a circular medallion.[77] The National Museum has two stone images of standing Siddhaikavīra, belonging to the seventh century from Sarnath and Nalanda. The Sarnath image has Akṣobhya on the crest and Keśinī and Upakeśinī on its sides. The Nalanda image has to its right the figure of Yamāntaka.[78] The Indian Museum has three stone images, two from Nalanda and one from Bihar Sharif, belonging to c. ninth-tenth century, all two-handed. The Bihar image has *abhaya* in place of the usual *varada* pose. The Nalanda Museum itself contains two standing stone images, the ornaments and hair style of which justify their identification with Siddhaikavīra. The Asutosh Museum has an eleventh-century stone image from Bhangor, 24 Parganas. It is two-handed, the right hand in *varada* and the left holding a manuscript on a lotus. On the stele on the top there are five Dhyānī Buddhas with Akṣobhya in the middle and two companions on the two sides. Siddhaikavīra images are very common in metal, and they are found mostly from Nalanda. Of the metal images two, belonging to the Indian Museum, deserve special mention. One of them is seated in *padmāsana* with the left leg tied to the waist by a band. The right hand holds an indistinct flower-like object and the left a manuscript on a lotus. The other is a standing image in a somewhat *bhaṅga* pose on a double petalled lotus within a decorated *prabhāmaṇḍala* with the right hand displaying the *varada* pose and the left holding the stem of a lotus. The Nalanda Museum has three bronze images, seated respectively in *ardhaparyaṅka*, *lalita* and *sukhāsana*. Their hands show lotus and *varada*, excepting the one in *sukhāsana* whose right hand is in *vitarka mudrā* and the left on the knee holds a lotus stalk. All of them have ornaments befitting a Kumāra. A bronze image in an unconventional attitude from Nalanda is now in the National Museum. It is seated cross-legged on lotus, right hand resting on the raised right knee and the left holding a lotus. The Kurkihar hoard contains two bronze images. One of them belongs to the ninth century. Its right leg is pendant, the right hand in *varada* on the right knee, the left hand resting on the lotus pedestal with a stalk of *nīlotpala*. The other belonging to the eleventh century stands on a lotus, the left hand raised with *nīlotpala*, the right hand pendant with *varada*.[79]

The Arapacana form of Mañjuśrī is not uncommon.[80] A few of his images have been found even in Indonesia (cf. the Javanese Arapacana of the Leiden Museum). The god is described as being white or red in colour, seated in *vajrāsana* with four companies, his symbol being a book and a sword.[81] An image of this god, which is found at Jalakundi in Dacca, represents him as seated in *vajraparyaṅka* pose on a double-petalled lotus supported by the Nāgas. He is two-handed, the right forearm carrying the sword is missing, and the left hand holding a manuscript is placed against his breast. Four miniature replicas of him known as Jalīnī, Upakeśinī , Candraprabha and Sūryaprabha are shown, one on the top centre and the other three below and on the two sides of the seat. There are four miniature figures of Vairocana, Akṣobhya, Amitābha and Ratnasambhava on the top section of the *prabhāvali*. The figure belongs to the twelfth century.[82] Khiching in the Mayurbhanj district of Orissa has yielded a few stone images of Arapacana.[83] Arapacana is frequently represented in Nepalese bronzes in which the manuscript is placed on the stem of a lotus. The National Museum contains a bronze image of Arapacana. It is seated in *vajraparyaṅka* on the lotus seat over a high pedestal. The right hand is upraised brandishing a sword and the left is clinging to breast with a manuscript. This image, which has a jewelled crown, belongs to c. tenth century. The Banpur hoard of Orissa contains at least two bronze images of Arapacana. The Indian Museum bronze image of Arapacana is in *vajrāsana* on a lotus pedestal, carrying in his right hand a sword and in the left a manuscript, both the hands being held against the chest. The image is without any attending deity.[84]

Sthiracakra is another rare from of Mañjuśrī. In iconographical texts he is described as of white colour, the right hand in *varadamudrā* and the left holding a sword, seated with his own Śakti. Often he is viewed as having a sword and a manuscript in his two hands.[85] The Vaṅgīya Sāhitya Pariṣat (Calcutta) sculptutre of Mañjuśrī, seated in *ardhaparyaṅka* on a double-petalled lotus, probably depicts this variety. The special feature of this image is that the sword appears on a lotus, the stem of which is held in the left hand of the god, while the right hand exhibits the *varada* pose. He is accompanied by his Śakti on his left side.[86] The National Museum has a tenth-century bronze image of Sthiracakra from Nalanda. It is seated on a lotus over a high pedestal in *lalitāsana.* The right hand contains an upraised sword. The left is on the knee holding an *utpala* (lotus) by its stalk. The right knee is clasped to waist by a scarf. There is an elaborate aureole topped by a parasol with streamers.[87] The Indian Museum has a bronze image of the god seated in *ardhaparyaṅka* on a double petalled lotus. The right hand is in *abhaya* posture while the left hand resting on the left knee holds a lotus stem which contains a sword. Another stem stretches out from the back of his right shoulder. Around the image is a *prabhāmaṇḍala*, the top of which contains the paternal deity, probably Amitābha.[88]

The Vāgīśvara form of Mañjuśrī is more than one. His head contains the image of five Dhyānī Buddhas. He is decked in all ornaments and looks like a prince. His vehicle is the lion. He holds a *nīlotpala* in his left hand while the right is displayed artistically. Another form of Vāgīśvara is Dharmadhātu who is four-faced and eight-handed.[89] The Indian Museum stone image of Vāgīśvara from Nalanda belonging to the tenth century carries a bell in his right hand and sits on a lion-throne instead of a lion. The left hand carries a stalk of lotus. The image of Vairocana is on the *jaṭāmukuṭa* and a *stūpa* replica on the stele to the right of the head.[90] The bronze Vāgīśvara of the Kurkihar hoard is seated on a lion with Prajñāpāramitā manuscript on a blue lotus in the left hand. A bunch of hair forms chignon on apex. The yellow variety of Vāgīśvara which is known as the Mahārājalīlā Mañjuśrī is nicely represented on a bronze image belonging to the Kurkihar hoard. It is seated in *ardhaparyaṅka* on a lotus pedestal. The left hand is on the lotus seat holding a stalk of blue lotus on which the Prajñāpāramitā manuscript is laid. The right hand is pendant on the raised right knee. The image belongs to c. twelfth century.[91]

Mañjuvara is another form of Mañjuśrī. He is of golden yellow colour showing the images of five Dhyānī Buddhas on the crest. His hands display the *dharmacakra-mudrā* and a blue lotus bearing the

Prajñāpāramitā manuscript.[92] A beautiful stone image of the two-handed Mañjuvara, found at Talanda in Rajshahi, and now in the Rajshahi Museum, is shown seated in *lalitāsana* on the back of a lion. The hands are shown in *dharmacakra-mudrā* against the breast, and a book is placed on a full blossomed lotus which is held by the stalk in its left arm. It belongs to the eleventh or twelfth century.[93] The Rajshahi Museum has three Mañjuvara images in stone, more or less similar to the one mentioned above, but they have in addition companion deities. A Mañjuvara image has been found from Mainamati, five miles to the west of Comilla in Bangladesh.[94] From Nalanda five stone images of Mañjuvara have been recovered, four of which are in the Nalanda Museum and the remaining one in the Indian Museum.[95] An image of this god discovered from the Birbhum district, West Bengal, also follows the aforesaid description. It contains miniature figures of five Dhyānī Buddhas on the head and two divinities to the right and the left. One of the two Indian Museum images of Mañjuvara has on its either side two female figures, Keśinī and Upakeśinī.[96]

Four *sādhanas* in the *Sādhanamālā* describe the Mañjughoṣa variety of Mañjuśrī. In his general form this god is golden yellow in colour. His vehicle is lion, he exhibits the *mudrā vyākhyāna* and the symbol lotus in the left.[97] Two stone sculptures, one from Magadha now in the Indian Museum, and the other from Nalanda now in the Nalanda Museum, represent Mañjughoṣa. In the former the god is seen to be seated in *lalitāsana* on a lion throne with two hands in *vyākhyāna-mudrā* with a stalk of blue lotus passing between the left forearm and the upper arm. The lower portion of the other image is lost, but the upper portion corresponds to the description given above. A tenth century stone image of Mañjukumāra has been found from Nalanda which is now in the Indian Museum. It is seated in *satvaparyaṅka* (an attitude in which the legs are gathered up on the seat, but not locked) on lotus supported by lions. It has three faces and six hands. The two right hands have a sword and an arrow while the third is in *varada* pose and the left have a manuscript, a water-lily and a bow. Akṣobhya is on the matted crest and Vairocana on the top of stele. The aureole is edged by flames.[98]

In the Kurkihar hoard we come across five bronze images of Mañjuśrī Kumārabhūta as pot-bellied, wearing sacred thread round earrings with jewels and *jaṭāmukuṭa*. They are seated on a single or double throne in *mahārājalīlā* pose with left leg pendant and supported on a lotus. The left hand is raised in front of the chest and holds the book. The right hand rests on the right knee in *varada-mudrā* and holds *akṣamālā* in one case, and in all other cases a more or less rounded object resembling a fruit. Attendant deities are also present.[99] The association of Mañjuśrī with Kumāra-Kārtikeya of the Puranic tradition is significant. Frequently he is described as Kumāra, Kumārākara, Kumārabhūta, etc. Peacock, the vehicle of Kārtikeya, has also been described as his mount.

Among other Bodhisattvas Vajrapāṇi is widely represented in sculpture. Very often he is represented as a companion divinity of the Buddha along with Padmapāṇi. In cave reliefs of Kondivte, Nasik, Ajanta, Aurangabad, Ellora, etc., the Buddha is attended by Padmapāṇi and Vajrapāṇi. A beautiful stone image of Vajrapāṇi can be found on the side wall of the front porch of the temple in Monastery I complex of Ratnagiri. In images he is shown carrying a lotus on which is placed the *vajra*. Sometimes he holds a *vajra* in one of his hands against the chest. He is enumerated as one of the eight principal Bodhisattvas, who is of white colour, carrying the *vajra* in one hand and displaying the *abhaya-mudrā* on the other. He is the Bodhisattva of the Dhyānī Buddha Akṣobhya.[100] A ninth century bronze image of Vajrapāṇi has been discovered from Ratnagiri in Orissa. Another bronze image is found from Sirpur in Madhya Pradesh. Amravati has yielded a nice specimen in stone. An interesting sculpture from Nalanda shows Vajrapāṇi as surrounded by four seated female figures. His left hand is placed on the left thigh, while he holds a *vajra* in his right hand against the breast. Each of the two seated female figures at the upper two ends of the slab is seen holding a garland. The figure at the right lower end of the slab has her hands placed against the hip, while the one at the left is seen in a playful mood.[101] A few seated bronze images from Nalanda represent him as seated cross-legged on a double lotus pedestal, his left hand resting on the left knee holds a *vajra* while his right hand has a *cāmara* or fly-whisk. He wears a crown, earrings, a necklace and bracelets.[102] In Kurkihar hoard, there is a bronze image of Vajrapāṇi, belonging to the ninth century A.D. Its left hand is pendant and holds a stalk of *nīlotpala* issuing from root-scroll. On the lotus is placed *vajra*. The right hand is in *abhaya-mudrā*.[103] Minor Bodhisattvas are rarely represented in sculpture. The Patna Museum contains a bronze image of Bodhisattva Gaganagañja recovered from Nalanda which belongs to the ninth century. It is in *lalitāsana* on a *triratha* pedestal. The right hand is in *varada-mudrā* with a jewel on it. In the left is the root of a Kalpavṛkṣa. The halo is broken. The Museum also contains a bronze image of Trailokyavaśaṅkara seated in *vajraparyaṅka* with upraised hands holding an indistinct object. It belongs to c. tenth century.[104]

Among other gods, Hayagrīva has several forms, in one of which the effigy of Amitābha is borne on his crown. He is thus regarded as the spiritual son of Amitābha and commonly known as Saptaśatika Hayagrīva.[105] He is of red complexion, three-eyed and brown-bearded. He is angry-looking, with a protruding belly and wears a garland of skulls and ornaments of eight serpents. Clad in a tiger skin, he holds a thunderbolt and a staff in his two hands.[106] As an attendant deity Hayagrīva is very often represented along with the Bodhisattvas in sculpture. Another form of this god emanates from Akṣobhya whose effigy he bears on the crown. He is of red colour, with eight arms and three faces with three eyes in each face. He is clad in a tiger-skin and shows in his four hands a thunderbolt, a staff, *karaṇa* pose (outstretched hand with index and little fingers erect, while the thumb presses the two remaining fingers against the palm of the hand), and a raised arrow. Of his four left hands one has the raised index finger, the second touches the breast and the two remaining ones hold the lotus and the bow.[107] Hayagrīva, according to the Purāṇas, was a demon. Viṣṇu assumed the horse-headed form to kill him. Viṣṇu is also called Hayagrīva. The special cognizance of Saptaśatika Hayagrīva is the scalp of a horse over his head. A bronze image of Hayagrīva, gold plated with verdigris in places, is found in the Kurkihar hoard.[108] It is of the Saptaśatika type mentioned above.

Heruka is one of the most popular deities of the Buddhist pantheon whose worship is described in the *Herukatantra.* He stands on a corpse in the *ardhaparyaṅka* attitude, is clad human skin with *vajra* in his right hand and a *kapāla*, full of blood, in the left. From his left shoulder hangs a *khatvāṅga* with a flowing banner. Decked in ornaments of bones, his head is decorated with five skulls. He bears the effigy of Akṣobhya whose emanation he is.[109] Nairātmā is the Śakti or female consort of Heruka. When in embrace with this Śakti, Heruka is known as Hevajra. A stone image of Heruka has been discovered from Amaravati. Two-armed varieties of Heruka found in Eastern India are characterised by the dancing pose on a corpse below, with emblems like *vajra* and *kapāla* in hands, a *khatvāṅga* along the left side of the body, garlands of skulls, etc. The Sarnath Museum contains a stone image of Heruka, found at the same place, dancing in *ardhaparyaṅka* on a human corpse. The raised right hand, though damaged, holds a *vajra*. The left forearm, containing a *kapāla* is missing, the portion having *khatvāṅga* may, however, be seen. He has a grinning face and a garland of human heads. The Nalanda Museum contains a tenth century stone image of Heruka, much mutilated, with hands and legs gone.[110] A unique specimen of this deity in black chlorite, hailing from Badkamta in Tippera and belonging to the eleventh century is now in the Dacca Museum which agrees in all details with the description given above.[111] A stone image of Heruka has been found in Ratnagiri. The Banpur hoard contains one bronze image in *ardhaparyaṅka* on a corpse, with a skull cup in the left hand and a garland of skulls showing a fierce attitude. It contains a *khatvāṅga* on the left shoulder with flowing banners and a miniature Akṣobhya on his head.[112] A sixteen-armed Heruka in union with his Śakti is now in the Nahar family collection of Calcutta. The Indian Museum has a unique image of Heruka in bronze.[113] The Hevajra form of Heruka in *yuganaddha* is popular in Tibet.[114] Hevajra is also blue, one- or three- or eight- faced, two- or six- or sixteen-armed.[115] The name of his Śakti differs according to the number of his heads. Their names are Nairatmā, Vajravārāhī and Vajraśṛṃkhālā. Images of Hevajra are comparatively rare. The Paharpur image of Hevajra has eight heads, and sixteen arms which hold skull cups. Each of the eight hands has third eye on the forehead. The image is represented in *yuganaddha* with his *śakti*. Miniature dancing figures are carved round the main pair and beneath them are a number of corpses.[116] A similar image, without the Śakti, has been found in the Dharmanagar subdivision of Tripura.[117]

Nairātmā, the Śakti of Heruka-Hevajra when represented singly, is two-handed, conceived as dancing in *ardhaparyaṅka* on a corpse, the right hand holding *kartari* and the left a *kapāla* with *khatvāṅga*.[118] A stone image Nairātmā from Nalanda, belonging to the tenth century is now in the Indian Museum. The image is one-faced and two-armed, the right hand containing *kartari* and the missing left apparently had a *kapāla*. It is represented as dancing in *ardhaparyaṅka* on a corpse, and wearing a garland of skulls, having a fierce mien with a third eye, upraised hair and Akṣobhya on crest.[119] The Vaṅgīya Sāhitya Parisad bronze image also shows the above characteristics, but the *khatvāṅga* is lost.[120] Vajrayoginī, another Śakti of Heruka-Hevajra, is of yellow or red colour, standing in *ālīḍha*, carrying her own severed head in her upraised left hand and *kartari* in her right hand. One should not fail to recall here the Śākta-Tantric conception of Chinnamastā. Vajrayoginī has a number of varieties. In one variety she is said to be standing in *pratyālīḍha* on a corpse and to have two hands. She has a terrific mien with frowning round eyes, three in number, bare fangs and protruding tongue and red hair rising up like flames. In another description she is said to have a *vajra* in the right hand and *karota* (skull cup) and *khatvāṅga* in the left. In another, she is said to have a *kartari* in the right hand and a *kapāla,* filled with blood of Devas and Asuras, in the left.[121] A supposed eleventh century stone image of Vajrayogīnī is now in the Patna Museum which is standing in *ālīḍha* on a corpse placed over a lotus pedestal. The right hand contains a *kartari*, and the left a *kapāla* with *khatvāṅga* between forearm and the upper arm. Having a fierce mien with three eyes, the image is represented against the background of flames with the Dhyānī Buddha Vairocana on the top section of the pointed stele.[122]

Sambara is not very much different from Hevajra, since he is also Heruka in *yuganaddha* i.e. in union with his Śakti Vajravārāhī.[123] Representations of this deity are well-known in Nepal and Tibet, but they are extremely rare in India. An image of this deity, belonging to the ninth century, made of stone, from Nalanda is in the Indian Museum. It has three heads and twelve arms of which two are crossed on the heart, holding a thunderbolt and a bell in the attitude known as *vajrahuṅkāra*. The god is standing in *ālīḍha* posture. His heads bear matted hair, the front one having three eyes. In the hands we can recognise a long magic wand with skulls at the upper end known as *khatvāṅga*, a skull cup, the severed head of Brahmā etc. Above his head appears a four-armed female standing in the same pose as the god, and his figure is repeated thrice below, between the legs of the central figure and at the sides. The attributes are not very much clear, but there is no doubt that she is Vajravārāhī.[124] A stone image of Sambara from Ratnagiri, now in the Patna Museum, has three heads. The principal hands are in *vajrahuṅkāra mudrā*, the right hand holding a *vajra* and the left a *ghaṇṭā*. The uppermost hands hold the hide of an elephant. The remaining right hands carry a *ḍamaru*, a *triśūla*, a *kartari* and a *paraśu* while the left ones have *vajrapāśa*, the head of Brahmā, a *kapāla* and a *khatvāṅga*. Bhairava and Kālarātri are under the feet.[125]

Yamāntaka, also known as Yamāri, regarded as a god of the eastern direction, has two forms, Rakta and Kṛṣṇa. The Tibetan tradition explains the origin of this fierce god, 'most complicated and terrible of the northern Buddhist divinities'.[126] An emanation of Akṣobhya, Raktayāmāri is depicted as one-faced, two-armed, standing in *pratyālīḍha* with a *kapāla* full of blood in the left hand and a staff in the right, decked in ornaments of snakes, clad in a tiger skin and embraced by his Śakti.[127] Kṛṣṇayamāri has three varieties : (1) one-faced, two-armed, a staff marked by *vajra* in the right hand; raised index finger with noose against the chest in the left; (2) three-faced, four-armed, *mudgara* and sword in the right hands, lotus and jewel in the left, in union with Śakti; (3) three- or six-faced, six-armed; *vajra*, sword and *muṣala* in right hands; *vettali* (goblin?), axe and lasso in the left hands; according to a different version, sword, *mudgara* and *vajra* in the right hands; *ghaṇṭā, muṣala* and *vajrapāśa* in the left hands.[128] A tenth century stone image of Yamāri from Nalanda, now in the Nalanda Museum, shows the god as standing in *pratyālīdha* on a buffalo. The god has six heads and six hands, right hands holding a sword, a *vajra* and *mudgara* and the left ones a *pāśa*, a *ghaṇṭā* and a *kapāla*. Dwarfish and pot-bellied with three round rolling eyes in the main face which is bearded and whiskered and hair rising up in curls, the image bears Akṣobhya on the crest, a garland of human heads, snake ornaments and a canopy of snake overhead.[129] An interesting sculpture in the collection of the Rajshahi Museum, hailing from Vikrampur, represents Kṛṣṇayamāri.[130] A form of this god has also been traced in a bronze image from Ratnagiri.[131]

Corresponding to the Hindu Kubera, Jambhala is regarded as an emanation of Akṣobhya as well as of Ratnasambhava. He is regarded as the god of wealth. Usually he has one face and two hands, the right hand holding a citron, and the left a mongoose vomiting jewels. Also he is described as three-faced, six-armed, carrying in right hands a citron, a goad and an arrow and embracing his Śakti, i.e., Vasudhārā, with the first hand, the others carrying a mongoose and an arrow. He has a protruding belly. Eight petals of his lotus seat are occupied by eight Yakṣas. In some representations he tramples upon two semi-divine beings, Saṅkhamuṇḍa and Padmamuṇḍa. In *Yab-Yum* Jambhala has another form with three faces and six eyes and embracing Vasudhārā with two principal hands, while others contain a *vajra*, a sword, an emerald and a lotus. A variety of Jambhala is known as Ucchuṣma Jambhala and another is known as Vaśya Jambhala.[132] Images of Jambhala are found in Gandhara, Mathura, Sarnath, Magadha, Orissa, Tamilnadu, Bengal and Nepal. The Jambhala figures found in Bengal are depicted as pressing the neck of a mongoose vomiting jewels with his left hand. We may refer to two typically representative specimens of Jambhala, now in the Rajshahi Museum, originally found at Dhurail in Rajshahi district, Bangladesh.[133] The image of Jambhala is common in Orissa where we come across his pot-bellied form in Ratnagiri, Ayodhya and the Prachi Valley.[134] A Jambhala image has been found in Mayurbhanj which is now in the Khiching Museum. A bronze image of Jambhala has been found in a hoard near the Puduveli-gopuram at Nagapattinam in Tamilnadu.[135] A number of stone and bronze images have been discovered from Nalanda. Two stone images from Nalanda, now in the National Museum, belonging to the ninth century, show Jambhala in *maṇḍala*, that is, in the company of other male and female deities.[136]

The National Museum also contains a tenth century image from Nalanda standing with two feet on two overturned pots. An eleventh century bronze image from Nalanda, now in the Nalanda Museum, represents the god along with his consort Vasudhārā, both seated in *lalitāsana*. Metal images of Jambhala from Nalanda, sitting with feet resting on lotus or on *kalasa*, holding a citron in the right hand and a mongoose in the left are very common, and the same also holds good in the case of stone images.[137] The Indian Museum has also a few Nalanda metals showing the pot-bellied god with a citron and a mongoose. The Patna Museum also contains two bronze images from Nalanda and one from the Kurkihar hoard.[138] A bronze image of Jambhala is found in the Banpur hoard which has a flabby appearance with a bulging belly. It is well-decorated with jewellery and ornaments. The right hand is in *varada* pose and the left has a mongoose.[139]

Vasudhārā is the consort of Jambhala and bears the image of either Akṣobhya or Ratnasambhava on her crown. Originally she was an earth goddess of the simpler people. Her Brahmanical counterpart is Śrī-Lakṣmī. Conceptually she was also connected with Hārītī, the protectress of children, who was also a popular goddess that subsequently came into the folds of Buddhism. Vasudhārā is yellow in colour. Her symbol is the ears of corn which she holds in her left hand. Her right hand is in *varada mudrā*. She is sometimes represented as one-faced and six-armed, and as sitting in *lalita* attitude. In the three hands she exhibits *namaskāra* and *varadamudrā* and ears of corn. In the three left hands she has a book, ears of corn and a vessel containing jewels.[140] Vasudhārā images are fairly common and they may easily be identified because of the corn symbol. A tenth century Nalanda stone image, now in the Nalanda Museum, does not, however, show the ears of corn. Instead, it has in the left hand a vase with sprouts of foliage indicating plenty, the emblem of the goddess. Similar seated sculptures of the goddess have also been found at Nalanda.[141] The Lucknow Museum contains a fourteenth century metal image from Nepal, elaborately jewelled and containing a sheaf of corn, a manuscript and an auspicious jar. A similar one from eastern India dated year 36 of the reign of Rāmapāla, is now in the Victoria and Albert Museum, London.[142] The Indian Museum contains several metal images of Vasudhārā all seated in *lalitāsana* with the right hand in *varada mudrā* and the left either holding the sheaves of corns or resting on the pedestal in which case the bunch of corn sheaves is upraised from the pedestal almost parallel to the left hand. A nice bronze specimen has been recovered from Nagapattinam. In Orissa Ratnagiri and Mayurbhanj districts have yielded Vasudhārā images.[143] The Patna Museum contains a Nalanda bronze of Vasudhārā and also four bronzes from Kurkihar. One of the Kurkihar images is four-headed. The upper right has no object; the lower right is in *varada* attitude; the upper left contains a *kamaṇḍalu* and the lower left a lotus. The ears of corn are absent.[144]

Four-faced and eight-armed Trailokyavijaya is an emanation of Akṣobhya. The front-face is fierce-looking and wrathful, the right imprinted with anger and the left with disgust, whereas the face behind exhibits heroic disposition. He makes the *vajrahuṅkāra mudrā* with two hands holding *ghaṇṭā* and *vajra* against the chest; three right hands carry *khatvāṅga*, a goad and an arrow and three left hands have a bow, a noose and *vajra*. Standing in *pratyālīḍha* pose he tramples upon the head of Maheśvara with his left leg while the right leg rests upon the bosom of Gaurī.[145] A few Trailokyavijaya images have been found at Nalanda. One of them, in stone, is four-armed and is seen trampling on a prostate figure of Śiva who holds his usual symbols. The two frontal hands of the deity are held against the breast. The upper right hand holds a *vajra* while the upper left one some indistinct object.[146] The National Museum contains an eleventh century stone image of this god standing in *pratyālīḍha* on prostrate figures of Śiva and Pārvati.[147] In the Nalanda collection of the Patna Museum we have a bronze image of a four-faced Trailokyavijaya in *pratyālīḍha* trampling upon the head of Śiva with his left leg and the body of Gaurī with his right, wearing a garland of severed heads, a *kīrtimukuṭa* and four Akṣobhyas placed on the four side, holding a *vajra* and *ghaṇṭā* against the chest in his two main hands and a half broken noose in the middle and a broken *vajra* in the lower left hands. The remaining three hands and the upper hands are broken. This image belongs to the seventh century.[148] The Trailokyavijaya bronze image of the Banpur collection is the biggest and the most interesting of all bronze images. Here the trampled Śiva image under the left foot is eight-handed, one-faced and three-eyed, garlanded with skulls of human heads and decked with the head of a serpent and the crescent of the moon. Gaurī with four arms lies flat with her face upwards. The round halo at the back of the image with clear signs of flames make the image more fearful. The main figure is in *pratyālīḍha* attitude, with two hands clasped against the chest in *vajrahuṅkāra*. He has a crown on the head, *kuṇḍala* in looped ears, broad necklace, armlets, bracelets, a waist-band, a girdle, a will-fitted embroidered garment for the lower limbs, etc. The crown on the head is decked with five Dhyānī Buddha figures, of which only four are visible. The image belongs to c. eleventh century.[149] A similar deity is Bhūtaḍāmara who is very rarely represented in Indian art though four *sādhanas* are attributed to him in the *Sādhanamālā*. The Indian Museum has a tenth century stone image of this god from Nalanda. It is standing in *pratyālīḍha* on the prostrate figure of Śiva. It is four-handed, the principal pair is joined near the breast showing the *bhūtaḍāmara mudrā* (characterised by finger combinations). The other right hand holds an upraised *vajra* and the left a *pāśa*.

A form of Tārā, Kurukullā is a goddess emanating from the Dhyānī Buddha Amitābha. She is one-faced, but may have two, four, six or eight arms. She has several varieties. Śukla or white Kurukulllā is two-armed with symbols of rosary and a bowl of lotus. She sits on an animal in *vajraparyaṅka*. Tārodbhava Kurukullā is four-armed, the left hands showing *abhaya mudrā* and an arrow and right hands a bow and a red lotus. Uḍḍiyāna Kurukullā is red in colour and sits in *ardhaparyaṅka* on a corpse. She is four-armed; the first pair is in the attitude of discharging an arrow from the bow while the second pair holds a goad of flowers and a red lotus. The goddess has five skulls on the head, protruding teeth and tongue, garments of tiger skin and brown hair rising above her head in the shape of a flame. There are other varieties also like Aṣṭabhūjā of Māyājālakrama.[150] The Banpur hoard contains two bronze images of Kurukullā. One is in sitting posture, six-armed, three-faced, three-eyed, blooming with youth. The lower right hand is in *abhaya mudrā*, the middle one holds a *vajra* and the upper an arrow, whereas the left hands hold from lower to upper a stalk of *utpala*, *pāśa*, and a bow respectively. She has on her crest the image of Amitābha. The second image stands for Uḍḍiyāna Kurukullā. It is fierce in form and has the garland of skulls stretching to the waist. It is four-handed; the left upper hand holds a bow, the lower a stalk of lotus, while the right upper hand holds an arrow of flowers and the lower a goad. She is in *ardhaparyaṅka* pose dancing on a corpse. The hair of her head rises above in the shape of a flame.[151]

An emanation of Amitābha, Bhṛkuṭi is one-faced, three-eyed, four-armed, yellow-coloured with a very youthful appearance. She shows the *varada-mudrā* and rosary in her two right hands and carries *tridaṇḍī* and *kamaṇḍalu* in the left hands. She bears an Amitābha image on the crown.[152] Bhṛkuṭi is also regarded as a form of Tārā and is often identified with Khadiravanī Tārā and Dhanada Tārā. Cave 10 of Ellora contains the image of Bhṛkuṭi along with the images of other Buddhist divinities. A four-armed image of Bhṛkuṭi has been obtained from Salihundam in Andhra Pradesh.[153] The Nalanda collection of the Patna Museum contains a bronze image of the four-armed, crowned and standing Bhṛkuṭi. She holds a rosary and some unknown objects in the two right hands and the branch of a tree and *kamaṇḍalu* in the two left hands. There are two unidentified animals on either side. In front of the pedestal are two *makaras*. A female devotee is sitting to the right in *añjali-mudrā*. It belongs to c. ninth century.[154]

The goddess of epidemic, Parṇaśabarī, who was evidently a tribal adaptation, as her name implies, is regarded as an emanation of Akṣobhya and/or of Amoghasiddhi. In one conception she is described as three-faced, the front one being of yellow complexion. In her six hands she holds a *vajra*, a *paraśu* and an arrow on the right ones and in the left noose, cluster of leaves and bow. Her *jaṭāmukuṭa* is decorated with flowers and an image of Akṣobhya. She stands in *pratyālīḍha* trampling under her feet the Vighnas (i.e. *Gaṇeśa*). In another conception she has a green complexion, three faces, three eyes and six hands. The attributes of the six hands are the same as above. Here she tramples under her feet various diseases and pestilences and bears the image of Amoghasiddhi on the crown.[155] The Indian Museum image of Parṇaśabarī with three faces and six arms trampling upon Gaṇeśa corresponds to the first type mentioned above.[156] Bhattasali discovered two stone images of Parṇaśabarī from Nayananda and Vajrayogīnī villages of Dacca district, both belonging to the tenth century, now in the Dacca Museum, which correspond to the second type where the prostrate figures under her feet are diseases and pestilences in human shape.[157] The Kurkihar hoard contains seven bronze images of Parṇaśabarī assignable to a period between tenth and twelfth centuries. The first one is seated on a single lotus throne in *mahārājalīlā* attitude with the right leg pendant resting on a small figure of Gaṇeśa. The upper right hand holds a *vajra*, the lower right in *varada*, the upper left holds *pāśa* and the lower left is pendant on left knee.[158] The second one is seated cross-legged with a slight *bhaṅga* pose of her body. It is four-armed, the upper right holding an arrow instead of *vajra*. The goddess wears a *karandamukuṭa*. The third one is seated in *vajraparyaṅka* in *tribhaṅga* on a single lotus. The remaining ones mostly follow the aforesaid types.[159]

Prajñāpāramitā is regarded as the personified form of the Mahāyāna treatise *Prajñāpāramitā* which is said to have been recovered by Nāgārjuna. She is usually recognised by *vyākhyāna-mudrā* and the manuscript of *Prajñāpāramitā* on a lotus. She is of three types—*sita* (white), *pīta* (yellow) and *kaṇaka* (golden). Having the image of Akṣobhya on the crown, she is one-faced, two-armed, generally represented in *vajraparyaṅka*, carrying a lotus in her right hand and the manuscript in the left. In another form, her two hands display the *vyākhyāna-mudrā*. On a lotus to her left rests the manuscript. In some cases there are two manuscripts on two lotuses rising from under her two armpits.[160] The Vajrayoginī copper plate of Syamala-varman, a section of the Varman dynasty of eastern Bengal, speaks of his gift to the temple of Prajñāpāramitā. One of the finest images of this goddess, originally from Java, is now in the Leiden Museum. It has only one lotus bearing the manuscript in her left, but the Indian Museum image has two lotuses on either side, each bearing a manuscript. The Maldah Museum contains a very fine stone image of this goddess, cross-legged and two-handed.[161] The Nalanda collection of the Patna Museum has four bronze images of Prajñāpāramitā, all four-handed and in *vajrasāna*. In the two upper right hands are a rosary and a stalk of lotus on which is placed the manuscript. The lower right hand is in *varada-mudrā* and the left holds a bowl.[162] Two inscribed bronze images of the same type are in the Kurkihar hoard.[163] The site museum of Nalanda has five bronze images corresponding to the forms mentioned above, i.e., two hands in *vyākhyāna-mudrā* and the manuscript on the lotus. The Indian Museum contains a bronze image from Nalanda belonging to c. tenth century which is represented as seated in *vajraparyaṅka* on a lotus seat with hands in *vyākhyāna-mudrā*. On either side of the image a lotus is shown passing between the forearm and upper arm, each supporting a manuscript. The image has a flamed aureole topped by a parasol.[164]

Chastiser of all wicked beings, Aparājitā is described as trampling upon Gaṇeśa. She has a single face, yellow complexion and two hands, the right hands shown as if giving a slap (*capeṭadāna*), and the left held near the breast with noose together with the gesture of a threat.[165] On the strength of this iconological description, a Nalanda fragment showing only the lower half of a full image was first identified with that of Aparājitā. This identification was confirmed when subsequently the Indian Museum image was discovered. Though mutilated, it represents the goddess in *pratyālīḍha* attitude.[166] The Nalanda Museum, apart from the first-mentioned one, has two stone images of Aparājitā, one in *capeṭadāna* and the other in *ālīḍha* attitude. The National Museum also contains one from Nalanda.[167] The Patna Museum contains two stone images, trampling over a prostate Gaṇeśa, one hailing from Banaras and the other from Pachar, Gaya. Both the images belong to the seventh-eighth century A.D.[168] Aparājitā images occur in relief in the smaller Stūpas which stud the precincts of the main Stūpa and also in the sculptural finds of Ratnagiri.[169] A three-faced, six-handed and white-complexioned goddess is described in the iconological texts as Sitātapatrā Aparājitā.[170] No representation of this form of Aparājitā has so far been known in Indian Buddhist art. The bronze image of an eight-handed goddess originally found in Tippera and now in the Dacca Museum has been tentatively identified by Bhattasali with Sitātapatrā Aparājitā.[171]

One of the most interesting iconographic types is the goddess Mārīcī, an emanation of the Dhyānī Buddha Vairocana. She is usually represented with three faces, the left one being that of a sow, eight hands holding *vajra*, an *aṅkuśa*, a *śara*, an *aśoka* leaf, a *sūci*, a *dhanu* and a *pāśa*, the other hand being in *tarjanī* pose, with the figure of Vairocana in her crest, and riding in *pratyālīḍha* pose on a chariot drawn by seven pigs, driven by the charioteer Rāhu. She is also generally accompanied by four other subsidiary goddesses, viz. Vartāli, Vadāli, Vārāhī and Varahamukhī.[172] She has as many as eight forms some of which are met with in the extant images. Images of Mārīcī were discovered form Sarnath, Sanchi, Salihundam and other Buddhist sites. An eight-armed stone image of Mārīcī from Khiching now in the Baripada Museum deserves special mention. Belonging to the eleventh century, this three-headed (one sow-like) image mostly corresponds to the iconological description given above.[173] An eighth century stone image from Ratnagiri, seated in *lalitāsana*, with the right hand in *varada* and the left holding *aśoka*-twigs flanked by Vidyādharas on either side indicates her Aśokakāntā form.[174] The Banpur hoard contains an image in bronze which is in *pratyālīḍha* pose, one faced and two armed, the left hand holding a flower bunch and the right a *vajra*. The eight-handed form, mentioned above is known as Sīta Mārīcī, corresponding images of the type having been found in Ujani and Panditsar, now in the Dacca Museum,[175] and one from Vikrampur, now in the Rajshahi Museum.[176] They are all in stone and belong to c. tenth century. Pīta Mārīcī is also eight handed having the same emblems and companions as those of Sīta Mārīcī. The difference is in regard to the complexion of the goddess; the former is white and the latter bright yellow, and in the prescription of a sow's face for each of the companion deities by which the Pīta variety is characterised. The Indian Museum contains two eleventh century stone images from Nalanda of this type. The Nalanda Museum and the Rajshahi Museum has one each, the latter procured from Narkelberia.[177] Another form of Mārīcī is Picuva with three faces and eight hands as above, but without the attendant deities.[178] This form is represented in three Nalanda stone images, two belonging to the National Museum and one to the Indian Museum. The latter also contains a bronze image of Picuvā. The Patna Museum contains two images, one from Bihar and the other from Sonepur, Orissa, both belonging to c. tenth century.

The former is on a round pedestal with seven pigs and the face of Rāhu in the centre. The latter is in a chariot drawn by seven boars, arms broken and faces damaged.[179] A tenth century stone image from Nalanda, now in the Indian Museum, shows the goddess as standing in *ālīḍha* on a chariot drawn by pigs (six shown on the pedestal with Rāhu in the middle), three-faced (right and left ones of sows) and six-handed, the right hands holding a *vajra*, a *śara* and a *śucī* and the left a *tarjanī* with *pāśa*, a bow, and probably an *aśoka*-leaf in the broken one. This has been identified with Mārīcī Ubhaya-Varāhananā.

Mahāmāyūrī is one of the *pañcarakṣā* deities (five protectresses) in the Buddhist pantheon. She is of green colour, has three faces and six hands and is affiliated to Amoghasiddhi.[180] Rock-cut images of this goddess are found in the Ellora caves.[181] The one in cave 8 stands in *samapādasthānaka* on a lotus, the right hand broken and the left holding a globular object. A peacock in outspread wings is on the right, and below it is an ascetic reading scripture. To the left is an attendant goddess with a flywhisk. In the upper are two hovering gaṇas on two sides of the head. The cave 7 figure is almost identical with the one mentioned above, though it is of a coarser workmanship.[182] One other goddess of the *pañcarakṣā* group known to have been represented in sculpture is Mahāpratisarā. She has two varieties—one of them is three-faced, ten-armed, and the other four-faced and eight-armed.[183] Two images, one in Dacca Sāhitya Parisat and the other in the Dacca Museum correspond in essential details to the iconological descriptions of this goddess.[184] A goddess of wisdom, besides Prajñāpāramitā, is Mahāsarasvatī who has white complexion, with the right hand in *varada mudrā* and the left holding a white lotus, a smiling countenance, and an ornamented maiden body.[185] A ninth century stone image of this deity has been recovered from Nalanda and is in the Nalanda Museum. The image is seated cross-legged on a lotus supported on a *ghaṭa*. The right hand is in *varada* while the left is broken. Hair is in neat chignon clasped by a pearl tiara with a crescent moon on the right side. The deity is attended by four companions each seated on a lotus bearing a manuscript in hand.[186] Uṣṇīṣavijayā is an emanation of Vairocana whose image she bears on her crown which is often in the form of a miniature *caitya*. She is white-complexioned, three-faced and eight-handed.[187] The Indian Museum contains an eleventh century stone image of this goddess from Nalanda. The goddess is seated in *vajraparyaṅka* on a lotus over a high pedestal. She has three faces each with three eyes. The four right hands show a *vajra* (missing) *varada* pose, *bāṇa* and Buddha on a lotus held by stalk while the left hands hold a *kumbha*, a *pāśa, abhaya* pose and *cāpa*. Dhyānī Buddha Vairocana is substituted by Akṣobhya on the stele above head. Three *stūpa* replicas are shown in the upper section of the stele, one is on top centre and two on two sides.[188]

The goddess Cundā is the embodiment of *Cundā Dhāriṇī*.[189] A four-handed form of this goddess is more frequently seen in sculptures and paintings, though forms with six, twelve, sixteen, eighteen and even twenty-six hands are also known. In her common four-handed form she is one-faced, bearing a pot in the main pair of the hands, the other pair holding a book on a lotus in the left hand and the right is in *varada* pose.[190] A two-armed variety of this goddess is in the Indian Museum. It is a bronze image representing her in *vajraparyaṅka*, the right hand resting on the knee in *varada* pose, and the left hand in *samādhi*, probably with a saucer. The manuscript is on a lotus issuing from her left side. Among the four-handed images of Cundā mention may be made of a tenth century stone image from Nalanda, now in the National Museum, showing the goddess seated on a lotus in *vajra-paryaṅka*, the main pair of hands placed on crossed soles of the feet holding a bowl. Of the remaining two hands the left holds a rosary and the right a lotus by the stalk. The Indian Museum and the Nalanda Museum have similar Cundā images in metal.[191] A six-handed metal image of Cundā from Chittagong area of about ninth century is now in a private collection at Calcutta. The goddess is seated in *vajraparyaṅka*. She has her main pair of hands joined in *samādhi-mudrā* and has rosary and *varada pose* (with jewel of palm) in two other right hands and the manuscript and a waterpot in the two left.[192] A tenth century twelve-armed bronze image of Cundā which comes from Nalanda is in the Indian Museum. It corresponds to a stone image from Orissa which is now in the Patna Museum, the difference being only in the posture of sitting.[193] A miniature painting of the sixteen-armed Cundā is found in a Cambridge manuscript of *Prajñāpāramitā*[194] which bears the label 'Paṭṭikere Cundā Varabhavane Cundā'. A metal image of the sixteen-armed Cundā is in the Baroda Museum; another image of the same type has been recovered from Bodhgaya.[195] An eighteen armed bronze image from Nalanda is now in the National Museum. Seated in *vajraparyaṅka* the principal hands are in *dharmacakra-mudrā*, the other right hands showing from top *vandana*, a *vajra*, a rosary, a pen, *abhaya*, a bell, a jewel and *varada* and the left hands a manuscript, an inkpot, an indistinct object, a *cakra*, a *patākā*, an indistinct object, a noose and a waterpot.[196] The Patna Museum contains one of the same type in *vajra-paryaṅka*. The two principal hands are in *dharmacakra-mudrā*. The remaining right hands show from the top *abhaya-mudrā,* a broken, indistinct object, a thunderbolt, a discus, a club, a dagger and a rosary. One of the left hands has a *kamaṇḍalu* and others are broken. It belongs to the seventh century.[197] Another sixteen-armed stone image from Niyamatpur, belonging to the tenth century, now in the Rajshahi Museum, also deserves mention. It is seated in *vajraparyaṅka* on a lotus upheld by a Nāga couple shown on a pedestal which has, besides, two pot-bellied female figures.[198]

Originally a primitive protectress of children, Hārītī was admitted in the Buddhist pantheon and her cult became very popular even among the Hinayanists. She and her consort Pañcika have been represented all through in Indian art, from the Gandhara sculptures onwards. According to the Buddhist legends she was the guardian deity of Magadha, who was in the habit of stealing and devouring children. But this ogrees was converted into the protectress deity of children under the Buddha's influence. She is also represented as holding a pomegranate which the Buddha gave her as food as a substitute for the human flesh.[199] The images of Hārītī are often associated with mango fruits. Excavations at Kosambi have yielded a temple of Hārītī. The Stūpa complex at Takht-i-Bahi contains an image of Hārītī and her consort. This holds good also in the case of cave 6 of Ajanta, cave 7 of Aurangabad and cave 2 of Ellora. There was a Hārītī temple complex at Nagarjunikonda. Hārītī images have been found also in Ratnagiri. The Banpur hoard contains five bronze images of Hārītī. Each of them are shown as seated on a lotus pedestal carrying a child on her lap. One composite relief of the twelfth century hailing from Deopara and now in the Rajshahi Museum shows Hārītī and her consort in *lalitāsana*, their right hands holding Vijapurakas and the left a seated child in each case. In the middle of the *pañcaratha* pedestal squat four children.[200] The Patna Museum contains a second century stone image from Silour, Saran, and a twelfth century bronze image from Kurkihar.[201] It also contains a squatting Hārītī-Pañcika combine on a rectangular slab discovered from Mathura. A sandstone relief from Bhita belonging to the Kuṣāṇa-Gupta period is also in the Patna Museum. It is in *pralambapāda-āsana* with legs wide apart and an infant on her left leg.[202]

Tārā is the most important goddess of the Buddhist pantheon. She appears to be a very ancient protectress deity (derived from the root *tār* which means 'to save' or 'to protect' who was adopted in both the Buddhist and non-Buddhist pantheons in the early centuries of the Christian era. Several goddesses, Indian and non-Indian, merged in Tārā in course of time. She was introduced in Buddhism as the Śakti of

Amoghasiddhi but became more famous as the consort of Avalokiteśvara. As the supreme female principle of Tantric Buddhism she was elevated to such a position that all other Buddhist goddesses came to be regarded as her manifestations. There were famous centres of the Tārā cult in different parts of India such as those of Vaisali (Tirabhuktau Vaiśāli Tārā), Potalaka, Belligave, etc. Rock-cut images of this goddess are found in the caves of Karle, Kanheri, Aurangabad and Ellora. Stone and metal images have been discovered from numerous sites such as Sarnath, Sravasti, Sirpur, Nagapattinam, Salihundam, Ratnagiri, Banpur, Nalanda, Kurkihar, Mayurbhanj, Paharpur, Mainamati and many other places. Cave 12 of Ellora represent a rock-cut Tārā-maṇḍala belonging to the seventh century. In two adjacent panels there appear two group of goddesses, three in each. Each of the goddesses is seated in *lalitāsana* on a lotus, this being upheld by a couple shown below. Each has a halo around the head. In the same cave there is another panel also showing a group of three goddesses similarly treated. Tārā in her early and simple form is endowed with two hands and is generally found seated in *vajraparyaṅka* (or *lalita* in some cases), the right hand exhibiting *varada* (rarely *abhaya*) and the left holding a stem of lotus. In course of time with the multiplication of her forms, the number of her hands increased, and variations appeared in respect of cognizances, sitting postures, etc. She was also attended by accessory figures, the number of which extended up to ten. Some of the well-known varieties of Tārā are described below.

The Śyāma Tārā or the Green Group consists of Ārya Tārā, Vaśya Tārā, Khadiravanī Tārā, Mahattarī Tārā, Varada Tārā, Durgottāriṇī Tārā and Dhanada Tara. Jāṅguli and Parṇaśabarī also belong to this group. Ārya Tārā is described as seated in *vajraparyaṅka* with *varada* in the right hand and *utpala* in the left, having the effigy of Amoghasiddhi on her crest. A slightly variant form is that of Vaśya Tārā in which the goddess is enjoined to be seated in *bhadrāsana*. When the goddess is accompanied by Aśokakāntā Mārīcī and Ekajaṭā we have another form known as Khadiravanī Tārā. Mahattarī Tārā may be distinguished by the *vajraparyaṅka* attitude in which she sits, and also by the fact of her being represented without any companion whatsoever. Varada Tārā sits in the *ardhaparyaṅka* attitude like Ārya Tārā but she can easily be recognised by the presence of four goddesses—Aśokakāntā Mārīcī, Mahāmāyūrī, Ekajaṭā and Jāṅguli. Durgottāriṇī Tārā has a green complexion, the lotus for her feet, and garments are of white colour. She has four hands and carries in the first pair of hands the noose and the goad and display in the second a lotus and the *varada mudrā*. Dhanada Tārā carries a book and a rosary in the first pair of hands, while the second pair carries objects similar to those held by Durgottāriṇī. She has an animal for her *vāhana*, is accompanied by eight goddesses originating from the eight syllables of her *mantra* and bears the image of Amoghasiddhi on the crown.[203]

The National Museum contains two bronze images of Ārya Tārā from Nalanda, belonging respectively to the seventh and tenth century A.D. Both the images are, however, standing. The Lucknow State Museum on the other hand has two bronze images from Nalanda belonging to the tenth-eleventh century which are seated in *ardhaparyaṅka* having *varada* pose and *utpala* in hands and Amoghasiddhi on the crest.[204] The Nalanda collection of the Patna Museum contains a few bronze images of Ārya Tārā, belonging to the eighth-ninth century.[205] The Kurkihar hoard of the same Museum also has a good number of two-handed images of Tārā. There are twenty standing bronze images, nine standing with a slight bend and eleven standing in *samapāda-sthānaka*.[206] Some of these goddesses are described simply as Śyāma Tārā.[207] There are stone images of this goddess as well in the Patna Museum. A rock-cut image of Khadiravanī Tārā is in cave 7 of Ellora. The Indian Museum has a stone image of this goddess from Nalanda which corresponds to her iconological description mentioned above. The Asutosh Museum of the Calcutta University contains one eleventh century image from Agradigun in the Dinajpur district.[208] The Patna Museum has a good number of Khadiravanī images in *lalitāsana*, showing *varada mudrā* and a lotus in two hands and accompanied by Ekajaṭā and Aśokakānta Mārīcī. Particular interest attaches to one inscribed stone image dated the 35th year of Devapāla.[209] Another stone image from Ratnagiri in Orissa shows Khadiravanī Tārā accompanied by the same two goddesses seated in *lalitāsana* on separate lotuses.[210] A metal image of Khadiravanī is also there. A four-handed stone image of Dhanada Tārā from Nalanda belonging to the tenth century is in the Indian Museum. The Nalanda Museum has one image of this goddess in metal which belongs to the tenth century. It is standing with slight flexion on a lotus, right hands holding a rosary and exhibiting *abhaya mudrā* and the left hand holding a lotus stalk and a manuscript. The Patna Museum contains a four-armed image in bronze from Nalanda. Its upper right hand is broken and the left holds a *kamaṇḍalu* from which emerges a *nāgakeśara* flower. The lower right is in *abhaya mudrā* and the left holds *nāgakeśara*. Its identification with any particular form is uncertain. The Banpur hoard has eleven Tārā images in bronze, all in *lalitāsana* carrying *utpala* in the left hand and exhibiting *varada* in the right.

Among the goddesses of the Sīta Tārā or white Group, the Aṣṭamahābhaya Tārā sits in *ardhaparyaṅka* attitude and is surrounded by ten goddesses originating from the ten syllables of the Tārā *mantra*. These ten deities are identical in appearance with the principal deity. Mṛtyuvañcana Tārā bears a wheel on her chest. She is absolutely unattended and sits in *vajraparyaṅka* attitude. Caturbhūja Sitatārā, an emanation of Amoghasiddhi, has four arms and exhibits in the first pair of hands the *utpalamudrā* and a lotus and the *varada* pose in the second. She may be recognised by the presence of two goddesses, Mahāmāyūrī and Mārīcī. Ṣadbhūja-Sitatārā bears the image of Amoghasiddhi on the crown. She is three-faced and six-armed. Among other Tārās of White Group mention should be made of Viśvamātā, Kurukullā and Jāṅguli. In the Red Tārā group there is only Kurukullā whose various forms we have already had the occasion to refer. The Blue Tārā group comprises Ekajaṭā and Mahācīnatārā. Ekajaṭā has several forms, and she bears the image of her sire Akṣobhya on her crown in all cases. The Yellow Tārā group comprises Vajratārā, Jāṅguli, Parṇaśabarī and Bhṛkuṭi. Vajratārā is yellow, has four faces and eight arms and bears the image of Ratnasambhava on her crown.[211]

Images of Aṣṭamahābhaya Tārā have been found in Ratnagiri, Nalanda and Somapara. They are all in stone belonging to the ninth-tenth century and are in the Patna, Nalanda and Dacca Museums respectively.[212] The one in the Patna Museum is standing in *tribhaṅga* on a lotus pedestal, with hands broken. Five Dhyānī Buddhas are on the top. On two sides are eight scenes, four on each side describing, perhaps, the dangers which the goddess in this form is said to remove.[213] The one in the Dacca Museum has eight miniature figures of goddess on the *prabhāvali*, four on each side, and the figure of Vajrasattva on the extreme right corner of the pedestal.[214] The Nalanda Museum contains a tenth century metal image of Mṛtyuvañcana Tārā, seated in *vajraparyaṅka* on a lotus over a pedestal. It has a long necklace with *cakra*-like clasp between the breasts. Another image of this deity in stone is in the Rajshahi Museum. In Indian art representations of Vajra Tārā are very rare. Reference may be made in this connection to an image of this goddess from Khiching.[215] There are two notable representations in metal, one form Patharghata, now in the Indian Museum, and another from Majvadi in Faridpur district, now in the Dacca Museum. The Patharghata image is seated on the pericarp of a lotus. Its eight petals can be opened and closed at will. There are eight goddesses, each against a petal, forming a *maṇḍala* round Vajra Tārā.[216] The one from Majvadi is much mutilated and only partly preserved. The figure is within an eight-petalled lotus, with the figures of eight attendants carved on the inside of the petals.[217] The National Museum contains an eleventh century four-headed stone image from Sarnath which is often identified with Vajra Tārā. One image of Mahāśrī Tārā hailing from somewhere in Bihar is in the Indian Museum. It is endowed with two hands in *vyākhyāna-mudrā* and has four attendant deities in accordance with the iconological description of the goddess.[218]

NOTES

1. See A. Cunningham, *The Stūpa of Bharhut* (London, 1887); B.M. Barua, *Bharhut*, 3 Vols.(Calcutta, 1934-37); M.C. Maisey, *Sanchi and its Remains* (London, 1892); J. Marshall, A. Foucher and N.G. Majumdar, *The Monuments of Sanchi*, 3 Vols. (Delhi, 1940); Debala Mitra, *Sanchi*, 2nd ed. (New Delhi, 1965); A.H. Longhurst, *The Buddhist Antiquities of Nagarjunikonda*, MASI 54 (Delhi, 1938); C. Sivaramamurti, *Amaravati Sculptures*, BMGM IV (Madras, 1942); etc. For the views of Coomaraswamy see *Arts Bulletin*, IX (New York, 1927), 287-328; *Elements of Buddhist Iconography* (Cambridge, Mass., 1935).
2. "In early Indian Art, so far as the cult images are concerned, one iconographic type stands out predominant, that is the standing figure with right hand raised, the left hand on the hip....Of this type are early images of Yakṣas and Yakṣis, whether independent or attendant. And it is also this type which provided the model for cult images of other deities, such as Siva or Buddha, when the necessities of *bhakti* determined the appearance of all deities in various forms". Coomaraswamy, *Yakṣas*, 2 Vols. (Washington, 1928, 1931, rep. New Delhi, 1971), I, 29.
3. K.K. Dasgupta in *Ananda Coomarswamy : A Centenary Volume* (Calcutta University, 1981), 60-61.
4. Sculptors of Mathura worked in Kasia, Bodh-Gaya, Sarnath and other places of northern India even during the Gupta period. The colossal recumbent Buddha figure of Kasia made by Dinna of Mathura in the early Gupta period deserves special mention in this connection. A Bodhisattva from Bodh-Gaya dated in the year 64 of one Mahārāja Trikamala is also of Mathura inspiration. S. Kramrisch, *Indian Sculpture* (Calcutta, 1933). fig. 54. The same holds good in the case of a seated Buddha image at Mankuwar in the Allahabad district, belonging to A.D.448-49, which preserves partially the conventional treatment of hair found in early Mathura

images. V.A. Smith, *History of Fine Arts in India and Ceylon* (Oxford, 1911), 173, fig. 119. In the Buddha and Bodhisattva images of the Sarnath school we come across an improvement upon and sublimation of the Mathura types. These images are more sophisticated, characterised by more refinement and clearer delineation of features discernible in the curly hair, robes covering one or both shoulders, absence of *urṇā*, greater varieties of *mudrās*, elaborately decorated nimbus, lotus or lion pedestal usually with figures of donors. J. Ph. Vogel, *Catalogue of the Archaeological Museum at Mathura* (Allahabad, 1910); 'The Mathura School of Sculpture' in *ASIAR*, 1906-07, 137-60, 1909-10, 63-70; V.S. Agrawala, 'Buddha and Bodhisattva Images in the Mathura Museum' in *JUPHS*, XXI, 1948, 43-98; *Sarnath*, second ed. (New Delhi, 1957); D.R. Sahni, *Catalogue of the Museum of Archaeology at Sarnath* (Calcutta, 1914).

5. For the crowned Buddhas see R.D. Banerji, *Eastern Indian School of Medieval Sculpture* (Delhi, 1933), Plates XVII (b), XXI (c), XXII (b,c), XXIII (b), XXIV(c), XXVI (d).
6. Debala Mitra, *Buddhist Monuments* (*BM*) (Calcutta, 1971), 59, pl. 62.
7. *ASIAR*, 1934-35, 40, pl. XVII e-f; N.N. Bhattacharyya in *East Indian Bronzes* (*EIB*) (Calcutta University, 1979), 74, 101.
8. *BM*, 230, 232, pl. 27.
9. *Bronze Images of the Patna Museum* (*BIPM*) (Patna, 1961), fig. 12.
10. *BM*, 67,76, pl. XIV.
11. *Ibid.*, 97, pl. XVI.
12. *Patna Museum Catalogue of Antiquities* (*PMC*) (Patna, 1965), 126,pl. XXVII.
13. N.N. Bhattacharyya, *EIB*, 75.
14. R.D. Banerji, *op.cit.*, pl. XXIX (a); Barua, *Bharhut*, III, pl. XLVII.
15. *BM*, 73, 97, pl. XV.
16. *Ibid.*, 71, 204, pl. XVII.
17. *Ibid.*, 116, pl. XIX.
18. *PMC*, 53-54.
19. *ASIAR*, 1908-09, 157.
20. The *Mañjuśrīmūlakalpa* (*MMK*) IV describes him in the garb of an ascetic with a crown of matted hair and *tripuṇḍraka* on his forehead, wearing a red cloth with the skin of a black antelope on his left shoulder, having four hands and a golden complexion. In *Sādhanamālā* (*SDM*) 560 he is described as three-faced, three-eyed and four-armed, having a golden complexion, seated with both legs tucked up on a lotus seat; two of his principal hands exhibit *vyākhyāna-mudra*; of the other two hands the right is in *varada* and the left holds a cluster of *nāgakeśara* flower. The *Niṣpannayogāvali* (*NSP*) 50 also gives a similar description But such four handed

forms are not generally available, although we have many two handed representations in which the right hand is in *varada-mudrā* and the left holds the *nāgakeśara*, his recognition symbol. This two-handed form is also described in *SDM* 49 and *NSP* 66.

21. S.K. Saraswati, *Tantreyana Art : An Album* (*TAA*), (Calcutta, 1977), figs. I-IV.
22. *ASIAR*, 1920-21, 42-46, 1927-28, 159.
23. For Kurkihar images see *JISOA* II, 1934, 1ff. Pls. XXIX-XXXIV; *ASIAR*, 1930-34, pls. CXLVII-CLXIX.
24. *EIB*, 76.
25. B.T. Bhattacharyya, *Indian Buddhist Iconography* (II) (Calcutta, 1968), 81.
26. *History of Bengal* (*DHB*), ed. R.C. Majumdar, (Dacca University, I, 467n.
27. *TAA*, fig. 199.
28. Iconological descriptions of the Dhyanī Buddhas are to be found in the *Advayavajrasaṃgraha* (*ADV*), 40ff.
29. *NSP*, 8.
30. *ADV*, 41.
31. N.K. Bhattasali, *Iconography of the Buddhist and Brahmanical Sculptures in the Dacca Museum* (*IBBSDM*)(Dacca, 1929), 22-23. pl. III, a.
32. For the Banpur hoard see Debala Mitra, *Bronzes from Acutarajpur*.
33. A. Getty, *The Gods of Northern Buddhism* (*GNB*), 58.
34. *SDM*, 27ff.
35. Coomaraswamy, *History of Indian and Indonesian Art* (*HIIA*) fig. 264.
36. *TAA*, figs. 83-84.
37. *PMC* 119; for Nalanda bronzes see *ASIAR*, 1920-21, 42-46.
38. *EIB*, 78-79.
39. *TAA*, figs 43, 44.
40. *DHB*, 468, pl. XXII, 56.
41. *IBI*, figs. 99-102.
42. *PMC* 140.
43. *SDM*, 39-40.
44. *IBBSDM*, 24ff. Pl. VII.
45. *TAA*, figs. 60-62.
46. *EIB*, 80.
47. *TAA*, figs. 46, 57.
48. *IBI*, fig. 105; Dikshit, 'Six Sculptures from Mahoba' in *MASI*, VIII.
49. *Ibid*., fig. 107.
50. *TAA*, figs. 48, 54-56.
51. *IBI*, fig. 106.
52. *EIB*. 80.
53. *JISOA*, II; 1934, 70ff.

54. *IBI*, 124-25.
55. *TAA*, figs. 64-67, 69.
56. *EIB*, 81.
57. *SDM*, 88.
58. *TAA*, figs. 71, 72, 75.
59. *DHB*, 468.
60. *EIB*, 81.
61. *SDM*, 85-86.
62. *TAA*, figs. 80-81.
63. *IBI*, 141.
64. *SDM*, 33.
65. *SDM*, 65-66.
66. *SDM*, 137.
67. *PMC*, 121.
68. No. Add. 1643 dated A.D. 1015.
69. No. A. 15 dated A.D. 1071.
70. *MMK*, 40-41, 60, 64, 111, 304, 315, 317-19, 322, 447, 460.
71. *NSP*, 48.
72. *DHB*, 466, pl. XLIV, 111, 113.
73. *SDM*, 129.
74. *IBI*, 103.
75. *SDM*, 140.
76. *IBI*, 114.
77. *MMK*, 44, 48, 51, 54-56, 70.
78. *TAA*, figs. 12-13.
79. *EIB*, 84.
80. *GNB*, 111.
81. *IBI*, 120.
82. *IBBSDM*, 28-29, pl. VII, B.
83. *BM*, 233.
84. *EIB*, 92.
85. *IBI*, 122.
86. *DHB*, 470; *Pariṣat Museum Catalogue* 33.
87. *TAA*, fig. 29.
88. *EIB*, 85.
89. *SDM*, 128.
90. *TAA*, fig. 30.
91. *EIB*, 86.
92. *IBI*, 175-76.
93. *DHB*, 469-70, pl. XXII, 57.
94. *BM*, 244.
95. *TAA*, figs. 36-40.
96. *EIB*, 86.
97. *IBI*, 104-05.
98. *TAA*, fig. 31.

99. *PMC*, 143.
100. *IBI*, 98-99.
101. *ASIAR*, 1930-34, 278, pl. CXLI, 9.
102. *Ibid.*, 1927-28, 159, 1929-30, 201, pl. XXXIII d.
103. *PMC*, 144.
104. *Ibid.*, 120-21.
105. *IBI*, 146.
106. *SDM*, 509.
107. *IBI*, 165.
108. *PCM*, 144.
109. *SDM*, 473.
110. *EIB*, 89.
111. *IBBSDM*, 37, pl. XXII.
112. *BM*, 225, 232.
113. *EIB*, 89.
114. *GNB*, 142-43.
115. *NSP*, 14-15.
116. *ASIAR*, 1927-28,107, pl. XIXa.
117. *EIB*, 89.
118. *SDM*, 451.
119. *EIB*, 89.
120. *IBI*, fig. 149.
121. *SDM*, 452-53.
122. *EIB*, 89.
123. *IBI*, 160-62.
124. *ASIAR*, 1934-35, 80, pl. XXIV, c.
125. *BM*, 232, pl. 33.
126. *GNB*, 152-53, 164.
127. *SDM*, 530.
128. *IBI*, 167-78.
129. *TAA*, fig. 176.
130. *EIB*, 90.
131. *BM*, 232.
132. *SDM*, 564, 577.
133. *DHB*, 471, pl. LXV. 158.
134. *EIB*, 91.
135. *BM*, 197.
136. *TAA*, figs. 150-51.
137. *ASIAR*, 1920-21, 42-46; 1927-28, 159; 1928-29, 146; 1933-34, 278.
138. *PMC*, 123,144.
139. *EIB*, 92.
140. *SDM*, 421.
141. *EIB*, 92.
142. *TAA*, figs. 154-55.

143. *BM,* 197, 232-33.
144. *PMC*, 149-150; *JISOA*, II, pl. XXXII; *BIPM*, No. 30.
145. *SDM*, 511.
146. *ASIAR*, 1934-35, 278, pl. CXLI.15.
147. *TAA*, fig. 178.
148. *PMC*, 121, pl. XXIII.
149. *EIB*, 91.
150. *IBI,* 147-52.
151. *EIB*, 94.
152. *SDM*, 341.
153. *BM*, 184, 222.
154. *PMC*, 122, pl. XXV.
155. *SDM*, 306-07.
156. *IBI*, fig. 140.
157. *IBBSDM*, 58-61, pl. XXIII a-b.
158. *BIPM*, No. 31; *ASIAR*, 1930-34, pl. CXLIX, 7.
159. *PMC*, 151; *BIPM,* No. 32.
160. *IBI*, 197-199.
161. *DHB*, 472, PL. XXVI. 62.
162. *PMC*, 122, pl. XXV.
163. *Ibid*., 149, JISOA, II, pl. XXXII, fig, 1.
164. *EIB,* 95-96.
165. *SDM*, 403.
166. *IBI*, figs. 189-90.
167. *TAA*, figs. 185-87.
168. *PMC*, 66.
169. *BM*, 228, 232.
170. *SDM*, 395.
171. *IBBSDM*, 53-54, pl. XVIII.
172. *IBI*, 207-09.
173. *BM*, pl. 140.
174. *SDM*, 306; GNB, 133.
175. *IBBSDM*, 43-44, pl. XIII-XIV.
176. *TAA*, fig. 118.
177. *EIB*, 97.
178. *SDM*, 297-98.
179. *PMC*, 65-66.
180. *SDM*, 400.
181. *BM*, 182, 184.
182. *TAA*, figs. 180-81.
183. *SDM*, 401-02.
184. *IBI*, figs. 184-85.
185. *SDM*, 329.
186. *TAA*, fig. 182.
187. *SDM*, 394.

188. *IBI*, fig. 156.
189. *Ibid.*, 221.
190. *SDM*, 271, 352; *NSP*, 49, 57, 89.
191. *EIB*, 97-98.
192. *TAA*, XLVIII.
193. *PMC*, 85.
194. No. Add. 1643.
195. *IBI*, figs. 163-64.
196. *BM*, 89, pl. XXVIII.
197. *PMC*, 123, pl. XXVI.
198. *DHB*, pl. XXVI, 64.
199. *GNB*, 86.
200. *EIB*, 102.
201. *PMC*, 22, 95, 152.
202. *ASIAR*, 1911-12, pl. XXXI, 8; HIIA, pl. IV.13.
203. *IBI*, 307; GNB, 123.
204. *EIB*, 99.
205. *PMC*, 121, cf. pl. XXIV.
206. *ASIAR*, 1930-34, pl. CXLIX.3; CXLVII; *JISOA*, II, pl. XXVIII, XXX; etc.
207. *BPIM*, Nos. 29-30, etc.
208. *TAA*, figs. 104-05.
209. *JBORS*, X, 1924, 31-36.
210. *PMC*, 88, pl. XVII
211. *IBI*, 308-09; *GNB*, 122-26.
212. *TAA*, figs. 101-03.
213. *PMC*, 85.
214. *IBBSDM*, 56-57, pl. XXI.
215. *IBI*, fig. 181.
216. *BM*, 17, pl. XXX.
217. *IBBSDM*, 45-53, pl. XXV-XXVII.
218. *SDM*, 244-45.

INDEX